44 Hyde Terrace

Returns in person or by post to:
Mental Health Library; The Mount Annexe
44 Hyde Terrace; Leeds, LS2 9LN

**Renewals by phone, email or online via
library catalogue:** 0113 3055652
libraryandknowledgeservices.lypft@nhs.net
www.leedslibraries.nhs.uk

shown
on, by

**Books should be returned or renewed by the
last date shown above.**

PATHWAYS OF GROWTH

ESSENTIALS OF CHILD PSYCHIATRY

Volume 1
Normal Development

WILEY SERIES IN CHILD
AND ADOLESCENT MENTAL HEALTH

Joseph D. Noshpitz, Editor

PATHWAYS OF GROWTH

ESSENTIALS OF CHILD PSYCHIATRY

Volume 1
Normal Development

JOSEPH D. NOSHPITZ
Chesapeake Youth Centers

ROBERT A. KING
Yale Child Study Center
Yale University School of Medicine

A Wiley-Interscience Publication
JOHN WILEY & SONS, INC.
New York   Toronto   Chichester   Brisbane   Singapore

Library of Congress Cataloging-in-Publication Data

Noshpitz, Joseph D.
    Pathways of growth: essentials of child psychiatry / Joseph D.
    Noshpitz, Robert A. King.
        p.   cm.—(Wiley series in child and adolescent mental health)
    "A Wiley-Interscience publication."
    Includes bibliographical references.
    Contents: v. 1. Normal development—v. 2. Psychopathology.
    ISBN 0-471-09917-1 (v. 1).—ISBN 0-471-53177-4 (v. 2).—ISBN
    0-471-53178-2 (set)
        1. Child psychopathology. 2. Child development. I. King,
    Robert, 1943–   II. Title. III. Series.
        [DNLM: 1. Child Development. 2. Child Psychiatry. 3. Mental
    Disorders—in infancy & childhood. WS 350 N897p]
    RJ499.N68   1991
    618.92'89—dc20
    DNLM/DLC
    for Library of Congress   90-12693

To the memory of Bruno Bettelheim,
Fritz Redl, & Reginald Lourie
Dear friends and inspired teachers
Whose voices spoke to the era

Series Preface

This series is intended to serve a number of functions. It includes works on child development; it presents material on child advocacy; it publishes contributions to child psychiatry; and it gives expression to cogent views on child rearing and child management. The mental health of parents and their interaction with their children is a major theme of the series, and emphasis is placed on the child as individual, as family member, and as a part of the larger social surround.

Child development is regarded as the basic science of child mental health, and within that framework research works are included in this series. The many ethical and legal dimensions of the way society relates to its children are the central theme of the child advocacy publications, as well as a primarily demographic approach that highlights the role and status of children within society. The child psychiatry publications span studies that concern the diagnosis, description, therapeutics, rehabilitation, and prevention of the emotional disorders of childhood. And the views of thoughtful and creative contributors to the handling of children under many different circumstances (retardation, acute and chronic illness, hospitalization, handicap, disturbed social conditions, etc.) find expression within the framework of child rearing and child management.

Family studies with a central child mental health perspective are included in the series, and explorations into the nature of parenthood and the parenting process are emphasized. This includes books about divorce, the single parent, the absent parent, parents with physical and emotional illnesses, and other conditions that significantly affect the parent–child relationship.

Finally, the series examines the impact of larger social forces, such as war, famine, migration, and economic failure, on the adaptation of children and families. In the largest sense, the series is devoted to books that illuminate the special needs, status, and history of children and their families, within all perspectives that bear on their collective mental health.

JOSEPH D. NOSHPITZ

Chesapeake Youth Centers
Cambridge, Maryland

Preface

This work is designed to introduce the discipline of child and adolescent psychiatry to the graduate student. Child and adolescent psychiatry is a branch of medicine, but it is also a common ground where many diverse fields intersect and interact. Within medicine, psychiatry and pediatrics are its primary sister fields; outside of medicine, social work and psychology are the chief siblings. In addition, sociology, anthropology, education, pastoral counseling, public health, law, and city planning are only some of the adjacent realms whose interests will at times intersect with child and adolescent psychiatric theory and practice. One of the formidable barriers to communication among such various realms is the lack of a common, jargon-free language. Our goal in this work to try to bridge this gap, to avoid the use of in-group language, and to explain the relevant ideas without use of the necessary shorthand that every field develops—and that eventually leads to an exclusive argot.

This has proved to be no mean undertaking. Many passages had to be rewritten several times to achieve the necessary mixture of scientific rigor and literary felicity. This was especially true because we sought to retain our affiliation to our primary discipline in an intensive and comprehensive manner.

Throughout this book we have used the traditional pronoun *he* in referring to the child. This stylistic convention is for ease of reading only; the information herein refers impartially to girls and boys unless the specific content states otherwise.

The book is not a once-over-lightly kind of effort; we routinely referred to recent and technically advanced studies, and we have summarized this information in the text. At the same time, we have made every effort to couch this material in language that would be transparent to and communicative with graduate students of any adjacent discipline. The outcome is thus the product of much arduous address to the literature as well as considerable soul-searching and self-questioning. But the effort itself has been rewarding, and we can only hope that those who chance to read our work are as gratified and stimulated by that encounter as we were in its writing.

JOSEPH D. NOSHPITZ
ROBERT A. KING

Cambridge, Maryland
New Haven, Connecticut
February 1991

Acknowledgments

Many friends and colleagues have contributed to the creation of this volume. No small measure of the emotional support necessary to proceed with a long and arduous undertaking came from the warmth and frequent infusions of interest by Dr. Jack Davis, Director of the Grove School, and his wife, Helen Davis. Much of the research was accomplished within the framework of the Children's Hospital National Medical Center of Washington, D.C., and the hospital made many resources available to help in producing and editing the original document. Of first importance were the medical library and its two skilled and devoted librarians, Deborah Gilbert and Shirley Knobloch. They produced bibliographies, sent away for arcane references, and repeatedly offered their cheerful and unstinting support to a sometimes grumpy and demanding author.

Then there were the members of the extraordinary group of physicians and other professionals who staffed the hospital. Kenneth Rosenbaum, M.D., reread the chapter on genetics twice to help verify facts and correct errors. Anne Fletcher, M.D., reviewed the chapter on prenatal development and offered many constructive comments. Dana Czapanskiy, M.S.W., read through the document with great care and advanced both general and textual critiques; he then reread the corrected manuscript for a final polishing. His comments were invaluable. Tomas Silber, M.D., was very helpful in reviewing the biology of adolescence. Others, outside the Children's Hospital, helped as well. Dean Coddington, M.D., a friend and colleague, critiqued the document, offered excellent suggestions, and posed many thoughtful questions, all of which helped give form and polish to the final product.

Finally, a particular debt and a proportionate sense of gratitude are owed to one of the researchers in the field who inspired several sections of the text and who set a model for felicitous writing about child development. Daniel Stern has produced some enormously enriching studies of infancy and early mother–child interaction, and his influence has been a preeminent presence in several chapters of this volume.

J.D.N.

Contents

PATHWAYS OF GROWTH

ESSENTIALS OF CHILD PSYCHIATRY

Volume 1
Normal Development

Introduction

This book seeks to lead the student toward an understanding of the principles that underlie child psychiatry and toward an awareness of its accumulated wisdom. The most important of these principles is that the clinical discipline of child psychiatry is an application of the basic science of human development. Accordingly, we have started with an exposition of the nature of development in both its biological and psychosocial dimensions. We then recount current views about the principal syndromes known to the discipline.

In keeping with this approach, Volume 1 first describes our genetic makeup, with illustrations of how genetic issues increasingly concern mental health practitioners. The focus then shifts to the way the embryo and fetus grow in the womb, and to the ways in which the unborn baby is both vulnerable and aware.

We then look at the developing brain and describe a little of what is known about the relation of structure to function. Following this, we study the newborn to see what the child brings into the world and what his potentials are for subsequent growth.

The initial overview is based largely on the kinds of data acquired by direct observation. Following this, we review development from the standpoint of psychoanalytic theory. And we close Part II of the book by looking at the work of a major theorist who has studied the development of the sense of self.

The account proceeds stepwise through the first months, the first year, toddlerhood and the preschool years, the grade school and pubertal epochs, and early and late adolescence. At each stage we seek to integrate biological, psychological, and social factors to illuminate the experience and the vicissitudes of that time of life.

PART I

Background

Chapter 1

The Genetic Base

INTRODUCTION

As a field of research, genetics has recently shown extraordinary activity and unusual promise. In respect to human biology, the discoveries pouring out of the geneticists' laboratories may overturn the entire present conceptualization of disease. Researchers have already unraveled many great mysteries of the past regarding aspects of physical illness; they have identified new syndromes, provided new therapies, and gained powerful insights. In addition to remarkable advances in pathology, an even more exciting emergent is work directed toward the origin of personality traits and the biological basis for our attitudes, competencies, and capacities. Behavioral genetics is a relatively new field that is just now beginning to burgeon.

GENETIC FACTORS

For a century or more, knowledge of genetics was superficial and fragmentary. The great flood of knowledge that currently bears this field forward is at best only a few decades old. For example, for many years children in school and scholars at the university were taught that human cells possessed 48 chromosomes. Human cells, in fact, contain 46 chromosomes, yet it was not until 1956 that the correct figure was discovered by Tijo and Levan (1956). Prior to that date, generations of microscopists had failed to ascertain the correct figure, and for decades the textbooks had continued to pass along the erroneous number as hard scientific fact.

From the view of the geneticist, there are two kinds of cells in the human body, the sex cells, which transmit the genetic message from generation to generation, and the somatic cells, which make up the body proper, with all its structure and functions.

The somatic cells reproduce by splitting, a process called *cell division,* or *mitosis.* During such cell division, under appropriate observational conditions, the genetic material of the cell is visible within the nucleus in the form of pairs of rod-shaped bodies, the *chromosomes.* (They have long been known to microscopists because they take stains readily and appear as highly pigmented bodies; hence the name *chromosome* or "colored body.") These chromosomes are present in pairs that represent the matched genetic contributions of the mother and father. The ovum and sperm each bear a single set of 23 chromosomes; their merger brings the chromosome count up to the normal 46.

When studied under the microscope during cell division, the chromosomes have the appearance of cruciate bodies, that is, variations on the letter X. This is a bit deceptive because an X usually appears to be two intersecting lines. In the case of chromosomes, each X is formed by two angled arms that join in the middle as though each chromosome had the shape of a letter *V* tipped on its side. The two Vs face away from each other and meet at their points (Riccardi, 1977). When stained appropriately and observed more closely, each chromosome has a characteristic size, shape, and, even more striking, a distinctive pattern of different colored bands along its length that makes it readily distinguishable from the others.

It was this patterning that enabled Tijo and Levan to find the correct chromosomal number. These investigators first cultured cells to boost their rate of multiplication, then chemically arrested the process in the stage of division when the chromosomes have doubled and have begun to move away from one another (the metaphase). After staining with dye, the investigators found that each pair of matched chromosomes displayed alternating bands of different colors that permitted definitive classification—and thus an accurate count.

If researchers go beyond the chromosomes' usual microscopic appearance, by enlarging them enormously and looking into their chemical makeup, they can detect that the chromosomes are composed of literally millions of small subunits, chained together in a linear array; these are, in fact, great, extended ribbons that coil around one another in serpentine fashion. Chemically, these curious helixes are designated as *deoxyribonucleic acid* (DNA). The DNA in each chromosome is different, which allows the individual chromosome pairs to have highly specialized functions, that is, to convey unique quanta of information.

Proteins and DNA

The mission of the DNA is to carry the information necessary to build the body. This includes both its structural components (e.g., the various tissues of which we are made) and its functional regulators (e.g., hormones and enzymes). In practice, this reduces to building a group of substances called *proteins.*

Proteins are a familiar part of everyday experience. A typical protein is gelatin, the basic ingredient of Jell-o. It is a coherent but rather soft and squishy stuff; under certain conditions it can be ropy and sticky. Nasal exudate is largely protein; the muscles that compose the human body (and that of other animals as well) are of similar constitution. Protein can have many forms. Much of the basic material of the human body is one form of protein or another. The information necessary to create each of these proteinaceous forms in the right amount and at the right time and place is encoded in the DNA.

It is important to have some grasp of the composition of this class of substances. Proteins are complex aggregates of a group of chemicals called amino acids. The amino acids are relatively small, simple compounds that are present in most foods. They are essential factors in the human diet; if they should be unavailable, serious consequences can follow. The key to identifying the individual proteins is the choice and the number of specific amino acids employed in their composition, and the three-dimensional way these amino acids link together. Only 20 amino acids are essential to human nutrition and enter into the formation of our proteins. On the one hand, this is not a great number; on the other, it allows a huge assortment of possible arrangements. If the proteins are to form bone or cartilage or muscle, the arrangement has to be of one kind; if they are to produce insulin or thyroid gland secretion, they will clearly have to link together in quite a different way.

Body proteins are of two kinds: structural and functional. The structural proteins are the building blocks for bone, cartilage, connective tissue, muscle, tendon, ligament, the capsules and sheaths around the various organs, the materials from which blood vessels and organs are formed, and the like. The functional proteins are called *enzymes;* they are the chemical regulators of the body and help specify the rate, the order, and the quantity of the various metabolic processes. For example, these enzymes regulate the kind, the quantity, and the rate of production of each of the neurotransmitters within the many neurons; they regulate the production of the endocrines within the endocrine glands; they initiate and maintain the many cycles of metabolism that allow the body to process oxygen, sugar, food molecules, and waste products. The proteins are key players in the drama of being alive; our bodies are composed of them and our activity and vital processes depend on them. We grow by producing and organizing ever-greater quantities of protein and elaborating these products into new tissues. We also use them up (in the course of jogging or worrying the body consumes them at a great rate), and as we do so, our DNA can manufacture more.

One of the great breakthroughs of the 20th century was the discovery of the form and constitution of DNA; this feat was accomplished by Watson and Crick (1953), who received a Nobel prize for their achievement. Because genetics promises to play an ever more important role in understanding human development, it seems appropriate to review some of these investigators' findings as well as more recent discoveries.

The constitution of DNA allows for many subtle variations in composition. It is, in effect, a *very* long, linear chain of simple compounds that repeat over and over but in varying and quite specific sequences. The sequence holds the information.

Watson and Crick discovered that the DNA molecule is structured as a sort of hyperextended ladder. Like any ladder, it has two parallel side rails linked by a series of transverse rungs. In this instance, however, compared with the rungs, the side rails are immensely long—long enough, indeed, to allow for approximately 3 billion connecting rungs. (The image of a ladderlike structure is not entirely accurate; in fact, the two side rails wind around each other in a double helix. Perhaps the truer analogy is a spiral staircase, but for purposes of clarity of presentation, the ladder image will be retained here in referring to the different components of the DNA molecule.) Chemically, these long side rails are composed of an endlessly repeating, alternating series of phosphate and sugar molecules. (The sugar is called *deoxyribose* and gives DNA part of its name.) The rungs of the ladder are, as noted, relatively short; they are each composed of two different small compounds (called *bases*) that vary in composition. They do not vary a great deal, however; in fact, only four different molecules of this kind enter into the formation of these rungs. Each rung is composed of a pair of these chemicals (base pairs), so that only a limited amount of variety in their make-up is possible (see Figure 1.1).

The four bases are usually designated by initials. They consist of *adenine* (A), *cytosine* (C, *guanine* (G), and *thymine* (T). As they come together to form the base pairs in DNA, adenine always pairs with thymine, and guanine with

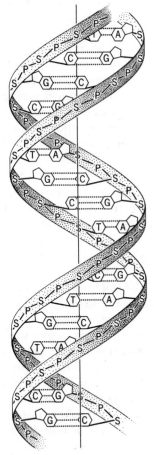

Figure 1–1. The DNA molecule.

cytosine. Each strand (or section of the long side rail) of DNA can then be thought of as a sequence of bases (e.g., TGACCTGA) connected to one side rail that is linked to an exactly complementary strand (on the other side rail) by the appropriate matches (e.g., ACTGGACT). It is as though all the words in a language were written in pairings of only four letters; this is enough, however, to allow for endless variation in their sequencing. And for this language, the sequencing is the essential bearer of information. (It may help to recall that Morse code has only two units of communication, *dit* and *dah*. Again, their sequencing carries the message.) Functionally, the ordering of the base pairs actually provides a set of instructions to be carried out by the appropriate chemical operators.

The long double strands of DNA carry the master program for a great many operations. Along the length of the DNA molecule, each segment of the extended ladderlike arrangement bears a different message. As noted earlier, there are about 3 billion base pairs in each such strand of DNA; hence, the amount of information carried is very great indeed (White & Lalouel, 1988).

Considerable research has made it evident that a given unit of information is ordinarily composed of large numbers—typically about 10,000 but sometimes extending to millions—of base pairs. These units correspond roughly to what are conventionally called the genes. On the other hand, only about 10% of the original DNA material participates directly in encoding proteins. Many extended sequences of base pairs are apparently silent, that is, so far as can be ascertained, they do not find expression in form or function. It may well be that these unexpressed portions of the DNA chain either are serving as regulators of the action of the more active portions (the genes), are vestiges of our primate ancestry (such as the determiners of a tail or body fur) that have fallen into disuse, or are playing a role that is not yet understood in the processes of growth and developmental regulation. The active sectors, at any rate, give rise to the body's structure and function. These processes involve a great many additional steps.

How does the DNA in the cell nucleus become a human being? One key to what happens is the preservation of the DNA molecules as master prototypes that do not themselves enter into the formation of body substances. Anyone familiar with computers knows that when an individual obtains a new program disk, the first instruction is always to make a working copy of the master disk and then to preserve the original in a safe place; only the working copy will be used thereafter for actual service. Evolution seems to have found it expedient to pursue a similar course with DNA; hence, when it is to be used, the first step is to make a working copy.

This the body does very neatly. Ordinarily, the work of body-structure building and functioning does not require using all the data available in a particular DNA molecule; on any given occasion only a certain portion of these data is likely to be called for. Hence, the first step is to select the necessary segment of information-bearing material and to make a copy of that.

In effect, the body sends out a message: Such and such a substance is currently necessary. (Perhaps the person has been exercising and requires more muscle protein; or the individual has ingested a great deal of sugar, which needs insulin for its proper metabolism, but insufficient insulin is available.) The information necessary for producing that substance is encoded in a particular sequence of bases somewhere along the length of the DNA molecule. The appropriate segment (which contains the desired information) must then be located along one strand of the DNA helix. Once found, the two long rails of the DNA molecule are temporarily pulled apart at just that spot, the information encoded in the appropriate base sequence is immediately copied, and the two side rails are then neatly rejoined. Thus the DNA molecule is preserved intact.

The copy gives rise to a new type of nucleic acid molecule called *ribonucleic acid* (RNA), which differs from DNA in important ways. It is also a long strand with bases along its length, but the copy's form is no longer a double helix; instead of a ladderlike arrangement, this RNA molecule resembles an extended comb. That is to say, the bases, instead of being paired companions in the helix, are now located along the long strand of RNA somewhat the way teeth are set along the spine of the comb. In addition, although three of the constituent bases (adenine (A), cytosine (C), and guanine (G)) are the same, the fourth base in RNA is *uracil* (*U*) rather than thymine. But these bases are now attached to a different sort of material than was present in the DNA; in the new configuration, the spine of the comb is made up largely of the sugar *ribose* (and again the name of the substance reflects this). This ribonucleic acid (RNA), in turn, is not only structurally different from the DNA, but is processed in a somewhat different way.

The ensuing process resembles building a plastic airplane model, which starts out as an array of parts that must be fitted together by following the provided set of instructions. The DNA operates on a similar principle: For the manufacture of a particular protein, it is necessary to have both a model to copy (one segment of the DNA molecule), and a set of instructions about where the model-segment begins, where it ends, and how it is to be clipped out (these plans for construction are contained in the adjacent DNA segments). At some point, of course, the model and the instructions must in turn be separated from one another. As a result, certain parts of the new single strand are removed, and the appropriate segment is retained as the template for the formation of the new protein. As for the site from which they were removed, because a gap has been created, the dangling ends at each extremity of the gap are rejoined. Meanwhile, for the template-to-be segment that has been separated out, a cap is put on the front end, a tail on the back end, and the shortened molecule is tidied up and made ready for its final mission. Because the DNA resides in the nucleus of the cell, all this is taking place in the nucleus as well.

The completed model molecule is now ready for travel; at this stage it is therefore called *messenger* ribonucleic acid (mRNA). This mRNA will presently leave the nucleus and travel into the cytoplasm, where it will transmit instructions to the cell's synthetic machinery for assembling the specified protein. For this reason Caspari (Plomin & Daniels, 1987) defines a gene as "a stretch of DNA that can be transcribed into RNA" (p. 21).

The translation of mRNA into the protein for which it codes must take place within a rather specialized chemical environment provided by a number of small spherical bodies in the cell cytoplasm called *ribosomes*. Each ribosome functions as a device for reading the mRNA template and transcribing the specific sequence of mRNA bases into a corresponding array of amino acids. As noted earlier, these amino acids are the true building blocks. Albeit relatively simple substances commonly present in the food we eat, they can be chained together in large numbers to make huge, very complex molecules indeed. This is what takes place at this point; the amino acids are linked together to form a specified protein.

To review this information, the chromosome is a long-chain molecule of DNA serving as a carrier of communicable data. Along its length are the different loci for storing these bits of information; at each locus there is an informational unit composed of a series of base pairs. Certain groups of bases carry the data necessary to build proteins. Many of these base pairs are flanked by other sequences that do not get translated into proteins, but that act as regulators of the associated processes. Part of what happens when RNA is transformed into mRNA is the removal of these associated "silent" areas. The geneticist calls such informational units of base pairs and regulating components *alleles*, and they probaby come closest to the older concept of gene.

Because the human body deals with lengthy sequences, there can be a near infinity of different varieties of DNA, some of them diverging one from another by tiny differences in the arrangement of their base pairs. To give some sense of scale, return for a moment to the image of the chromosome under the microscope. As noted earlier, with proper staining different colored bands are visible along the length of the chromosomes; each tiny band, however, is thought to contain some 2 million to 5 million base pairs (Patterson, 1987).

The DNA in human cells can code for (offer a template for) about 500,000 proteins. That is to say, on the basis of what each human being inherits, the cells have a built-in capacity to produce that many different proteins. In fact, however, only about 10% to 20% of these genes are active, and the reality is that the multiplication and interactions of some 50,000 to 100,000 proteins determine our substance, growth, and functioning (Scarr & Kidd, 1983).

Such a complex array of intricately formed materials, which constantly undergoes replication and recombination, is subject to a certain amount of error. Such errors are called *mutations,* and these mutations are not inherently unlikely; on the contrary, they are statistically inevitable. The estimated statistical probabilities of such errors are about 1 in every 10 million reproductive cells. Most mutations produce some insignificant change that is probably indetectable. Indeed, they may well contribute to the enormous genetic variability of our species. Some, on the other hand, make for radical changes that are incompatible with survival; by and large, their products lead to infertile sex cells or to ova that do not implant or that are aborted so early as never to be recognized as pregnancies.

All these aside, however, a group of mutations remain that do make a difference and are clinically significant. Although each such mutation is compatible with survival, it produces an alteration in a specific site that either deleteriously affects anatomical structure (e.g., cleft lip and/or cleft palate) or disturbs the functioning of the mind or body (e.g., inborn errors of metabolism that cause seizures, mental retardation, autism, or psychosis).

Once a mutation has been established, it may be transmitted from generation to generation and become a recognized syndrome. In general, there are two types of such disorders: those due to the pathological form of a single active genetic locus, and those resulting from the simultaneous presence of two or more such aberrant genes. It is important to distinguish these genetic disturbances from those caused by chromosomal aberrations. The gene-borne conditions are inherent in the material that composes the chromosomes; the chromosomal illnesses arise from things that go wrong in the formation and/or replication of the larger chromosomal bodies. Some of the disorders caused by anomalies in the structure or number of chromosomes are discussed below.

When a single gene has gone awry, a defective template will then be offered for forming a particular protein, and as the body grows, its constitution will reflect precisely this discrepancy. Just how devastating this can be becomes evident with the realization that this mechanism is the basis for all the cases of sickle cell anemaia (where the structural defect is in the formation of hemoglobin) and hemophilia (where a defective clotting factor is the culprit) to name just two. Cystic fibrosis and thalassemia are additional examples.

Because proteins are deployed for either structure or function, when a genetic locus fails in some way, the ensuing sequence of disturbance will reflect either the one type of problem or the other. For example, the expression of a mutation may have an impact primarily on the developing *body organization* of the fetus, in which case it leads to a congenital anomaly (Graham, 1983). Unfortunately statistics indicate that this state of affairs is not uncommon; malformations are the leading cause of death in infancy. Alternatively, the end product of the genetic difficulty may be a disturbance in the formation of a chemical regulator, which results in skewing some vital *function*. For example, such a defect may alter the functioning of an enzyme, which in turn determines the character of a biochemical process; the resultant condition (perhaps one of the many forms of mental retardation) will then express the aberrant genetic message in terms of a deviant biochemical pattern. In recent years, researchers have identified more than 200 such genetic conditions, called *inborn errors of metabolism*, and new ones are constantly being discovered. Each of these conditions is the outcome of a change in a specific gene, which in turn disturbs the formation or structure of the specific functional enzyme coded by that gene. Lacking this properly functioning catalyst or regulator, what should be a routine metabolic process does not proceed normally, with unfortunate results. In the nature of things this event is again, by no means, truly rare; 1 in every 1000 newborns has an inherited metabolic disorder. There are many conditions of this sort (some with formidable names, such as the aminoacidurias or the mucolipidoses, and others with eponymic titles, such as Tay-Sachs, Wilson's, Lesch-Nyhan, Menke's, and Hartnup's disease).

In sum, in single-gene disorders the pathogenic gene may lead to alterations in key structural proteins, or may produce defects in the absorption, transportation, utilization, or excretion of crucial biochemical substances. Given the genetic nature of this group of disturbances, not surprisingly they often cluster within a particular ethnic group and/or become associated with specific families.

The polygenic disorders (i.e., those involving several sites of genetic aberration) are even more frequently encountered. Multiple-gene involvement underlies such relatively common conditions as diabetes mellitus and essential hypertension. These particular examples are usually diagnosed later in the course of development; often, however, this kind of genetic pathology becomes apparent much earlier in the life cycle. Serious anomalies such as congenital heart disease, cleft palate, clubfoot, pyloric stenosis, and other such conditions are recognizable at birth (or very shortly thereafter). Major congenital malformations (classified as major because they interfere with normal living and usually require surgery) are estimated to occur in 2% of all newborns (Graham, 1983). Moreover, at one year of age, the incidence is likely to be even higher, because some occult problems, previously undiagnosed, by then have come to attention. It has been suggested that 20% of all pediatric hospital patients suffer from clinical problems involving a genetic dimension. Indeed, so common and so serious are these conditions that congenital malformations constitute the third most common cause of death in both sexes, up to the age of 14 years.

Because the inborn errors of metabolism contribute so largely to severe mental handicaps, it is useful to study them in greater depth. A well-known metabolic condition called *phenylketonuria* ("fe-nyl-key-tone-u-ri-a"), or *PKU*, can serve as an example.

Phenylketonuria

As just noted, PKU is due to an error in the formation of a single protein that functions in the body as a specific enzyme. Because protein formation is so basic to all that follows, it is essential that the processing of these amino acids within the body be letter perfect.

One of these amino acids is called phenylalanine. This is a naturally occurring compound found frequently in nature and ordinarily present in many foods. The human body, however, can utilize only a small (albeit essential) amount of phenylalanine directly. Any amount in excess of this basic level can become a serious problem. Hence, most of the ingested phenylalanine must be converted into something that can be handled more readily by the body. Properly metabolized, phenylalanine serves as an essential ingredient of functioning. On the other hand, if something blocks the necessary metabolic sequence, the results can be catastrophic (Leroy, 1983).

The first step in the chemical metabolism of phenylalanine falls to a particular substance, an enzyme (structurally, itself a protein), named phenylalanine hydroxylase. This enzyme converts phenylalanine into another amino acid named tyrosine. This is a critical step in the metabolism of phenylalanine; if it is not properly carried out, then the phenylalanine will simply accumulate. More than that, after a while, part of it will form toxic breakdown substances. If such a state of affairs persists for any length of time, dire consequences follow. Unfortunately, in about 1 person out of every 10,000, the necessary gene that specifies the structure of phenylalanine hydroxylase is defective; as a result, the properly functioning enzyme does not form. Without this metabolic enzyme, the phenylalanine ingested by the affected baby accumulates in the body, and some of it spills over and is diverted into an alternative metabolic pathway to form phenylpyruvic acid (and other noxious substances called phenylketones). These, in turn, spill out into the urine (hence the name phenylketonuria). Indeed, this illness was first discovered when Folling, a Scandinavian physician, noticed a peculiar odor arising from several severely retarded patients (including several siblings). This led him to discover abnormally large amounts of phenylpyruvic acid in their urine.

It is of considerable interest that at birth, such a baby's brain is essentially normal. Despite the absence of the critical enzyme, as long as the fetus remains in utero a number of factors protect it from an excess of phenylalanine. For one thing, it has not yet eaten any food. For another, the mother not only supplies nutrients via the placenta, she is also able to metabolize the phenylalanine sufficiently to prevent the buildup to toxic levels. To be sure, the mother is a carrier and is only 50% metabolically competent, but that is enough; toxic levels of phenylalanine do not get through and, as a result, at birth, the clinical aspect of the problem is not yet manifest. Because the genetic template for the enzyme is lacking, however, once the baby starts to eat, he cannot handle the phenylalanine that he ingests in the usual fashion. Lacking the appropriate enzymatic tools to deal with it, the baby's body metabolizes the phenylalanine by converting some of the phenylalanine into phenylpyruvic acid, which in turn gives rise to a series of toxic breakdown products. More serious still, above a critical level, the unmetabolized phenylalanine is in itself a very toxic substance. In particular, these toxins interfere with the normal myelination of nerve cells in the brain. Hence, as these substances (both the phenylalanine itself and its breakdown products) continue to accumulate, the developing brain is damaged, and a severe form of mental retardation ensues. In effect, the food the child eats poisons him and damages his brain.

Once this chain of events was understood, it became possible to devise a relatively simple test for this enzymatic defect. Those newborns whose blood showed a positive response to the test could then be placed on a low-phenylalanine diet that provided the necessary minimum but avoided the danger of excess. Thus protected, the children would grow up with relatively little deviance. Indeed, such preventive measures have led to a dramatic reduction in retardation due to PKU, which formerly accounted for as many as 1% of institutionalized retardates. (Most states currently employ a blood test that screens for five genetic conditions: phenylketonuria, thyroid deficiency, galactosemia, homocystinuria, and maple syrup urine disease. This is done routinely before the baby leaves the hospital.)

In propionic acidemia the villain is a deficiency in the enzyme, propionyl-CoA-carboxylase (PCC). Again the issue is the poisonous effect of normal nutrients; in essence, the child is unable to break down ingested protein in a wholesome fashion, and the protein he does ingest becomes toxic. Accordingly, the solution for at least some of the affected (PCC-deficient) children has been to limit dietary protein, with a resultant normal instead of severely damaged nervous system (Brandt et al., 1972, cited in Scarr & Kidd, 1983).

In brief, with at least some genetic disorders, understanding their underlying mechanisms permits interventions with a reasonable hope for a successful outcome. In the future, advances in genetic engineering may permit direct replacement or supplementation of the defective genetic material.

CHROMOSOMAL DISORDERS

As noted, there are in general two kinds of cells, the sex cells, which subserve reproduction, and the somatic cells, which compose the rest of the body substance. The sex cells, or gametes, contain 23 chromosomes each. Their union at fertilization brings the chromosomal count of the fertilized ovum up to the usual 46.

Gender is, of necessity, reflected in chromosomal structuring. In 1923 it was discovered that in terms of their genetic constitution, men and women differ in a characteristic fashion: In all of their somatic cells women have two matched sex chromosomes called *X*, whereas men have only one X matched against quite a different and smaller sex chromosome called *Y*. Men thus lack the full double complement of X-related genes, and women do not have a Y chromosome. This allows for certain characteristics that are carried on either the X or Y chromosomes to be transmitted to or carried by chiefly males or chiefly females. This has been of unique importance in unraveling the genetic transmission of many conditions.

It should be noted that, until 1959, gender was thought to be determined by the presence or absence of two X chromosomes; at that time, however, the role of the Y chromosome came to be recognized. Thereafter, it was assumed that some gene or genes on the Y chromosome trigger the cascade of events that ultimately determines male gender, or, by its absence, allows the basic propensity for establishing female gender to emerge. This Y-borne gene has been called the *testis determining factor* (TDF). Up to the 6th or 7th week of gestation the embryo has a gonad without identifiable sex differentiation; after that the die is cast one way or the other. When the TDF is present, the fetal gonad was thought to develop into testes; when absent, ovaries would form. But until recently the nature of the factor (or factors) on the Y chromosome that, by its presence or absence, determined gender was totally unknown. Analysis of chromosomal material from a number of aberrant cases, however, led to the detection of a relatively short stretch of DNA (140,000 base pairs long) located on the short arm of the Y chromosome (technically in an area called 1A2); this genetic material appears to be critical. Essentially this is thought to be the gene for sex determination. (This kind of genetic arrangement is found in a great many mammals.) This gene encodes for what are called *finger* proteins (because of their shape); these are essentially regulators that influence the actions of other genes.

Paradoxically, this gene is found on the X chromosome as well. It is speculated that when the genes are located on the two X chromosomes, one gene turns off; but when they are located on an X and a Y, both are active. Thus, the normal female would have only one effective gene of this kind, whereas the male has two. Whether this mechanism or some other is the critical factor in sex determination is yet to be discovered; in any case, the basic processes leading to sex determination are apparently close to being unraveled (Page et al., 1987).

Thus far this chapter has dealt with the effects of very small disturbances within the material of the chromosomes, those involving one or several genes. However, an all-too-common state of affairs arises from the disarray of larger segments of the normal chromosomal architecture. This can occur in many ways; however it happens, the inevitable outcome is that the genetic material transmitted from one generation to the next is passed along in some erroneous fashion (Gerald & Meryash, 1983).

Geneticists have designed a mapping system to describe the structure and sequence of the chromosomes in very precise and minute detail. Because even the most minor alterations in the arrangement of this genetic material can have major consequences, a very complex language has been developed to specify the histological nature of disturbances in terms of both the location and the ordering of the chromosomal structures. This language addresses both the count of chromosomes present and their distinctive form.

The structural aspects of each chromosome are unique both in form and function. As noted earlier, the various pairs can be distinguished simply by studying their size, their form (in particular, the location of the centromere), and the bands of different color that appear along the arms in a typical and identifiable sequence. With regard to the larger contours of the chromosomes, every person has a more or less identical set, so that it has been possible to designate each chromosome pair by number (with 1 representing the largest pair and 23 the smallest) and to describe their subsidiary parts in minute detail. Currently, investigators are exerting enormous efforts to locate and to define the function of each gene on the human chromosomal aggregate. This mapping of the chromosomes is one of the great scientific advances of our era.

Chromosomes can undergo many different changes that affect the developmental outcome. There can be too many chromosomes, or too few. There can be transposition of part of a chromosome from a normal to an aberrant location. There can be fragile sites, where breaks occur in the continuity of one of the arms. Any change in the architecture of the chromosomes is likely to have disturbing effects on subsequent growth. The process of mitosis has many hazards, for example, there can be a doubling or tripling of one of the chromosomes, or the separation of the chromosomal material may be incomplete so that extra pieces cling to one or the other of the newly formed chromosomes. If this occurs early in the division of the fertilized ovum, then an individual emerges with some radical alteration in the constitution of the chromosomes of all—or of a majority—of the body cells.

Insofar as anomalies of number are concerned, a common chromosomal misarrangement is called *trisomy;* it involves the *doubling* of a particular chromosome so that instead of there being two of each kind, there is one extra (or three in all, hence the term trisomy). Another aberration involves the loss or *deletion* of part or all of a chromosome so that one large set of genes is missing. Where an entire chromosome is lacking, the effect is so severe that the fetus usually does not survive. Indeed, chromosomal abnormality is probably the greatest single cause of spontaneous abortion. Where there is an excess of chromosomal material, the effects are less lethal as a rule, but neither are they benign. Many serious conditions (which usually include mental retardation) flow from this source, such as *Down syndrome* (trisomy 21) or *cri du chat syndrome* (trisomy 5).

The exceptions to this generalization involve the X and Y chromosomes. In these sex-linked aberrations, the doubling of either of the sex chromosomes or, in the female, the loss of one X chromosome is far less destructive than is the case with the nonsex chromosomal bodies (the autosomes). In particular, in a female, the loss of one of the X chromosomes leaves that individual with a solitary X chromosome, which gives rise to *Turner syndrome*. On examination, such a patient has only 45 chromosomes in each autosomal cell instead of the normal 46. The condition usually exists in partial form, that is, when examined microscopically, the body tissues display two kinds of cells, some with the normal complement of two X chromosomes alongside other cells with only one (a state of affairs called mosaicism). Under such conditions the clinical picture is mixed and may well approach the normal. Where Turner syndrome is present in pure form, however, then a number of distinctive findings are likely to be present. In particular, on cognitive tests these individuals show a marked loss of spatial ability, although their verbal ability is usually unaffected; indeed, they can be intellectually quite successful. Their spatial difficulties may beget problems with sense of direction, visual memory, handwriting, drawing, or copying. They have also been found to have difficulty in discriminating cues from facial affective expression (they cannot read the "meanings" of another person's facial expression), and many display a certain immaturity in their social and emotional development (some of which may be associated with this failure to read emotional cues). Some investigators (McCauley et al., 1987) feel that these traits suggest a possible right brain hemisphere deficit. Physically, such girls tend to be short and to display a curious sort of "webbing" around their necks; their ovaries are defective, and they need hormonal help to go into puberty and mature.

The opposite kind of disturbance, where one of the X chromosomes is doubled leading to an XXX female, is not accompanied by striking patterns of physical abnormality. The intellectual functioning of these individuals is somewhat affected, however; their speech development is likely to be delayed, and they may have problems forming speech sounds. They usually have an impaired short-term memory and numerous learning deficits. Careful examination will also reveal problems with balance, equilibrium, and the integration of sensory data. Some degree of social dysfunction is likely to be present as well, and the girls have difficulty making friends.

When males have a doubled X chromosome (i.e., an XXY complement), they will display the signs of *Klinefelter syndrome*. Here again the deleterious effect on intelligence and development may not be severe; verbal ability may lag behind spatial skills and general performance. In about half the cases, there is a lag in the development of language and later reading difficulties may arise. One study (Berch & Bender, 1987) reports that they "have difficulty decoding what is heard, storing this information in memory, and then retrieving the appropriate words to express an idea." In perhaps one-third of the cases emotional development is retarded, and at puberty sexual development is incomplete. By and large, their parents and teachers find them to be passive, unassertive, and withdrawn.

Another possibility for males, the XYY condition, has enjoyed ill-deserved notoriety. XYY males were found to be excessively represented within the prison population and therefore were presumed to be aggressive. However, further data suggest that they may be somewhat taller than average, have a generally lower IQ, and tend to be social isolates, but that they are not more aggressive than other men. As children, about half of this population have language problems and difficulties with reading. However, they do not show more behavior problems than average. Their higher rate of imprisonment as adults may reflect their intellectual or social inadequacies (Achenbach, 1982).

On the other hand, the threat to normal development is far greater where the count of autosomal (non-sex-linked) chromosomes is disturbed. Down syndrome is the commonest form of mental retardation, occurring at a rate of 1.0 to 1.2 out of every 1000 live births. The classic description of this condition was published by John Langdon Down (1866/1983). However, its chromosomal origin was not discerned until 1959, when it was found to occur in connection with the doubling of the 21st chromosome (Pueschel, 1983). As noted earlier, this doubling means that three exemplars (trisomy 21) of that chromosome are present in each body cell instead of the normal two. Trisomy has also been described in association with other chromosomes such as 13 and 18; these also result in retardation, but the associated physical findings are different.

In the course of cell division chromosomes can break so that part of one remains attached to a place from which it should have separated. Various other maldistributions of chromosomal material are also possible; these will often have profoundly disturbing consequences for the developing human being. Deletions, translocations, inversions, the presence of extra chromosomal material, and the simultaneous presence of different types of cells within one individual (mosaicism) have all been described. As each of these may affect any one of 23 chromosomes at a large variety of locations, an enormous number of possible anomalous conditions may emerge. A large number have already been described.

It is important to keep in mind that the genetic information necessary for the correct structuring of the brain is not localized to a few limited sites on a small number of chromosomes. On the contrary, the genetic contributions to brain formation are apparently distributed throughout *all* the chromosomes, so that each contributes to the organization of the brain. Moreover, the distribution of brain-related chromosomal material is not only widespread but massive as well; approximately one-third of all the chromosomal substance is directly concerned with brain structure. This is a tribute at once to the critical importance and the immense complexity of the human brain. It is therefore understandable that a disturbance anywhere in the chromosomal geography can have very serious consequences for brain growth and function, and any one of a wide variety of chromosomal aberrations can result in mental retardation, autism, speech disturbance, or some other untoward effect of brain abnormality.

The fragile X syndrome illustrates the intimate connection between chromosomal structure and brain function (Hagerman et al., 1983). Although this condition is usually confined to men, it can appear in women as well. It is relatively common, with an incidence estimated at 0.92 per 1000 male births (Herbst & Miller, 1980); next to Down syndrome it is the commonest chromosomal cause of mental retardation. Fragile X is characterized by severe psychological aberrations, including speech disturbance, a classic autistic syndrome, psychosis, and mental retardation. Some investigators have considered the speech pattern—described as jocular, narrative, staccato, and repetitive—to be so characteristic that it is almost diagnostic. Abrupt bursts of repeated three-to-four-word phrases have been noted. Some of the behavioral difficulties have included violent outbursts, hyperactivity, and self-mutilation. A number of physical stigmata are variously present: prominent ears, very large testicles, a long face, a prominent chin, and a relatively undeveloped mid-face. However, the phenotypic manifestations of this condition are highly variable. There are cases on record without these features, and, in a few instances, the chromosomal condition has been identified, but no psychological abnormality has been described (Bregman et al., 1987).

BEHAVIORAL GENETICS

Many kinds of behavioral syndromes are associated in whole or in part with genetic disorders (Leroy, 1983). For example, one psychotic condition resembling schizophrenia may be part of an inborn disturbance of copper metabolism (Wilson's disease); another kind of psychosis (Huntington's chorea) may be associated with a lack of neurotransmitter availability in a critical site (the basal ganglia) in the brain. In some instances, the behavioral symptoms form only a single facet (albeit often a significant one) of a widely disseminated medical condition with life-threatening implications.

In a great many maladies serious behavioral disturbances are themselves genetically transmitted disorders without accompanying medical illnesses. The patient with a major mental illness (e.g., schizophrenia, manic-depressive psychosis) may be physically robust, yet the psychological disturbance may be overwhelming.

Finally, some aspects of behavior, such as personality traits, intelligence, or temperamental characteristics, are not inherently pathological but may well be under the sway of genetic influences in their formation and appearance. A number of critical dimensions of adjustment fall into this category. For ethical reasons, much of the research in this realm has been conducted with animals of various kinds.

Animal Studies

A host of behavioral traits whose appearance is clearly linked to genetic transmission have been identified in various laboratory animals. Only a few of these will be mentioned.

Drosophila. The fruit fly, *Drosophila*, has frequently been the object of genetic studies, and its anatomic variants are familiar to every student of the field. However, a number of behavioral dimensions of genetic change have been charted as well, indicating that here, too, hereditary influences can dominate the appearance of specific patterns. Some of the genetically regulated behaviors that have been described thus far are homosexuality, lack of courtship success, and a mutant condition called "stuck" (inability of the male to withdraw after copulation). Avoidance learning and habituation in *Drosophila* are influenced by different mutations, as in the case of the "dunce" mutation, which results in the failure of both habituation (the ability to get used to a recurring stimulus) and avoidance learning (the ability to learn from experience).

The genetic defect responsible in this condition is the lack of any enzyme to metabolize cyclic adenosine monophosphate, a substance suspected of playing a central role in invertebrate habituation. Currently, in fact, four single-gene mutations (called *dunce, rutabaga, turnip,* and *Ddc* by the investigators) disrupt associative learning—and all produce disturbances in the internal chemistry of the receptor neuron (specifically, in the monoamine-stimulated adenylcyclase pathway). Two other mutations (*cabbage* and *amnesiac*) interfere with memory retrieval. In short, individual genes are being identified that have specific behavioral effects (Tully, 1986).

Learning in Rats. The maze-running ability of rats is clearly influenced by training and experience. Different strains of rats, however, will absorb the training and experience in different ways and at highly diverse rates of acquisition. Certain well-known genetic lines are outstanding in their ability to perform in maze tests. It is important to recognize that the rats achieve this level of success only under specific environmental conditions; if the conditions change, for example, if the degree of heat or cold, light or sound, satiety or hunger vary above or below specific thresholds, then the quality of their performance can vary radically (Searle, 1949, cited in Achenbach, 1982; Tryon, 1934). Mouse strains, too, differ not only in learning to run mazes for food, but also in their avoidance learning. Selective breeding produces strains of mice that differ in respect to anxietylike behavior; these divergences have been correlated with differences in the density of certain neurotransmitter receptor sites in the brain (Fuller & Thompson, 1979). Many aspects of cognitive functioning in rodents are decidedly influenced by inherited factors.

Primates. Inevitably, the experiments and the observations holding the greatest interest are those made on humans or other primates. The observations that ethologists and primatologists have been able to make both in the field and under controlled conditions have richly amplified the evidence for the genetic transmission of human behavioral patterns.

Of special interest are the isolation studies in which experimenters have taken infant monkeys and reared them apart from their natural caretakers. I.Charles Kaufman (1982) initiated this line of research, and Harold Harlow carried it forward brilliantly (Harlow & Harlow, 1965). It is hard to complete almost any college course in behavioral science without seeing some of the movies that Harlow made of his baby Rhesus monkeys and their wire-frame mothers.

These babies were separated from their mothers at birth or shortly thereafter and were reared in some form of isolation (Sackett, 1982). Such youngsters tended to develop a characteristic pattern of deviant behavior that was stable and readily recognizable. It involved the following:

- Body rocking.
- Stereotyped locomotion.
- Self-clutching.
- Oral activity directed toward the self.
- Withdrawal from possible social contacts.
- Low level of exploration (in males).

In adulthood, an additional set of behaviors appeared:

- Self-directed aggression.
- Incompetent sexual behavior.
- Inadequate maternal behavior.

Taken together, these symptoms constituted the *isolation syndrome* and were a highly predictable outcome of such solitary early experience. Although the basic cause of this condition was obvious, the mediating events that led to the behavior's particular form were not. Various theories have been formulated to explain this outcome: biochemical deficits, anatomical abnormalities, lack of stimulation, failure to learn social skills during critical periods, and failure to develop affectional systems. Some or all these of elements may indeed be present, but just what brings the isolation syndrome into being is not yet known.

A number of additional observations, however, suggest a genetic influence. Male and female Rhesus monkeys differ somewhat in the particular way they express this syndrome—and the differences between males and females are, in the final analysis, a matter of genetics.

The results of similar experiments with other kinds of monkeys were more striking still (Sackett, 1982). Several species resemble the Rhesus, such as the Pigtail Monkeys and the Crabeating Macaques. When reared in isolation, the behavior of these other species differs reliably from that of the Rhesus. For example, when young Pigtails were separated early and reared alone, they showed a much less intense form of the isolation syndrome. They were able to resume socialization when it was offered to them, and, as adults, they had little of the difficulty in mating and caring for young displayed by their Rhesus cousins. Moreover, in respect to gender differences, the males displayed none of the disturbances in exploration that were so striking in the Rhesus.

The Crabeating Macaques occupied a position midway between the other two species. The isolation pattern was more evident and certainly more strongly present than in the Pigtails. Nonetheless, it was a great deal less severe than was true for the Rhesus.

Such data seem to indicate that genetic factors affect the degree to which monkeys are at risk for developing the isolation syndrome. The species differences are genetic in origin, as are the gender factors; finding species differences in this group of behavioral responses demonstrates the significant role of genes in influencing behavior. Furthermore, these experiments tell something about the interaction of genotype (the underlying genetic character of an individual) with environment. Like other individual differences in genetically determined vulnerability to stress, these interspecies genotypical differences become apparent only when the individuals are exposed to the necessary environmental conditions.

Mental Traits

A host of mental characteristics, long suspected of being at least partially under genetic influence, are now the objects of intensive exploration. Suggestive studies may shed light on some of these psychological elements, and it is likely that the short list currently available will grow much longer.

Among the possibilities are stress response, intelligence, and personality traits.

Stress Response. In one project (Tennes, 1982), researchers studied infants' reactions to brief separation. It was possible to define three different patterns of response. One group, the *active responders,* cried lustily when the significant caretaker left them for a moment. Another group, the *low responders,* did not manifest any striking distress reaction under these circumstances. And the third group, the *ambivalent* ones, showed some elements of dismay, but were, on the whole, not nearly as upset as were the active responders.

The investigators then examined the biological aspect of this response by measuring these children's level of urine cortisol excretion (cortisol is one of the important hormones associated with the human stress response). The highest level of cortisol excretion was found in the active responders, the lowest was in the low responders, and intermediate levels were present in the ambivalent group. Similarly, Suomi and colleagues (Suomi, 1986; Suomi et al., 1981) have shown that infant monkeys differ in both their behavioral and their glandular (specifically, their pituitary-adrenal axis) responses to separation (as well as to other stresses). These patterns of response remain stable for a given individual over much of the life span. Moreover, in monkeys it has been possible to demonstrate that relatives, such as siblings and half-siblings, tend to have similar response patterns, even when they are reared apart or are cared for by adoptive mothers with quite different response styles. Taken together, these data suggest a genetic basis for an infant's profile of stress responses, of which the crying and protest behavior are really only the most visible part. Thus, underlying constitutional differences that appear in the patterning of the organismic stress reaction are presumably determined to a significant degree by genetic makeup.

Intelligence. Some well-designed twin and adoption studies speak strongly for the heritability of intelligence. There is an important developmental dimension to this. Attempts to assess intelligence in the first year of life have generally proved to be of little prognostic value. Various functions can indeed be measured, but they do not correlate well with what is tested for at later stages of childhood. During infancy, children from the same biological parents seem to be closer together in intellectual scores (in a statistical sense at any rate) as well as closer to their biological parents than they are to nonrelated individuals, such as adoptive siblings or adoptive parents. The difference becomes more marked in adolescence when the effect of the parental environment begins to diminish and the youngster becomes more independent (Scarr & Weinberg, 1978).

The question of heritable mental traits stirs many intense political and philosophical controversies. Nowhere has this been more heated than in the area of the inheritance of intelligence (as measured on IQ tests); indeed, this has been the subject of stormy debate for decades. It has involved both scientific and political dimensions, generated enormous passions, and embroiled many people in intense, bitterly fought confrontations about issues that are still largely unresolved. Much of the furor has centered on the tormenting question of race: Are some racial groups more (or less) intelligent than others?

In the United States this question has been addressed largely within the framework of white–black comparisons. Many thousands of black and white children and adults have taken psychometric tests, and large collections of data are accordingly available for analysis. These show that in aggregate, blacks have scored about 15 points (one standard deviation) lower on standard IQ tests than have whites (Jensen, 1969); inevitably, this has reinforced the stance of those who claim that racial differences in IQ do exist. It has led others to reexamine the fairness and the appropriateness of the testing itself; in particular, whether or not the tests have been culturally skewed in favor of whites.

Some of the positions taken by the participants in this debate have been startling in character. Thus, after the death of a distinguished English psychologist, Dr. Cyril Burt, investigators discovered that he had created a mass of false data, had written papers with fictitious authorship to support his thesis, and had thoroughly hoaxed the world of scientific psychology by reporting a series of fraudulent twin studies that "demonstrated" conclusively that blacks were less intelligent than whites.

But the issues need not take on a pseudoscientific character; they can be more directly political. The largest and perhaps the most detailed study of American youth to date (Bock & Moore, 1986) reviewed the factor of intelligence from a number of different views. During 1980, in the course of testing approximately 12,000 participants between the ages of 15 and 23 years, the authors found that Hispanics scored $\frac{1}{4}$ to $\frac{1}{3}$ standard deviations below non-Hispanic whites, and that blacks scored another $\frac{1}{2}$ standard deviation below Hispanics. In attempting to determine why this was so, the authors examined a number of theories and asserted that the data ruled out the possibility of genetic transmission; moreover, they dismissed the likelihood that language difference affected the scores. The authors suggest:

> A more satisfactory explanation [of the group differences] is simply that the communities represented by the present more-or-less exclusive subcultural subpopulations in the United States maintain, for historical reasons, different norms, standards, and expectations concerning performance within the family, in school, and in other institutions that shape children's behavior. Young people adapt to these norms and apply their talents and energies accordingly. (p. 158)

In effect, the authors place the onus for the differences in IQ scores on cultural shaping rather than on genetic transmission (quoted in *Science*, by Catterall, 1987). Other highly qualified experts also assert that no compelling evidence demonstrates the existence of racial differences in IQ (Kamin, 1981). Because many voices assert the opposite view, for the unbiased reader the measurement of intelligence remains confused and confusing. The search is on for culture-free tests, and no truly satisfactory instruments are universally accepted. More to the point, the concept of intelligence as a unitary invariant factor (Spearman's *g* factor, for "general intelligence") has come under considerable question (Gould, 1981). IQ scores have lost their magical absoluteness, and competent psychologists now advance their findings far more tentatively than was the practice a generation ago.

It may indeed be true that some aspects of intelligence are genetically transmitted, but environmental (subcultural and intrafamilial) influences also play a considerable role. Perhaps a majority view (among behavioral geneticists) holds that about half of current differences in IQ among individuals in U.S. and European white populations is the product of genetic influence (Scarr & Kidd, 1983). But there are certainly important reasons for questioning whether current methods of determining both the intelligence quotient in general and its heritability in particular will bear thorough scrutiny (Tizard, 1979). The field is lapped in controversy, and at this point it is too early to make any kind of declaration. On the other hand, as Scarr and Kidd (1983) point out:

> If current differences in intelligence are attributable half to genetic differences, about 10% to differences among family environments, and the rest to differences among individuals within families, are we led to abandon a commitment to improve children's lives? We fail to see the connection. (p. 394)

Personality Traits. The heritability of personality traits has been known to animal breeders for centuries. Some dogs have been bred to be gentle companions for children; others, to be viciously aggressive and to attack ferociously; still others, to hunt or to herd. Cocks have been bred to fight; horses, to race; and draft animals, to be stolid and to pull. A variety of behavioral patterns and personality traits have been known to "breed true," to appear in generation after generation, and, through inbreeding, to be capable of genetic enhancement. Demonstrating that this holds true for humans as well has been more difficult. It has involved carefully defining what a potentially heritable trait *is* and how it is to be reliably identified and measured (i.e., specifying the phenotype to be studied). It has also required fairly elaborate research conditions to allow distinguishing the genetic component from possible environmental influences. Indeed, the separation out of genetic and environmental factors as contributors to behavioral and attitudinal patterns has been the central task of the discipline of behavioral genetics.

To accomplish this mission, the involved scientists have worked with rather large populations and have developed complex mathematical tools to marshal the emerging data in a rigorous fashion. The traditional techniques of behavioral genetics have been the twin study method, the adoption and/or separation method, and the family study. Dramatic advances in molecular genetics are now supplementing these older techniques with linkage analysis. This methodology (termed *restriction fragment length polymorphism* analysis) makes it possible to determine quite precisely the position along a chromosome of the gene responsible for a given condition relative to a "marker" gene whose locus is known. And even newer and better techniques that utilize X rays are being promised.

The older methods of study, although producing strong suggestive evidence for the genetic transmission of various behavioral traits and conditions, have serious limitations.

By their nature, the proofs that they attain are essentially statistical—and hence subject always to the challenge that they might be spurious. Their critics assert that no underlying etiologic mechanism is being adduced and that the statistical conclusions might have alternative explanations.

The greatest difficulty is that the older methods cannot completely control for environmental factors (Vandenburg, 1984). For example, twin studies comparing monozygotic (identical) and dizygotic (fraternal) twins reveal genetic differences only if it is assumed that the two types of twins have comparable rearing environments. Studies comparing twins separated from birth or contrasting the biological and adoptive relatives of adoptees are interpretable only if there are not systematic biases in where and how the children have been placed. In family studies it may be impossible to distinguish genetic transmission from the effects of a shared familial environment.

The response offered by the investigators in these territories is twofold. First, in the case of a few pathological behavioral syndromes (e.g., several varieties of manic-depressive disorder), older family studies have been confirmed by newer linkage studies. Thus, in various families, linkage techniques have been able to locate the responsible gene on particular chromosomes with considerable precision. In these instances at least, the proof of their genetic character has thus acquired a biological basis to support the statistical dimension. Second, even for traits such as extroversion, altruism, or political conservatism, which have no known genetic locus, the accumulated evidence of a genetic contribution is becoming so large and so consistent that it can no longer be easily relegated to the merely hypothetical. It is becoming plausible.

The methods employed to establish such conclusions are of considerable interest. One of the earliest studies, the Louisville Twin Study (Wilson,

1977), undertook to follow two populations of twins, one identical and the other fraternal, from birth to age 15 years. Among other behavioral items, observers rated temperamental characteristics, such as activity level, sociability, and emotionality. A principal finding has been to trace out the genetic influences on the style of behavioral development. The data indicated that as the children grew, the rate, the order, and the quality of their developmental changes were genetically determined. By comparing the character of development in the two populations, the investigators were able to document that the tempo and sequence of *how* each individual twin developed was as much under genetic control as was the character of the individual traits that appeared and persisted.

Thatcher et al. (1987) reported on a study of brain development that suggests the kinds of neuromaturational factors underlying such developmental patterns. Using a complex mode of electroencephalographic analysis, they examined a sample of 577 individuals ranging in age from 2 months to 26.42 years. On the basis of their findings, the investigators concluded:

> Discrete growth spurts ... appeared in specific anatomical locations at specific postnatal periods. The left and right hemispheres developed at different rates and with different postnatal onset times, with the timing of growth spurts overlapping the timing of the major developmental stages described by Piaget. (p. 1110)

Hence, the notion of a predetermined course for neurobiological development is now receiving at least suggestive support from these anatomical observations.

The tactic of comparing identical and fraternal twins has been supplemented by another technique, the comparison of twins reared in a single household with those reared in separate households (e.g., one twin is reared in his family of origin by the biological parents, and the other grows up within an adoptive or, in any case, different family in some other setting). This method allows for controlling both the subjects' genetic makeup and the environment of their rearing. As a result, it meets the basic criterion of behavioral genetic research, that is, it allows for sorting out environmental and genetic differences. In addition, it makes for a considerable degree of cross-validation, because the two groups of identical twins (those reared together and those reared apart) can be compared with each other as well as with a population of fraternal twins. It thus permits some ingenious and powerful observations.

Yet another important methodological tactic employed in these investigations is the use of adoptive as against biological families, where once again the interweaving of biology and environment may be more clearly distinguished. One such study was spurred by the 1973 discovery in Texas of an adoption agency that had routinely done psychological tests on the biological mother of each of the children they placed (Horn et al., 1979). This allowed researchers to utilize a large pool of data that they could explore in many ways.

One surprising conclusion of such work is that similar traits or personality characteristics among children in a given household have very little to do with the youngsters' being reared in the same environment. Instead, these similarities are far more a function of the children's degree of genetic closeness, on the one hand, and the *uniqueness* of their experience on the other. This flies in the face of the dominant attitude of social scientists for much of the late 20th century: the concept that shared environment is the primary force shaping development. The behavioral geneticists stand firm, however, on the solid bank of data that they have laboriously but methodically collected through the years, which strongly suggests that within the population studied, approximately half of the variance of many characteriological behavior patterns is genetically determined, and the rest is due largely to environmental factors that the individuals do *not* have in common.

Methodologically, these scientists have addressed the nature of environment and the behavioral differences of their subjects with questionnaires and various objective tests. By and large, their subjects have included white, middle-class families, automatically introducing a certain statistical stability in the environmental component of their work. Through the years, these investigative methods have become increasingly sophisticated and precise. Today many behavioral geneticists are convinced that a strong suggestion of genetic determination is associated with a variety of behavioral factors. J. Phillip Rushton (1984) listed them as follows: activity level, alcoholism, anxiety, criminality, dominance, extroversion, intelligence, locus of control (personal autonomy), manic-depressive psychosis, political attitudes, schizophrenia, sexuality, sociability, values, and vocational interests.

In most instances, the behavioral geneticists find that for any given trait, about 50% of its variance is genetic in origin. The environmental influences that determine the other 50% might be anything from mother–infant interaction to subcultural orientation to traumatic events; in any case, an unpredictable quantity. Thus, when identical twins reared apart were compared to fraternal twin pairs reared apart, as well as to identical and fraternal twins reared together, the correlation among the observed behaviors was 0.49 for identical twins reared apart and 0.52 for identical twins reared together. The difference is tiny and is presumably due to the environmental influences at work. The equivalent correlation for fraternal twins reared together was 0.23—about what could have been expected from the degree to which they shared genes. Again, the environmental influence is near the vanishing point.

The heritability of social attitudes was also explored in this study, and it was found that the estimate for "traditionalism," that is, a conservative outlook on political and social attitudes, was 0.45% (Holden, 1987). In an international study that involved twin subjects in England and Australia, the correlation between the views of both the identical and the fraternal male twins on such items as attitudes toward the death penalty was accounted for entirely by the genetic loading and was not affected by their environmental experience. Thus, heritability bids fair to assume new dimensions in the formulations of social scientists.

Similar results were obtained by Rushton (cited in Holden, 1987) who studied 573 pairs of adult twins in respect to traits such as altruism, empathy, nurturance, aggressiveness, and assertiveness. Here again, as the distribution of these characteristics in identical and fraternal twins was measured and compared, altruism and aggressivity (which would presumably have been strongly influenced by parental attitudes) turned out to be present according to a genetically determined pattern—with virtually no discernible environmental effect.

There are many difficulties with this type of research. Critics have been quick to point out (Kamin, 1981), for example, that when twins are reared apart, they often live in adjacent dwellings, share similar environments, and have a great deal of contact with one another. Again, the reality of their twinship may affect the way their environments respond to them, thus creating unique conditions. Alternatively, within adoptive situations, parents may have very different expectations of biologically related children (whom they may expect, consciously or unconsciously, to imitate them) than they do of children whom they perceive as being totally unrelated. Hence, investigators still debate the interpretation of some of these data.

Another emerging realm of study is a beginning clarification of the nature of environment. With the data described, it has been possible to compare certain aspects of the twins' environment in terms of how much of it was shared (essentially identical) and how much was unique and different for each twin. The investigators' (Plomin & Daniels, 1987) rather startling conclusion is that the differences between children growing up in the same family are influenced to a far greater extent by circumstances that are different for each than they are by elements of the environment that they share. The factors that the children experience in common are considered the *shared* components of their environment, and those that are unique for each child are the *unshared* elements. Thus, in the extreme case, identical twins who share all their genes in common are nonetheless likely to be different in certain behavioral respects. Particular environmental influences that they share would *not* lead to differences in attitude or comportment; on the contrary, with identical genetic makeup, identical twins should respond in exactly the same way to common stimuli. But differences between such twins *do* indeed exist; hence, *nonshared* environmental forces must affect their development.

Investigators have offered the proposition that for *any* children growing up in the same home, the key influences affecting their developmental profiles in ways that make them different from one another are the unshared aspects of their environments. Thus, that they have the same mother and the same father and that these individuals have certain consistencies in child rearing are thought now to be *less* important in shaping development than are the *differences* in the parents' attitudes toward individual children as well as other unique events and interventions experienced by each child that other family members do not share. In effect, the somewhat unexpected conclusion is that within the same family, the siblings are likely to be as different from one another as any of them may be from children reared in some other family. In brief, "the most important source of environmental variance is nonshared environment" (Plomin & Daniels, 1987, p. 4).

In addition to adaptive mental traits that may be under genetic influence (stress response, intelligence, and personality characteristics), there are a number of pathological conditions with accompanying mental aberrations of one sort or another. Several categories lend themselves to study. On the one hand, a variety of conditions associated with known physiological disturbances are characteristically accompanied by psychiatric disorders. On the other hand, there are a group of conditions where a biological component is either totally unknown or at best imperfectly defined, and where behavioral manifestations form the prominent and significant symptomatology.

Hereditary Medical Conditions with Behavioral Symptoms

These illnesses pose the psychiatrist a real dilemma because prominent or distressing psychiatric symptoms may mask the presence of a profound physiological disorder. Thus, a patient suffering from such a condition may appear to have a straightforward psychiatric problem and may be diagnosed and treated as such. In some instances, the full nature of the illness does not become manifest until much later. The diagnosis does not suggest itself at the outset because the symptoms seem so consonant with some recognized psychiatric syndrome; weeks or months may pass before the underlying illness becomes evident.

Illnesses with Autisticlike or Psychotic Symptoms. Inborn errors of amino-acid metabolism such as homocystinuria can give rise to certain cases of childhood autism. This is only one of several such conditions.

Other Genetically Determined Metabolic Disorders. Such conditions as Wilson's disease, intermittent porphyria, and Fabry disease are often accompanied by behavioral symptoms similar to those of childhood schizophrenia.

A partial listing (Levine et al., 1983) of conditions involving inborn errors of metabolism with known effects on behavior (such as symptoms simulating those of psychosis) would include:

- *Disorders of Lipid Metabolism.* These include Niemann-Pick disease, Types A and D; Gaucher disease, noninfantile, nonneuronopathic type; Fabry disease; Refsum disease; "adolescent" types of hexosaminidase A deficiency; and some "chronic" types of Beta-galactosidase deficiency.

- *Disorders of Oligosaccharide and Glycoprotein Metabolism.* Examples are cherry-red-spot-myoclonus syndrome; sialidase deficiency; mannosidosis; and aspartylglucosaminuria.

- *Mucopolysaccharidoses.* This group includes Hunter disease and Sanfilippo disease (Types A, B, C, and D).

- *Disorders of Amino Acid or Organic Acid Metabolism.* This includes the aforementioned phenylketonuria (both that due to the classic hyperphenylalaninemia and that due to biopterin deficiency); hyperhydroxyprolinemia; hyperargininemia, Type V; histidinemia; and methylmalonic acidemia with deranged sulfur amino-acid metabolism.

- *Disorders of Purine and Pyrimidine Metabolism.* These include Lesch-Nyhan disease (where among other distressing symptoms the patients are given to self-mutilation); orotic aciduria, Type I; some of the porphyrias (congenital erythropoietic porphyria and acute intermittent hepatic porphyria); and hepatolenticular degeneration (Wilson's disease).

Disorders Caused by Malfunction of the Endocrine Glands. The endocrine glands (e.g., the hypothalamus, pituitary, thyroid, adrenal, ovaries, testes, even the brain itself) act as primary regulators of growth and organizers of structure; they thus have a profound influence on the growth and functioning of the body. Their secretions (called *hormones*) are poured directly into the bloodstream and act as chemical messengers regulating the rates of growth and metabolism of all tissues. For example, the sex hormones (estrogen, progesterone, and testosterone, to mention a few of the best known) affect the reproductive organs and tissues responsible for the secondary sexual characteristics, but they also exert a potent and at times irreversible organizing effect on the brain. As a result of their activity at critical periods, the brain becomes masculinized or feminized. Such critical periods exist throughout development so that certain functions mediated by these endocrine glands must be initiated at their proper metabolic moment. Should they arrive too early or be delayed for too long, then the fate of these endocrine glands becomes uncertain; they may never develop properly, and more serious still, the functions they subserve may, in turn, grow awry. This is especially true during periods of rapid growth and differentiation; during such periods, the effects of hormones are decisive.

Of special interest is the fact that thyroid hormone also affects brain growth and organization. This substance influences the formation of myelin, the growth of dendrites and synapses, the structure of the cell membranes, and the metabolic competence of the neurons. The lack of this essential secretion during a period of particularly rapid brain development can have catastrophic effects on brain growth, intellectual advancement, and personality unfolding in general. The person with congenital hypothyroidism (who at birth suffered from inadequate thyroid secretion—and who used to be called a cretin) is usually seriously mentally retarded, stunted in growth, and otherwise altered in physical appearance. In the past, the condition was so widespread and so devastating in character that the term *cretin* is still a commonly employed pejorative for a stupid or incompetent person.

Clinically, the first 3 months of postnatal life are critical for developing this condition. In the infant genetically deprived of thyroid hormone, replacement therapy during that interval will prevent the appearance of the condition, or restrain its advance. Despite an inborn propensity toward hypothyroidism, a child so treated will often achieve full health and function. If, however, the necessary replacement therapy is not immediately forthcoming, the hypothyroidism will progress, causing irreversible mental retardation.

Psychiatric Illnesses without Medical Disturbances

The major mental disorders comprise a group of serious and common illnesses whose most prominent symptoms are disturbed behavior. Any associated physiological disturbances are not as yet well understood. Many of these maladies are transmitted in a fashion that is evidently familial, with direct genetic patterns of vulnerability either strongly suggested or already largely worked out. The following subsections describe some of the more important members of this group.

Schizophrenia.   Scarr and Kidd (1983) have commented, "Perhaps no other disorder has such a testy literature about the nature of its genetics" (p. 382). Although still subject to debate, recent findings have supported the probable presence of a genetic component in the etiology of this condition. Three kinds of data have now focused on the heritability of schizophrenia: twin studies, adoption data, and the study of various neurobiological markers in the relatives of schizophrenics.

The twin studies repeatedly show that the concordance of monozygotic twins for the development of the symptoms of schizophrenia is characteristically higher than the concordance of dizygotic twins. That is to say, when one of a twin pair with the same genetic makeup develops schizophrenia, the other is far more likely to do so than is the case for twin pairs with different genetic inheritance (O'Rourke et al., 1982).

The adoption studies are equally suggestive. In Denmark, where excellent adoption records are maintained, several long-term studies have been carried out. A consistent finding has been that elevated frequencies of the disease occur in the biological relatives but not in the adoptive relatives of schizophrenics. For example, one such investigation involved locating pairs of siblings where at least one of the natural parents had identified schizophrenia, and where the children had been reared apart from an early age. The incidence of the appearance of schizophrenia in these children was then compared. Whether reared by the natural parents or away from them, the likelihood for the appearance of this condition in these siblings was essentially the same. With the environmental factor controlled in this way, the powerful influence of the genetic component was thus confirmed.

The environment plays an enormous role in determining whether the syndrome becomes manifest, even within a genetically inclined individual. Thus, the coefficient of genetic relationship for first-degree relatives is .50; the actual concordance of such relatives for the appearance of schizophrenia is, in fact, less than 10%. Compared with the likelihood of schizophrenia appearing in the population at large, this is a very large number; but it is much less than it could be in terms of the genetic loading. The difference is thought to be due to the environmental forces at work; favorable circumstances can apparently protect many vulnerable individuals from the full appearance of the condition. The results of this and other adoption studies have been convincing to most—but not all—serious students of the field (Kessler, 1980).

Having a parent who is schizophrenic dramatically increases an offspring's chances of developing schizophrenia. Several large prospective studies of children with a schizophrenic parent or parents reveal that even prior to the onset of any overt schizophrenic symptoms, many of these youngsters show significant deficits in the areas of attention and information processing (Neuchterlein, 1986). Offspring with marked deficits are at high risk for development of schizophrenic symptoms in later life.

Researchers have invested much effort toward seeking a dependable marker that would characterize carriers of a genetic predisposition toward schizophrenia. To date these investigations have not borne fruit. One of the more likely possibilities currently being studied (associated in particular with chronic schizophrenia) is eye movement dysfunction (Holzman, 1987). Disturbances in eye tracking and other eye movement disabilities are more common in the near relatives of certain schizophrenics, even when those relatives display no symptoms of the disorder.

In a sizable percentage of monozygotic twins both siblings develop schizophrenia, but what about those cases of identical twins where the illness in one twin is not echoed by its appearance in the other? Important protective or exacerbating environmental factors have a profound influence on whether or not the disease appears. What these factors are, however, is not known. By the same token, the nature of the genetically transmitted element that makes for the disease is equally unknown. Attempts to develop a model for the transmission of schizophrenia (e.g., single-gene inheritance as against polygenic transmission) have led to a multitude of possibilities; the current view is that no available model really fits the data.

There may well be a number of different genetic sources for the appearance of this condition (in effect, there may be a number of different schizophrenias). In any case, it is probably most accurate to say that what is, in fact, transmitted genetically is a vulnerability for schizophrenia rather than the illness as such. The goal of present research must be to single out the nature of that vulnerability.

Manic-Depressive Illness.   There is now little doubt that a genetic predisposition exists for the major affective disorders in general and for manic-depressive illness in particular (Gershon & Nurnberger, 1983). A number of different sources of data converge to support that conclusion (Scarr & Kidd, 1983). The characteristic drug responsiveness of these illnesses (along with the discovery of other biochemical findings) speak for a biological base to the conditions—and therefore a likely genetic etiology. In addition, family studies reveal the consistent appearance of an increased prevalence of the illness in close relatives of the target patient (Gershon et al., 1975). Surveys of adopted-away offspring of affected parents also show an increased incidence of the condition despite the change in family milieu (Cadoret, 1976). A least one twin study suggests a similar conclusion (the monozygotic twins were about five times as likely to show the disturbance as were the dizygotics) (Gershon et al., 1977). And finally, females are far more prone (by a factor of 1.5 to 3.6 depending on the study) to the impact of affective illness than are males; although alternative hormonal or sociocultural explanations are possible, this finding raises the question of X-linked inheritance.

With this wealth of evidence, the issue becomes not so much one of genetic versus environmental transmission; the question instead becomes: Just what is the pattern of genetic inheritance? Kidd (1982) reviewed the genetic data and suggested the existence of at least 3 genetic forms of the disorder: an X-linked form (Baron et al., 1987; Mendlewicz et al., 1987), a link on chromosome 11, and an unspecified form. Recent studies of large Amish families with several generations of relatives afflicted with manic-depressive illness seemed to permit localization of the responsible gene to a site on chromosome 11 (Egeland et al., 1988; Gerhard et al., 1984). Shortly thereafter, however, a reevaluation of their population challenged the accuracy of this finding (Kelsoe et al., 1989). In any case, the disorder is clearly heterogeneous (caused by disturbance on more than one genetic locus).

Of special interest is the accumulating evidence (Cytryn et al., 1985) that the infants born to parents with major affective disorders are demonstrably different from the babies of normal comparison parents. At one year of age the offspring of manic-depressive parents are significantly different in respect to their difficulty in regaining their composure once they have become upset; they display a strikingly different pattern of self-consolation; and their attachment behavior is also different from that of control babies. Zahn-Wexler et al. (1984) found that the disturbances such infants manifested were evident in the social but not in the cognitive domain. These investigators report that when they observed such youngsters in the Ainsworth Strange Situation, it was possible to document an increasing press of attachment problems between 12 and 24 months of age. Emotional dysregulation and an inability to share hinted at future peer difficulties. It is possible that the vulnerability that will later take form as a propensity toward alternating swings of manic and depressive cycles of behavior is manifested early on by these disturbances of emotional and interpersonal regulation. The difficulty with these findings is that the mothers often show disturbed responses to their infants. Hence, it is still not clear whether the infants' behavior is an expression of genetic difference or a response to disturbed mothering.

Genetic factors also influence the transmission of depressive illness (unipolar depression), but its heritability is different from that of bipolar illness. Determining the degree of genetic influence is complicated because the illness takes different forms under different environmental circumstances. Thus, when the usual methods are employed for the factor analyses of personality traits for sizable populations, symptoms of anxiety and symptoms of depression tend to form distinct clusters. However, in a study of 3798 twin pairs with multivariate genetic analysis, Kendler et al. (1987) found:

... genes act largely in a nonspecific way to influence the overall level of psychiatric symptoms. No evidence could be found for genes that specifically affect symptoms of depression without also strongly influencing symptoms of anxiety. By contrast, the environment seems to have specific effects, i.e., certain features of the environment strongly influence symptoms of anxiety while having little influence on symptoms of depression. These results, which are replicated across sexes, suggest that the separable anxiety and depression symptom clusters in the general population are largely the result of environmental factors. (p. 451)

In other words, the same genetic makeup can find expression as a depressive illness or as an anxiety disorder depending on the milieu within which the condition develops. If this thesis is accurate, it would profoundly affect the demographics of affective disorder.

Alcoholism. During the 20th century, alcoholism has moved from its traditional role as a prime example of human weakness to the status of a disease, and, more recently, to acceptance as another condition to be explored for inherited vulnerability. The web that binds together the generations of alcoholics has become ever more strongly woven. Today the accumulated evidence suggests that some genetic factor may make a sizable percentage of the population extremely susceptible to the use and abuse of this substance (see material on drug abuse in Volume 2, Chapter 13). Again, little is known about the precise nature of the underlying mechanism that might determine such inherited vulnerability. On the other hand, the work of Cloninger (1987) has begun to illuminate this formerly obscure area of study.

In particular, this investigator has employed the findings of a great many observers in several different fields. Using this multifaceted approach, Cloninger has begun to build an integrated picture of distinct subtypes of alcoholism that can be differentiated by their genetic, neurophysiological, and psychosocial characteristics. For years, there have been reports of two types of alcoholics, one with an early onset (often beginning with puberty) and the other with a later point of initiation (often in the third or fourth decade of life). An inability to abstain from alcohol characterizes the early-onset type; the youngsters seek it avidly from an early age and cannot readily be restrained from its use. In contrast to this, the late-onset group is marked not so much by a quest for alcohol as by an inability to stop drinking once the pattern is initiated. But the differences do not stop with the relationship to alcohol use; there are profound personality differences as well. The early-onset type do not seem to respond to rewards nor to learn from failure; they seem rather to be driven to seek novelty and are variously noted to be excitable, distractible, impulsive, and disorderly. They drive when drunk, have accidents, and are often involved in delinquent behavior. Again by way of contrast, the late-onset group will avoid getting hurt and learn from experience. Moreover, such individuals are seldom delinquent and tend rather to be dependent, sympathetic, sensitive, and persistent.

EEG studies and other biological measurements also distinguish the two groups. Most important from a genetic view is that the members of the early-onset group show a high rate of familial transmission of the condition, whereas the late-onset group members show little such uniformity in incidence. In adopted-away sons of early-onset alcoholic fathers, the risk of alcoholism is nine times that of the sons of all other fathers. In the adopted-away sons of late-onset alcoholic fathers, there was no problem with alcoholic abuse unless the adoptive father showed a strong tendency to abuse alcohol. This is comparable to the fate of boys whose biological parents did *not* abuse alcohol but who were adopted into a home with an alcoholic father. Under those conditions the children show no tendency to drink excessively. For children of the early-onset parents, no matter what the external environmental conditions, the vulnerability is strongly inclined to find early expression; whereas for the offspring of a late-onset parent, the vulnerability will not be realized unless the necessary external conditions are present to evoke it. In short, it is necessary to go beyond such crude categories as alcoholism per se and to break down the behavior into specific patterns of adaptation. There in turn must take into account not only the genetic tendency, but the particular environmental conditions that evoke its expression.

Learning Deficits. Albeit a complex and confusing realm, the broad area of learning deficits is subject to the influence of genetic transmission. Because the etiology of such difficulties is often of intrauterine or perinatal origin, there are obvious limitations to the generality of this statement. Nonetheless, for a long time it has been known that learning difficulties have a familial tendency. If in the course of working up a child for learning problems, the investigator takes a careful family history, he or she often discovers that a parent or close blood relative displayed similar problems during childhood (DeFries & Decker, 1982). Indeed, studies of one group of families with histories of dyslexia (Smith et al., 1983) have permitted investigators tentatively to localize the gene responsible for dyslexia in those pedigrees on chromosome 15. More than that, in twin studies, monozygotic twins show a high concordance rate for dyslexia ranging from 84% to 100%. Clearly, in many cases of learning difficulty, aspects of brain architecture or the organization of its function are subject to genetic control, and these aspects determine the way cognitive functioning develops—and maldevelops—in particular areas. Nonetheless, a recent review suggests that in those cases where a genetic factor is present, the genetic origin is more likely to be heterogeneous than due to single-gene transmission (Smith et al., 1990).

Panic Attack Proneness. Recent research into the biology of panic attacks has revealed that individuals with this condition can be precipitated into such an attack by administering intravenous lactic acid; moreover, evidences for a similar chemical vulnerability can be found in close relatives of the afflicted individuals. However, the injection of lactic acid has no such effect in nonvulnerable subjects. This suggests that panic attacks are both familial and associated with a particular neurobiological vulnerability. More than that, many studies of family trees reveal a strong familial linkage of panic disorder. In constrast to this, when the distribution of generalized anxiety disorder is studied in similar fashion, no such familial trend is discernible. Together, these findings suggest that panic disorder may well be subject to the laws of inherited transmission (Judd et al., 1987).

Stuttering. Careful studies of the family characteristics of stutterers yield a pattern that suggests genetic transmission. The distribution of stuttering across families is clearly nonrandom. Investigators have considered the likelihood of stuttering being learned behavior but have pointed out that many adults stop their stuttering before they have their children. Scarr and Kidd conclude that "at this time definite proof is elusive, yet all available evidence suggests that susceptibility to stuttering is genetically transmitted" (Scarr & Kidd, 1983, p. 391).

Tourette Syndrome (TS). This disorder is manifested by multiple motor and vocal tics, usually with an onset in childhood, and characteristically pursuing a variable course during development. Although apparently non-familial cases do occur, the relatives of TS patients have an increased incidence of the syndrome, multiple motor tics (without vocalization), and obsessive-compulsive syndrome. Recent studies (Pauls & Leckman, 1986) indicate that certain cases of obsessive-compulsive disorder are etiologically related to TS and to chronic tic disorder and are inherited as an autosomal dominant trait. Linkage studies currently under way in several large pedigrees afflicted with TS may soon produce more precise information concerning the genetic loci for the condition; currently about 25% of the genome (the total mass of genetic material) has now been excluded from the search and the field is narrowing down (Pauls et al., 1990).

Autism. Hereditary factors have now been implicated in the etiology of autism. The classic findings are present: Both siblings of monozygotic twin pairs are more prone to develop the syndrome than is the case with dizygotic twins, and the siblings of autistic children are far more likely to have autism than are members of the population at large. Of considerable recent interest, however, is the finding that close relatives of autistic children tend to have far higher rates of psychopathology than expected. This has suggested to Piven et al. (1990) that autism, cognitive disorders (such as specific learning deficits), and severe social dysfunction and isolation ". . . represent expressions of a common underlying genetic abnormality" (p. 181). In other words, a single genetic factor finds different expressions in different children, that is, in one child as a learning deficit, in another as shyness and isolation, and in a third as autism.

Attention-Deficit Hyperactivity Disorder (ADHD). Children with ADHD have been found to have a high incidence of minor physical anomalies that are usually unremarked by the casual observer; generally speaking, these anomalies are without clinical significance. (They include such phe-nomena as eyes set too wide apart, a single crease across the palms, unusual architecture of the ears, etc.) Studies of the families of children with ADHD reveal that the close relatives of these children often have such anomalies as well, usually without the accompanying cognitive problems of the target population. In brief, the children can have ADHD alone, anomalies alone, or anomalies along with the attentional deficits; and their family members can show a similar scatter. To account for this, Deutsch et al. (1990) postulate a hidden latent factor that can take form as either brain pathology (and give rise to the cognitive attentional difficulties) or as minor physical anomalies. Because the genetic tendency could find either kind of expres-sion, some children would have the attentional problems without the anom-alies; others would show anomalies without the concentration difficulties; and their family members, too, could have anomalies without the cognitive findings, or vice versa. Then there could be individuals who display both findings. Given this formulation, a previously puzzling distribution of ADHD began to make sense. Indeed, an analysis of familial data suggested that the latent trait was transmitted in an autosomal dominant mode.

Chapter 2

From Conception to Birth

INTRODUCTION

The underlying principle of all developmental thinking asserts that at each stage of growth, the emerging configuration is the product of an active, reciprocal, and continuing exchange between the genetic potential and the environmental menu of actualities. No development takes place in the abstract; the genetic schema is always realized within some environment. More than that, the process is always dynamic; the growing developer influences the surrounding milieu just as surely as the surround impinges on the developmental processes that it enfolds.

FETAL BEHAVIOR

People are not used to thinking of the unborn baby as behaving, that is, as manifesting recognizable adaptive/responsive patterns. Behavior, as it were, begins at birth. But to a surprising extent, very early in life indeed, striking sequences can be identified that speak for both adaptiveness and responsiveness, and even for a measure of self-regulation. As a result, a host of intriguing studies have now been conducted in an attempt to better understand the fetus as a behavioral entity.

Early Studies

Between 1936 and 1958, Hooker studied the behavior of 140 human embryos and fetuses (Hooker, 1952; Richmond & Herzog, 1979). His subjects were almost invariably the products of abortions as these were delivered at (or were brought to) the hospital. When be began his work, neonatology was almost nonexistent, and all the embryos (as well as the younger fetuses) regularly died. Nonetheless, he applied himself systematically to studying those that became available to him, and only in the wake of his pioneering research have researchers begun to gain some insights into the organization of fetal behavior.

Genetics and Function

It had always been assumed that after the structure of an organ was initiated by the nature of the genetic patterning, the organ would have to be complete before it was ready to function. Embryologists have learned, however, that once specialized cells appear, they begin to function immediately, well before the entire organ has elaborated. This functioning is not incidental; it will influence and, indeed, may be essential for the subsequent development of that organ or organ system. Thus, the genetic component may begin the process, but the activity of the cells themselves is necessary to bring it to fruition. In particular, among Hooker's recorded observations were notes about the presence of spontaneous movements of the newly formed muscles, which began to move long before their innervation was complete. There was no sensory stimulus present, and no valid reflex arc was even possible as yet, but the muscles moved, as it were, on their own volition. This muscle contractility is a functional presence that is of considerable import in the development of subsequent processes. When muscles contract, their tone is maintained, contractures are avoided, and their exercise encourages fuller growth. More than that, when the fetus has developed enough, the movements signal life to the mother with many consequent emotional ramifications. The earliest point in the gestational cycle at which mothers have reported feeling life is the 16th week. This means that when she is less than halfway through her gestation, such a mother may already experience her baby directly.

Earliest Findings

Through systematic study, Hooker was able to document a number of significant developmental trends:

1. Using the tip of a very fine hair as his stimulating instrument, he found that before the age of 7 weeks, the embryo did not respond to his probe. In the middle of the 7th week, however, stimulation of the mouth and perioral area caused the embryo to flex its neck away from the hair. Thus, the embryo's very first responses were connected with stimulation of the mouth region.
2. As development proceeded, this capacity to be excited by touch gradually spread over the head and downward to encompass the trunk until a touch anywhere would beget a movement response.
3. In the 10th week, swallowing movements appeared, and (as was subsequently discovered) with embryos of 12 weeks gestation, this action was already functional; they were regularly imbibing amniotic fluid. Initially, this involved taking in from 15 to 40 milliliters per hour, a substantial factor in the embryo's fluid regulation. This swallowing behavior served both to adjust amniotic fluid balance and to provide the growth process with an important source of protein (18% of the necessary protein and 14% of the nitrogen intake).
4. The first reflexes noted in response to stimulation were the palmar flexion and the plantar toe curl, which could be elicited by Week 10. Fetuses of 14 weeks showed a more elaborated capacity to grasp with their hands, and by the 18th week they could be found with their thumbs in their mouths.
5. Fetal breathing movements appeared early.
6. Crying was observed in the amniotic sac.

7. The thumb sucking and other types of contact demonstrated that self-stimulation was a significant presence from early in the second trimester.

Governing Principles

From these several observations Hooker could deduce a number of principles regarding development:

1. As noted above, muscles can contract before they are fully innervated.
2. In general, motor nerves develop before the sensory nerves.
3. Presently, a series of reflexes is formed wherein a given stimulus automatically begets a given response. If a person touches a hot surface, he or she will snatch away the hand before even feeling the burn; a reflex arc has closed and the sensation begets the defensive movement. If something suddenly approaches a person's eye, he or she blinks—without thought, plan, or intention. The circuitry is built in. Many such reflexes are present at birth; those who have studied the embryo and fetus have been able to identify such responses well before birth. However, for a reflex to appear, the necessary connections must be made, that is, a receptor cell must be in place and must connect to an effector cell, which can then get a muscle to act. Developmentally, this means that reflexes will appear when the nervous system is well enough advanced to allow for the completion of such a loop. There must be a sensory axon leading from the surface of the skin into the spinal cord, a spinal ganglion where the cell body is located, a number of intercalated neuronal links within the cord itself, and finally an outgoing motor nerve to complete the response. The initial reflex movements tend to be isolated, jerky, and relatively uncoordinated.
4. As time goes on, higher brain centers link up and take over; with this, a sequencing of contractions and a patterning of reactions are introduced, and the movements become smoother, more sustained, and more complex.
5. These spontaneous movements play a role in establishing the sleep–wake cycle as well. There are different stages to sleep. The relatively active and movement-filled part of the sleep experience (REM sleep), is present in the premature infant about 70% of the time. This early in development REM sleep is not well differentiated from non-REM sleep; the distinction becomes firm only later when, at about 3 months of postpartum life, the REM events become confined exclusively to the sleep state. Only then can full muscle relaxation be attained during sleep (Metcalf, 1979). (See also Chapter 3, pp. 83–84, for a discussion of the organization of sleep.)

Sensory Functioning

In recent years investigators have directed a good deal of effort toward ascertaining the level of development reached by the growing embryo and fetus at different points in gestation. New techniques have been elaborated that explore these questions in utero. Animal experimentation has contributed its moiety of illumination, and a rich pattern of information has emerged.

Hearing. One ready barometer of fetal response is movement; another is heart rate. Hence, in determining whether or not the fetus is sensitive to sound, the monitoring of these behavioral variables has been invaluable. In one study, pure tones were sent through the mother's abdominal wall at various stages of fetal growth; the first responsive changes in heart rate were noted at 26 weeks (Murphy & Smyth, 1962). Evidently, at that point, the total response apparatus is sufficiently integrated to allow this to happen. It has been demonstrated that at 20 weeks, the cochlea (the hearing part of the inner ear) does show detectable function.

Postmortem examination of infants born at term and measurement of electrical-activity responses to sound in the brains of living newborns reveal that the part of the brain that mediates hearing (the *medullary cortex* of the acoustic area) is already myelinated at birth. The remainder of the acoustic pathway (e.g., a part of the brain called the *inferior colliculus*), however, does not complete its organized development until the second year of life.

It is not altogether surprising to learn that multiple sources of sound exist in the womb. Indeed, it has been possible to place a transducer next to the ear of a fetus in utero; 72 decibels (approximately the sound level of adult conversation) have been recorded at that point. The mother's heart, her vascular system (in particular, the *souffle*, the sound produced by the movement of blood through the placenta), and the mother's digestive apparatus all contribute to the volume of apparent noise that regularly impinges on the fetus.

Touch. As noted (Hooker, 1952), the earliest responses were elicited at about $7\frac{1}{2}$ weeks in the perioral area; by 14 weeks, a touch anywhere on the body brought about a reaction.

Taste. It seems a trifle absurd to talk of fetal taste, but, in fact, responses of a predictable kind have been observed. Because the embryo starts to consume amniotic fluid rather early, it offered investigators a ready behavioral measure for ascertaining the presence of taste responses. Thus, saccharine introduced into the amniotic sac was found (DeSnoo quoted in Bradley & Mistretta, 1975) to increase the swallowing of fluid; presumably, even at that early age, the young developer already had a sweet tooth. Iodinated oil, on the other hand, generally agreed to have an unpleasant taste, diminished the intake of amniotic fluid. Taste preferences apparently appear early (Graves, 1980).

Vision.   Within the womb visual functioning is not likely to be extensive; nonetheless the precursors of visual experience must be there as well. In fact, from 29 weeks the eyes have been observed to open. More than that, experiments with the maternal abdominal wall have revealed that it does indeed transilluminate to some extent, and that dim but measurable changes in the degree of intrauterine illumination can be recorded.

THE FETAL ENVIRONMENT

Many of the difficulties experienced by newborns are attributable to events taking place during gestation, an outcome of the interaction between the fetus and its total surround. The study of the character of that surround and of the factors that influence its nature has been richly productive. This has involved not merely a study of pathological elements, but an understanding of the fundamental character of that environment in its many dimensions.

The Fluid Container

The fetus lives as an entity of ever increasing weight bobbing within a totally liquid envelope (Graves, 1980).

Gravity.   As the fetus grows, it gradually shifts from a condition of weightlessness to an ever closer approximation to the experience of normal gravity.

- *The Floating World.* At the outset, the relative proportions of the volume of amniotic fluid to the volume displaced by the fetus are in the order of four or five to one. In effect, the developing human is a small mass floating within a much larger container of liquid. As the fetus approaches term, however, the proportions change so that eventually they are equal. The level of flotational support diminishes in equivalent degree, and as the fetus enlarges, it gradually comes to feel the sense of weight.
- *Growth and Space.* As the fetus comes to occupy an every greater fraction of the intrauterine space, it comes into more and more contact with the wall of the womb so that many touch experiences begin to occur. Researchers conjecture that the mother's movements gradually assume ever more meaning for the contained developer.

The Fetus as Regulator.   As noted, the fetus is not altogether passive in respect to the dynamics of fluid exchange. Toward term, it is ingesting between 210 and 760 milliliters of amniotic fluid every day. Moreover, its kidneys have begun to function, and it is urinating actively, usually somewhere between 1 and 17 milliliters per day.

The Endocrine Environment

Because most human births produce only one offspring, the issues attendant on bearing litters do not crop up very often in human affairs. Animal research, however, tells something of the immediate and direct effects that littermates have on one another. Thus, a rat fetus born as the unique female within a litter of several males will predictably display a considerable degree of masculinization. It is evident that the increased testosterone flowing from the bodies of the siblings has impinged directly on the female and affected her development.

SOME GENERAL PRINCIPLES

The Developmental Gradient

An innate response readiness seems to be present that can be triggered by the right stimulus. Thus, at birth the infant must perform a variety of functions for the first time. Ordinarily, he can manage them quite well and takes them in stride.

Vision.   The fetus has seen only light and shadow in utero, knowing light primarily as diffuse transillumination. Nonetheless, at birth or very shortly thereafter, the newborn can fix his gaze and, to some extent, is able to follow a moving stimulus. More than that, researchers have found that the infant will select among available visual patterns and fix upon a preferred one. Clearly, the mechanism for visual response has been well prepared and requires only the proper triggering experience to become functional.

Smell.   So far as has been determined, the fetus is unable to smell. If, however, an observer offers a 2-day-old nursing infant a choice of breast pads from a number of different women, the infant will turn preferentially toward that of his own mother (MacFarlane, 1975).

Fetal Learning

The question arises as to whether any real learning can take place prior to birth. Because premature babies are surviving ever younger deliveries (many are being saved despite a birth weight of 1000 grams or less [2.2 pounds]), the question of their brain status is becoming an increasingly serious issue. Any technique that could help assess their learning capacity might give valuable hints about the necessity for intervention at critical moments.

Auditory Learning.   A series of ingenious experiments suggests that the fetus can both hear and recall what it hears in a functional way. Investigators (DeCasper & Fifer, 1980) developed a sucking test that offered the child a choice. The arrangement allowed the baby to suck more or less actively, depending on the result he preferred. The investigators then had pregnant women close to term read passages out loud to the fetus from a particular children's book, *The Cat in the Hat.* During the last 6 weeks of their pregnancies, 16 women read in this way twice a day. By delivery time, it was estimated that the fetuses had had about 5 hours of exposure to the reading.

Once born, the babies were given a choice; they could command the mother's voice, now on tape, reading the *Cat in the Hat,* or they could elect to hear her reading a different passage, with quite a different meter, from another work. The results were unequivocal; the babies sucked to hear the familiar reading. Evidently, the prenatal experience could influence postnatal choice.

Taste—Aversive Learning.   From animal experiments, it is known that lithium chloride makes rats feel sick. The investigator injected this substance into the amniotic sac of a rat when the fetus was 20 days old, and followed it 2 days later with an injection of apple juice. The young were delivered by Cesarean and allowed to develop normally for 16 days. At that point, the newborn's favorite teat was known and the investigator proceeded to paint it with apple juice. The baby immediately switched to another nipple. At the same time, control rat infants who had not had the benefit of the lithium chloride did not switch nipples. Other attempts to get the rat to come near a feeding situation with apple juice nearby failed as well. It was evident that the prenatal experience had left a considerable impression (Smotherman, 1982, as reported by Kolata, 1984).

Future Studies.   Other techniques are being developed: One involves externalizing fetuses so that they hang free in a saline bath with the umbilical cord intact and functional; in another, a plastic window is placed in the wall of the uterus so that fetal reactions can be observed directly (reported by Kolata, 1984).

The Tendency to Repeat

One of the striking aspects of development is the proneness of many sequences to recur throughout the progressive advance from stage to stage. It appears as if some built-in template is realized again and again under different conditions and at different levels of maturity. Perhaps this represents an economy of means or some basic conservatism of the developmental process. In any case this tendency is apparent very early and persists throughout the life cycle. Freud noted certain aspects of this and called it the *repetition compulsion*. There are many examples.

The Repetition of Grasping. The rudiments of the pincer movement of the hands are apparent early in fetal life. At birth, however, the baby cannot hold objects in this manner, and, in effect, must rediscover the ability to use his thumb in an opposable fashion when he is several months old.

The Recurrence of Separation–Individuation. The same sort of repetition takes place within the framework of the separation process. There is a first biological separation at birth. An initial psychological differentiation from the primary attachment to the mother follows during the first year of life; a more complex and sophisticated separation process occurs during the second and third years; yet another movement away, this time of more mature character happens when the child enters grade school; once again there is a separation at puberty; and finally, for the last time, separation occurs at the end of adolescence. Psychologically, each of these stages has much in common with its predecessor, and indeed, with the events of the first year. In many ways, then, throughout development repetition is the rule.

The Competent Fetus

What emerges is a picture of the fetus as a competent and unique individual, sentient, active, capable to some degree of monitoring and regulating its own environment, and relatively independent of its caretaker in a number of rather important ways. At the same time, it is subject to the effects of many environmental stimuli and responds readily to the appropriate inputs. This makes for a certain vulnerability to stimuli, especially those of noxious character, and these can have a primary impact on the way the fetus continues to develop. A few of the important classes of such stressful events will be reviewed here.

Biological Stressors.   These include malnutrition, infections (especially viral), and drugs such as alcohol, tobacco, methadone, and many others (Richmond & Herzog, 1979).

Psychological Stressors.   The pioneer in this realm has been L. W. Sontag (1940) who has been conducting research on the effects of maternal stress on the fetus since the 1930s. He has noted that maternal upset results in many measurable changes, the most prominent of which is an extreme increase in fetal activity. This can reach a point where the kicking becomes literally painful to the mother. Infants subjected to a great deal of maternal stress will also display measurable differences at birth. They are often irritable, hyperactive, have a tendency toward frequent stools, and manifest feeding problems.

ANIMAL EXPERIMENTS.   Studies with Rhesus monkeys have produced additional evidence bearing on this phenomenon. When pregnant monkeys were exposed to severe stress, major changes were noted in the fetus's vital signs. Under certain circumstances these turned out to be irreversible, leading to speculation that the response was due to impaired maternal circulation. On the other hand, another important finding was that in the face of less severe threats, the unborn infant had a very real capacity to adapt to the changes. For example, if the mother's blood pressure fell, the fetus could act, as it were, to maintain its own pressure independently. It is likely that a dynamic relationship exists between the emotional state of the mother, the fetus' capacity for self-regulation, and the ultimate outcome. This is especially likely if the maternal state induces demands that exceed the fetus's ability to adapt.

SOCIOLOGICAL FACTORS.   In 1951 Pasamanick and Knobloch (1961) showed that the incidence of prematurity was 11% in black newborns, compared with 8% in lower-class whites and 5% in upper-class whites. The incidence of complications of pregnancy was even more striking: 5% in upper-class whites, 15% in lower-class whites, and 50% in blacks. With this it became evident that socioeconomic level was a crucial factor in the health of fetuses and newborns. Nor is this merely ancient history. Sad to relate, the passage of the years has not altered this state of affairs appreciably. The *Vital Statistics of the United States* (1986, p. 296) reveals that among black infants born that year nationwide, 0.12% had Apgar scores of zero, whereas among white infants, only 0.06% scored that low. Again, 5.6% of white newborns were classified as "low birth weight," (p. 91) but 12.4% of black babies arrived in that condition. Because nearly three times as many pregnant black women, as against pregnant whites, had no prenatal care (3.03% vs. 1.16%) (p. 70), one source of these figures is easy to discern.

• *Maternal Nutrition.* Once the importance of class issues had become clear, the search was on for how they translated into the hazards that the pregnancies and the babies had to face. A series of studies in Scotland (Scott et al., 1956) suggested that one crucial variable was the mother's background. Statistically, her father's class or her former class were critical to the outcome.

More to the point, however, were the considerations that pointed to maternal nutrition as a crucial variable. For one thing, it was thought to influence the mother's pelvic status (e.g., inadequate vitamin intake can cause rickets, with a resulting distortion of the bony structure of the pelvis). For another, malnutrition early in pregnancy can affect the synthesis of DNA and thus influence brain growth and the possible appearance of malformations. For example, during World War II the Germans had occupied the Netherlands, and starvation was rampant. In the wake of this crisis, there had been a considerable increase in the incidence of prematurity and stillbirths. On the other hand, the deprivation in nutrition had no measurable effect on intelligence. Indeed, the investigators commented, "Poor prenatal nutrition cannot be considered a factor in the social distribution of mental competence among surviving adults in industrial societies" (Stein & Susser, 1979, p. 257). Another kind of data arose within quite a different quarter and involved a careful survey of the occurrence of birth complications at various times during the year in certain areas of the United States. This study showed a slight but significant increase in the number of retarded children born in the winter. Pasamanick and Knobloch (1961) suggested that this might be due to the poor appetites of pregnant women during the hot summer months when the embryo's brain was forming. At best, researchers can say only that the full effects of maternal nutrition on subsequent cognitive development remain to be established. The evidence, nonetheless, suggests that the nutritional status of the pregnant woman is a significant factor in determining the integrity of fetal growth. Whether it is the primary reason for the impact of socioeconomic factors on the outcome of pregnancy is still unknown.

• *Maternal Age.* There is a clear relationship between the age of the pregnant woman and the statistical probability that she will bear a child with Down syndrome (Smith & Berg, 1976). Overall, the incidence of Down syndrome is about 1 in 700 births. For a woman in her early 20s, the likelihood is 1 chance in 2300 that her baby will display this condition. For the 40-year-old mother, however, the probability has risen to 1 chance in 100, and by 45, to 1 chance in 54. The incidence of congenital hydrocephaly is of similar proportions with respect to maternal age. It is fair to say that 1 chance in 50 is still pretty good odds; considering what the parents and child face if they lose, however, the possibility has given many women pause.

Chapter 3

The Structure and Development of the Brain

INTRODUCTION

Most behavioral scientists believe that brain activity and mental functioning at every level are integral one to the other. To convey this approach, the following material will seek to depict the structure and development of the brain. This is one of the richest areas of current scientific investigation. Almost weekly, new discoveries and novel insights claim the attention of the interested student, including such vital issues as the unraveling of disease processes underlying the major mental illnesses; new insights into how children learn, or what blocks them from doing so; and an understanding of what happens to the brain—and the mind—with increasing age. This body of data is constantly expanding and becoming ever more rich and complex. Hence, in attempting to sum it up, only a brief overview is possible, and much of the following material has been selected on a rather arbitrary basis. It does, however, convey some sense of the richness and promise of the field. This branch of study—the continuing growth and integration of human psychology and human biology—shows considerable potential for radically changing the human condition.

ANATOMY OF THE MATURE BRAIN

The brain is a large mass of specialized tissue that fills the bony cranium. Albeit a single organ, the brain is divided front to back by a long, deep, central fissure that partitions it into two large hemispheres. These two masses, roughly equal in size, are actually the presenting surfaces of two rather sizable bulbous outpouchings of tissue that have formed around a hollow core. They resemble two great balloons, whose thick walls are made of spongy, gelatinous material that has been folded over and tucked under. On the surface of each hemisphere the observer sees a much-pleated, irregular terrain where soft, rounded ridges are separated by evident creases and indentations. The mounded folds are the *gyri;* the many valleys between the folds are called *sulci.*

In addition to the great longitudinal fissure that divides the brain into right and left hemispheres, the major infoldings have created two additional fissures on each of the brain's lateral surfaces, dividing off a prominent smaller lobe on the side of each of the hemispheres. These great creases are the Sylvian fissures, and they demarcate the right and left temporal lobes.

An illustration of the brain in profile shows the traditional arbitrary division of both hemispheres into an anterior, middle, and posterior region, each with its own name and functions (see Figure 3–1). The front end of each hemisphere is called the frontal lobe; the middle-to-back part, the parietal lobe; and the posterior end of each hemisphere, the occipital lobe.

(On the lateral surface of each frontal lobe the temporal lobe runs backward to flow into the parietal lobe.)

The surface of the brain is gray (the famous gray matter), and in fact, most higher mental functioning resides precisely in this outer covering of the brain. This gray tissue gets its coloring from a 2-millimeter (about one-eighth of an inch)-thick layer of nerve-cell bodies (and their connections). This gray layer spreads over the entire surface of the brain like an outer wrapping, following all the contours of the sulci and gyri and tucking under the various lobes to form a continuous sheath. This outer wrapping of cells is called the *cerebral cortex.* If the observer could peel off this cortical layer, smooth out its folds, and spread it out flat, it would cover an area of about 1.5 square feet (Hubel & Wiesel, 1986).

The contours of the hemispheres (the lobes, sulci, and gyri noted above), despite inevitable individual differences, are quite standard from one human being to another; they have been carefully studied and described, and each bit of brain surface has a name of its own.

MICROSTRUCTURE OF THE MATURE BRAIN

A microscopic examination of a cross section of cortex from almost anywhere on the brain surface shows that this gray mantle, thin as it is, is nonetheless divided into 6 discrete layers of cells. Each layer lies parallel with the surface of the brain and is continuous over all its area. Of the many different kinds of cells involved, the nerve cells proper, or neurons, are the primary action cells of the brain; they accomplish all the perceiving, know-

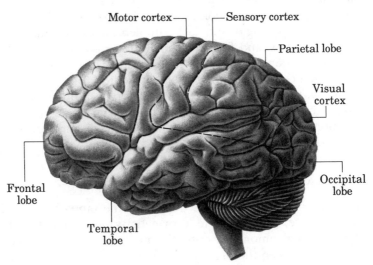

Figure 3–1. Regions of the brain.

ing, thinking, and feeling that the human experiences. Within the cortex are huge numbers of neurons; in fact, each square millimeter contains about 100,000 of these cells, and the sum aggregate for the entire cortex is approximately 10 billion neurons. Although that may seem to be a large number, it represents only the thin outer layer; the actual count of neurons throughout the entire brain is probably closer to 100 billion.

A great many other prominent structures are present in the underlying substance of the brain. Indeed, the array of tracts and nuclei is so complex that one thinker (MacLean, 1969) has spoken of the triune brain, suggesting that the human brain is really a system of 3 brains set one inside the other. According to this theory, on the innermost level is the *reptilian brain*, the basic core of survival functions involving the centers that regulate respiration, elimination, cardiac action, blood pressure, digestive activity, body temperature and water balance, and the most primitive urges for fight or flight, food quest, and sex.

These compose the brain stem. Sitting atop them is a labyrinthian complex of structures, the primitive mammalian brain, with many large centers and their connecting tracts; prominent among these are the *limbic system* and *basal ganglia*. The limbic system (including various discernible cell clusters such as the thalamus, hypothalamus, hippocampus, and other structures) is the great generator and regulator of emotions. It connects indirectly to both the endocrine and the autonomic nervous systems. It allows for producing graded and highly discrete emotions that can be attached and give affective color to percepts, memories, and experience in general. The basal ganglia, also called the *striatum*, are a group of paired cell masses that regulate and integrate motor action, allowing particularly for habitual and automatic movements such as walking, smiling, or skilled activities of many kinds. When this kind of functioning is impaired (as in Parkinsonism), the body movements are rigid and lack suppleness, the characteristic *pill-rolling* tremor appears, and facial expressiveness disappears. MacLean calls this part of the brain the *old mammalian brain;* it allows for stalking behavior and other such complex motor patterns as well as for emotional expression.

Finally, the *new mammalian brain* sits topmost, dominated by the cortex. This is best developed in human beings and makes possible the higher functions, such as impulse regulation, language, and abstract thought, that characterize the species.

The Neuron

The neurons, in many ways, represent the pinnacle of evolution. They gather, store, and distribute information; they stimulate and inhibit; and they rank high among the critically important, finely tuned communication devices that keep the organism conscious, sensate, functioning, and integrated. Neurons come in several sizes and shapes, with corresponding specializations of function. These different varieties are layered out in distinctive patterns in different parts of the brain, an arrangement that has been termed the cell *architecture*. Among their other characteristics, the neurons are quite irregular in outline and give off many processes. There are two classes of such outgrowths: the dendrites and the axons.

The Dendrites.   These are irregular projections on the surface of the individual cells. Although they can be long and sinuous, as a rule they are short, stubby, and have many branchings. The dendrites function primarily to receive incoming messages. To this end, their surfaces are dotted with tiny, mound-shaped protoplasmic nodules, the dendritic *spines*, each of which forms one working face of a junction with another cell. Developmentally, the dendrites grow extensively during the first 2 years of life. They start out as relatively smooth, cone-shaped mounds swelling up on the surface of the nerve cells. Presently the mounds bud out branches that extend, divide, and subdivide, and grow ever more complex until they are arborizing and ramifying to an enormous extent. Ultimately, their bushy perimeter comes to occupy twice and three times their initial area at the time of birth. Meanwhile, the internal intricacy of the multitudinous branchings and rebranchings are advancing from a sketchy outline of tendrils to a dense mat of intertwining and overlapping processes. It is an arrangement very much like the back of a telephone switchboard, obviously designed to form a rich pattern of connections and communications. This is a particularly important aspect of brain growth (Freedman, 1980).

Numerous incoming, message-bearing fibers converge on a single dendritic area to deliver their message. Curiously, however, these fiber terminals do not touch the dendritic spines; instead, a single incoming fiber nears a single dendritic spine closely enough so that only a tiny gap remains between incoming and receiving surfaces. But it is of the essence to maintain this gap. The junction that occurs is called a *synapse;* it is the basic communication device of the central nervous system.

Because of this critical gap, in humans, the nature of transmission across the synaptic cleft is chemical in nature. When a nerve fibril brings a message to a receptor neuron, the incoming nerve impulse travels along the nerve process and gets as far as the synapse—where it stops. At that point the nerve ending acts as a *secretory* organ; instead of an electrical impulse crossing over, the fiber terminal releases an appropriate *chemical* messenger (called a *neurotransmitter*). This secretion, in turn, must *cross* the synaptic gap in order to reach the correct receptor on the dendritic spine surface. There are evidently a host of ways to influence this sequence of events. First, it is possible to augment or diminish the formation of the necessary neurotransmitting chemical in an individual, even by diet. Then, the process of release can be manipulated; for example, some drugs augment the release of specific transmitters. In turn, once the transmitting substance is released, the nerve terminal can stop the neurotransmitter back up—or can be blocked from doing so. (Normally, most of the material released is, in fact, reabsorbed by the releasing surface; blocking such reuptake is a powerful way to influence the chemical working of the brain.) Again, the neurotransmitting substance can be destroyed by chemical (enzymatic) activity within the synaptic cleft. Finally, as another means of affecting synaptic transmission, the receptors on the dendritic spines can be either increased or decreased in number, thus allowing for heightened or diminished receptivity. Or the receptors can be blocked, inactivated, or otherwise interfered with. Because most modern psychopharmacology depends on being able to influence the processes taking place at the synapse, this discussion will refer to that structure again and again.

Recent research has focused on the receptors and on the events within the cell after a neurotransmitter molecule has been accepted by a receptor. This is particularly important from the view of devising medications that will accomplish specific tasks. Thus, if a given medicine achieves its effect by binding to a particular set of synaptic loci, it might be ideal for its purpose if it could confine itself to that single task. Most medications, however, attach to more than one receptor site and thus produce undesired side effects. For example, the clinical phenomenon of depression is associated with a decrease in the amount of two important neurotransmitters, noradrenalin and serotonin, in the synapse. To remedy this, a number of antidepressant medications have been devised that block the reuptake of serotonin and noradrenalin by the cells that secrete these substances. Because reuptake is the major mechanism that reduces the quantity of available neurotransmitter, blocking this action enhances the amount available in the synapse to reach the receptors—and this, in turn, relieves the depression. Unfortunately, many of the medicines that connect so nicely with the reuptake sites also have a strong affinity for certain receptor sites on the other side of the synapse. Some drugs, for example, attach all too readily to histaminergic receptors that when stimulated, make patients sleepy and sometimes cause them to gain weight. Others connect preferentially with muscarinic acetylcholinergic receptors, which give patients dry mouths, constipation, blurred vision, sometimes urinary retention, and sometimes even memory disturbances. Alpha adrenergic receptors cause the patient to get dizzy, especially when standing up suddenly and to complain of a racing pulse. Different medications thus connect with different receptors, and the prescribing physician has to decide, first, whether to try to block noradrenalin or serotonin uptake, and then, which side effects will be the least troublesome to which patients. In fact, there is no way of telling in advance who will experience what, and a great deal of trial and error goes into formulating an optimum medication regimen.

The Axons. In addition to the receptor dendritic processes, the neurons give rise to another class of outgrowths, the *axons*. These protoplasmic processes carry messages away from the cell body and are thus called neural *efferents*. Because they function differently, their structure and appearance differ from the receptor dendrites. Examining a neuron under the microscope, reveals that from one aspect of the cell a single long fiber (usually a much more slender filament than even the longer dendrites) extends out and away. Here the word *long* should be taken quite literally; the axon serves as a distance communicator and may extend from one end of the brain to the other, or it may go from the surface of the brain down into the spinal cord and be several feet in length. In somewhat the same manner as the dendritic pattern, the tip end of the axon may also subdivide and ramify, so that the message arising within a given neuron can spread throughout the brain, or even beyond that to several points in the spinal cord impinging on many cells at once. Often, a group of axons arising from a cluster of similar neurons acting in concert will extend and ramify together; this gives rise to many of the tracts of the brain.

However, the targeting of the axon terminals is never random. It is a highly specific process, determined both by genetic ground rules and by the facilitating or inhibiting effects of experience (Georgopoulos et al., 1986; Hubel & Wiesel, 1986).

Functionally, the long slender axons have many tasks. Among them is to link up neurons residing within the central nervous system (CNS), which comprises the brain and spinal cord, to the appropriate peripheral gland or muscle cell (effecter). Within the brain proper, however, most axons have a different mission: to connect nerve cells with other nerve cells. To function effectively, the thicker axons must carry their messages at a certain minimum speed, that is, in the neighborhood of 15 meters per second. Before they can do this, however, they must be sheathed with a fatty chemical substance (a phospholipid) called *myelin,* a coating whose net effect is to facilitate the passage of the nerve impulse to a remarkable degree. At the time of birth the process of myelinization is largely incomplete. A microscopic examination of the newborn's brain shows that many of the axons are in place, but they are as yet unmyelinated and hence in no condition to transmit messages with anything like the necessary rapidity. To be sure, some axons are thin enough not to need the facilitation that the myelin offers, and other pathways are already mature and ready to carry messages. But a goodly percentage of the available fibers are not yet fully functional; they are still in the process of receiving their myelin. As the baby grows, the efficiency of the nervous system is dependent, to a considerable extent, or which nerve tracts are being myelinated, to what extent, and in what order. A major factor in brain growth and functional organization, then, is the progressive myelinization of the axons linking up the various centers; in effect, this is what wires up the brain.

Literally thousands of incoming signals impinge continuously on any one neuron. As a rule, it takes a host of such incoming impulses, some of which may be stimulant and some inhibitory, to allow the neuron to sum up these collective messages and thus to determine whether or not to fire off a signal in its turn. Thus the individual neuron is capable of quite sensitive and complex response patterns to the multiple wash of impulses that continuously cross and recross the neural network.

Neurotransmitters

Functionally, each neuron is a kind of chemical factory producing various neurotransmitters. As noted previously, the specialized surface of the neuron is also a target of such chemical messengers. More technically, the cell membrane covering the dendritic spines has discrete receptor sites and each such receptor is a protein (usually a glycoprotein) that is exquisitely sensitive to the presence of even tiny amounts of its specific neurotransmitter. Once the receptor has received an appropriate chemical messenger, this initiates the next phase of function within the receiving cell.

Different neurons produce different groups of transmitters, each of which has a particular functional task. In a number of sites, cell clusters exist where each member cell produces the same neurotransmitter. Elaborate systems of such clusters are interlaced and distributed throughout the brain (and to some extent throughout many other parts of the body as well) to subserve discrete functions. Specific neurotransmitters tend to concentrate in particular parts of the brain and to be utilized by nerve fibers running in well-established tracts. As a result, modern neuroanatomy speaks of different *neurotransmitter systems* that investigators are now busily mapping out. Specific forms of inhibition and excitation are mediated by these neurotransmitters, for example, signals conveyed by one neurotransmitter system might initiate a sensation of pain, whereas the activation of another might inhibit and obliterate the pain experience and/or induce a pleasure experience. One of the neurotransmitters associated with pleasure sensations is dopamine. If the reuptake pump for dopamine were to be blocked— especially within the forebrain—the person would experience the effects of higher than normal concentrations of dopamine. (Cocaine is thought to bind very tightly to this reuptake pump.) Or the lack of adequate amounts of a neurotransmitter at a crucial juncture might produce a state of depression, and its subsequent restoration would relieve the condition. Such a state of depression might arise if not enough of the necessary neurotransmitter is getting across the synapse (not enough is being produced, it is being resorbed too quickly, or it is being destroyed within the synaptic cleft). Another possibility is that the neurotransmitter does get across, but the receptor surfaces are blocked or otherwise down-regulated. In sum, it is by increasing the availability of, or blocking the action of, the neurotransmitter substances that psychoactive chemicals (whether distilled by a shaman for a religious cult, produced by a pharmaceutical company as a prescription medicine, or made in a basement as an illegal street drug) have so potent an effect on mood, arousal, emotion, alertness, and relaxation.

Overall Status of the Brain at Birth

The newborn infant comes into the world only partially "done" and with much remaining to be completed. The amount of growth necessary varies a good deal from system to system. Thus, the visual centers and tracts are in a relatively advanced state of maturation, and practically from the moment of delivery, the newborn displays a striking ability to engage visually. The auditory apparatus, on the other hand, lags behind the visual centers. It is reasonably advanced but will not approach completion until much later. The centers that maintain a sense of balance (the vestibular system with sensitive sites in the labyrinth of the inner ear) are also well along at birth, and the baby is accordingly quite sensitive to changes in position.

The tracts going to the higher centers of the brain (the sites in the cortex having to do with abstract thinking, with forming inner images, and with recalling associations) have still not been "wired in." Many of the long motor fibers (those mediating voluntary muscle action) that extend down into the spinal cord have not as yet been myelinated. In particular this is true for the great pyramidal tracts; these are long fiber bundles that begin at the primary sites in the cortex for initiating voluntary motor actions (the motor cortex) and extend all the way down to the spinal centers governing the peripheral musculature.

Functional Maps

During most of human history, people have had very little understanding of how the mind works or what the brain comprises. Toward the latter half of the 19th century neurologists discovered that there was a definite association between a given brain area and a specific function, such as speech, perception, or motor control. A host of careful clinical and postmortem examinations revealed that if damage occurred to one brain area there was aphasia; if to another, there was paralysis; if to yet another, the individual could only see things in the right visual field of each eye and not in the left. This led to a hugely exciting effort to study brains postmortem in ever greater detail and to chart the functions of the different brain areas. Eventually all this moved into the laboratory. Tremendous technical advances followed; presently, electrodes could be placed within individual cells and their potentials measured, and EEG brain waves could be recorded from discrete areas and in response to specific stimuli. Different parts of the brain surface of experimental animals could be precisely anesthetized,

ablated, treated with various active chemical agents, or electrically stimulated. Ultimately a host of studies were carried out to find out what
anatomical area causes what behavioral or experiential effect. (Much of this
has involved animal research, but some work on humans has been done in
collaboration with neurosurgical treatments.)

Eventually researchers learned that in a number of ways, the body and
the sensory world were clearly mapped out on different areas of the cortex.
Thus, a researcher studying the sense of touch would find that a specific bit
of brain surface was associated with the hand, an adjacent area with the
arm, and yet another patch with the trunk. Destroy any one of these
surfaces and the sensation of touch would be lost in just that region.
Elsewhere, another extent of cortical brain surface bore a similar map of the
body having to do with the ability to initiate movement. If any part of that
area were injured or disconnected, the specific muscles it represented were
thereupon paralyzed. Contrariwise, if that bit of cortex were electrically
stimulated, the appropriate muscle would twitch; placing the electrode
where a sensory map had been traced would elicit the associated sensation.
For unknown reasons, the motor and sensory maps for the right half of the
body project onto the left hemisphere, and those for the left side, onto the
right hemisphere. As noted, each particular sensation or motor function
has a special part of the brain surface reserved for it. Thus, the visual field
maps out on the occipital lobe, but the left half of the visual field of each eye
projects onto the right occipital cortex and vice versa.

All in all, it is speculated that there are somewhere between 50 and 100
specialized cortical areas ("maps") of this kind (Hubel & Wiesel, 1986, p.
42).

EXAMPLES OF FUNCTION

The following subsections will illustrate the way the brain works by describing two kinds of brain functions: vision and memory.

Vision

The construction of an image of the outside world from the light signals
that enter the eyes involves transmitting a visual stimulus through the brain
along the pathways leading to an actual percept. Each eye perceives a
certain delimited area called a *visual field*. This field has definite boundaries—an individual cannot see to the left or the right of that field or above
or below it without changing the position of the eyes, by moving them,
moving the head, or changing body position. Although the individual
perceives it as one, this visual field is, in fact, divided in two. Images arising
from the left half of the field impinge on the right half of the inner surface

of each eye, and the images from the right side of the field hit the left half of the inner eye. The images entering the eyes are focused (by the lens in that eye) on a light-sensitive organ at the back of the eye called the *retina*. The retina is a tissue rich with specialized neurons; the fibers arising from those neurons gather together at the back of the eye and form the optic nerve.

The retina of the eye is actually a kind of outpouching of the brain itself, so that the optic nerve is not a conventional nerve so much as it is a tract of the brain. Thus, the retina already contains a great many neurons layered in complex arrays; the light signal that comes in initiates a sequence of synaptic connections and information transfers among them; and these interneuronal activities in turn accomplish the first steps in image processing. The resulting partially processed signal then goes back along the optic nerve (there are about 1 million fibers in each nerve), which presently divides so that some fibers from *each* optic nerve go to the right, and others to the left. In each case, the fibers proceed until they arrive at a first internal way station, a pair of brain areas called the *lateral geniculate bodies*. Although these are midline structures, one on the left, one on the right, each gets fibers from both eyes. (A pair of medial geniculate bodies subserve the function of hearing in much the same way as the lateral geniculates process vision.)

Within each geniculate body, the nerve fibers (from both the right and left eyes) encounter a new array of neurons and form yet another set of synapses. Having processed the retinal signals, the lateral geniculate neurons now give rise to another set of nerve fibers that cross the midline and travel back to connect with the primary visual cortex of the occipital lobe on the opposite side—left lateral geniculate body to right occipital cortex and vice versa. (The same sort of arrangement takes place with the medial geniculate bodies, except that they send their fibers to the superior temporal gyrus where hearing is mediated.) The result of this partial crossover is that the right cortex gets messages from the right part of the retina of both eyes (which perceives the left visual field), and the left cortex from the left halves of both retinas (which perceive the right visual field). It has been determined that the two visual fields are, in fact, mapped on the cortex in such a way that each portion of the retina (the light coming from each point on the visual field) excites a specific cluster of neurons on the surface of the appropriate occipital lobe (Hubel & Wiesel, 1986).

In this way, an assemblage of images forms that offers a first level of perception; it is, however, far from being a full-sense impression; in fact, the pattern of light and dark elements available at this stage is rather primitive. A true visual image, as it is experienced by a person, needs considerably more elaboration: It needs contour and shape delineation, color and texture, orientation in space, recognition of motion, and affective coloring. To have meaning, it also needs to be integrated with memory, other sensory experience, and linguistic data. Achieving all these requirements means that the message must continue to be processed well past the primary visual (occipital) cortex. All the necessary ramifications and inputs necessary to achieve a full perception are not yet known; however, many of the pathways have been traced out (Mishkin & Appenzeller, 1987). Starting from the visual cortex, the signal must now pass forward along a number of additional way stations (each of which adds certain elements such as color, texture, shape, and other necessary qualities). The flow of information from the occipital lobe cortex actually breaks up into three main streams, each with several way stations of its own. The rule seems to be that some 10 neurons in one way station impinge on one neuron in a later station. Thus, as a signal proceeds, each cluster of neurons sees a more and more complete and true-to-life image. The neurons have complex connections, both in series and in parallel; as the signal feeds forward, the image becomes more and more complete. As it establishes lateral connections with adjacent neurons, the functions of attention, memory retrieval, and other forms of modulation are perfected.

The three main streams of neuronal information terminate respectively on the lower surface of the temporal lobe, on the posterior part of the parietal lobe, and on the parietal sulcus. This latter area is important for the detection of motion; the posterior part of the parietal lobe serves for orientation in space. As a result of the several processing operations at these way stations, the information that arrives at the temporal lobe site (100 microseconds after the signal arrived at the first way station) provides a far more complete image; it begins to resemble what can be conceived of as "out there." Each of the way stations has filters that screen particular images. Thus, the signal that finally gets to the temporal lobe is so constituted that rather complete images are now impinging on the temporal lobe neurons. But these are also specialized; one neuron set in the temporal lobe may be responsive to full-face images, and another only to profiles. The representation that is finally screened out by temporal lobe neurons is thus fairly developed and detailed. Nonetheless, it is not as yet well located in space; to add this component, the parietal lobe cortex must send a measure of input into the lower temporal cortex. (Among other things, the parietal lobe is associated with the organization of the sense of form and spatial relationships; it can be demonstrated that animals whose parietal cortex is ablated cannot recall the location of objects in space.)

The U-shaped fibers of white matter that lie just under the grey matter of the brain and connect one area of cortex with another are called *association fibers.* They link together different areas of cortex so that the entire cortex is involved in associational functions. Ultimately, these information-carrying fibers cross the midline so that messages from *both* sides of the brain impinge on given temporal lobe neurons and contribute to the formation of the final visual image.

Beyond the construction of the immediately visual aspects of the image, this temporal region also connects directly with a number of other sites.

There are links to those portions of the thalamus and hypothalamus associated with the generation and registration of emotion. It is apparently here that the appropriate emotional coloring of the percept is elaborated and integrated. The thalamus is part of a larger limbic system that is located at the very center of the brain. From the limbic system a radiation of fibers to the prefrontal lobe may well be responsible for attaching additional qualities of meaning to the percept. Properly speaking, all of these are part of the visual pathway, so that what started out as a mere sensory experience involving the retina/optic nerve/lateral geniculate body/occipital lobe linkage becomes a highly complex, organizational network requiring the participation of numerous loci. In effect, it pulls in much of the cortical and subcortical brain. Despite the linear fashion of the above description, these events actually take place not so much as an assembly-line operation with the percept traveling along and having the necessary qualities added one by one (as the term *way station* might suggest), but rather it is a series of simultaneous parallel processes, with a great many mutually interactive, oscillating feedback loops resonating and integrating with one another in constantly varying dynamic interplay to produce the final perceptual outcome. It is likely that the individual cells actually function as part of neuronal ensembles. Thus, when a particular face is flashed before an individual linked up to an appropriate scanning device, it activates a given array of neurons (about 10% of the whole). Flash a different face before the same individual, and again about 10% of the neurons light up—but a different 10%.

Memory

This tendency toward total brain involvement with significant functions is even more marked in the case of memory. Here, numerous brain areas must work together to subserve the needs for recall that are so essential for human (and, for that matter, for animal) adaptation. One such site is the temporal lobe; another, the limbic system; yet another, the frontal lobe. The recall of habitual patterns involves the cerebellum, motor cortex, and basal ganglia.

The temporal lobe, the large, lateral brain mass on the side of each of the hemispheres, is a rather elaborately curled-under part of the original great neural pouch. Within the substance of the temporal lobe, one of the lumpy curls was thought by the early anatomists to have an almond shape; it was accordingly called the *amygdala* (Greek for "almond"). It is the part of the temporal lobe most directly connected with memory functioning.

The term *limbic system* describes an array of brain nuclei and pathways that cluster at the center of the brain, with many complex interconnections among them and with numerous radiations to other parts of the brain. As noted earlier, emotions are generated and regulated (gated) in the limbic system; the connections with this system attach emotional qualities to percepts, memories, or thoughts of any kind. One of the largest and most central of the brain nuclei in this system is the *thalamus*. Certain parts of the thalamus are involved with the limbic system and are vitally associated with memory functioning; indeed, if the medial ventral thalamus is destroyed, severe memory deficit follows.

Another part of the limbic system was thought by the older anatomists to resemble a seahorse and was therefore called the *hippocampus;* this structure is also essential for memory functioning. Finally, the frontal lobes, the site of the great regulatory and inhibitory centers of the brain, are also of critical importance in forming and retrieving memories.

Much of what is known about memory has come from exploring memory loss in many individuals. These studies have come about in various ways. In some instances they were carried out during and after surgical removal of parts of the brain (either in an effort to control unrelenting seizures or to excise tumors). In other cases there have been careful follow-up studies of individuals suffering accidental injuries. Another source of information has been the postmortem study of brain lesions of affected individuals, who, during their lives, had demonstrated significant memory deficits (e.g., those with conditions such as Korsakoff's syndrome or Alzheimer's disease). Such studies initially implicated the amygdala and the hippocampus as parts of the brain subserving memory. In addition, a great many laboratory studies using experimental animals have carried the research far enough forward to warrant some firm conclusions about the anatomy of memory.

The formation of memory has been studied by training animals to perform a variety of tasks and then surgically removing various elements in these systems, for example, the amygdala may be ablated on one side, on both sides, or the white matter connecting the amygdala to other structures may be cut. Or both amygdala and hippocampus may be surgically removed on one or both sides, with the animals being tested for memory and for learning before and after each such procedure. Or the thalamus may be selectively damaged, or the frontal lobes, or the connections among them. Thus, by slow and painstaking work, researchers have determined some of the anatomic underpinnings of memory.

There seem to be two different kinds of memory: habit and recall. *Habit* is noncognitive in the sense that it does not involve thought but is instead a sort of stimulus–response sequence that connects particular sense impressions with specific motor patterns of reaction in a routinized, automatic way. *Recall,* on the other hand, is cognitive in nature and has several dimensions. First, there is simple recognition, that is, initially the individual has an experience of seeing, feeling, or smelling something; then, when he or she has a reencounter, the experience is familiar and recognizable. Second, there is cross-modal recognition, that is, the individual hears a voice and immediately visualizes the person, hears a melody and thinks of a scene, or smells a kitchen odor and immediately experiences a taste image (and perhaps a visual image as well) of the associated food. The underlying neuroanatomy for these different kinds of memory is demonstrably different. A third form is long-term memory. The ability to bring to mind an event, a scene, a phrase—to think of something and then recreate the memory—is an invaluable element in human mentation. It differs from recognition memory in that the person need not encounter the stimulus to recognize it but can evoke the memory set as he or she wishes.

The actual structure of recall memory requires these anatomic elements: (1) the critical centers (i.e., the hippocampus, the amygdala, the limbic system, the thalamus and hypothalamus, and the prefrontal cortex), and (2) all the many connecting fibers that mesh these several brain regions into a unified network that records and encodes memories. The amygdala acts as a site for sensory integration; it receives fibers from the cortical representations of all the senses—touch, taste, smell, hearing, and vision—as well as from the emotion-generating and affect-regulating limbic system. The amygdala is thus a great mixer; among other things it serves as the switching center that permits cross-modal perception. On the other hand, it is not in itself a final storage site for most forms of memory; once it has constructed the full meaning-laden, affectively charged percept and made all the connections, it sends fibers back to different sites in the cortex so that the percepts thus formed can there be stored and kept available for recall.

If the amygdala is surgically removed from an experimental animal, the animal does not suffer a loss of simple recognition memory. However, the animal does lose its normal fear of people, and it even loses its reaction to such unpleasant experiences as being pinched. Contrariwise, it is hard to teach such an animal to associate an action with a reward. With the loss of the amygdala, the visual memory of an experience, the emotion associated with that experience, and the motivation generated by that experience no longer link together. Moreover, the fact that the amygdala connects back to each of the sensory areas mapped on the cortex suggests that it not only helps *store* memories at these sites, but that it might be able to transfer back to these sites the emotional messages from the limbic system. In this way, it could affect what a person selectively remembers and selectively forgets in keeping with the dictates of his or her feelings.

With the ablation of the amygdala, another kind of loss becomes evident: cross-modal memory, that is, the ability to translate impressions from one sensory modality into recognition of another (e.g., to recognize something visually that the individual has previously felt or heard but has never seen). Because such cross-modal memory is basic to much adaptive learning (a person needs to be able to say what he or she reads, to write what he or she hears, etc.), this deficiency, albeit subtle, is very important (see, e.g., the later discussion of Stern's concept of *amodal perception*) (Stern 1985, pp. 47–53).

The ability to recognize familiar aspects of experience is so obviously valuable, that it finds wide representation in several brain areas. On the other hand, if the amygdala and the hippocampus are *both* removed from *both* sides of the brain, then a massive and global memory loss does ensue. With so massive an injury, the entire capacity for subsequent recognition memory is lost, and regardless of whom the person has just met, what he or she has just encountered, or even whatever he or she has just learned (surprisingly, individuals with such lesions can still learn), a moment later it is forgotten. This, however, only applies to new experiences; older established memories had previously been stored in the cortex and are therefore preserved.

This, briefly, describes some of the mechanisms underlying recall. Habitual memory, the other type, operates through quite a different mechanism. It involves at least three parts of the brain: the striatum, the cerebellum, and the motor cortex. The *striatum* is a large mass of cells deep in the brain that serves to regulate and smooth out muscular movement. In particular, this site maintains habitual motor patterns such as walking or smiling. The cerebellum is one of the major divisions of the brain, located just under the occipital lobe (at the rear of the brain mass); among its very specialized functions are coordination of muscular movements and balance. Finally, the motor cortex is part of the frontal lobe; it contains one of the mappings on the gray matter of the brain referred to earlier, where the musculature of the body is represented in a characteristic fashion. Thus, all of these neural arrays are concerned with patterning and regulating muscle control. Because in the course of individual development the striatum matures long before the cortex, infant lab animals can learn habitual patterns of movement at a very early age. By the same token, if the striatum is destroyed, motor habits can no longer be acquired (Mishkin & Appenzeller, 1987).

BRAIN GROWTH

The newborn brain weighs about 300 to 400 grams; it increases in mass until, at 12 months of postpartum age, it weighs about 900 to 1000 grams—a two- or threefold expansion in a relatively short time.

The hallmark of the brain is its huge concentration of neurons; these nerve cells generate, record, transmit, and exchange the information that the brain acquires, manufactures, and stores. It might be thought that some of the brain's growth is due to an increase in the number of neurons, but the reality is that by the time of birth, most individuals have all the neurons they will ever possess. From that point onward it is a matter of the child's learning how best to use what he has been given. This is not a trivial observation; it underlines the vital role of child rearing, training, and education in the formation of the human being. To be sure, recent research has demonstrated the presence of new cell growth in the brains of birds

(Nottebohm, 1984); although this is not a very likely model for what happens in humans, it does prove that neuronal cell growth (neocytosis) is possible well after birth. Recent literature at least suggests that in the human, cell division continues after birth for as long as 5 months (Winick, 1976).

An even more pertinent finding, however, has been that the actual *thickness* of the cortex varies in experimental animals depending on the experiences to which they are exposed early in life (Diamond, 1987). With a more stimulating kind of environment about them, baby rats demonstrate measurable increases in the thickness of the gray matter on the brain surface (as compared with peers who were not so stimulated). Hence, the impact of environmental stimulation receives extraordinary confirmation in the form of anatomic change.

During the first 12 months, the newborn's brain experiences unique and unparalleled growth, accompanied by equally momentous functional transformations. Indeed, it has been suggested that at least five-sixths of human brain growth takes place after birth (Dobbing & Sands, 1973, quoted in Diamond, 1987). Many disparate elements take part in this striking elaboration of structure and function. Because the process of new cell formation is largely complete by the time of birth, all of the subsequent growth must reflect changes in the connecting and supporting structures. But such changes are profoundly influenced by the amount, the kind, and the sequences of stimulation—or lack of stimulation—that a given infant receives. The impact of early environment is therefore likely to be critical.

EMBRYOLOGY OF THE BRAIN

It is important to have some sense of the actual formation of the brain structures during embryological development. Hence, the following material will depict some of the details of this sequence of events along with an account of a number of the underlying processes that seem to be at work.

The Neural Tube

The fertilized ovum immediately begins a process of almost frantic activity. It simultaneously moves down the oviduct to the uterus and enters into a sequence of rapid cell division. At length, it embeds itself in the uterine wall and sets about building the embryo. In a short time, the precursors (anlagen) of the several organ systems and anatomical structures begin to appear. The usual way of talking about this early developmental sequence is to speak of how many days old the embryo is when a particular emergent can be identified. This chapter will concentrate on only part of this process, the developmental embryology of the human central nervous system (CNS).

By 3 weeks of age, the embryo resembles a hollow ball. There is an outer surface (ectodermal) layer of cells and an inner lining layer (endoderm). Together they form a shell around a center filled with fluid.

Approximately 21 days after fertilization, a groove becomes evident on the outer surface of this tiny ball. Differential growth occurs at the edges of the groove so that the cells composing the groove margins proliferate ever more rapidly until they heap up into two long mounds or ridges. Presently these ridges push toward each other until they touch, whereupon they proceed to fuse over the groove so as to create an enclosed tube. The original groove is called the *neural groove* and the tube, the *neural tube*. This tube form is the basic precursor—as well as the permanent pattern—of the CNS. To be sure, it will undergo many changes: It will subdivide into a series of pouches; it will fold upon itself in complex ways; its walls will thicken and differentiate; and many other things will happen. But the fundamental tubal arrangement will be discernible throughout. In time, one end of the tube will expand to form the brain, and the rest of it will become the spinal cord.

An important early step is for the ends of the tube to close off. If they do not, the baby will be born with serious birth defects. In particular, if the forward (rostral) end fails to seal off as it should, the upper portion of both brain and skull will not form, and the baby will be born as an *anencephalic.* Such infants display a type of malformation in which the skull stops at the level of the eyes, the infant has no forehead or upper cranial bulge, and the upper portion of the brain is missing. Babies born with such a defect do not long survive; that they live at all is due to the more or less intact status of the lower portion of the brain. Because this contains the centers that regulate and support respiration, heart beat, blood pressure, water balance, and the other vital functions, life can be temporarily sustained.

Where the front end of the neural tube does close off as it should, and brain development begins normally, this forward portion of the neural tube continues to elaborate and presently shows three bulges, one behind the other. These will become the several divisions of the brain; in a short time each division will undergo further complex subdivision and give rise to a characteristic set of brain elements. This initial dividing up is important because to fit into the cranium, the tube will have to fold over upon itself in a predetermined fashion, so that in its final form, the brain is an angled, folded tube with thickened walls and an inner, fluid-filled lumen.

At the three-bulge stage, the rostral bulge will, among other things, give rise to the cortex; the middle bulge becomes the diencephalon (the thalamus and hypothalamus), and the posterior bulge, the cerebellum and medulla oblongata. Throughout all of this, the basic tubular character is never lost. The inner lumen of the tube will presently expand to form the large, fluid-filled spaces within the brain mass known as the *ventricles;* these contain the special blood vessels that generate the spinal fluid. The walls of the rostral end of the tube become the substance of the brain (the caudal end becomes the spinal cord).

Microstructure. During the ensuing weeks, brain growth proceeds at a rapid rate. Examination of a mature brain under the microscope reveals a complex massing of specialized cell clusters in various parts of this extraordinary organ, plus a layering of numerous different cell types within these clusters and throughout the cortex. How this arrangement develops from the simple neural tube has been the subject of considerable study. Researchers have determined that as the tube elaborates, the actual brain substance is formed out of the tubal wall by three processes: cell proliferation, cell migration, and cell differentiation (Nowakowski, 1987). These processes account for most of the ensuing brain architecture.

PROLIFERATION. As noted, both in humans and in other primates, all the neurons that are present throughout life have been formed and put into place before birth. (This is true for many other species as well, although there are some notable exceptions.) Within the early human embryo new nerve cells form largely within the tissue that lines the inner surface of the tube. Because this inner space will give rise to the brain ventricles, the inner tubal lining is known as the *ventricular zone.* Microscopically, this is the only site that shows evidence of neuronal cell division (mitosis). As development proceeds and new cells form, large numbers of these young neurons will move away from the inner lumen of the tube, some merely pushed away by new growth, but many moving out in a series of waves of migration. Presently these migrant cells will find their way into the various clusterings throughout the brain, and, especially, into the several layers of the cortex. In a few places along the length of the neural tube a second, subventricular site of neuron mitosis can be identified; it is speculated that the newer, phylogenetically more recent groups of neurons (presumably those associated with speech and thought and higher level functioning in general) arise from this source.

An analogy of the process would be a population of humans, all of the same age, who settle at the banks of a lake and begin to raise families. As time goes on, the firstborns all are born at about the same time. When these babies grow up into young adolescents, they must move inland because the lakefront has been filled by the initial settlers. In short order a second wave of younger siblings come along who have to pass through the first group of inlanders and settle even farther inland. Then the third-born group of the original settlers has to pass through both their older and middle siblings to settle still further out. And so for wave after wave of migration, each starting at lakeside, and each having to move farther and farther away.

The cells of the brain form only at the margins of the central lumen and move out in waves, each succeeding group passing through and beyond those who came before. Eventually, just as a human population might come to the edge of the sea and be able to move no further, the latest arrivals cluster at the surface of the brain in the six layers of the cortex.

This process has been studied intensively. An example of the extent of cell growth in the brain is a particular class of large cells in the cerebellum called *Purkinje cells*. During early brain growth, once one of the original specific precursor cells at the lumen starts dividing, it will eventually produce about 10,000 mature Purkinje cells. The Purkinje cells are only one of a great many different types of neurons present throughout the central nervous system, and large numbers of these diverse cell types are being produced at the same time. Whether as migrants or as displaced masses of cells moved about by the pressure of adjacent growth, all of them must find their proper place. So complex a process must have numerous associated vulnerabilities, and many pathogenic factors can impinge on the growing brain. Toxins or traumatic events can injure large masses of brain tissue. On the other hand, genetic defects or viral infections may affect only one cell type while sparing the others. Specific deficits—and the accompanying syndromes—may then occur.

CELL MIGRATION.   As noted, the majority of the nerve cells formed by the cell division at the lumen do not remain there. They are either carried outward passively by the next generations of cells that press them from below, or they actively climb up, as it were, as migrants, and make their way through the existing brain substance until they arrive at their proper destination. Thus a series of waves of outward cell migration pass through the layers already established and come to rest beyond them. As a result, in some areas of the cortex, the outermost layers are formed by the latest arrivals, and the overall architecture is a laminated one, with layer after layer of neurons lying one atop the other in orderly strata.

While this is going on, the *supporting tissues* of the brain are elaborating as well. These cells, the *glia*, are not neurons and neither generate nor transmit nerve impulses. They do, however, form the basic scaffolding along which the neurons migrate and within which they come to rest.

If something happens to disturb the process of migration, cells may arrest their progress in the wrong area (heterotopia), and abnormal function will follow (Friede, 1975, pp. 300–303). Such aberrations (misplaced patches of cells from failed migration) have been described in certain cases of schizophrenia, in a number of dyslexics, and in a variety of other conditions (Galburda et al., 1985; Jakob & Beckmann, 1986).

DIFFERENTIATION.   Under normal conditions, however, once the migrating neurons arrive at their destination, they change their character and begin to assume their final form. This metamorphosis involves several processes. The neurons must elaborate the communication devices—the axons and dendrites—that will fit them into the information exchange system. The axons must frequently travel long distances and traverse many complex regions to reach their final location. Then these axons must deal with such issues as whether and when to myelinate and how and when to synthesize and to store the neurotransmitter substances. The dendrites in their turn must bud, subdivide, and arborize; and simultaneously with these anatomic changes, they must develop the postsynaptic receptor sites on their surfaces appropriate to the designated functioning of that neuron. Indeed, the entire chemical arrangement that will permit the elaboration of enzymes, neurotransmitters, and receptor mechanisms must ripen within the framework of the neuron cell body and become functional. In short, a great many complex processes must proceed at once.

The Strategies of Synapse Formation. One of the most striking recent advances has been the recognition that during the initial laying down of all this complex organization, two quite different strategies are at work. The first involves producing a superabundance of connections in predetermined areas so that the excess can then be winnowed and thinned to the desired specifications as a kind of fine tuning. The other strategy is the elaboration of specific new connections of a unique sort to cope with novel or unexpected challenges.

EXCESS. Initially, the neurons elaborate far more connections than necessary, and they then allow the extra ones to die off. In the flush of their first growth, the axonal (and dendritic) webs spread exuberantly, with far more nerve processes extending through the network than will finally remain part of the system. As a result, early on, there is both a more diffuse deployment of these fibers and a heavier concentration of their endings on given cells. Thus, any one axon may subdivide into far more filaments than will presently be necessary, and for a time, more axon terminals will impinge on many cells than will ultimately remain in place. (To give some sense of proportion, in a normal area of the visual cortex, a single neuron would have some 20,000 to 30,000 synapses occurring on its surface.) The cutting back that eventually occurs takes place in two ways as well. One is simply neuronal death. At the outset there is a superabundance of neurons so that large numbers of these cells will normally die out, both during gestation and through the first two years of postnatal life.

The other method of thinning out does not involve cell death as such; instead it operates by cutting down on the number of collateral or terminal axon filaments so that the density of the axonal web is thinned directly. The pruning of superfluous neurons and connections does not occur at random; rather the emerging pattern is the result of many concurrent forces. It reflects genetic and hormonal factors on the one hand but is profoundly influenced by experiential and environmental factors on the other (Barnes, 1986).

The thinning-out phenomenon has been called a regressive maturational process. Theorists have speculated that some important pathological conditions arise because of disturbances in the way this thinning out takes place. Thus, it has been used to account for attention deficit disorder: If the advance in cognitive maturation depends on an ability to focus attention in more concentrated fashion, and if this ability in turn requires the elimination of excessive branch points in the neural network in the brain, then a failure to thin out enough connections at the right time might produce a child with serious difficulties in concentrating and maintaining attention.

Of even greater interest is the application of this finding to explain why the major mental illnesses such as schizophrenia and manic depressive disorder do not assume their typical form until after puberty. According to this hypothesis, in some individuals the normal process of thinning out that takes place at puberty may go wrong in some way. Too many cells may be lost, and/or they may be lost in the wrong place. For example, if important internal regulatory systems are eliminated, then the ability to distinguish between inner and outer stimuli may be lost, and thought disorder will ensue. Such conceptualizations are still essentially theoretical, but they indicate how rich an area of study this finding opens up (Feinberg, 1987).

NEW SYNAPSE FORMATION.   Although thinning out is an essential maturational process, it is also true that new synapses form with remarkable rapidity in the face of stimulating experiences, presumably to encode the learning, memories, and feelings evoked by these experiences. An important measure of the brain substance's functional ability is the number of synaptic connections within a given volume of tissue. To appreciate the remarkable rate at which brain growth proceeds, consider that even in the small rat brain, during the later stages of brain development approximately 250,000 synaptic connections are forming *each second* (Greenough et al., 1987). Within the much larger human brain that number is likely to be multiplied manyfold.

At any rate, the infant's experiences profoundly influence the establishment and the maintenance of the synaptic network. Certain patterns of stimulation may enhance the formation of specific synapses and facilitate their functioning. Contrariwise, the absence of appropriate stimulation may allow given sets of synapses to fall into desuetude and disappear. Hence, the density and the patterning of synapses are particularly sensitive to developmental issues.

It is the object of considerable research whether the initial synaptic map is determined by genetic prestructuring; whether on the other hand it is a malleable presence to be written on primarily by experience (this readiness of brain formation to be influenced by experience is called *plasticity*); or whether it is some combination of both. The impact of various hormones (particularly the steroids) on this array of processes is also being studied in depth.

In this connection Greenough et al. (1987) have suggested a way of considering plasticity within the framework of how the brain grows. They suggest that two underlying mechanisms make for plasticity: experience expectant and experience dependent. *Experience expectant* refers to processes that facilitate the emergence of essential competencies, such as those that underlie the species' long-term adaptation to its environment (within which natural selection has been at work). Geographic, seasonal, and ecological predictables provide certain cues to which the particular species has phylogenetically become accustomed—and in response to which its neural circuitry has evolved. For an arboreal species (e.g., tree-living monkeys) the neural circuitry underlying the ability to cling during infancy, the maintenance of balance under rapidly changing conditions, specialized kinds of visual–motor coordination, rapid orientation in space, refined estimation of distance, and so on would all need to be innate and potential in each individual from the time of birth. Investigators associated these abilities with the factor of early neuronal excess; the animal is preset for life high above the ground where survival might depend on the ability to swing rapidly among swaying tree branches. The intrinsic pattern of thinning out would then refine this particular set of competencies for achieving optimum adaptation to the particular trees in which the animal developed, to the specifics of the local food supplies, and to the character of most immediate predator threats.

Experience dependent refers to processes that permit the unique experience of any given member of the species to influence the storage of information and shaping of behavior. It might mean the ability to deal with novel threats to survival that have not been part of the species' history or to recall where specific food sources are located in the immediately surrounding territory and how to gain access to them. This kind of learning and recall is vitally important if a given individual is to survive and reproduce. Within the brain, this ability depends on the formation of new synapses that encode the novel experiences.

Experiences and Synapses

Environmental influences on brain development have been studied by rearing animals in a series of special environments and then examining these subjects postmortem to compare the effects of the different life courses on the anatomic and functional structure of their brains. Such an experiment was carried out by exposing one group of rats to a complex social environment and another group to individual cage occupancy, and then taking rats from each group and measuring the degree of cortical thickness in their brains. Under these conditions, the complex-environment rats developed much thicker cortexes. Moreover, the neurons in their brains were larger and developed up to 20% greater surface for synaptic connections, which amounts to about 2000 more synapses per neuron in the complex-environment (and presumably more stimulated) rats. Translated into human terms (where hundreds of millions of cortical neurons are present), such a difference would mean trillions of additional synapses. In addition, the different environments are reflected differentially in the brains of males and females (in the males, the differences are most marked in the visual cortex; in the females, the differences are greatest in the hippocampus).

The capacity to form new synaptic connections in response to new experiences does not merely characterize early development; it persists throughout life. It also occurs in response to specific learning experiences. Rats trained in complex mazes show more increase in brain substance than rats trained in simple mazes. Moreover, where one of a rat's eyes has been occluded before training the animal in a maze, subsequent examination of the brain shows increased dendritic growth in the visual cortex serving the unoccluded eye—a specific response on the part of the stimulated cells.

All in all, the evidence suggests that new synapses form directly in response to new experiences. For example, certain kinds of high-frequency stimulation make the neurons of the hippocampus much more responsive to subsequent stimuli, a phenomenon called *long-term potentiation;* underlying this process is synaptic formation, with new synapses forming within 10 to 15 minutes.

This can be verified not only by the laborious process of counting the number of synapses in a given volume of tissue, but also by the presence of polyribosomal aggregates that appear to be a marker for new synapse formation (as may be recalled, the ribosome is the apparatus within the cell responsible for synthesizing protein). This material appears in the dendritic (postsynaptic) spines only during periods of rapid synapse formation; it is far more frequent in the dendritic spines of animals reared in complex environments than it is in the equivalent site among control animals. This tends again to confirm that rich patterns of stimulation lead to extensive synapse formation.

Brain Growth and Stimulation

Experimentally, the effects of limiting sensory input have been studied in greatest depth in connection with the visual system. Thus, von Senden (1960) reported on the surgical restoration of sight among human adults with long-standing cataracts, who had never before been able to see. For the first two weeks after the bandages were removed, these patients could discriminate between a triangle and a square only by counting corners. Many animal experiments have been conducted that involved suturing or masking the eyes of newborns and then studying later patterns of visual response. Early deprivation in kittens leads to a permanent deficit in the animal's ability to recognize patterns and to orient itself visually. The longer the early deprivation, the more severe the ensuing deficit. Associated studies of neuronal cell architecture reflect this finding; examination of the brains of animals subjected to visual deprivation demonstrates that there are fewer dendrites and fewer synapses in the visual cortical areas. Other experiments have involved limiting the kinds of visual experience permitted an experimental animal (e.g., a kitten might be allowed to see only vertical lines, or only horizontal lines, or only brief stroboscopic flashes, etc.). Subsequently the researchers would study the animal's behavior and eventually subject its brain to exploration as well. These studies have led to the following conclusion: Not only is the *number* of connections influenced by the early visual experience, but the *patterning* of these connections is also a product of the early stimulus configuration.

Evidently there is a phylogenetic advantage to having the genes rough in the expected patterns of neural connections and then allowing experience to refine the details of the basic organizational pattern. The fundamental adaptability of the animal is thus preset for the larger phylogenetic exigencies and then adjusted minutely to the individual circumstances in that creature's immediate surround. Winnowing out the optimal connections from an oversupply of diffusely spread axons and synapses allows a highly organized pattern to emerge from a much less orderly one. In short, where a particular kind of experience is expectable, an available excess of neurons, axons, and synapses allows experience to carve out the most adaptive pattern for that animal in that environment. Contrariwise, however, if the experience of the animal is abnormal (as in experimental situations), the resulting anatomic and functional configurations will be abnormal as well.

In the human, the investigator might speculate that such preformed potential organizations might underlie the social smile or the capacity for speech. Thus the innate potential to engage in social smiling would be predetermined by the genetic map, but whom the baby smiles at and when he smiles would be determined by experience. Similarly, the capacity for language would be innate; the specific language the individual learned to speak would be experiential. Moreover, because of the infant's predilection to develop in certain directions, he may initiate many cues to evoke stimulating responses from the caretaker. For example, the infant's temperament might be largely predetermined; this in turn would affect the initial messages and cues that he offers the caretaker, as well as the stimuli to which he preferentially responds. The particular synapses that thin out and the new ones that form would reflect the "fit" between infant and caretaker.

In humans, another great weeding out of synapses occurs during puberty; thus, as the pubertal years advance, cortical synaptic densities drop from about 15 trillion per cubic millimeter in the child to less than 10 trillion per cubic millimeter in the adult (Huttenlocher, 1979). This pruning may be the neuroanatomic basis for the postpubertal loss of certain types of plasticity; for example, beginning with puberty, new languages are more difficult to acquire and the brain is less able to recover from or to compensate for certain types of injury. As previously noted, disturbances in the pruning process may explain why serious mental illnesses (schizophrenia, manic-depressive disorder) do not usually appear in typical form before puberty.

Critical (Sensitive) Period

This gives new definition to the concept of critical interval or sensitive period. Such an interval now becomes the epoch during which a particular set of axonal and synaptic connections can potentially become established and other possibilities can be discarded.

NEUROPHYSIOLOGICAL DEVELOPMENT—THE FOREBRAIN

The sequence in which centers attain their full development and the choice of which centers come to be connected to which will determine the functions of the brain that are operational at any given time. The process resembles the opening of a new communications center. All the apparatus is now in place in the working area, but a lot of it is not yet unpacked, some of what has been unpacked is not yet assembled, and the initial connections among the various units are just being plugged in. According to the triune concept referred to earlier, the brain is actually organized on a number of different levels; each level has a somewhat different evolutionary history, and each is in a different state of maturation at the time of birth (MacLean, 1969). Thus, the lowest level, the reptilian brain (anatomically, the brain stem), develops first and contains the centers that govern the elementary functions vital to life (respiration, heart-rate, blood pressure, temperature regulation, water balance, etc.). The next level, the old mammalian brain (anatomically, the midbrain), is concerned with integrating sound and sight and other sensory modalities and elaborating experiences on a reflex level. Not until the new mammalian brain (the forebrain and the lateral and anterior parts of the cortex) is functional, however, can language and thought become possible in the sense that we ordinarily know these functions. Indeed, in some areas of the brain, such as the prefrontal lobes (which are responsible for many high-level, cognitive, affective, and social functions), myelination continues until the third decade of life (Weinberger, 1987) and in some cases perhaps even longer.

It is important to perceive that the newborn is in many ways still largely a *midbrain animal,* with many important centers in the cerebral cortex yet to be connected. This process will progress rapidly during the first weeks and months of postgestational life.

As noted, the brain mediates a host of functions that are only partially operational at birth. The observer can almost chart the actual process of myelinization of the tracts leading to and from the various higher centers by observing such changes as alterations in reflex patterns, sleep patterns, social engagement patterns, and a host of other behaviors associated with essential brain functions, all of which come into play during the first year.

Inhibiting Function

One of the most vital activities of the anterior part of the brain (the frontal and temporal lobes in particular) is inhibiting the activity of lower centers to allow the expression of higher level functioning. The two large axonal trunks, the aforementioned pyramidal tracts, are a prime example of this hierarchical ordering. Lower centers (e.g., the brain stem and spinal cord) are active and functional at birth. Under their influence, when the investigator strokes the sole of the foot, the baby's toes will fan out and the big toe will cock back in a reflex fashion. In time this will give way to quite a different reflex response; stroking the sole of the foot at this later stage, will cause the toes to clench forward. For this more mature pattern of plantar toe curling to supervene, however, the lower level (toe fanning) reflex must be suppressed by the establishment of higher order cortical control. This does not happen until the myelination of two major bundles of fibers (the pyramidal (or corticospinal) tracts), a consummation generally achieved near the end of the first year. These large tracts are several feet long; they run from the motor cortex of the frontal lobe down to the lowest centers in the spinal cord (which control the peripheral musculature). This reflex response to stroking the sole of the foot in the adult, remains one of the neurologist's cardinal tests and enables him or her to determine whether the full length of these corticospinal connections is intact. Starting at 12 months of age and throughout the rest of the life cycle, any lesion that either impinges on these conduits or damages the higher cortical centers so that they cannot exert their influence will cause the inhibitory function to fail. The infantile pattern will then reappear, that is, when the sole of the foot is stroked, the toes will fan out instead of curling in. The examiner will then report a *positive Babinski.*

From one perspective, the theorist may configure the entire advance from primitivity to maturity as an expression of inhibitory function. In MacLean's (1969) metaphor, the lower centers represent the reptilian and primitive mammalian primary urges for survival and reproduction, whereas the higher centers offer the possibility of containing impulses and transforming the crude and the pristine into the social and the humane. But to accomplish their civilizing task, these higher centers must be able to inhibit the more drive-related animal impulses and the selfish and infantile urges arising from limbic and midbrain structures. Much of the basic drama of what it means to be a human being can be construed as a recounting of this inner conflict between developmental levels.

The infant's neurological organizarion and early reflex phenomena continue to play a role in later development, so it is important to consider their basic functions.

The Early Reflexes

Several primitive reflexes that are readily demonstrable during the early weeks disappear more or less quickly as they become inhibited and masked by more mature patterns of function. As already noted, the Babinski reflex takes about a year to come to maturity; the grasp reflex ripens much earlier in the neonatal period.

The Grasp Reflex. The hands of the very young baby are typically clenched. If the observer opens the fingers and places his or her finger or a pencil in the newborn's palm, the infant's fingers will tighten about it immediately and cling to it with tenacity; indeed, people often remark how strong the baby is. Phylogenetically, this reflex is probably a residual trace of the clinging reflex that helped primate ancestors hold fast to their mothers' fur; in any case, after about 3 months it usually fades out. Thereafter the baby's hands tend to remain open, and the automatic grasping behavior is no longer present. In point of fact, the reflex has not been eradicated, but it has been suppressed by the inhibitory activity of the developing cortex; under normal conditions it should never again appear. In place of this automatic reflex grasping, the infant's volitional grasp becomes increasingly better modulated so that he can explore and manipulate the world of objects about him. A similar series of events alters many other early reflex patterns.

The Rooting Reflex. This term describes the baby's quest for the nipple. If the baby's face is brushed, especially on the cheek area, he begins to seek back and forth with his mouth, trying to attach to the source of stimulation and sustenance. As with the grasp reflex, this behavior too will fade out (be inhibited) and will be replaced by an increasingly directed search for the breast. (As with the grasping and Babinski reflexes, the rooting reflex may reappear in the adult when pathological conditions interfere with cortical inhibition.)

Other Reflexes. A great many other reflexes have been discerned as normal properties of the newborn; these response patterns have a similarly transitory existence during early infancy and are then inhibited by more advanced functioning. Among them are the following:

- *The Parachute Reflex.* The baby is held in the air face down with his body parallel to a table top. As he is lowered toward the table his arms and legs thrust out.
- *The Stepping Reflex.* If a baby is held in the air in a vertical position so that his feet just touch a tabletop, he will make stepping movements with his feet as he is moved forward.

Many other reflexes persist for varying lengths of time but end fairly early in the first year of life. If they do not disappear when they should, or if they reappear later in life, it is usually a sign of significant and often serious nervous system disease.

The Organization of Sleep

Among the many other functions initiated by lower centers and ultimately regulated by the frontal lobes is the structure of the sleep–wake cycle. The nature of sleep, like other functions, undergoes important changes during development. The actual sequences of sleep development can be seen by observing the character of this function at different levels of the maturational process. To convey this clearly, however, it is best to start with the endpoint—the nature of sleep as it occurs in the fully mature individual—and then look backward to see how it was arrived at. There are two major types of sleep in the adult, REM and non-REM. (The acronym *REM* stands for *Rapid Eye Movement,* a characteristic finding that accompanies REM sleep and gives it its name.) These REM/non-REM phases are cyclical and alternate with one another; with the polygraph and the electroencephalogram investigators can chart their waxing and waning quite precisely during any normal night's sleep. In adults, most of the night is ordinarily spent in non-REM sleep, with REM cycles arising and subsiding at predictable intervals. Adult sleep usually begins with non-REM sleep; it slides gradually from light (Stage 1, non-REM) sleep through ever-deepening phases (Stages 2 and 3) until deep (Stage 4, non-REM) sleep is attained. About 90 minutes or so after falling asleep, the first REM cycle appears. This may last for about 15 minutes and is accompanied by complete body relaxation, by rapid eye movements, and by active dreaming. Subjects have reported dreams in Stage 4 sleep as well, but such dreams are not consistently present and their character is usually far less active than is true for the typical—and quite predictable—REM dreaming. The average adult has about four or five such REM episodes during a given night's sleeping. As a rule, the REM periods are more widely spaced early in the night and begin to come at closer intervals toward the end of the sleep period. All this is very different from the pattern seen in early life.

The Sleep of the Premature Infant.   When electroencephalographic electrodes were placed on the heads of premature infants (Bernstine et al., 1955; Metcalf, 1979), the ensuing tracings were notably different from those obtained from adults, and even from more mature babies. Instead of the cyclic patterns that would later be the norm, the preemies showed a rather variable record with intermittent sharp and slow bursts (the so-called *trace alternative*). Apparently, the capacity to have an organized sleep–wake cycle is not present at this early stage; it appears only with further maturation. Instead, for about 70% of the time, the preemies showed an irregular buzzing of low amplitude fast waves that suggested REM sleep; for most of the remaining time poorly organized slow waves predominated. It appeared as though, for extended intervals, these preemies were in a state of constant REM. Clinically, many observers have remarked that it is often hard to tell whether preemies are awake or asleep; they seem to remain somewhere in between. Anatomically, this low amplitude, fast-wave discharge is associated with midbrain (diencephalic) activity. It has been speculated that the early appearance of this diencephalic buzzing is, in fact, an important functional presence for the CNS. This electrical activity seems to act as a source of self-stimulation just when the newly forming neural array may be in great need of such stimulus input to begin functioning and to continue to grow well.

Sleep Patterns of the Newborn.   By the time the fetus is close to delivery, the sleep architecture has changed considerably. Although the relatively advanced premature infant is still much given to REM patterns, at term these are present only 50% of the time; they alternate with definite periods of non-REM functioning. Once born, the full-term baby sleeps about half to two-thirds of each 24 hours (Emde & Robinson, 1979); now, however, there are sharper differences between the sleep state and wakefulness, and sleep itself is no longer so uniform. The baby still differs considerably from what he will become, but the harbingers of change are clearly present. Among the major distinguishing features of this newborn period is that sleep is initiated by REM patterns instead of the Stage 1 non-REM sleep so typical of later life. Moreover, REM patterns can still be recorded at times during the baby's waking day rather than exclusively during sleep. Thus continuous tracings have revealed REM configurations when the baby is crying or sucking. Before many months have passed, however, REM patterns are confined exclusively to periods of sleep.

Sleep Patterns at Three Months. The 3-month-old infant has a far more well-developed sleep pattern. By 12 weeks, the baby is no longer sleeping half the time; instead, he is likely to have settled into a routine and sleeps primarily at night. Most important of all from the parents' view, he usually manages to remain asleep all through the night. The EEG tracing is different as well. For one thing, the baby no longer begins his night's sleep with the REM pattern; instead, there is a gradual slide through the earlier stages (Stages 1 through 4 of non-REM sleep) so that REM sleep appears only after a while. For another, a new element emerges: Once the baby has fallen asleep, a rhythmic recurrent pattern of high-amplitude wave bursts appears, the so-called sleep spindles. This pattern is characteristic of frontal lobe dominance and, hence, of more mature functioning. With the advent of frontal lobe influence, a new order of regulation has supervened.

PART II

Birth and Infancy

Chapter 4

The Baby Is Born

INTRODUCTION

In all of adult experience scarcely any event has an impact comparable to that of the birth of a baby. (Death may perhaps be the sole claimant to an equivalent call on human sensibilities.) A baby's birth sends a clarion call to the adult's inner orientation and causes almost everything else to be set aside.

In one sense this is quite expectable. Our early primate ancestors were a highly social species who ran to long gestations, small litters, and high levels of infant mortality. For such a group, the arrival of a new member of the tribe was bound to have had profound survival meaning. Among such prehuman and early human groups, surely some individuals were more strongly inclined to accept newborns with pleasure, to protect them, and to offer them support. Logically, these group members would have been most likely to keep their infants alive and thus to transmit their genetic constitution over the generations. The investigator can but surmise (it seems reasonable) that pleasurable responsiveness to the newborn would have had profound survival value; for that reason, if for no other, the advent of a baby was likely to have been an important event. Thus, the arrival of a newborn has become a complex and enmeshing emotional happening.

Aside from the emotional overtones of the birth process as such, the baby has an impact as baby. The vast majority of people have a strong tendency to respond to infants in a fairly stereotypic and predictable way. As a rule, a person has but to whip out a baby picture and pass it around to evoke a familiar series of comments about how cute, how adorable, how fetching the infant is. This is not a true releaser in the strict ethological sense; the response is not totally automatic. But the ubiquity of this reaction does suggest some innate, biologically determined basis for its appearance.

Babyness and Negative Evokers

Lorenz (1943; quoted in Fullard & Rieleng 1976; also in Stern, 1977) suggested that out of their very helplessness, the vulnerable young needed some means for evoking the social reactions in their parents that would make for survival. Indeed, such an ability to elicit adult attention and caring would be a requirement for most mammalian species. The young of certain phyla are protected only by their numbers; huge quantities of eggs are laid, and probability rather than care determines that some get through into maturity. For the weak and immature babies of most mammals to survive, however, requires protection, feeding, tenderness, transportation, stimulation, instruction, and other elements of care. For that matter, until very recently the history of our own species suggests that infant mortality has always been the primary limiting factor on the growth of human population.

Seen in that context, Lorenz's observation is a most powerful one. Human young are all too fragile; great care and attention are necessary to see them through; and there must indeed be some traits associated with the mere appearance of babies that can arouse intense nurturant and protective feelings in adults. Lorenz called these qualities *babyness;* he was able to describe a set of distinguishing physical characteristics present in immature birds, dogs, cats, and humans that tend to have this kind of evocative character. These include a number of cephalic features: The infant's head is large in relation to the size of the body, the eyes are large in relation to the size of the face, the forehead is prominent and protruding, and the cheeks are round and puffed out.

Together these features make for the quality of cuteness so typical of babies, kittens, and Disney chipmunks. The appeal is nearly universal; advertisers are all too aware of this and proceed accordingly.

A number of additional factors may enhance these basic traits. Thus, the baby's smile, the brightening of his eyes, or a posture that involves thrusting out the tongue with the mouth open and the head thrown back will often take the viewer by storm.

Such a response to babies is not confined to a single gender or to any epoch of the life course; it is not prominent during the preschool years, but by age 6 or 7 years it is apparent as a recognizable reaction. It will typically achieve specially high intensity at puberty and will continue thereafter. Thus, all members of any given society (except for the very youngest) are likely to participate in infant care (although in particular societies, custom might rigidly confine it to some members and forbid it to others).

Ugly or deformed babies inhibit the appearance of these responses. Many animals who are otherwise good caretakers will abandon deviant infants, as will many primitive human societies. Human myth is filled with tales of the imperfect infant exposed on the hillside who was rescued by a shepherd or forester and survived to become king. In present-day American society, reference to the ugliness of a baby will characteristically elicit uneasy laughter. The underlying anxiety is probably based on powerful evolutionary forces that impel abandoning such infants, and that people must then struggle to override. Such a struggle often fails, and impaired or physically handicapped children are especially prone to be abused (see Volume 2, Chapter 21).

THE BEGINNINGS OF NEWBORN EXPERIENCE

However, aside from the meanings of the baby as baby, another dimension to the birth process has its own set of emotional overtones. This is the moment when the baby severs his organic connectedness to the mother and begins one of the most moving and dramatic of human psychological experiences, the knowing of separation.

This aspect of birth struck many early psychoanalysts as the prototype for all later experiences of stress. Some thinkers, for example, Otto Rank, believed that to be born left ineradicable traces on the human psyche, and they regarded it as the first encounter with basic organismic anxiety. From Rank's standpoint, the experience of being born thus anticipated, and indeed, gave form to all later responses to profound distress. As he configured it (Rank 1924/1929), humans were fated endlessly to relive and to reexperience the trauma of birth in various guises. Ultimately they had to master that event in order to achieve true autonomy and individuality, or, in sum, mental health.

Rank viewed existence as beginning in a state of bliss; this was the hallmark of fetal experience. Within the womb, the child was totally enveloped and sustained by the mother, gratified, protected, and without unsatisfied desires. In that safe haven the baby enjoyed a knowledge of perfection without disturbance or unfulfilled need. Given this state of affairs, the birth experience had to be traumatic. It meant the interruption of a sense of total gratification, a sudden and unwelcome termination to the paradisiacal state that had for so long prevailed. Rank regarded it as a terrifying experience that thrust an overwhelming bout of panic on the newborn as his first conscious experience. The theory of birth trauma thus sought to account for all later anxiety in terms of the primordial events of this time.

Professionals may criticize Rank for a sort of romantic extremism, but in fact, his view of separation as a central aspect of human psychology and psychopathology indeed foreshadowed many later concepts. The theory of separation–individuation is one of the most powerful and seminal hypotheses today. The essential difference from Rank's theory is that the core conception of the modern theory deals with the birth of the sense of self rather than with the birth of the baby. There are many other differences as well, but the key conception in both approaches continues to be the central role of separation as a primary psychological experience.

Plato's dialogue, the *Symposium* (Hamilton & Cairns, 1961) suggests a curious parallel to Rank's views. The *Symposium* tells the story of a dinner party where, as part of the entertainment, each guest must describe the nature of love. One of the many views presented places special emphasis on the issue of separation. Aristophanes, a guest at the feast, tells of a time when all humans were, in effect, double creatures. They had four arms, four legs, two heads—doubles of everything. In addition, because they were powerful and fortunate, they challenged the gods. Zeus responded by splitting each of these double creatures in two. Since then and forever after, the two halves have sought one another in their fervent desire to reunite and thus reachieve the quintessential bliss that once they knew. Although told tongue in cheek, the key role of separation and the power of the urge to reunite form the heart of the tale.

Constitution

Earlier thinkers often had to confront the fact that a particular set of distressing circumstances caused one child to develop a neurosis whereas another tended to react with some disturbance of conduct. Why the difference? The usual reply was that it had to do with *constitution,* with something innate that came, as it were, with the package; and determined that, faced with similar environmental stresses, each child should develop along quite a different path.

As research went on, constitution turned out to be very much like the weather; everybody talked about it but no one did anything about it. Investigators, it is true, made some attempts to define different typologies and described certain personality sets that they felt were predictable and would determine such important variables as symptom choice and characteriological style. However, none of the suggested schemata held up satisfactorily. Occasionally they continue to be referred to; professionals still encounter terms such as *pyknic, asthenic,* and *athletic,* or *oral, anal,* and *phallic* personalities, but they are chiefly of historical interest. Still earlier physiological character typologies belonging to the humoral theory are enshrined in such terms as *phlegmatic, sanguine, choleric,* and *melancholic.* More recent work on these issues employs the term *temperament,* which will be discussed later.

Personality and the Nursery Experience. People at any age are clearly different in fundamental ways; they have unique configurations of style and response that mark them off from the rest of humankind; and these traits are present from early on. Indeed, differences are readily discernible among babies at the very beginnings of life.

The observer has but to go into a well-baby nursery and spend some time there to encounter striking verification of early individual differences (Bennett, 1971). As the new babies arrive at the nursery door, the nurses and the aides greet them with characteristic pleasure and, often enough, with a naming ceremony of sorts. The babies are dubbed according to intuitional rules of unknown character, and each receives some cognomen. Thus, one is *Little Romeo;* another, *Fancy Pants;* the next, *Droopy Drawers;* and the following one, *Pollyanna.* There is a cutesy quality to this naming, but the designations also possess a certain core of validity. If the investigator studies the babies in question, it turns out that Little Romeo is unusually appealing, whereas Droopy Drawers is just that, a Droopy Drawers, and nothing else will say it quite so precisely. The babies communicate a specificity of character makeup from the outset; there is an inherent profile, identifiable and, to some extent at least, describable, that the nicknaming captures. In short, babies bring with them into the world notable differences in constitutional endowment. The problem becomes how to specify and measure the particular dimensions of temperament, so that initial subjective intuitions can presently become scientific and reliably measurable expressions. In addition, it is essential to ascertain which early differences are evanescent, which persist, and what are the implications of each for later development. These are crucial problems for current research, and much work remains to be done.

Temperament.   The above discussion of constitution noted that many innate factors are present at the time of birth. Presumably, the majority of these have genetic origins, but significant elements can be introduced during gestation by such influences as maternal nutrition, illness, smoking, alcohol intake, and medication. In any case, by the time a child is born, he has many readily discernible traits that are thought to persist and that establish important configurations of behavioral style. This "style" is a way of describing the *how* of behavior rather than its *what* or *why*. Some thinkers (Thomas & Chess, 1977) have called this matter of persistent behavioral style *temperament.* Temperament breaks down into a number of discrete components, and investigators are currently pursuing the identification and study of these components.

The focus of this kind of study, however, falls on the specification of individual differences. It does not attempt to observe or to establish normative states. The observers of temperament are, for the most part, not interested in an average or majority typology; they seek instead to study variance, the factors that distinguish individuals from one another. As a result, temperament has not been easy to define. A number of different formulations have now been offered. Rutter (1987), for example, speaks of

> . . . the general notion that there are simple, non-motivational, non-cognitive, stylistic characteristics that represent meaningful ways of describing individual differences between people. For the most part, such differences appear early in childhood, show substantial stability over time after the preschool years (although the particular behavioral manifestations may change), represent particular modes of response (although these may require particular situations to bring them out), and possibly have fairly direct neurobiological correlates . . . there is general agreement that some variant on the features of emotionality, activity and sociability is needed. (p. 447)

OVERVIEW.   Researchers are currently elaborating a number of different theories of temperament. In the future this line of study is likely to play an ever more important part in clinical thinking; it therefore seems appropriate to summarize at least a few of these views.

For some investigators, temperament does not refer to a single trait so much as it indicates a *group of related traits*. It refers to behavioral *tendencies* rather than to particular acts and is usually thought of as having a biological basis. One of its most important qualities is its stability, that is, at least to some extent its phenomena are continuous over time. Given its innate character, only in infancy is it likely to be visible in relatively pure form; as the child grows, later developmental acquisitions and interactions may make its outlines harder to see.

Various investigators have approached temperament in different ways. Some, like Kagan, have been content to study a single trait at a time and to sort out its form, frequency, and physiological correlates. Others have worked with temperament by winnowing through numerous possible traits and seeking to define a cluster that would meet the necessary criteria.

Kagan and his colleagues (1988) have recently reported longitudinal observations on a sizable population of children. As they sorted out their data, the investigators found that 10% to 15% of the large cohort displayed excessive shyness, whereas another 10% to 15% were unusually outgoing. Both the shy and the outgoing cohorts were followed from age 21 months or 31 months (2 different study populations) up to 7 years of age. To establish the kind and quality of their behavior—inhibited and withdrawn or spontaneously expressive and engaging as the case might be—the researchers observed the children in a number of social situations.

Because animal studies have revealed that withdrawn subjects show greater arousal in certain brain areas (the limbic areas, the hypothalamus, and especially the amygdala), it seemed appropriate to check the functioning of these areas in the study population of children. As these children were followed from 2 years of age to 7 years of age, it became clear in the more extreme cases that these patterns were stable over time. The authors concluded that this is not just a matter of random distribution of a trait, but, in fact, reflects a qualitative difference between shy children and the larger body of randomly selected youngsters.

Measurements of vocal cord tension, cardiovascular behavior, pupillary size, urinary norepinephrine, and salivary cortisol showed good correlations between most of these levels and the index of inhibition at every age. In conclusion, the authors suggest that "most of the children we call inhibited belong to a qualitatively distinct category of infants who were born with a lower threshold to limbic-hypothalamic arousal to unexpected changes in the environment" (Kagan et al., 1988, p. 171).

Investigators who consider *clusters* to be the essential characteristic of temperament designate different boundaries for the definition of temperament. They have considered long lists of possible traits and pared these down to a select few; only a few of the proposed traits have been accepted by all who work in the field. In fact, in a recent exchange of views (see following paragraphs), the only traits that attained general agreement were *activity level* and *emotionality;* no other dimensions were supported by all theorists.

Not long ago, four of the major thinkers in the field met for a roundtable discussion of temperament (Goldsmith et al., 1987). Although these four theories by no means exhaust all the perspectives currently being advanced, a summary of this exchange provides some sense of the nature of the issues now under debate:

• Buss and Plomin define temperament as a set of *inherited personality traits* that appear during the first year of life and persist thereafter as continuing influences on personality. Individual characteristics (such as intelligence or talents) that are not properly regarded as personality traits are excluded; more transient characteristics, such as rhythmicity (which is no longer readily observable after early infancy), are also excluded. After all the pruning, for these theorists temperament boils down to three traits: emotionality (distress), activity (tempo and vigor), and sociability (preference for being with others rather than alone). All these appear to be heritable, and thus meet the necessary condition. (Originally, impulsivity had been included as well, but its heritability could not be sufficiently demonstrated and it was accordingly dropped.) As the child develops, these three traits continue to grow and to differentiate. Thus, primordial *distress* differentiates into *fear* and *anger,* so that by 2 years of age three traits are present: distress, fear, and anger. In a parallel fashion, as growth proceeds, sociability becomes both *sociability* (the desire to be with others) and *responsiveness* (how a person behaves with others), and so on. In considering how temperament affects interpersonal exchange, Buss and Plomin take the surprising position that it is a mistake to think in terms of the impact of the environment on the individual. Instead, within their framework, the important determinant is the impact of the individual on his or her surround. On the basis of temperament, the person (even the small child) both selects the elements of the environment toward which he directs himself and shapes that environment in keeping with his own organization.

• Thomas and Chess emphasize the stylistic aspect of behavior; its *how,* in contrast to its *what* (content) or *why* (motivation), defines their concept of temperament. For them, temperament is an independent aspect of personality, not derived from any other attributes (such as cognition, motivation, etc.), that is always expressed as a *response* to an external stimulus. It can therefore be understood only in terms of the social context within which it arises, and that context will affect its form and degree of expression. The child's temperament will influence the environment, and vice versa, in reciprocal fashion. From this emerges the notion of *goodness of fit.* Chess and Thomas take the position that clinicians always deal with an interplay of caretaker and child temperaments rather than with the characteristics of either individual as such.

These investigators were able to sort out nine traits that clustered into three patterns of special functional significance. They regard temperament as being innately determined in the newborn brain, the product of some mix of genetic factors and intrauterine experience. They postulate that the developmental nature of temperament will give rise both to periods of stability and to discontinuities.

● Rothbart defines temperament in sparer, and perhaps more compelling, terms. Within this framework, the essential quality that distinguishes temperament is its biological character. Rothbart views temperament as a group of relatively stable individual differences in *reactivity* and *self-regulation* (where reactivity is the central concept, and self-regulation consists of processes that serve to enhance or to inhibit reactivity). Temperament is thus observable as individual differences in the patterning of emotionality, activity, and attention. This concept goes beyond behavioral style to specify predispositions to particular reactions. As an example, for Rothbart, the fully formed fear reaction comes into being piecemeal. Developmentally, different components mature at different times: The reaction that will come to be known as fear is present at birth, but at that point it is a more generalized distress reaction. During the first 6 months after birth it will continue to develop; in particular, autonomic components such as heart rate acceleration will undergo evolution. In contrast to this, behavioral inhibition (e.g., stranger anxiety) usually does not emerge until the second half of the first year and may increase thereafter. Thus, several elements contribute to the fully formed fear response that presently appears.

In any case, temperament gives a specific environmental stimulus its import and impact; and the individual will accordingly seek out or avoid particular environmental sets depending on temperamental proclivities and vulnerabilities. This will affect everything from problem-solving tactics to occupational choice. In particular, it will also govern the choice of strategies for enlisting others to serve as sources of excitement or emotional security.

In this connection, personality is regarded as "a far more inclusive term than 'temperament.' Personality includes important cognitive structures such as self-concept and specific expectations and attitudes" (Goldsmith et al., 1987, p. 510). Within the framework of this approach, temperament provides the biological base for the developing personality.

● Goldsmith and Campos assert that temperament is essentially emotional in character, or, more precisely, that it consists of individual differences in the probability of experiencing and expressing the primary emotions and arousal. These theorists add the qualification that the emotional nature of temperament refers to behavioral *tendencies* rather than to emotional behavior as such; nonetheless, it is possible to study temperament through the expressive aspects of emotion. This concept of temperament extends beyond transitory states and does not include cognitive or perceptual elements. Basic emotions are thought to utilize a noncodified communication process that finds expression in unique facial, vocal, or gestural patterns. These emotions regulate both inner psychological and outer social processes. In particular, the expression of emotions rather than their reception is identified with temperament.

Emotions are associated with goals (or needs), with an awareness or an appreciation of what attaining that goal requires, and with action toward realizing that goal. Of particular cogency for interpersonal functioning is the role of emotions in achieving communicative exchange.

In sum, the different schools of thought overlap in many ways, but their differences are real. Buss and Plomin accentuate the heritable nature of temperament; Thomas and Chess, its stylistic qualities; Rothbart, its regulatory biological character; and Goldsmith and Campos, its emotional nature.

In addition to these descriptions of theories of temperament, a number of different typologies of personality are currently being developed. One of the most interesting is that of C. Robert Cloninger (1987). His approach is based on integrating the current knowledge of brain neurotransmitter systems with observed patterns of behavior in humans and laboratory animals. Although literally dozens of neurotransmitters are known, three major substances of this kind are associated with a pattern of anatomic structures and associated neurophysiological functioning. The three neurotransmitters (and their contexts) are dopamine (and the dopaminergic system), norepinephrine (and the noradrenergic system), and serotonin (and the serotoninergic system). As researchers have proceeded in this area, they have correlated these neurophysiological systems ever more closely with specific modes of behavior. They have tested their findings by observing the responses of subjects (animal and human) to specific brain lesions, to the stimulation of discrete brain areas (including single cells), and to a variety of chemicals that simulate, enhance, block, or inhibit neurotransmitter function. As a result of many observations, various behavioral clusters have emerged that are associated with the activation or inhibition of given neurotransmitter systems and that are apparently stable, predictable, and genetically transmitted.

The three major neurophysiologically based and genetically transmitted behavioral clusters that have thus been identified have each received a different title: Cloninger calls them *reward dependence, harm avoidance,* and *novelty seeking*. In adults high reward dependence would characterize individuals who are eager to help others, emotionally dependent, sympathetic, sentimental, sensitive to social cues, and persistent. The individual with a high level of harm avoidance would be cautious, apprehensive, pessimistic, inhibited, shy, and susceptible to fatigue. High novelty-seeking behavior is impulsive, exploratory, excitable, disorderly, and distractible. By way of contrast, low harm avoidance characterizes the person who is confident, relaxed, optimistic, uninhibited, carefree, and energetic; low reward dependence typifies the person who is socially detached, emotionally cool, practical, tough-minded, and independently self-willed. Finally, low novelty-seeking is the hallmark of the person who is rigid, reflective, loyal, orderly, and attentive to details.

These trait clusters will find specific expression in various syndromes and personality types. Thus, the passive-dependent or anxious personality is characterized by high reward dependence, high harm avoidance, and low novelty seeking, whereas the antisocial personality is likely to display just the reverse, namely, high novelty seeking, low harm avoidance and low reward dependence. Each of these traits is quantifiable, each varies independently, and, as noted, each presumably reflects differences in brain systems.

This entire approach has not yet been studied in childhood, but as research continues, the links among behavioral clusters and underlying heritable, neurophysiologic profiles will undoubtedly give the term *temperament* enriched meaning and will open new doors to understanding, classifying, preventing, and treating psychiatric disorders.

THE NEW YORK LONGITUDINAL STUDY. Within the clinical universe, the best known study of temperament is the New York Longitudinal Study initiated by Thomas et al. (1968). During the 1950s, these investigators collected a sample of 133 infants born to 85 upper-middle-class families. Starting when the babies were 3 months old, the parents were interviewed regularly and repeatedly: 4 times the first year, twice a year thereafter until age 6, and then once a year into the teens. There has been a subsequent follow-up into adulthood. Later, the investigators added another sample of children from lower-income families who were similarly studied. As their investigations proceeded, these authors defined nine components of temperament that observers could reliably identify and could then explore systematically in terms of their implications for further development. Several clusterings of these factors (or "temperamental profiles") emerged from this study; these groups of temperamental traits commonly occur together and appear to influence the course of development even into adult life (Chess & Thomas, 1984).

Categories

The nine individual *categories of reactivity* used to classify the infants are:

1. *Activity Level.* The energetic motility—or lack of it—that the child displays.
2. *Rhythmicity.* The regularity and predictability of the child's biological patterns (sleep–wake, hunger, feeding, etc.).
3. *Approach or Withdrawal.* The child's response style in the face of the unfamiliar.

4. *Adaptability*. The speed and ease with which the child's current behavior adjusts to changes in the environment (not the initial so much as the overall behavioral response).

5. *Quality of Mood*. The amount of pleasurable, as against distressed and unhappy, feelings displayed by the child.

6. *Intensity of Reaction*. The energy level (either positive or negative) of response.

7. *Threshold of Responsiveness*. The amount or the level of stimulation necessary to evoke a response.

8. *Distractibility*. The readiness with which extraneous stimuli can alter ongoing behavior, both in terms of sensitivity to others and in terms of ability to complete a task.

9. *Attention Span and Persistence*. The length of time the child can pursue a task and the strength of his resistance to abandoning it.

Clusters

As noted, researchers have studied these factors for their co-occurrence in the same child. A number of these traits do, in fact, tend to cluster together frequently enough to allow for defining various childhood patterns. Based on these traits, Chess and Thomas delineated three kinds of children:

1. *Easy Children*. Youngsters who are regular and predictable; their reactions are of mild intensity; they are adaptable; and they are positive both in mood and in their approach to new situations.

2. *Difficult Children*. These respond negatively to new stimuli; they do not adapt well to change; they are intense in their responses and irregular in their biological functions; and they usually display a troubled mood. (These children are highly vulnerable to later conduct disorder, probably because the special difficulties they pose to those who rear them beget hostile and punitive responses and thus initiate a vicious cycle.)

3. *Slow-to-Warm-Up Children*. These youngsters are slow to adapt and tend to react negatively to new stimuli; at the same time they are not excessively intense and, given time, will "come around."

An issue that concerns the student of temperament is the question of validity. How closely do the categories that have been derived and listed above actually fit the realities of the observed children? In the psychological literature there are many kinds of validity, but in this connection the researcher must consider three kinds in particular (Plomin, 1982). One is *statistical* in nature, the outcome of the attempts to cluster the rating scales scores along with the various answers parents and subjects give to questionnaires. If, in fact, the dimensions of temperament are valid, all these bits of data should appear in a consistent way in some relationship to one another. This is called a factor analysis, and "there is as yet little evidence supporting the factorial validity of the nine New York Longitudinal Study dimensions of temperament" (Plomin, 1982, p. 59). Second-order studies of the easy/difficult/slow-to-warm-up child types have shown better results.

A second type of validity involves the extent to which the observations of different commentators (mother, father, teacher) agree with one another. This is called *concurrent validity,* and in this respect the results, at best, have been modest. One concern has been the extent to which parents can give "objective" observations about their own child. All sorts of interactive issues arise, for example, do difficult children create anxious parents? Contrariwise, do anxious parents create difficult children? Are anxious mothers, in fact, a later version of difficult children? Much remains to be learned.

The final aspect of validity to be considered is called *predictive,* that is, the ability of temperamental categories to predict later behavioral problems. Some relationships of this kind do exist, although not for temperamental traits assessed in infancy. It should be recalled that not even intelligence ratings obtained in infancy are predictive of later IQ. Brazelton's Neonatal Assessment Scale (BNAS), although widely used to assess newborns, is only marginally related to infant behavior at 4 months (Sameroff et al., 1978). All in all, in terms of the discrete categories, temperament correlations are not very robust during the first 5 years.

On the other hand, the more global assessments, particularly those of the difficult children, tend to be more stable. There is some firm evidence now linking difficult temperament in childhood (not in infancy) to later behavioral problems (Wolklind & DeSalis, 1983). However, the issue of goodness of fit always remains as a confounding variable. The child's temperament alone cannot be predictive; the caretaker's temperament and the fit between child and caretaker are critical.

Professionals in the field have given much attention to the heritability of Chess et al.'s (1984) list of temperamental characteristics. At present, very little evidence upholds the view that the several dimensions of temperament are genetically transmitted. Some indications suggest that aspects of parental personality, such as mood, may be genetically related to children's behavior. Parental child-rearing attitudes, on the other hand, are not. Twin studies have assessed these issues, and they suggest that most of these traits (those thought of as elements of temperament) are not significantly transmitted. It did seem that social behavior addressed toward strangers is heritable, whereas social behavior addressed toward the mother is not, and that after the first year, activity level is heritable.

All in all, the important outcome for temperament research is to focus on the individuality of each child and on the salience of parent–child interaction as the crucible for interventional activity.

On a clinical level, in the original New York Longitudinal Study, about 10% of the children manifested the difficult profile. On the one hand, *most* parents found this array of traits to be difficult; more to the point, however, the authors observed that specific mothers came to view their children as problematic in this way. Again, the issue of fit repeatedly came to the forefront.

But it would be a mistake to regard such an adaptive style as simply undesirable. In his work with a Rhesus monkey colony, Suomi (1983) reported that as early as 1 month of age, about one-fourth of the babies born to the colony showed unusual fearfulness and anxiety in the face of stress. This propensity is stable over time but is not necessarily observable until the animal is challenged in some way. By and large, these babies are more difficult to rear; on the other hand, they do elicit more maternal care and holding, which may well be adaptive.

This finding is particularly striking when studied in conjunction with another report. In 1984, De Vries published an account of an observation made in East Africa during a time of severe malnutrition. In brief, most of a group of difficult infants survived the episode, whereas almost the entire cohort of easy infants perished. Alongside the Rhesus report, a possible survival component emerges, associated with the difficult adaptive style.

In effect, these categories of temperament imply different levels of vulnerability. They delineate specific needs implicit in the several realms of reaction. These factors should in turn dictate the necessary response styles of caretakers.

Indeed, the investigators emphasize that the factors of parental temperament are as critical as those that the child brings to the interaction: The ultimate outcome is very much a matter of how the styles of parent and child fit together. Thus, a compulsive mother will respond very differently to a cyclically regular baby than she will to an unpredictable one, whereas a more hysterical type of caretaker may have just the opposite reaction. Although less well researched than temperament itself, this issue of fit is evidently of primary import for the character as well as the eventual result of any given rearing process. These categories are currently being used by pediatricians (Carey, 1982) and mental health workers at once to educate parents, help them understand the role of temperament in affecting their child's comportment, and lead them to learn techniques that could help the difficult child or the slow-to-warm-up child handle stress in more effective fashion.

Attachment

The concept of attachment has become one of the most important theoretical ideas in child development. It is usually associated with the work of Bowlby, a psychoanalyst who developed his thinking over a lifetime of research and scholarship (Bowlby, 1969, 1973, and 1980). From the outset, he was much influenced by the work of the ethologists. These students of animal behavior were beginning to describe the innately determined aspects of infant–caretaker interactions in ungulates, birds, primates, and other animals. Concepts such as imprinting had appeared in the literature and offered Bowlby a possible model for the description of human mother–infant interactions. As Bowlby described it, the child's tie to the mother was the product of the activity of a number of intrinsic behavior systems that developed within the infant (and mother) as a matter of course. The predictable outcome of the activity of these systems was proximity to the mother. Attachment behavior follows activation of these innately determined behavioral systems. It is important to note that although this formulation invokes the notion of instincts (i.e., an innate, species-specific repertoire of potential behaviors), it involves neither needs nor drives; it implies an "autonomous propensity to behave in a certain kind of way toward objects with certain properties" (Bowlby, 1969, p. 180). Although invoking phylogenetically determined inclinations, the model also emphasizes the importance of the infant's actual experience and environment as *releasers* of these behavioral propensities.

Attachment and Proximity. The concept of attachment was an attempt to answer a general biosocial question. Everywhere in nature the observer finds young birds and mammals in proximity with their mothers. The question is: What causes these animals to remain in each other's company? Why do they stay together in the first place, and why do they seek each other out if separated? As attachment behavior was studied, two main features of this behavior became specially salient: the *action to maintain proximity*, and the *specificity of the object* being sought. The action of the infant may involve calling, ambulation, or other means designed to achieve proximity; together, these several activities constitute *attachment behavior*. Some of the infant's actions, such as clinging or following, attempt directly to maintain proximity; other behaviors, such as crying or smiling, serve as elicitors (or releasers) of parental proximity-maintaining behavior. (The parental equivalent is called *caretaking behavior*.) Attachment behavior is thus defined as seeking and maintaining proximity to another individual.

Evident attachment behavior by a human infant begins early and, under ordinary circumstances, comes increasingly to be directed specifically toward the mother. However, it can take as its target the father, sibling(s), or some other relative(s). Organismic factors (illness, hunger, tiredness, etc.) and environmental factors (mother absence, appearance of strangers, and the like) can introduce many variations.

Once it begins to be manifest, attachment behavior continues to be ever more evident until about the third birthday. It changes in form with cognitive advance, for example, a baby may begin to wail only when he actually experiences separation, that is, when he is physically put down; later on, the child may initiate a verbal protest at the sign of an impending separation (mother puts on her coat). But not until about the third birthday will many children comfortably adapt to playschool if the mother is absent. However, although less urgent and less predictable, the pressure for attachment remains active and persists into adolescence. Indeed, even in adult life its action is discernible under conditions of change and uncertainty, and in conjunction with stress.

Imprinting.   Historically, the introduction of the attachment concept challenged existing psychoanalytic theory. The accepted wisdom of the day was that babies attach to caretakers because they meet the babies' needs, particularly their oral needs for suckling and nurturance. Thus the attachment phenomena were considered to be secondary to the primary drive for sustenance. Bowlby had observed that very serious psychopathology arose in patients who had a history of lacking not so much nourishment as closeness. He sought animal research that might cast light on this concept and came upon the work of Konrad Lorenz (1935). Lorenz was a student of ethology (the study of the rules governing animal behavior), who had described the phenomenon of imprinting. Although this work appeared in 1935, it did not become well known to the broader scientific community until the early 1950s. The nature of imprinting suggested a biologically determined need to remain close to an object to which a young animal was exposed during an early critical period. Thus, if shortly after hatching, ducklings were placed in contact with a person or a red balloon, they would subsequently follow this "other" (be it person or balloon) wherever it led them. As Lorenz put it, they imprinted on this other, and, thereafter, that became and remained for them a primary site of attachment. Under natural conditions, the "object" they were most likely to be exposed to shortly after hatching would surely be the mother duck; hence the survival value of this form of adaptation. (From an evolutionary perspective, the selective advantages of attachment behavior include protecting the young from predators and other dangers, and, in the case of higher mammals, fostering social learning.) The attachment behavior does not arise as a consequence of anything but the presence of the two participants; the attachment is direct and immediate without any other intervening "instincts" (feeding or other caretaking behavior). The question now arose whether attachment developed this way in mammals.

Harlow's Experiments: Early Social Contact.   A series of observations supported the idea that after an initial engagement, many young mammals would strive to maintain closeness to their caretakers out of a primary need for attachment. They do not seem to be motivated by hunger, and they are not easily discouraged; indeed, they will persist in this pattern even in the face of noxious stimuli. Harlow's experiments with baby Rhesus monkeys showed that on the one hand, these babies clung to mechanical, terry-cloth "caretaking figures" that offered the possibility of tactile closeness, and that on the other, these baby monkeys did not attach in nearly the same way to mechanical wire-mesh figures that primarily offered nourishment. Such observations, along with the accumulating mass of evidence indicating that infants are highly social creatures practically from birth onward, suggest that humans, too, fall within the scope of this concept. In a variety of ways, literally from the moment of birth, human infants seek and respond to interpersonal contacts with a primary organismic urgency having nothing to do with nourishment or other such need systems. Thus, small children will become attached to other small children who have obviously done nothing to meet any biological needs. Infants will also display attachment behavior toward adults who have had no part in their care, but who have reacted to their social gestures with intensity. Indeed, when attempts are made to condition youngsters, social rewards (a smile, a hug, a compliment) are among the most powerful rewards available. In the nature of things, however, the primary caretaker (usually the mother), in the course of feeding, changing, soothing, carrying, and watching over the child, has the most prolonged and intimate social contact with it.

In speculating on the survival value of attachment behavior, Bowlby suggests that its contribution to evolutionary development might consist of either its facilitation of social learning or its role in avoiding predators. Of the two, the predation hypothesis seems by far the more likely. In its simplest form, the suggestion is that the child who stays close to the caretaker is more likely to survive predation (and to transmit his genes) than the one who wanders off.

Attachment, Dependence, Sexuality, and Distancing. Attachment must be distinguished from both dependence and sexuality. If dependency is the absolute reliance on another for essential aspects of care, dependency is clearly greatest at birth and diminishes gradually thereafter. In contrast, in the human, attachment is at a relatively low ebb at birth, but begins to increase as the baby grows older; it is at its height at about the age of two years and begins gradually to diminish thereafter.

This pattern is the opposite of the way sexuality develops; sexuality is minimal during the early years but takes a progressive course just as attachment begins to subside. In some animals attachment behavior persists throughout the life-span, but sexuality is an episodic affair that comes with periods of heat (estrus). In general, attachment figures are selected much earlier than sexual objects.

In the actual living out of these sequences, attachment behavior appears to develop in parallel with certain tendencies toward distancing. For the child exploratory behavior and play will have the effect of distancing him from the caretaker. In a sense, the mother's retrieving behavior resembles the child's attachment pattern. The mother's hormonal state, her responsiveness to signals (such as hearing the infant's cry or seeing the child get too far away), and her anxieties about dangers from the environment will all play a role in her behavior. At the outset, it is the mother who maintains proximity; this is especially true once the child becomes mobile (in the sense of crawling or walking). With the passage of time, however, it becomes more and more the act of the child. For the child, signaling and approach behavior make for attachment. (*Signaling* involves calling, crying, smiling, babbling, arm raising, and otherwise trying to catch and to hold the mother's attention. *Approach behavior* includes following, clinging, and non-nutritive sucking.) The development of a secure attachment to the mother is one of the important prerequisites for the infant's (and older child's) ability to explore without excessive anxiety, inhibition, or recklessness.

For Bowlby, the outcome of the early interactive process is the development of a specific, mutual attachment between the child and his primary caretaker. Although Bowlby's ethological theory concerns the behaviors that facilitate and maintain this bond, as a psychoanalyst Bowlby was also interested in its internal representations in the child's mind.

Attachment and the Child's Inner Life. The concept of attachment had important implications for models of the child's inner life; as such, the concept had a profound influence on the development of what came to be known as object-relations theory. First, as already noted, the attachment concept postulates that the impetus toward interpersonal involvement is as compelling as hunger and thirst. Second, Bowlby proposed that, based on actual experiences, in the course of attachment to a specific caretaker, the infant came to organize a series of expectations concerning the caretaker's availability and propensity to respond to the baby's cues. These were elaborated as an "internal working model" of the caretaker, a construct that exerted a powerful influence on the attitudes and expectations the child would ultimately bring to future important relationships.

The Biology of Attachment. Turning to a more biological view, attachment behavior has been subjected to a series of penetrating investigations with some rather surprising findings. In particular, Hofer (1987) has worked with newborn rat pups and has studied the details of the way they have attached.

On the level of direct observation, it is evident that by the end of the second week of life, the rat pup will make its way back to mother from a distance of more than 30 centimeters (one foot). This is entirely consonant with the concept of attachment as an impulse to seek closeness. A biological mediator is at work here: a substance in the mother's excreta called *caecotrophe*. This acts as a chemical messenger affecting the young rat's smell receptors (technically, a pheromone); the net effect is to draw the pup back to mother.

Behaviorally, the mammalian infant's characteristic response to separation is some form of vocalization. Human babies cry, and rat pups vocalize in the ultrasonic range, but the behavior is ultimately the same: It is the emission of a distress call designed to regain proximity. In addition to the vocalization, other kinds of behavior are often (but less predictably) present, namely, locomotion (in the form of restlessness, pacing about, or agitation), self-grooming, rocking, or apathetic withdrawal. Thus, if a pup is isolated by abruptly removing mother and littermates, the pup emits a burst of vocalization. This occurs even if the pup was asleep when the move occurred. Once awake, the pup engages in a great deal of locomotion and self-grooming. Adding even an anesthetized mother, or a group of littermates causes the agitation to settle down. Moreover, various surrogate "mothers" (such as a piece of fur) can reduce vocalization in proportion to the degree of body contact they afford. It would seem that the young rat adds up sensory inputs and obtains relief from separation distress in that way.

All of this behavior, however, represents the immediate reaction to separation. When separation is not merely acute but is maintained over time, quite a different state of affairs ensues. The *protest* phase slowly gives way to a phase of *despair* (this is true for many mammalian species). Thus, in both rats and certain species of monkeys, after the acute phase has passed, decreased body temperature, slowing of the heart rate, and sleep disturbance characteristically occur. Nor is it hard to understand why such patterns may have developed: In the course of evolution, those animals who could protest effectively enough were likely to have had their caretakers return to nurture them; on the other hand, if the immediate protest failed, then the ensuing quiet depressed behavior of the despair phase ("conservation withdrawal") would have protected against the loss of metabolic energies and the kind of behavior that would attract predators—once again making for survival.

In fact, the two phases are quite separate and their appearance can be evoked or suppressed independently. For example, the protest behavior can be inhibited by providing surrogates, but the despair phase nonetheless appears on schedule.

Indeed, the despair phase represents a mosaic of independent processes that collectively give rise to the final behavioral picture. The warmth of the mother's body is one source of influence, her smell another, and direct tactile contact with her body yet another. Each of these appears to influence the infant's responsiveness, and the degree of the presence or absence of these factors has the effect of up- or down-regulating the pup's behavior.

A particularly striking example of the differential effect of such regulation emerged from a study of Plimpton (1981, quoted in Hofer, 1987, p. 641). Plimpton raised one set of bonnet macaque infant monkeys under conditions where the mother had to spend a lot of her time seeking scarce, hard-to-get food for herself and her family. Another set of infants was reared by a mother in a cage where food was supplied without limit. It was apparent that the mother who was hard put to obtain enough food became more tense, more rejecting, and more inclined to encourage independence in the infants at an earlier age.

But the striking differences between the two groups emerged when both were subjected to separation experiences. The immediate effects of separation were identical; the protest behavior was essentially the same. When the separation persisted long enough to bring about transition to the slowly developing despair phase, however, two quite different patterns ensued. In particular, the infants of the stressed mothers became much more depressed and showed far less complex behavior with the passage of time. Clearly, regulating factors emerge from the interplay between mother and infants that become increasingly internalized and come into prominence under suitable conditions.

A more precise example of such mutual regulating came about in the study of the nursing behavior of rat pups. The investigators were surprised to discover that the infant rats sleep through most of the nursing experience. Even more surprising was the discovery that a great deal of sucking takes place during sleep. With the sleeping pup at her nipple, the mother rat for her part secretes milk episodically. (In response to regular neural messages from the hypothalamus, a pituitary hormone, oxytocin, is released in pulses every 5 to 10 minutes; this contracts the walls of the ducts bringing the milk to the teat.) Whenever the milk comes down, the sleeping pup awakens, sucks rhythmically, and, most of the time, is asleep again in about 45 seconds. Hence, there is some connection between sleep, milk production, and milk consumption.

Studies of the mother rat showed that she is always in deep sleep at the time that milk release occurs. More than that, the trigger that causes her hypothalamus to initiate the milk-releasing cycle is the infant's sucking. In brief, the feeding transactions of the mother and infant rat are embedded in sleep (Hofer, 1987, p. 643). The infant sucks while he is asleep, and this sucking puts the mother to sleep as well, thus establishing the necessary conditions for milk release. Once the mother is asleep, the baby's continued sucking induces milk ejection. Indeed, only when the mother enters this state of deep sleep can her milk production ensue. Hence, a continuous reciprocal mutual regulation hidden within the nursing pattern is the key to its success.

This suggests that some aspects of attachment behavior do not a priori depend on high-level symbolic or cognitive processes. Numerous mutual regulatory behaviors between the mother and infant are present from early on, and they operate on diverse physiological and conceptual levels. These regulators may well underlie the structuring of subsequent attachment behaviors. Such a linkage of a maternal homeostatic system (milk production) and an infant's homeostatic system (suckling and intake of nourishment) creates a superordinate system of mutual regulation and may, in effect, offer a model for "symbiosis."

Hofer notes that what is thought of as attachment may, in fact, consist of a cluster of such systems. Although here observed on a physiological level, such a structuring of subsystems might underlie far more complex mutual social behavior that would emerge at a later date, for example, mother–infant play. Indeed, the investigator might now draw a general model for attachment using patterns of mutual biopsychosocial regulation.

The rat's response to prolonged separation can illustrate this point further. One of the consequences of such an experience is the loss of the regulatory contributions of the significant other. For example, Hofer has shown that the steady tactile stimulation of the mother rat licking her pup is essential for maintaining adequate levels of the growth hormone and catabolic enzymes necessary for metabolizing the milk that has been ingested. Hofer suggests that such a series of factors might also underlie the human response to long-term separations. Mutual social regulation, even in adult humans, may provide basic supports for health and mental equilibrium. In the face of bereavement, for example, these vital maintainer systems, which operate on both a biological and psychological level, may be severely disrupted or destroyed (depending on who has been lost and what the individuals meant to each other).

The Early Development of Attachment. This approach also sheds light on a major problem in attachment theory: It has never been clear how attachment develops during the first 6 months of life. Bowlby (1969, p. 265ff) had offered a 4-phase model. The infant begins with an inability to discriminate between people (during the first 2 months); he then becomes able to recognize his caretaker and to take special delight in her presence (3 to 6 months). Presently he begins to seek proximity to the caretaker and to react to separations and reencounters (in the latter part of the first year); and finally he begins to recognize the caretaker as an individual with an inner life and subjective characteristics like his own (perhaps by 24 months). This account leaves vague the nonperceptual aspects of attachment prior to Stage 3, that is, prior to the time the infant actually seeks proximity to the caretaker.

Internal Working Model. A conceptual structure that helps bridge this gap is the *internal working model* referred to earlier. Bowlby (1969, p. 80ff) and others had put this idea forward as part of the concept of attachment; it says, in effect, that the child's mind forms an internal schema, a representation of what the child has experienced and what he can expect from the world of others. Given the universality of such models (Pipp & Harmon, 1987) the infant, during the early months of life, may well establish such a model about the readiness of the social environment to play its part in mutual regulation. In response to appropriate cues offered by the baby, the caretaker can act to soothe, to comfort, to feed, to warm or otherwise to ease tensions and restore homeostasis. This would be the biological core of what might later be experienced as *basic trust.* It is thought that such internal working models appear at 3 or 4 months of age.

In any case, the mutual interdependence of mother and infant is key to understanding this view of attachment. The infant's cues are essential for the mother to carry out her mothering role; she is both stimulated and rewarded by the infant's behavior; her responses are intuitive and organismic; and, where the fit is optimal, she responds to the infant's several need systems (for closeness, stimulation, distance, sleep, help in changing state, etc.) with promptness and accuracy. The infant constructs a model about the reliability and sensitivity of the caretaker in performing the necessary regulatory functions; these encodings are likely to be particularly durable and resistant to change. In many of their significant aspects they are preverbal and sensorimotor in character and are deeply rooted in early biological organization; in a sense, they create or contribute to the form of early organization.

It is necessary to view Bowlby's work in the context of an important dialectic within psychoanalytic thinking, namely, between the drive–structure models and what has been termed the relational–structure models of the mind. (For an insightful discussion of these issues, see Greenberg & Mitchell, 1983.)

The Drive-Structure Model. As noted above, classic psychoanalytic theory saw intrapsychic structure as arising from the organism's need to deal with psychological tensions generated by phylogenetically based instincts, such as sex, aggression, hunger, and thirst. From this perspective, the infant experiences other human beings and represents them in the workings of his psyche only to the extent that they lend themselves to the gratification or the frustration of the internal needs. In effect, no inherent object and no preordained tie to the human environment exist. Instead, the object is "created" by the individual out of the experience of drive gratification and frustration. In short, psychic structure is formed around the efforts to cope with the drives (Greenberg & Mitchell, 1983).

Although this drive–structure model gives a powerful account of the organismic givens and passions that drive the individual, it is less satisfactory in accounting for how the individual construes and represents interpersonal experiences, and how they come to regulate and give form to psychological experience.

The Object-Relations Model. In contrast to the *drive–structure* model, the *relational–structure* model is represented by thinkers such as Sullivan, Kohut, and the British school of object-relations theorists (including Fairbairn, Guntrip, and Winnicott). In these various relational models the psyche is composed not of drive-derived but rather of relational configurations, that is, representations of the self in affectively laden interactions with others. Thus right from the beginning the other (or object) is present as a constituent part of psychic structure. Bowlby's attachment theory represents the ethologically most fully developed model built on the primacy of relational experience. As such, he is in accord with Fairbairn's insistence that the basic psychological imperative is not pleasure seeking (or tension reduction) but rather object seeking. On the other hand, Bowlby's internal working model deals primarily with expectations concerning the mother's physical availability. Although Bowlby makes reference to expectations concerning the mother's emotional availability, other object-relations theorists have given a fuller account of the more subtle aspects of how the mind subjectively experiences and represents relationships.

INNATE FACTORS

To grasp the nature of the many factors at work within a human infant, it is necessary to study the baby from a number of different standpoints (some of which may appear to be at a considerable distance from the direct experience of coming to know a child). Eventually, these narrative threads will come together, and the portrait of the youngster that emerges will be the richer for these diversions into apparently distant disciplines and foreign forms of description. The previous chapter has described the anatomy of the central nervous system, including references to the microanatomy, and has considered ways in which brain structure is reflected in function. There have also been a few additional observations about neurophysiology and the way the brain works to provide a sense of the coherence of structure and function.

One of the most telling developments of our epoch is the gradual convergence of neurobiological discoveries on the one hand, and the formulations and descriptions within psychology and psychiatry on the other. Although these two realms are not yet fully connected, the distance between them has narrowed dramatically in recent years.

There is as yet no way finally to bridge the still existing gap; the preceding material, however, has indicated some of the smaller connections that have been established. The observations about the very young infant that follow describe the health and quality of the nervous system including the character of the several organismic states that typify the condition of the young baby (alert, crying, sleeping, etc.). These initial bridging phenomena express the organization of the nervous system in recognizable behavioral terms. The discussion will then consider the more purely psychological aspect of the infant's adjustment and the relationship of the baby to stimulation, in particular, how the baby's need and hunger for stimuli affects his encounter with the visual (or, more generally, the sensory) world.

The Nature of State

When investigators first began to study the behavior and responses of very young babies, they noted that a given response had meaning only by taking cognizance of the baby's particular state at the time of the observation (Wolff, 1966). The sleepy or hungry baby was a very different fellow from the same baby when quietly alert and attentive, and investigators presently described other state differences of considerable importance. Investigators have now agreed on standard definitions for a set of physiologically and psychologically distinct states. This concern with the character of state has been basic to all subsequent work with young infants.

The States and State Stability. These states are genuinely different psychophysiological conditions, whose presence can be determined by objective examination. Moreover, for the baby, their regulation is an aspect of mastery and successful developmental achievement. Indeed, one of the early signs of healthy development is the baby's demonstrated ability to arrive at and to maintain each of these several states in an organized fashion and for an appropriate length of time. (As stated earlier, several dimensions of temperament concern the regulation of state.) Five states are commonly described including two sleeping and three waking conditions:

1. Alert wakefulness.
2. Quiescent wakefulness.
3. Crying.
4. REM sleep.
5. Non-REM sleep.

Some investigators add additional refinements, such as a state of fussiness, but all agree on the basic five.

The Character of the States. Within each state, the infant begins to differentiate a variety of behavioral patterns. For example, alert wakefulness may include hunger, feeding, playful social exchange, vocalizing, and so on. In a similar sense, each of the other states has its own dimensions of expression that the baby gradually elaborates.

Transitions among States. One of the major achievements of the infant is to begin to move smoothly from state to state. Thus, going to sleep, waking up, moving from a state of relative withdrawal to one of engagement with the outside world may all place certain demands on the child; hence, for a given infant, each may provide a source of potential stress as well as potential mastery. More to the point, each transition may require the support and facilitation of the attuned caretaker for successful accomplishment. For example, many fatigued infants become fussy and cannot make the transition to sleep without being rocked or sung to. Only later can the infant handle transitions in a more independent manner and display some measure of self-consoling and self-soothing behavior.

Stimulus Seeking

From birth on, infants are organized to need and to desire particular levels of stimulation. In effect, in the appropriate state of alertness, the infant experiences a measure of stimulus hunger and spontaneously engages in behavior designed to satisfy that need. As previously noted, this need is expressed in the diencephalic REM pattern of the premature's EEG; the stimulus generation referred to there may be an essential spur to development and the emergence of adequate functioning. Unused muscles and sensory systems begin to atrophy after surprisingly brief periods of immobilization, and that even well-learned languages tend to be forgotten if they are not heard or used. In short, all through the life cycle minimum necessary levels of stimulation are basic to many aspects of continuing good function.

Studies in Stimulus Seeking. Some of the earliest research done on the perception of infants is best understood in terms of this quality of stimulus seeking. Many examples are available.

In the early 1960s, Fantz (1963) tried to ascertain whether or not children were born with a built-in affinity for the human face. He devised an ingenious experiment to address this question. He placed a board over the head end of the baby's crib so that the child resting on his back could not help but look at the surface thus presented. On this board the investigator placed four designs: a sketch of the human face and three neutral geometric patterns of various kinds. He then proceeded to observe the infants' gaze in a measured fashion to determine how much time the child spent fixing on each of the several images. The infants chose the simulacrum of the face far more often than the other designs.

At first this was taken as a strong suggestion that from the outset humans are genetically prepatterned with some kind of innate affinity for the human face. Later research, however, demonstrated that the true driving force in the selection of that particular pattern was the baby's desire for stimulation. Interestingly enough, of all the visual arrays to which the baby is likely to be exposed, the one that most nearly satisfies the necessary criteria is the human face. That is to say, the face offers just the right combination of interesting curves and spaces to afford the visual apparatus the optimal stimulus level; the other patterns Fantz presented were either too boring or too complex. This became evident when subsequent investigations began to break down the perceptual performance into its component elements. Researchers offered babies a myriad of forms and patterns, among which were scrambled faces with the features all in a jumble (Goren et al., 1975). What emerged was that it was not the face as such to which the infant was drawn. The baby's visual apparatus needs and seeks a certain optimal level of stimulation by searching for and studying particular forms that offer the desired degrees of complexity. That the infant is preprogrammed to seek out the sorts of contours and configurations found in the human face is no doubt the result of evolutionary selection. Such a preprogrammed preference augments the possibilities for learning social, interpersonal, and affective cues in the context of a growing attachment to the mother.

Visual Following.   The interest in and the responsiveness to visual stimuli are evident at birth. From the moment of delivery, many babies will follow a moving object with their eyes. Nor is this merely a matter of eye movements. As the babies link to an image that they find interesting, a total body orientation accompanies the response. Their pupils dilate with interest, and their fingers, toes, and mouth all point toward the object.

Rhythmic Attunement.   An even more surprising finding that some researchers noted was the baby's tendency, shortly after birth, to move rhythmically in patterns synchronous with the sounds of human speech (Condon & Sander, 1974). These data were obtained with special photography that simultaneously recorded a moving image of the infant's movements and a continuous record of the rhythmic pattern of adult speech. When the two tracings were slowed down and matched against each other, the baby clearly moved in patterns that were directly responsive to the rhythm of the sounds produced by the adult. This was true regardless of the language in which the adult spoke, be it English, Swahili, or Chinese. This seemed to demonstrate that from birth on, the members of the human species are preprogrammed to attune themselves to cues from their social surround and are very responsive to such sensory input.

Several attempts to replicate this finding have been unsuccessful, however, and the prevailing opinion questions the presence of this response. The matter remains unresolved—but highly intriguing.

Entrainment

The responsivity people show to external rhythms is a commonplace observation. The toe tapping that accompanies hearing a "catchy" beat, the readiness to pick up the tempo of a dance, the power of group chanting to captivate people—all attest to humans' universal capacity to be entrained by a rhythmic message from the environment. What is not as popularly recognized is that many subtle biorhythms follow suit in less obvious ways. For example, McClintock (1971), noted that a group of young women who initially do not know each other but who enter a dormitory together at the beginning of a college year will presently begin to menstruate at about the same time. In effect, they will entrain one another, and unconsciously, but nonetheless inevitably, their biological rhythms will synchronize. The mechanisms underlying such entrainment are as yet unknown. Recent theories suggest pheromone involvement (Graham & McGrew, 1980).

It is possible to regard the infant–caretaker interaction as a biological system in which the mutual engagement of the two participants follows predictable patterns of entrainment. In time, researchers will be able to discern these interactions and systematically describe them. In particular, light will be shed on the manner in which the infant's responses cue in to the regularities of maternal signals and expectations. These responses tend to smooth out the baby's pattern and to make it synchronous with the maternal approach, or, more precisely, to cause the baby's rhythms and the mother's rhythms to mesh.

The Process of Entrainment.

Sander devised a situation where from the infant's birth, he was able to conduct 24-hour-a-day bassinet monitoring. In this way he could automatically record all the baby's movements and rhythmic patterns. In addition, during the waking hours, the infant–caretaker interactions were continuously monitored (Sander et al., 1982).

Immediately after birth, there was a progressive disorganization of the infant's biorhythms that peaked at 3 or 4 days. It appeared as if the previously established intrauterine patterns broke down in the face of the radical changes in biological circumstance that now prevailed.

The caretaker responded actively to the infant's crying and other demonstrations of need. These endeavors served as a sequence of signals that collectively began to organize and to give pattern to the infant's responses.

With this the process of entrainment began, and presently the infant was able to reorganize himself on a new level. His waking, sleeping, elimination, and food intake all began to regularize within the ambience of the caretaker's natural pattern of doing things. By about the 7th day, a new ordering of biorhythms was established.

It was notable that individual psychophysiological rhythms and social (interpersonal) rhythms developed together. Thus, during the next few months, an endogenous sleep–wake cycle would develop interactively along with the mother's social cuing, each influencing and shaping the other.

Imitation. Researchers had long thought that the capacity to imitate was a rather late development because it required the youngster to configure an image of the other within his own thinking and then to adapt his behavior to the established model (Piaget, 1962). It was therefore something of a sensational finding when Meltzoff and Moore demonstrated in 1977 that within days after birth, babies could imitate the facial expressions of caretaking adults. In particular, infants could open their mouths or thrust out their tongues after they had seen the adults do these things, and the babies could do it after the lapse of more than a minute. Hence not only could infants form an image and retain it, but somehow they were programmed to be able to translate it into action.

In any case, multiple small imitations occur during close early interactions, so that the baby takes on the facial characteristics, action rhythms, and some behavioral patterns of the caretaker. These form part of the process of growing maternal attunement between the mother and infant (Stern, 1985). Presently the child has these elements available as aspects of his own personality. Such primitive imitations have been called behavioral preidentifications.

Social Stimuli

All these discrete patterns, such as stimulus seeking, visual following, entrainment, and imitation, are part of a much larger and vital component of the infant's innate repertoire. The baby is preprogrammed to be a social being; in particular, to seek social stimuli. This has evident survival value, and the babies demonstrate such behaviors in a host of ways. The patterns alluded to are all part of this larger thrust of infantile adaptation; ultimately, they all make for ever greater degrees of attachment.

Among the many examples of the need for social stimulation is the kind of interactive behavior the baby regularly demonstrates. This is particularly apparent during feeding, which provides vital social aliment as well as food. Many mothers note that feedings sometimes take a long time because the baby keeps interrupting his ingestion of food "to play." And, indeed, babies do send many messages that they seek social exchange, even in the midst of so vital and preoccupying a pattern as eating. When investigators (Robson & Moss, 1970) studied the behavior of mothers and infants over time, they found that fully 50% of the exchanges between the two were initiated by the baby. Babies find many ways to indicate their desire for contact: They look, they gesture, they vocalize, they change facial expression, and they position their bodies in an expectant or a reaching-out fashion. The quest for such highly stimulating interactive experience is obviously a major component of the child's innate need set, and the availability of an adequate response to this seeking is essential for the baby's further growth and general development—especially in the realm of building trust and a sense of interpersonal competence.

Distress Reactions

Babies act in a number of characteristic ways to bring the caretaker to them. One of the most powerful is to indicate that they are unhappy or uncomfortable. Much of what is central to their growth depends on how their caretaking world perceives and reacts to these evidences of stress.

Crying. The most obvious and well-known reaction of this sort is the crying state. Typically, the early crying response is associated with hunger or chilling, and the image of a crying baby who responds to feeding or warming by becoming contented is a universal, established, accepted human sequence that cuts across time and culture. There is also a well-known pattern of nonnutritive crying where the baby cries for a time without any discernible biological reason. A possible explanation that has been offered is that this kind of cry has a social purpose; it brings the mother into a protective or meliorative contact with the baby in an attempt to soothe him, which fosters the process of mutual attachment. In particular, Bowlby states that in order of increasing effectiveness, the surest terminators of nonnutritive crying are: the sound of the human voice (especially mother's), nonnutritive sucking, and rocking at 60 cycles a minute or above (Bowlby, 1969, p. 294). Sixty cycles per minute would be the approximate rate of a slow walk; the average human gait goes somewhat more rapidly; and the rhythms at which babies are usually jiggled in an effort to comfort them are typically faster yet. In its more extreme forms, such nonnutritive crying may well be the basis of what is commonly called colic.

Withdrawal. A second mechanism, perhaps of more sinister import for development, is the infant's tendency to withdraw into non-REM sleep. This is particularly likely to occur in the face of an excess of stimuli that the baby finds unpleasant and that he cannot otherwise evade. This suggests that the usual means of coping are overwhelmed, and the baby, who finds no way out of his distress, just "turns himself off." For example, this can be observed during feeding when a misattuned mother–infant interaction reaches an impasse. The mother keeps shoving in food that the baby does not want or conducts the actual process of feeding in a way that the baby cannot tolerate; whatever the reason, the interaction brings the baby to a state of intense unpleasure. And with that the baby (some babies at any rate) turns off—and falls asleep.

Reflexes.   Motor reflexes have become recognized measures of the functioning and integrity of the central nervous system. Among innate patterned responses, a number of organized and predictable behavioral reactions have a social dimension as well and can readily be elicited from the young baby. They are, however, not merely neuromuscular phenomena; they are constitutionally determined responses that shape the way the infant deploys his attention, and they thus influence his engagement in social interaction.

MORO REFLEX.   Young babies show a characteristic startle response. This involves a sudden throwing out the arms plus a jerking of the body. This Moro reflex, so called, can occur in reaction to any sudden massive stimulus, such as exposing the baby to a loud jarring noise or letting the child abruptly drop a few inches. Neurologists often test for the reflex by simply letting the baby's head fall back without warning. Ordinarily the response is present only during the early weeks of life and then disappears. When activated, it sends a cautionary message to the caretaker: Baby has received a fright.

LOOMING RESPONSE.   All humans are sensitive to a social situation where some uninvited other gets too close, especially if this occurs suddenly. What is not generally recognized is how early this response appears. In about the second week of postnatal life, if someone looms over the baby, gets too close, or swings a hand down toward his face, the infant will show a very considerable reaction. His head backs, his eyes widen, and his face screws up in evident distress. This response appears early, and, in a measure, persists thereafter.

Subtle Reactions.   The baby can display a host of less obvious modes of responding that the attuned caretaker can readily discern (Stern, 1977). By the same token, the developmentally blocked or the constitutionally less sensitive caretaker will miss these cues, and much infantile distress will have to pile up before he or she gets the message. The emergent transactional experiences may have much to do with the pattern of interpersonal relationships that this child will later pursue.

HABITUATION.   A novel stimulus is interesting when the child first encounters it; after several experiences, however, it may lose its charm. This phenomenon is known as *habituation;* the baby simply does not show the same degree of interest and excitement in response to the fifth exposure to a given stimulus as he did to the first. Once a baby has habituated to a stimulus, if the investigator alters the stimulus a little, baby may not notice an infinitesimal change and may continue to be disinterested in the re-presented stimulus. If, however, there is a quickening of interest, that is, an absence of habituation to the new stimulus, it indicates that the infant is capable of discriminating the alteration of the particular perceptual element. This window into the infant's discriminatory capacities has been employed in numerous studies, that is, the researcher gets the baby to habituate to a particular stimulus set and then varies color, angle, thickness of line, quality of form, or loudness, pitch, overtones of sound, and so on to see which element the baby regards as novel and which he ignores as no longer interesting, "the same old thing."

For the caretaker, this becomes an important signal. If the caretaker is seeking to engage the baby, to interest him and bring him into a state of social exchange, then the sensitivity to habituation responses is crucial. To keep the baby interested, it is necessary to note the hints of flagging attention and to alter the stimulus set enough to quicken the baby's involvement. Tuned-in caretakers do this without realizing they are doing so; those lacking this kind of sensitivity need to have it demonstrated and to be taught how to respond.

GAZE AVERSION.   If a caretaker tries to force something on the baby that does not interest him, there may be an initial nonengagement followed by a turning away of the eyes. This is called *gaze aversion* and is one of the earlier demonstrations of a desire to disengage. Thus, long before the infant is able to move away physically from his mother, he can actively regulate his transactions with her by how he deploys his gaze. Gaze aversion is thus an important cue, and, if this behavior is not heeded, more strenuous efforts to distance the self will follow—which may set up many eddy currents within the dyadic relationship.

EYE CLOSING.   The beginnings of withdrawal behavior often take the form of the baby simply closing his eyes when he feels unhappy. This has been considered the earliest form of denial, the turning off of some unpalatable aspect of reality, or, perhaps more precisely, the turning off of the self when reality is too distasteful or unendurable. Babies who tend habitually to shut out external contact need extra support and active engagement to make the real world a more pleasant or, at any rate, a more tolerable place for them.

POSTURAL CHANGES AS INDICATORS OF AFFECTIVE STATE.   Many babies express their emotions through alterations in their overall muscle set, and the observer must note these larger order configurations to ascertain the baby's affective state. These behaviors can provide quite striking evidence of the child's state of happiness or distress.

● *Hitting and Kicking.* From early on some babies show a marked disposition to kick out or strike out in protest against the experience of the moment. At times of stress, they kick vigorously or flail away with all their limbs as though they were taking on an adversary and seeking to best it by force of arms.

• *Tensing Posture.* Here the postural response takes the form of a generalized increase in body tension. Movements become more rigid and jerky, and the facial expression usually indicates the baby's sense of stress. This is a total body state and involves the entire musculature; the overflow of tension from the affective experience translates itself directly into bodily terms.

• *Flaccidity.* A subgroup of babies who become altogether flaccid evince the opposite mode of adaptation. In effect, such a baby withdraws from his own musculature and abandons all effort to do anything; it is a quintessentially passive response, an assertion of total impotence, a giving up on the possibility of action. Its extreme form, the *floppy baby,* poses a complex problem in neuromuscular diagnosis (Dubowitz, 1980). In addition, hypotonia is a common finding in those rare infants who subsequently come to be diagnosed as having childhood schizophrenia (Cantor, 1982). In brief, the later sequelae of hypotonia are not clear and depend in large measure on the underlying cause. In general, however, such a response presages difficulties in this child's later adaptation.

THE BEGINNINGS OF POSTNATAL GROWTH

The neonate state is a transient phase, and the baby quickly begins to adapt to his new world.

Perception

The act of perceiving is no mere passive recording of stimuli that happen to fall on a receptor organ; to perceive is an active process involving not only the deployment of attention, but also the organization of the received message into some kind of inner context where it can be assigned meaning. Thus any attempt to study perception must take into account this larger sense of the process and the way it actually functions.

The Infant's Perceptual Repertoire—The Gaze. The infant arrives in the world with innately determined perceptual predilections, motor patterns, cognitive tendencies, and abilities for emotional expression. More than that, there are some built-in defensive structures as well. A great threat from the outset is too much stimulation—too much light, too much sound, too much interaction, too much of anything. The newborn is in some measure protected from this by his very "design." He can focus only at a fixed distance, about 9 inches, and visual events that are out of range probably do not affect him too much. During the usual pattern of breast feeding, however, the baby's face is just about that distance from the mother's. It has been observed that mothers, while nursing a child, spend about 70% of their time looking at the baby's face. Hence, the mother's face and not her breast is the initial point for both the visual world and a good deal of human relatedness. In any case, the baby does have some choice in whether or not he looks.

It is evident to even casual observers that, from the outset, the newborn is able to fixate his eyes on an object and to follow it when it moves. Less obvious is what the infant sees at this moment in development.

Stern (1977) quotes the work of Von Senden (1960) who found that for formerly blind patients, their first experience with the visual world was a painful one, an incoherent, chaotic sensory experience. They had formed useful and established sensory schemata for the configuration of objects; now they had to undo and to redo all these inner organizations. The newborn, on the other hand, has no preconceptions. His task instead is to create a set of schemata, a world view of a sort. He has a built-in predilection to seek sensation. The infant needs stimulation because of the way he is constituted, and he has an equally strong inner yearning to order his experience, to make some kind of sense out of it. There are inherent rewards of pleasure with these activities. Indeed, experiments in which rapid sucking on a nipple permits the infant to view an interesting image demonstrate that the infant will work for the pleasure of looking. The right kind of sensation at the optimal level of intensity is enormously rewarding, and the *aha!* reaction when something falls into place—some bit of the world can be figured out—yields an inordinate degree of satisfaction. This is especially true for visual experience; it is one of the more mature functions at this time and hence a particularly reliable source of data for constructing a map of reality.

Investigators doing animal research have explored this area. They have raised the question: Just what makes a newborn animal respond to stimulation? It is noteworthy that all infant animals have an apparently innate search pattern. Faced with a novel situation, their eyes begin to range in a characteristic way. Kittens, for example, seek laterally, whereas goats quest vertically, and all newborns, whatever their species, react to the character of visual stimuli in respect to such factors as intensity, contrast, and area of movement. Too low a level of stimulation fails to attract the attention of the infant, and too high a level will cause avoidance; the stimulus that falls in between, within the optimal range, is attractive. Most animal parents find the optimal range intuitively and try to keep stimuli within that confine. But within that good range, the parents will vary stimuli again and again to keep the infant interested and to prevent boredom and habituation. In the human, the baby initiates much of this interaction, and the mother enters into it after receiving the infant's signal. It is precisely here that the damaged baby may fail; he will not evoke the necessary interplay, and the critical amount of stimulation may thus never be achieved. This compounds the baby's deficits; he fails to achieve the stimulus input so vital to his development, and he fails to reward the caretaker, who may then, in some measure, defensively withdraw.

Other factors certainly enter into the picture, such as cultural and socio-economic conditions. A culture may dictate a certain type of swaddling behavior that could pose a barrier for a particular kind of caretaker, or poverty may weaken or preoccupy the mother so that she is functionally unavailable. Each caretaker brings her own fantasies and expectations to the nursery as well as her own (consciously or unconsciously) remembered experiences as a vulnerable infant in some other caretaker's hands—and her regard for her baby is a distillation of all these elements. How well or how poorly all this matches and interacts with what the baby brings with him defines the character of their fit. In any case, however, whether or not the stimulation is forthcoming, initially, at least, the normal infant will seek it and need it.

Perceptual Preferences.   As noted in the Fantz study, it is possible to determine from the very outset that infants have discernible perceptual preferences within each sensory modality. For example, when investigators sought to ascertain the pitch preferences of children, they began by offering the babies an arrangement that allowed the baby's sucking to determine the sound that was played. After that, there remained nothing but to record the sound that the infant sucked for most often; this presumably was the sound he preferred.

In addition to inherent preferences, the baby's capacity to distinguish among disparate stimuli and to discern certain global stimulus patterns is also evident early in life. Thus, by 4 weeks of age, the infant shows quite different kinds of attention to and involvement with persons than he does with things; he has learned the difference between the world of living entities and that of inanimate objects. This is no small achievement for so young a being (Brazelton, 1982).

But it is essential never to overlook the role of the caretaker within each aspect of the developing sensorium. Parents play a profoundly important role in helping the baby organize his experience. This role involves not only providing the infant with stimulation, but also helping him titrate his degree of excitement and arousal. For example, during the early weeks, mothers act to screen out too much noise, light, hunger, or stress of whatever variety; in general, they tend to keep stimuli at a low enough ebb to allow the baby to get only as much as he can handle. In effect, the mother acts as the external stimulus barrier shielding the baby from possible overload experiences. Some observers regard the father as acting the opposite way; in their play and interaction with the baby, fathers tend to increase the stimulus level (Parke, 1982).

Attunement

The mutual adaptation that characterizes the caretaker–infant interplay can be thought of as a kind of attunement of two rhythmic entities to each other's inherent pace, intensity, and cyclical propensities. The fit between them is a measure of the mutual adaptabilities that each brings to the interaction; it is a function of their flexibility and of their sensitivities to each others' signals. This attunement emerges in a variety of attentional, sensory, and affective areas.

Eye Contact. By 7 to 10 days postpartum, the mother can usually count on establishing regular eye contact with her baby. This is a consistent and rewarding arena of mutual engagement. As noted, the baby will usually fix on the mother's eyes during feeding, especially during nursing, feasting his eyes as well as his mouth. An initial sense of mutual engagement emerges that anticipates and, indeed, paves the way for many of the later aspects of attachment.

Body Language. Within a relatively short time, a regular pattern of response develops that allows for some predictability within the exchange between the two members of this nurturant dyad. In the average situation, by the time baby is 4 weeks old, the mother can sense cues that invite her to play. Although these may take form only as postural changes and facial expressions, they are nonetheless unmistakable in meaning, and the infant shows every sign of being richly gratified when the mother reads his cues correctly.

These early interchanges establish the organizing nuclei for what presently become real games. By 3 months of age, the baby and mother will be engaging in nonverbal (though often vocal) game sequences of stable character and predictable form; presently these games will become very important to both participants. The mother may, indeed, use words during these games, but she relies on the music rather than the denotative import of her language to convey what she feels. By 4 or 5 months the games are not merely predictable, they are formalized and must follow a definite routine. By this time the baby is beginning to understand some speech elements and is becoming capable of giving very clear signals (voiced, postural, facial, gestural, and various combinations thereof).

This ever more intricate organization of simple sequences into complex hierarchies is characteristic of how function elaborates. As individual capacities mature, for example, sending a message, receiving a message, performing a patterned act, or enacting any of the other requirements of game participation, each element of play becomes integrated into and coordinated with more complex behavioral capacities. In a similar fashion, both the early appearance of smiling behavior and the later ability to respond to verbal cues will gradually elaborate into social exchange repertoires of increasing intricacy and subtlety. So too, the separate abilities to coordinate visual orientation in space and motor control of arms and hands will presently be subsumed under reaching and grasping behavior, along with the capacity to manipulate objects.

The achievement of early pristine attunement between the two members of the nurturant couple will form the basis of later complex achievements, such as intuition, empathy, and, ultimately, perhaps compassion.

General Patterning

Researchers have devoted a great deal of effort to sorting out in what ways and to what extent the personalities of male and female babies inherently differ from one another. The findings to date have been relatively meager. Korner's studies (Korner, 1973) indicate that some differences may indeed exist. She reports that:

1. Girls tend to display more oral activity and greater tongue involvement during their early feedings than do boys.
2. Girls show more responsiveness to taste than do boys.
3. Girls are more reactive to oral comforting than are boys.
4. Boys display less tactile sensitivity than do girls.

To be sure, this is a difficult area because environmental influences in the form of gender role assignment begin at birth (sometimes earlier). Even within a given individual whose chromosomally determined gender is unambiguous, constitutionally determined predispositions may well incline that child more to maleness or to femaleness. There are certainly differences in the way caretakers address the babies of each gender. The signals the youngsters receive and the models they are offered may act early to shape response patterns and, conceivably, thus obscure native inclinations (Huston, 1983). Stoller (1976), a psychoanalyst who has studied this area extensively, has advanced the concept of primary femininity, an inborn proclivity that he suggests is part of the property of female humans from the very outset. Unfortunately, he has offered no rules for estimating the presence or absence of this element in personality structure, or for measuring the degree of its occurrence; the concept remains fascinating but slippery.

Learning

At this early developmental moment, many studies of infants' learning have involved conditioning experiments. A number of different efforts have been made to condition newborns and very young babies.

Classical Conditioning. Although classical conditioning is possible from the outset, it is weak and unstable early on and does not "take" very well. Ordinarily it is not successful until the baby is about 4 or 5 weeks old (Emde & Robinson, 1979). At that point the memory and associational functions are sufficiently advanced to provide the necessary physiological basis for conditioning.

Operant Conditioning. This form of conditioning does better at the outset and can often be demonstrated in the newborn using sucking as the primary reward (as in the pitch preference experiment described earlier). The response is short-lived at that time for some of the same reasons that classical conditioning doesn't work. However, operant patterns will usually show a certain amount of predictability by the 4th day. The use of such an approach as a means of conditioning social behavior is usually not possible before the 4th month.

Chapter 5

The Caregiver's Role

INTRODUCTION

It is important to note that, to an unusual degree, caretaking behavior is subject to cultural influence and traditional practices. Here, perhaps more than anywhere else, the old wives' tales reign powerfully over what people believe and what they do. It is likely that such qualities as cultural style and national identity are first instilled in the members of a given group by these same child-rearing techniques. More than that, the parents' own powerful identifications influence their approach with their children. These include identifications with their own parents, with the idealized images of their parents, and, curiously enough, with their child. They remember how they themselves were reared or would have wished to be reared, how they reacted to this experience or that, what they yearned for during childhood, and what things they wished could be different. Parents always rear their children against the backdrop of their own early experiences. Moreover, they know (more or less intuitively) what image their culture holds forth as the ideal child, the ideal man, and the ideal woman. These cultural images offer a goal for the parent, a model toward which to strive. Thus the culture and its traditional practices and motifs funnel down through the generations and reach into each home to affect the forming of the children who grow there.

DETERMINANTS OF CAREGIVING

Swaddling

During the early part of the century a group of anthropologists embarked on a study of national character. They based their work in part on the observation of child-rearing practices in various eastern European countries. Among other items, they investigated the practices attending the management of the newborn within each of the populations and, in particular, the assumptions behind those practices. They found that swaddling young infants was an almost universal custom among the populations of eastern Europe. This led the investigators to ask the mothers and grandmothers in these cultures to explain the meaning and purpose of this swaddling behavior. When thus approached, the Russian mothers explained that tight swaddling was necessary to protect the baby who might otherwise tear himself to pieces. In Poland, the swaddling had several meanings: to protect the fragile and vulnerable baby from harm, to toughen him in preparation for the rigors of existence, and to keep him from touching the dirty parts of the body (crotch and feet). The Polish-Ukrainian Jews swaddled to create a sense of warm intimacy for baby. And the Romanians sought to prevent the child from masturbating.

In brief, then, each cultural group had a different reason to swaddle and, indeed, carried out the practice in somewhat different ways. The important aspect of this illustration is that the initial attitudes toward babies and the form given to the earliest relationship with them are subject to powerful cultural determinants. The significance of these findings goes beyond custom and local practice; it is part of a culturally determined system of projective identification. In effect, a cultural myth is created, and each member of the culture then views the appropriate object as the exemplar of the myth. A woman who harbors such a myth and who bears a baby will inevitably view the baby as displaying the characteristics foretold by the cultural belief.

Today, although American society does not lack for myths, the commoner tendency is to discard previously held beliefs in the face of the newest theory that gains public attention. A particularly striking example of such popularly accepted innovations was associated with the bonding phenomenon.

Bonding

The term *bonding* and the associated theory were developed by Marshall Klaus, a pediatrician and pulmonary physiologist of note, who turned his talents in the direction of studying the early mother–child relationship. Initially, the theory that emerged from his formulations swept the field, and for a time it was a leading concept among investigators. Recently, however, a number of researchers have raised questions about its validity, and a vigorous debate is now under way (Klaus & Kennel, 1976).

Animal Models—Goats. Ethologists have observed a variety of activities on the part of animals that collectively suggest that for many species, immediately postpartum, a very extraordinary state of affairs prevails. The mothers show a set of characteristic behaviors that convey a striking sensitivity to their new offspring along with an intense sense of connectedness.

Taken together, these amount to a sensitive period—a postpartum interval of special attachment. This is best understood as a unique emotional relationship between the two individuals that is specific in character and whose consequences endure through time.

In goats, for example (Collias, 1956), there is a critical, time-limited period for such attachment. Under normal conditions, immediately after the birth of a baby, the mother goat will engage in intense licking of the newborn's body. If this licking is allowed to proceed for 2 minutes and the baby is then taken away, the investigator may thereupon substitute a different newborn baby goat (taken from another mother), and the first mother will accept it. If, however, the licking is allowed to proceed for 5 minutes before the baby is removed and replaced, then the mother will reject such a substitute kid and will accept back only her own.

More striking still, taking a newborn kid from its mother within the first few minutes after birth precipitates a hazardous state of affairs. If the baby goat is restored immediately, nothing untoward follows. But if the separation lasts any length of time, for example, a half hour, when the kid finally is restored, the mother will reject it outright, or, at best, neglect it thereafter. Clearly, something special about the immediate postpartum period has immense effects on the process of attachment between the mother and offspring. If accurate, these data illustrate the concept of a *critical period* as being a moment in development when a window of possibility opens for certain changes to occur. Given the appropriate environmental triggers or releasers (to use the ethological terms), the changes follow. Lacking them, however, the critical moment passes and the window slams shut; a *structural* change occurs. Development then proceeds along an irreversibly different route from the one it would have taken had the opportunity been grasped when available. Furthermore, once the favorable time has passed, subsequent exposure or experience will not bring about the change or development that might otherwise have been initiated.

The concept of critical periods is controversial. Lorenz (1935) considered the imprinting of hatchling birds on moving objects (described earlier) to be just that, a critical-period phenomenon. He believed that the period during which imprinting could occur was fixed and that it was limited to a few hours or days; once imprinting had taken place, it was irreversible. However, later work suggested that the limits of this period were not fixed and immutable, nor was the imprinting irreversible (Hinde, 1983).

As a result, the less absolute concept of *sensitive period* came into prominence. This concept implies that "a given event produces a stronger effect on development during or that a given effect can be produced more readily during a certain period than earlier or later" (Hinde, 1983, p. 41). Unlike the critical-period concept, the sensitive-period notion leaves open the possibility that similar effects can still be evoked later, albeit with greater difficulty.

Critical- and sensitive-period events may involve either behavioral or physiological development. An example of a critical-period phenomenon is provided by the observation that deprivation of contoured visual stimuli during the first few weeks of life (i.e., placing a translucent filter over a newborn kitten's eyes so that it cannot see clearly) prevents certain types of crucial topographical organization from taking place in the visual cortex of the kitten's brain. Once established, this state of affairs is not easy to reverse, and subsequent exposure to visual stimuli in later life has little or no ameliorative effect (Wiesel, 1982). Whether comparable phenomena occur in the realm of cognitive and personality development remains the topic of much debate.

Human Potential for Attachment.   The question arises then: Do humans show a time-limited potential for attachment to their infants, comparable to the animal experiments just cited? If so, how absolute is the time limit and how reversible are the consequences of missing it? It is quite evident that human mothers are intensely attached to their babies; when does this begin? At the outset, according to Klaus, "A cascade of reciprocal interactions begins between mother and infant which locks them together and mediates further attachment. This is the optimal although not the sole period for attachment to develop" (quoted in Klaus et al., 1975, p. 39).

A number of observations tend to support this view. There have been situations in hospitals where mothers have been inadvertently given the wrong baby for a time, and then, when the error was discovered, the mothers have had to give up the child they had received and accept their own instead. It has been noted that under such circumstances (in effect, experimental situations created by chance), the "wrong" mothers have expressed real reluctance to give up the baby to his correct mother and have made many declarations of longing for the ceded infant ("It was such a *beautiful* baby!") (Kennell, 1982).

Again, in the case of premature or high-risk babies, where early separation is necessary so that the child can receive the necessary intensive care, the initial attachment pattern cannot develop. In such instances, the mothers are later hesitant and clumsy in learning to feed and to diaper. Sometimes they forget that they have a baby or comment that they feel that the baby belongs to the head nurse or to the doctor.

Long-Range Effects of Early Separation. Klaus believed that the effects of early separation were all too likely to be long-lasting. Although many of the studies are retrospective and hence suspect, cumulatively they seem to suggest that such early experience could have a considerable impact on the developmental process.

PARENTAL FAILURE. As Klaus viewed it, prematurity and other early conditions (such as illness) that prevent the usual postpartum closeness carry with them a high risk of later relationship difficulties between parent and child. In their more extreme versions, this can include child abuse and failure to thrive. In Klaus' view, it were as though some protective factor in the early relationship would cushion the later interactive processes against the more destructive varieties of emotional discharge. Lacking this initial structuring, the essential inhibitory mechanisms did not form, and subsequent stresses made for the appearance of these serious syndromes.

BRIEF SEPARATIONS. Using more sensitive indices than the appearance of full-blown disorders, Kennel (1982) suggested that babies who had had even brief separations after birth (e.g., for short-term treatment for hyperbilirubinemia) were less warmly attended to by their mothers for as long as a year after birth than were children without this history.

EXPERIMENTAL FINDINGS. A now famous study (Klaus & Kennell, 1976) involved comparing how two groups of young mothers related to their children in the face of differing early circumstances. During the days immediately after birth, one group of mothers had contact with their newborn babies for relatively brief periods of time; the other group, for relatively extended periods. Subsequently, during the next 2 years, both groups were observed during well-baby visits and their behavior was charted. From the outset it appeared that the mothers who had had the extended contact experience talked more to their babies, asked more questions of the doctor, and seemed to have a better contact with their youngsters. In particular, they appeared to keep their babies in greater proximity, engaged in more soothing behavior, fed the babies with more fondling and eye-to-eye contact, had more success at breast feeding, and had babies who gained more weight. Thus a relatively brief period of different handling at the outset seemed to have the most far-reaching effects on the later relationship.

Similar findings ensued (Kennell, 1975) when an experimental group of parents were allowed early contact with preemies and were then compared with mothers who had had the usual, more restricted access to their infants. Here, too, when observations were made at one month, the early-contact mothers looked at their babies more during feedings than did the mothers assigned to the standard preemie pattern. At follow-up, when the children were $3\frac{1}{2}$ years old, the early-contact babies had a mean IQ of 99 as compared with the other group, whose IQ was 85.

Conclusion. Klaus and Kennell concluded from these observations that there was, indeed, an early sensitive period in the human: In the immediate postpartum state the mother was uniquely ready to form a close attachment to her baby, she needed adequate exposure to her child to do so, an attachment so formed was not easily given up, and the establishment of such early bonding had long-range effects. By the same token, the failure to establish adequate bonding would also have far-reaching implications for development.

Critique. When the concept of a sensitive period during which bonding took place was first reported, it took both the medical community and the lay public by storm. It became a dominant theme in styles of hospital management, and it had a considerable impact on the research area as well. Nurses were concerned about so ordering things that "bonding should take place" and would adjust schedules accordingly. The experimental studies comparing brief-contact and extended-contact mothering offered an especially striking and apparently convincing image that rapidly became a part of the dogma of child development.

However, attempts to replicate the findings raised various questions about the validity or at least the general applicability of the model. At present, there is real doubt whether the phenomenon of bonding exists in anything like the form in which it was originally described. Investigators have questioned the research methodology in particular (Svejda et al., 1982).

METHODOLOGY.   In Kennel and Klaus's study (1976), there was no random assignment or blind rating. That is to say, the persons who designed and carried out the postpartum segment of the project also observed and commented on the behavior of mothers and infants on follow-up. They knew which subjects were assigned to each category of the study, and their observations could have been influenced by what they hoped to see as the outcome. Furthermore, because the assignment to both the brief- and extended-contact groups was nonrandom, it is not clear whether other preexisting discrepancies between the two groups of subjects might have accounted for the differences noted at follow-up.

Researchers carried out a replication study using as subjects 30 lower-middle-class women who were having their first baby. These women were randomly assigned to the two groups and were rated blindly (i.e., by judges who did not know to what group they had been assigned). This approach failed to show significant differences in the care provided by brief- as against extended-contact mothering. Indeed, when the investigators compared maternal responses under the two sets of conditions, they observed minimal differences (Svejda et al., 1982).

CONCLUSION.   Critics reexamining the bonding hypothesis concluded that a host of postnatal events were collectively far more important in determining the long-term quality of mother–infant attachment than were the alleged early bonding experiences. Overall, the case for a sensitive period in human adaptation was considered weak. More than that, the socioeconomic factors affecting the subjects appeared potentially far more important in facilitating—or hampering—maternal responsiveness than was the presence of a sensitive period. Thus, the availability of a support system in the form of a grandmother, a father, a nurse, and so on could be far and away a more crucial variable in shaping the early mother–infant interaction than the issue of how much postpartum contact they had had. Moreover, the bonding model omitted the role of the infant as a contributor to the development of the mother–child relationship. Because the particular qualities offered by the infant are important influences on early attachment, this is a specially significant lack.

A more balanced approach is to regard mother–child attachment as an ongoing, unfolding, mutual process, a developmental emergent in its own right, and not the product of a single event or an initial exchange.

CONCERNS. Critics have also emphasized other limitations of the bonding hypothesis. The model reifies one particular component of the mother–child interaction detracting from the full richness of the process of developing a relationship. Thus, if the initial contact is overvalued, it could lead to a neglect of subsequent interactions. Due to adoption or to medical complications, many a parent is unable to be with his or her baby from the outset. The bonding hypothesis implied that having missed the critical moment, bonding now could never take place; as a result, many such parents were made to feel irretrievably hurt or guilty. In fact, the early development of attachment is not *transactional* (the consequence of an event or a number of events); it is *interactional* (the product of an ongoing process). There is therefore no reason to regard the lack of early contact as necessarily compromising future attachment.

Role of the Father

Engrossment. The father's early interest in touching and handling the infant has been called *engrossment* (Greenberg & Morris, 1974). From early on, fathers are often very active in the care and management of newborns; however, objective observers have described small but significant differences in the care-giving behavior of fathers and mothers during the first 48 hours. Evidently fathers can and do care for newborns in heartfelt ways, but these are nonetheless different in some measure from mothers' ways.

Paternal Bonding. If bonding does occur, do fathers bond as well as mothers? To explore this question, one group of fathers were given enhanced early contact with their new babies and were then compared with another group of fathers who had not had this experience. When the researchers evaluated the findings, no differences could be discerned between the subsequent caretaking behaviors of each; they therefore concluded that paternal bonding did not occur. However, such studies suffer from many of the defects noted in the work on maternal bonding (Greenberg & Morris, 1974).

It seems safe to say that father–infant behavior remains an insufficiently studied area. Margaret Mead once observed that fathers were a biological necessity but a social accident. This would imply that fathers have little to do with babies. On the other hand, when one group of investigators (Parke, 1982) conducted a study of middle-class parents' interactions with 2- to 4-day-old babies, the results were somewhat unexpected. These investigators observed the mother alone with the baby, the father alone with the baby, and the mother and father together with the baby. What emerged was that in the triadic situation, the father held the baby twice as much as the mother, vocalized more than the mother, touched the baby as much as or more than the mother, but smiled at the baby less than the mother did.

To test the effects of class and economic status, the investigators repeated the study at a general hospital with families of lower socioeconomic status (SES), who showed the expected higher rate of premature and high-risk babies. Most of the findings were comparable to those of the middle-class group, but in the triadic situation the low-SES fathers played a more dominant role and did more of the feeding.

The investigators concluded that although differences do exist between the ways that fathers and mothers interact with babies, fathers are, in fact, more involved with and responsive to their infants than our culture has acknowledged. Indeed, contrary to Margaret Mead, it can be said that fathers are social as well as biological necessities.

Modern family arrangements place a small but significant number of fathers in the role of primary caretaker for their children. Recent studies have begun to explore the impact of the father in that role (Greif, 1985). Some feminist neo-Freudian authors such as Dinnerstein (1977) have argued that only the father's assumption of a major role in child-rearing can transform what they see as men's deep mistrust of women.

Chapter 6

The First Six Months of Life

INTRODUCTION

Daniel Stern (1977)* has conducted sensitive, informative studies of the social interactions between young babies and their mothers and has ana-lyzed moments of one-to-one interplay. Stern's approach has included numerous dimensions such as direct observation, the study of filmed se-quences, and computerized evaluations of sound, gesture, and facial ex-pression. Stern concluded that this often playful social give-and-take is among the major determinants that shape how a baby learns to participate in human exchanges and to construe the interpersonal world.

In summary, Stern asserts that for the infant, the outcome of these early interchanges is the development of schemata of face-voice-touch that allow the child to identify the mother as a unique and specific responsive entity. She is at the same time the locus of intentions, affects, and interest, a veritable psychological other. Along with this, the baby is also acquiring the schemata for expressing and recognizing emotion. These acquisitions in-volve a mastery of signals and cuing systems as part of the infant's emotional equipment. The infant is also mastering the meaning of variations in the tempo and rhythm of human exchange and is learning the social cues and conventions necessary to initiate, maintain, terminate, or avoid interactions with the mother. As part of these exchanges, the baby learns such dialogic techniques as taking turns, waiting for the other fellow to finish, and the like. These techniques later become the underpinnings for what linguists call the *pragmatics* of language and social communication. All in all, the work of this social learning during the first 6 months results in the establishment of the conditions necessary for full object relationships later in develop-ment.

Following Stern's exegesis, the data in this chapter will first describe what the mother offers and then what the baby brings to the interaction.

WHAT THE MOTHER OFFERS AND WHAT THE INFANT EVOKES

A specific group of behaviors characterize the mothering of a young baby regardless of who is offering that care. Fathers, foster parents, nannies, wet nurses, grandparents, and other alternatives to the biological mother have nurtured babies from time immemorial. Sometimes this has been the result of happenstance, sometimes misadventure, and sometimes cultural prac-tice; in any case, certain aspects of mothering behavior remain essentially the same among all caretakers in all epochs and under a wide variety of different conditions.

---

*Much of the material in this chapter has been built on the framework of Daniel Stern's writing, in particular, on the opening chapters of his book *The First Relationship: Infant and Mother,* 1977, Cambridge, MA: Harvard University Press.

The infant has obvious biological needs. The point of the present observations however, is that the infant also has social needs that are, in their own way, as innately programmed as the needs for direct food intake and care of excreta.

Adults naturally and unconsciously perform a series of acts that are directed only toward infants. These behaviors are, moreover, as pleasurable as they are natural, and most people who participate in child care evidently indulge in them with a great deal of satisfaction. These activities, which can be summed up in the phrase "playing with the baby," are essential for the healthy development of babies. They include characteristic facial expressions, certain ways of speaking, a special quality of gaze, and a set of face and head movements that typify this kind of exchange.

Somehow interaction with an infant evokes in the adult a need to play out a sequence of stylized communication or, more precisely, very specialized communication. This highly functional behavior serves to prepare the baby for later communicative exchange.

Faces as Messengers

The study of mother–child interactions has yielded a set of rather typical expression-sets that are repeated (with some inevitable variation) by most people playing with a baby. They involve a quality of exaggeration—an extreme distortion of features—to portray some mock or caricatured form of emotion such as play-surprise, a deep frown, a huge smile, or mock-sympathy. Compared with ordinary emotional display, these telegraphed "performances" are much slowed down, are much speeded up, or may exhibit various combinations of rate change. The verbal concomitants are equally exaggerated, with heightened contours of pitch and intensity so that the behavior ranges from whispering to pretend-scary.

Speech

The caretaker employs quite a special form of speech in these exchanges. There is a pronounced stress on the different sounds and syllables, and the voice is produced with a marked rhythm so that a singsong quality is often present. The speed of communication is slowed with the vowel sounds in particular being stretched out, and the overall melody of speech is exaggerated, with many crescendos and glissandos.

The speech content usually takes the form of a monologue structured as though the mother were in an active dialogue with the baby. She poses her questions and then allows pauses for baby's simulated responses. This form of exchange plays a critical role in preparing the baby for later conversation: The timing, the phrasing, the tonal patterns of speech, the rhythmic structure of human exchange, the framework of alternation of speakers as a means of interaction, even such nuances as taking turns are all foreshadowed in this interplay. Such repeated interactions lay down the particular matrix of socialization for that baby. Such exchanges also play an active role in the progressive bonding of the two partners; as the play proceeds, it reaches ever higher pitches of intensity and excitement, and mother and infant begin to vocalize together, a phenomenon called *chorusing* (Stern et al., 1975).

On the whole, the mother's vocalizations are relatively few in number, exaggerated in degree, and repetitious in character. This array of elements, however, is easier for the baby to learn. Cross-cultural studies (Ferguson, 1964, quoted in Stern, 1985) show that wherever observations were carried out, mothers universally used some form of baby talk. It is simply part of the human way of relating to babies. This form of speech involves a number of distinguishing characteristics: Utterances are short, syntax is simplified, there are numerous nonsense sounds, and many of the ordinary forms of speech production are transformed, for example, "rabbit" becomes "wabbit." As the child grows, the mother tends to offer increasingly complex speech samples.

The way in which the mother inflects and accents her speech is also unique. Because playful switches of pitch delight the infant, mothers frequently raise their pitch, often to a falsetto, while accompanying their verbalizations with theatrical head movements that feature exaggeration and fullness of display.

The Meaning of the Mother–Infant Gaze

Stern (1977) calls mutual gazing between adults a potent interpersonal event and declares that if eye-to-eye contact is held for more than 10 seconds it means a fight or a bid to lovemaking. Although these alternatives may not exhaust the total array of potential meanings of fixed-gaze behavior, undoubtedly such prolonged locking of eyes is always an intensely charged and meaningful exchange. With babies, however, the mother–infant gaze may be joined for 30 seconds or more (although the average tends to be about 20 seconds).

Many face and head movements enter into this gaze-centered interaction. Verbalizations are often accompanied by changes in head position that tend either to reveal or to conceal the features. The presentation of an animated facial expression is part of many games. Peekaboo can start as early as 4 months, with baby initially an interested spectator and only later a participant (Kleeman, 1967).

Generally speaking, these facial expressions coupled with gaze invite interaction. In effect, they are a form of flirting, a way of initiating pleasurable and playful exchange. Further changes in expression maintain or modulate the ongoing interaction. Thus, a smile might invite more playful exchange, a frown or gaze aversion would suggest a wish to terminate the interplay, and a neutral or an expressionless face might signal a desire to avoid play engagement at that time.

In pathological situations, along with the other interactional difficulties that are likely to be present, these game-playing patterns are distorted as well. Thus, abusing parents typically have difficulty in creating or participating in any games with their babies. Or, parents of congenitally blind babies often find it very hard to play a game that does not implicitly depend on the presence of vision. The net result is that vital elements of parent–child interaction fail to be realized, and development is accordingly disturbed.

Personal Space

Most people possess a sense of a certain volume of space around the self that is altogether his or her own. This realm of personal space, which is sometimes called the *body buffer zone*, forms a sort of psychological bubble around the body. In the same sense, too close an approach on the part of another person bursts the bubble and gives rise to a sense of discomfort. The exact volume and extent of the personal space thus formed vary widely along individual and cultural lines. In American culture, the usual distance people maintain in face-to-face interaction is about 2 feet. A bid for intimacy is a request—or an invitation—to violate and to enter this personal area. The looming reflex mentioned earlier is an innate aversion to such behavior that protects the face and eyes. (Ethologists speculate that such reflexes served to protect against predators (Bowlby, 1969).) In the nature of things mothers occasionally encroach on this area. Such experiences help the infant prepare for later intimate encounters such as kissing and snuggling. How sensitively or disturbingly the mother titrates her "invasive" behavior helps shape the infant's tolerance (or intolerance) for physical intimacy.

Putting It All Together

For purposes of explorative study, investigators may distinguish such factors as speech, facial expression, or movements. In the baby's experience, however, these all come together. Aronson and Rosenbloom (1971) conducted experiments in which the mother's voice was directed toward the baby from somewhere in space other than her face. Up to 3 weeks of age, the babies could tolerate this reasonably well, but thereafter the infants found it upsetting. In another experiment mothers of slightly older infants were instructed not to respond to the baby's cues with their usual animated facial expressions. The baby would make repeated efforts to get the mother to respond and would then begin to display distress and aversive behavior (Tronick et al., 1978). These findings suggest that within the first few months of life, the infant integrates multiple channels of communication (e.g., facial expression, vocal intonation, bodily rhythm) into a set of expectancies and presumed meanings.

Thus, by the end of 6 months, the baby can identify the cues and "read" many of the meanings arising from others' behavior. He has learned the basic rules that regulate the ebb and flow of vocal and social interaction, and he is beginning to learn something about the communication of affect and intention.

ENGAGING THE WORLD

As the baby approaches the middle of the first year, a great many new acquisitions come to the fore; these will have a determinative impact on the ever-changing, ever-enriching relationship with the caretaker. The baby will learn how to communicate, control, and express emotions as well as to gauge the effects of smiling, laughing, and crying. Presently, he will begin to integrate these elements into more elaborate patterns of being arch and winsome, winning and coquettish, or clamorous and invasive. In particular, he learns—or doesn't learn—how to play.

Visual Maturation

By the end of the 3rd postpartum month, the baby's ability to look at, see, and track his world is remarkably advanced. The baby can now pursue visually, hold his gaze when interested in something, and accommodate to the image so that he can see it sharply—and he can do these things for all intents and purposes as well as the adult. The baby can also withdraw his gaze or shut his eyes and thus turn off a sensation that is too intense or that he no longer wishes to engage. (In this respect, seeing is very unlike hearing.) Compared with the relatively low level of the infant's achieved competence in speech, gesture, locomotion, or manipulation, his visual functioning is strikingly advanced. Indeed, this is perhaps the only realm where the infant and mother now meet as equals. The baby's ability to control what he sees and to turn off or adjust the amount and kind of input allows him to become a full partner in the social exchange with his mother.

Development of Interest in Objects

At about the 6th month, the baby's interest in people seems to reach a plateau. He knows what they look like, and he knows who interests him. But the infant's increasing capacity to control his hands and fingers now allows him to manipulate and cope with objects in a new way. Accordingly, his interest turns ever more to the world of things; he begins to grasp objects, to handle them, to unravel their mysteries, and to reveal their secrets. The developmental landmark of increased hand–eye coordination is the particular high-water mark that the infant reaches at this time, and he can amuse himself for long intervals by handling and manipulating a favorite item. His play with the caretaker is likely to become more and more triadic; toys become a third presence in mother–infant interactions and are frequently resorted to thereafter as part of their interplay. In a sense the infant is becoming able to take the caretaker's presence more and more for granted; his interest is turning outward beyond the joys of person-to-person interaction to the great world of physical possibility that he is beginning to master.

Communicative Expressions

At this stage a variety of communicative means are rapidly developing into a body of techniques that will increasingly enrich the infant's ability to send and receive messages. These are pervasive mechanisms; communication ultimately becomes and remains a total-body, total-personality organization with ramifications for every physiological system.

Head Behaviors.   Head posture is a potent signal, and the coordination of head and eyes can speak volumes. Adults have initiated and, in part, carried through many a seduction almost exclusively with such units of behavior. Direct eye-to-eye contact, lateral gazing out of the corner of the eye, or turning the head away can each betoken a state of mind and a message. Surrender, for example, might involve lowering the head and going limp (a strategy actually used by babies who have been overstimulated). As the baby matures, mixed or ambivalent behaviors of this kind are possible.

The Face as Social Cue

From the outset, the human infant possesses a surprising degree of facial neuromuscular maturity. It is possible to identify a great many emotional expressions on the baby's face in the newborn period—all the while recognizing that some of these configurations may have very little to do with what the baby is actually feeling and thinkng. These facial sets will become social cues at a much later date. Preferred facial expressions at birth or shortly thereafter may prompt some of the character typing by the nurses described earlier.

Smiling.   Spitz and Wolff (1946) accorded smiling the role of the first organizer of the mother–infant relationship. Indeed, by any reckoning, the baby's smile is a striking and early promoter of interpersonal inter actions. To be sure, this applies primarily to the social smile; reflex smiling can be present from birth onward, but its significance varies with the baby's level of development.

During the first 2 postnatal weeks, smiling occurs only during REM sleep and drowsiness. It arises from endogenous sources, essentially a reflexive response to some momentary aspect of the baby's inner state. Only rarely will the observer see the smile in the alert awake infant during these early weeks. Hence when a mother asserts that her baby smiled at her from the first week, she is partially accurate. The baby may well have smiled that early, but not at her. From the viewpoint of interpersonal relations, at that moment the smile is a meaningless act; it is responsive not so much to the outside world as to some inner twinge. Several weeks must pass before a consistent pattern of social smiling becomes established.

However, sometime between 6 weeks and 3 months the smile becomes exogenous. At that point social stimuli such as seeing a human face, meeting another's gaze, hearing a high-pitched voice, or being tickled will elicit a smile. Needless to say, getting the baby to smile is enormously rewarding to caretakers, and within a relatively short time the baby's smile becomes instrumental. He uses it as a means to an end—the baby smiles intentionally to evoke a predictable and desired response. Thus it is both a means of response and an instrument for enacting intentions or fulfilling needs.

Smiling, in turn, becomes part of more complex and elaborate communication sets. In effect, it becomes incorporated into those more complicated patterns that might express mixed emotional messages. As the baby matures, there will also be qualitative refinements, different smiles for different situations, along with different degrees of smiling in response to varying levels of social communication.

It is noteworthy that early smiling is largely innate. Humans are programmed this way, and smiling occurs under highly diverse conditions. The development of the subsequent transformations and elaborations of smiling, however, depends on the appropriate interactions with the mother. This is particularly evident with blind children. For the first 4 to 6 months such children follow the same course as sighted children. Unfortunately, because they cannot see the mother's smiles, they are unable to respond to her initiations, and they cannot imitate her facial behavior or be reinforced by it. As time goes on, this deficit leads to major disruptions of the normal cuing and exchange system so typical of this time of life. Hence, without intervention, after the 4th month, blind children begin to display a damping out of the smiling behavior in particular and of facial expressiveness in general. This experiment of nature suggests that after the 4th month the innate component of smiling behavior has run its course and that further development of this capacity depends on visual feedback. Without that stimulus (or an appropriate substitute), smiling behavior begins to drop out.

Laughing. This form of emotional expression is not present at birth and awaits a considerable advance in development before becoming manifest. It typically appears between the 4th and 8th month in response to some very exciting form of play, such as tickling. Later, between the 7th and 9th month, verbal play alone can evoke laughter, and, by the end of the first year, visual triggers are the best elicitors of this behavior. Presently, laughter too, becomes instrumental in rewarding others' behavior and inducing further interaction.

Crying. This is far and away the most dramatic and the most certain expression of unhappiness available to the baby. It is actually the final emergent in a sequence of facial contortions that the baby initiates when he begins to feel troubled. An observer might note that the baby first begins to look serious, and then he frowns; these are followed by flushing, the lips quiver and retract (a form of grimacing), the mouth opens, and finally the baby starts to cry in earnest.

As this proceeds, somewhere along the way whimpering may begin, but the true vocalization of crying generally awaits the full end-point state.

In general, the expressions of distress are present at birth; they are especially likely to be noted during sleep. As parents can attest, however, stressful stimuli elicit them earlier than appropriate stimuli elicit the smile, and they begin to play an instrumental role in influencing parental behavior as early as 3 weeks. They are fully present as active deliberate social messages by the 3rd month.

Integration of Behavioral Expressions

Thus, the various forms of expressive behavior begin as largely innate motor patterns that are present at birth and that quicky assume their characteristic social form. As development proceeds, these behaviors are gradually integrated to form higher order, more complex messages. This higher order integrative function is equally innate.

For example, at a given moment of pleasurable experience the baby may smile, gurgle, change head position, and reach out to the caretaker in a particular way. Each of these acts is a discrete element of behavior; together, they make for a highly engaging communicative signal that conveys a great deal of meaning about the baby's state, relationship feeling, and wish for further interaction. In brief, they operate together as "functional units of communication" (Stern, 1977, p. 48), which in turn act as releasers for various maternal behaviors. Still higher orders of yet more complex behaviors employ these organizations as their elements, for example, coyness, winsomeness, coquettishness, and withdrawal. In brief, by 3 months of age, the baby has a sizable repertoire of tactics that he can employ in the service of engagement and disengagement.

Affective Communication

Brazelton and colleagues (1973) have developed a method of assessing the affective communication system that develops between the infant and his caregivers during the early months of life. This approach enables the investigator to measure the caregiver's sensitivity and to identify failures in communication. Basically, it entails a precisely timed integration of two images viewed with a split-screen technique (the caretaker's image is juxtaposed to that of the infant so the observer can study them simultaneously).

The results of this method of study have been striking. By 3 weeks of age the infant appears to have two distinct sets of behavior along with the associated attention–nonattention cycles. One set is directed toward people and the other toward objects. The baby tends to subject objects of interest to a short, intense scrutiny. For a brief interval the baby is very interested, and then the interest flags. With people, on the other hand, his attention is cyclical, waxing and waning in intensity but enduring for a much longer period. During the moments of increased attention, all parts of the infant's body move outward toward the observed person. Then, as attention diminishes, the movement is backward toward his own body. Thus, he oscillates to and fro. Brazelton surmised that this alternating character of attention regulates the baby's stimulus input and prevents him from becoming overwhelmed by the intensity of his engagement.

During such an attentional cycle, the child slowly reaches out and coos, his eyes dilate, his arms jerk forward, and his face brightens. Then, as the nonattention part of the cycle supervenes, his eyes shift away from the mother's face, his hands grasp his shirt (an activity that has been designated *place-holding*), and he moves toward both relaxation-reduction and attentional release. After several seconds, the baby slowly returns his gaze toward the mother, lets go of his shirt, smiles a little, and starts a new cycle. There is thus a regular sequence of initiation, orientation, acceleration, deceleration, and turning away.

The interaction requires a double synchronization. The mother–infant exchange, in fact, forms a finely tuned system that is acutely alert to social response. As the baby's approach pattern nears its peak, the tuned-in mother increases the frequency and intensity of her responsive behavior; then, as the baby turns away, she diminishes the strength of her reactions and permits disengagement. Where the mother is insensitive to these delicate variations, by 6 weeks the infant is manifesting a pattern of prolonged nonattention interrupted only by brief periods of attention.

Tronick et al. (1978) studied the effects of altering maternal messages in a number of babies during their first months. In one such experiment mothers were asked to engage their babies in playful exchange and then to maintain a deadpan expression for 3 minutes. The mothers accordingly began to interact with their babies; once play got under way, however, the mothers stopped their responsiveness and assumed a neutral expression. Confronted with this, the infants sought eagerly for the mothers' accustomed interaction, only to realize that for some reason it was not forthcoming. In each instance, the baby made repeated attempts to elicit a response; each attempt was followed by a brief expectant waiting period before the baby tried again. The extent and the urgency of this search for interaction on the infants' part were impressive; indeed, so telling and so needy were their actions that several of the mothers were unable to continue with the experiment. In the other instances, where the mothers maintained the blank expressions, the babies eventually abandoned the quest as fruitless. They retired in defeat, nor did they try again. Happily, once the experiment was over and the mothers entered into the exchange as usual, the babies responded in turn. These infants' persistence stands in sharp contrast to what happens in cases of failure to thrive (see Volume 2, Chapters 1 and 21). In failure-to-thrive babies, their attempts to interact with their caretakers have had so dismal an outcome that the babies have stopped trying to relate, even to the point of no longer taking nourishment. They are brought to the hospital because of a failure to gain weight and to grow. In such instances, the baby's withdrawal is extreme and takes the form of wariness and aversion. For example, in one early intervention program, a therapist devoted himself to winning such an infant's confidence; it took 2 weeks of repeated efforts to learn the baby's rhythms and to overcome his defensiveness. So closely is such a baby's food intake connected to his receptivity to social stimuli, that an investigative group (Rosenn et al., 1980) successfully devised a test based on this relationship. They established a responsiveness scale that was sensitive enough to predict a baby's weight gain by measuring his reaction to therapeutic overtures.

These findings lead to several conclusions. First, by 6 months of age, babies learn to discern the meanings of human signals, especially those that communicate affect. Second, the establishment of synchronous parent–infant rhythms is essential for optimal development. This conclusion is reinforced by the evidence of what happens under pathological conditions such as perinatal brain damage. Among the other disturbing consequences that may ensue are a number of more or less subtle alterations in motor behavior. The outcome all too often is that the parents of such children are repelled by the babies' movement patterns, and this disrupts the basic groundwork of interaction. Similarly, impaired maternal responsivity caused by ill health, depression, or preoccupation with stressful life events may also disrupt the development of optimal interaction and mutual attunement. In the future, increased parental attention to and concern with the baby's rhythms have the potential to revolutionize infant care, particularly of more vulnerable babies.

From the baby's view, the cyclical patterns of attention and recovery enable him to monitor and thus to regulate the level of sensory input. In particular, they allow the baby to cope to some degree with the unpredictability of his partner and thus to adjust to disturbing interactions that may arise. Given the immaturity of the infant's regulatory system, this capability is central to his maintaining a sense of balance, mastery, and control.

Brazelton (1982, pp. 49–54) speculates that the pathways to synchrony are established in intrauterine life (as the baby encounters the mother's heart rhythms, digestive rhythms, the pace of her walking, and other motor rhythms) and are then entrained by the mother's active interventions immediately after birth.

COGNITIVE DEVELOPMENT

The infant is a busy stimulus seeker and, depending on his state, actively pursues all manner of sensory inputs. The baby has a wide variety of processes to "feed," including those arising from his perceptual, cognitive, and sensory-motor apparatuses.

The Nature of Stimuli

In general, there are two kinds of stimuli: external and cognitive. External stimuli are primarily sensory in character; they consist of sound and its qualities (amplitude, pitch, etc.), visual images with all their attributes, the angle and degree of vestibular displacement, light or painful touch, sweet, bitter, or salty taste, and the like. Structurally, these are associated with particular sensory organs (eye, ear, skin, etc.) wherein highly specialized nerve endings send messages back to relatively delimited (i.e., modality-specific) organizational components within the central nervous system.

Cognitive stimuli arise during the processing of external sensations, and they necessarily involve some kind of endopsychic evaluative process. As a rule, this means some analysis of the relationship between an external stimulus and an existing memory trace to which it can be referred. The infant's relating of what he has perceived to what he already knows gives meaning to the sense impression. At this early moment, sensation and cognition generally occur together; it is not until later that cognitive efforts can arise from memories, fantasies, dreams, and other inner sources of stimulation.

The Beginnings of Thought

Intellectual activity may be said to begin when the baby starts comparing sensations to some prior referent. This process undoubtedly gets under way very early, but it becomes a prominent part of the infant's mentation by about 3 months. Relatively pure sensori-motor experience precedes it; by and large, at the outset, the infant reacts to the immediately sensual, and the things that happen do not have much "meaning." They simply feel good or they feel bad. But very quickly more recognition of the familiar develops; the baby shows an interest in engaging with or avoiding specific items associated with particular values of pleasure and unpleasure—and thought of a kind is evident.

The shift to this kind of functioning is evanescent at first, a matter of emphasis rather than transformation, and for quite a while the infant remains essentially a sensory machine. Indeed, in a way this will always be true; whatever else the human being is, he or she is always a responder to sensory inputs. But in time, sensations begin to acquire additional increments of cognitive meaning as well.

The Schema. In Piagetian terms, from the outset, the infant actively undertakes "effortful assimilation" of stimuli to form internal schemata of his world (Piaget, 1952). The schema here is a tentatively organized internal arrangement that gives pattern and a measure of coherence to the flow of sensory inputs. If this tentative organizaton "works," that is, proves useful for prediction and understanding, then it will persist; it will become more elaborate, gain additional reinforcement and complexity, and in time will become a structural part of mind. Thus, for example, if a 6-month-old is shown a little red ball that he finds interesting, and the ball is then put behind a handkerchief, the child may cry because for him the ball no longer exists. But when he is a little older, the child may find that, by pulling the handkerchief aside, he can recover the ball. After a time or two this organizes as a schema; it the ball disappears, the infant seeks it by pulling at the handkerchief. If the ball is hidden, then revealed, and then hidden once again, only this time behind a *different* handkerchief, the child will persist in pulling away the first one. That arrangement has worked before; the act of handling the covering cloth has revealed the desired object. Why does it not make sense to employ the same schema of action to obtain it once again? It is in the sensory-motor process of seeking answers to such questions and elaborating such schemata that the infant comes to construct the world of physical objects and the laws which govern them.

Goldman-Rakic (1987) studied the neurological basis for this behavior in Rhesus monkeys (Goldman-Rakic, 1987). This investigator set up an experiment as follows: First, she allowed the monkeys to see a morsel of food. Then, while the monkeys still observed, she hid the morsel so that it was out of sight but within easy reach. Next, she lowered a screen to conceal the scene, then raised the screen, and allowed the monkeys to seek the food. In general, they recovered it immediately. Goldman-Rakic thereupon further refined the experiment by introducing a period of delay between the time of lowering the screen to conceal the scene and the time of raising it again for the search to begin. In effect, the investigator was measuring the ability of the subjects to form and store an image in memory, and then to act on the basis of this representational memory. When a monkey could do this, it was again shown a morsel of food being hidden, but this time the food was hidden in a *different* place. Again the scene was masked, then revealed, and the monkey allowed once more to seek the bait. Under such conditions, time after time the monkey was able to uncover the morsel in the new location on the first try.

After a number of monkeys had been tested in this way, they were operated on and the dorsolateral regions of the prefrontal lobe (the orbital prefrontal cortex, i.e., some of the grey matter from the front tip of the brain) were removed. After the surgery, the animals responded to this test like young humans, namely, if the object was hidden, then revealed, and then hidden once again in the same place, it was found again almost 100% of the times. But if on the second try the object was hidden in a *different* place (although in full view of the subject), then the tendency to look in the place where the monkey had found it the *first* time (i.e., to repeat the previous response) was very strong. In effect, the brain-lesioned monkeys acted like 7½- to 9-month-old human infants (whereas normal monkeys acted like 12-month-olds). Hence, this area of the cortex appears to mediate representational memory. Because this is the basis of "object permanence," it is a fundamental building block of all later cognitive growth. It may also be the key to certain kinds of "organic" behavior such as perseveration and the state of being "stimulus-bound." That is to say, if a child cannot guide his behavior by inner representations that he can keep firmly in mind, he must seek such guidance and such cues from external signals. As a result, the child is prey to all the distracting and evocative stimuli that arise in the periphery; accordingly his behavior is likely to appear fragmented and to lack coherent direction.

The sequence described by Piaget underlines the observation that as a species, humans are problem solvers. An approach to life along the axis of seeking solutions to problems appears to be a very elementary part of the human constitution. Bruner (1975) suggests that the central tendency of the infant's mental life is the "active process of hypothesis formation and hypothesis testing." The emerging mind is constantly preoccupied with trying out possible models, with attempting to account for why events happen, with striving to understand why things sequence as they do, and, above all, with seeking to make them happen as the child would like. This quality of searching is basic to such traits as curiosity, a readiness to explore, and an inclination to try things out, all of which are ultimately crucial for adaptation and survival.

Such stimulus seeking will also need some safeguards. Lacking any sort of built-in defenses, the infant's questing combined with his vulnerability may expose him to potentially damaging inputs and lead him all too easily into harmful or downright dangerous situations. At this early stage, the chief dangers arise from either too low a level of stimulation (which the baby may try to regulate by self-arousal as in rumination), too high a level of stimulation (which he can try to moderate by aversive behavior), or too many stimuli flooding in at once (which he may seek to master by regulating attention).

Attention-Input Intensity. The capacity of a child to turn his attention to a particular stimulus is inborn. However, the child's ability to maintain his interest and focus on that source of arousal can vary enormously and comes to be influenced by a host of factors.

The inputs that are likely to evoke a child's response come in many forms and possess different levels of intensity. If the level is too low, the infant barely attends to the stimulus or quickly loses interest. On the other hand, if there is too much stimulation, the infant does what he can to avoid this input (by turning away or closing his eyes); rather typically, the baby cries to evince his distress, and if he is old enough, he calls for help.

If however, the level is not extreme in either direction, that is to say, it falls within the comfortable range, the baby's attention tends to be captured by interesting stimuli and to be fixed for relatively extended periods. Within this working range, as the level of intensity goes up, so does the baby's interest. This continues until he arrives at a certain threshold where things become too much—and he turns off. (It is noteworthy that the pattern of increasing responsiveness to more intense stimuli is gradual, whereas, when things become too much, the turnoff is usually quite abrupt.) But it is not just intensity that the infant manages in this way; he also makes the same type of response to other parameters of perception, such as complexity, novelty or amount of contrast. Another factor that affects attention is the baby's level of development; a more interesting, more complex, or more intense stimulus is necessary to capture the attention of an older infant than is required for a less mature one.

Habituation. As noted earlier, the infant who encounters a new stimulus will at first show great interest. If, however, the stimulus recurs over and over again in exactly the same way, then the baby will become less responsive with each reencounter. In brief, there is a progressive response decrement to any repeated unchanging input, which is called *habituation*. To some extent this capacity is already weakly present at birth; it progresses rapidly during the early weeks and is strongly present by 3 months. Because it allows the individual to tune out familiar background noises to concentrate on the new and the novel, it is an essential component of attention.

A classic experiment (Kagan & Lewis, 1965, referred to in Stern, 1977) demonstrating habituation involves showing the baby an image (such as a bullseye) for a fixed interval of time, over and over again. If the investigator measures the amount of time the infant looks at the target, with each presentation this interval grows less and less. If, however, the target is replaced with a new image, the amount of time spent studying this new image shoots right back up to the original level. In effect, with each display of the stimulus, the infant "remembers" the previously seen stimulus and has less need to restudy it. The recognition of this tendency is an important component of maternal behavior; the mother must become aware that to keep the baby interested, she cannot keep doing the same thing over and over again. (On the other hand, monotonous rocking and a simple, rhythmically repetitious lullaby are just what is needed to soothe a fussy, overly tired baby to sleep.)

Cognitive Stimulation. The sensory quality of a stimulus commands the newborn's attention. For such a beginner, the world is filled with unique and heretofore unappreciated experiences; each new sensation (within the proper range) has the qualities of freshness and discovery. As time passes, however, certain configurations tend to repeat over and over again and become quite predictable. The baby knows that a certain holding position will be followed by play, another by nursing, yet another by changing, and so on and on. Not that these in themselves lack interest, far from it. But by 3 months their predictability as much as their immediate sensuous experience become fascinating to the baby. A curious sense of power and a special kind of reward follow from being able to foretell what will happen. Much later, children old enough to be read to ask to have the same story read over and over again, with no detail changed. Here too, part of the pleasure of such rituals is to be able to predict exactly what will happen. Autistic children, who have great difficulty processing novel stimuli, develop what Kanner (1943) termed "an obsessive desire in the maintenance of sameness."

Hence, two great opposing tendencies are simultaneously present and in many ways determine the nature of cognitive experience. On the one hand is the pleasure in the mastery of the familiar, and, on the other, the readiness to habituate and the hunger for novelty. The optimal balance between variety and stability will be a major goal and regulator of behavior.

Within this context, any change in stimulus set carries the possibility of novelty. This is particularly true if all the rest of the sequence is familiar; the one bit of change is then intensely intriguing. For example, the mother may play out a game sequence with the baby over and over again. If she sees the infant's attention flagging, however, she may intuitively vary the play in some small way. This alerts the baby who tries to figure out whether things really are the same, or whether there is, in fact, a change. The new source of stimulation lies precisely in the mismatch between the baby's expectations and the stimulus as delivered (or, more technically, in the stimulus–schema discrepancy) (Kagan, 1967, referred to in Stern, 1977). Just such matching work results in the growth, elaboration, and refinement of the various existing schemata. Frequently, it leads to new schemata.

Kagan (1967) observes that a predictable relationship exists between the degree of discrepancy and the extent and intensity of attention given to a particular cognitive stimulus of this sort. That is to say, the greater the novelty, the more the baby is likely to study it. When enough change is introduced, the whole message becomes a truly new stimulus that the infant regards as an entity in its own right, unique and unrelated to other stimulus sets, and hence meriting maximal attention.

The Discovery of Space. As the baby becomes accustomed to manipulating his world, initially he allows each hand to operate on its own side to reach out for objects. Somewhere around the 4th month, however, the baby masters bringing his hands together at the midline and grasping things there as well as to crossing the midline to obtain or to handle desired objects. This new ability is the essential precursor for the baby's orienting himself in space. Once he can do that, the baby has made a new and important discovery about the environment that immediately surrounds him; he knows how to reach for or to locate things by combined visual, tactile, and kinesthetic cues. For the blind child this is a truly critical issue; such a child cannot marshal the necessary organization of perceptions that would allow this mastery of the midline to take place spontaneously. As a result, most blind children will not develop a sense of the spatial organization of their immediate environment. They know what they can touch; whatever else is out there remains a great and unapproachable unknown. When the time comes, for example, they will make no attempt to crawl; they have no sense of the area immediately before them.

Selma Fraiberg (1977), Parmalee and colleagues (1958), and others, in pioneering work, discerned this subtle but powerful issue, and they have initiated methods to overcome this deficiency. Today, starting at 4 months, all blind children can be taught the necessary orienting in space that rescues their development from what previously had so often been a failure with far-reaching consequences.

Arousal and Its Sources. Several terms are currently employed to indicate a state of arousal and attention. Stern prefers the term *excitement* (1977, p. 61) to depict this state of affairs, with the understanding that this term refers always to overt behavior; the subjective experience is only presumed to be present. These times (when the baby shows increased attention and a heightened level of activity) have become the subject of much study.

The infant's level of excitement varies in response to either internal stimuli or external events. While asleep, for example, the baby has an internally regulated cycle of rhythmically fluctuating activity. When the

REM condition predominates, he frowns, smiles, and changes heart rate and other motor patterns, all in response to internal stimuli.

For the first few weeks, the baby's state is largely determined by internal patterns of discharge. Gradually, however, external stimuli begin to play an ever-increasing role.

The baby has available the several previously described states. At birth, REM sleep is present about 50% of the time. As the days go by this proportion rapidly changes, the baby sleeps less, and more and more time is spent in a state of awake active alertness (the stage during which the baby is most attentive and responsive to the outside world). With the advancing weeks, the baby begins to pay greater attention to what is going on around him, and by the 3rd month, his level of excitation is very much a function of his attention to external stimuli.

Indeed, by this point the infant can maintain a reasonably even state for as long as 15 minutes at a time (under favorable conditions). The most playful interactions with the mother now begin to take place; the baby is alert, available, and interested a great deal more of the time.

In this connection, certain differences exist between excitement and attention. For one thing, excitement lags behind attention in its rate of build-up; it does not mount as readily or turn off as abruptly. The child does have some control over the quantity of visual input; by closing his eyes or averting his gaze the baby can "gate" the intensity and the quantity of visual stimulation. Through this mechanism, the baby also has a modicum of control over the level of excitement. If, however, the stimuli come too rapidly or too intensely and the baby does become overexcited to the point of discomfort, the child possesses no internal regulating mechanism to turn this off in the way he does attention. The baby can only cry, flail, and express his agitation and distress until he wears himself out. This can take a long time and is clearly unpleasant; in this situation the baby is in particular need of the caretaker's soothing and comforting interventions. This then is a major component of maternal care. By the same token, however, a critical factor in any baby's constitutional endowment is his capacity to accept such soothing and to respond by relaxing and being comforted. As already noted, the infants of patients with manic-depressive illness can have special problems in this regard (either for genetic or environmental reasons); once they become upset, they cannot readily be comforted, and they will stay perturbed far longer than will control infants (Cytryn et al., 1985).

As time goes on, cognitive factors become more and more important sources of excitement. Thus, adding a note of novelty or surprise to a game makes it all the more arousing for baby; in and of itself the unexpected becomes a potent source of stimulation. As long as they respect the baby's tolerance for stimulation, creative adults can keep quite young babies fascinated for long periods of time by introducing carefully graded minor variations into their standard patterns of play. The baby will crow, kick, and evidently have a marvelous time as long as the excitement is not "too much."

Emotional Component. The influence of affect on cognition and, in fact, the development of affect in any sense are difficult areas to study because they entail achieving insight into a realm where the critical information is essentially subjective. What a fellow human being experiences by way of emotion can be known only inferentially; as a rule, those who conduct research in this area do so by taking some sort of reading on objective nonverbal behavior (in addition to whatever may be said). At the same time scarcely anything we "know" is more immediate and compelling than our emotions. Hence, this is another area of immense vitality and uncertainty.

FREUD'S ORIGINAL MODEL. When Freud first undertook to formulate a concept of emotion, his theory held that all stimulation gives rise to tension and that such tension is inherently anxiety provoking and hence unpleasurable. The ego was like a dam that filled up, a repository where undischarged affect accumulated; when the level began to crest, the dam threatened to overflow, the situation became hazardous, and the associated reactions were highly unpleasant.

This view, in turn, led to the theory of *real-anxiety*, the notion that excess undischarged emotion, especially of sexual character, would in itself act as a kind of toxin and beget emotional disturbance. By the same token, discharge would inherently give rise to pleasure; it always felt good merely because tension had been lowered. Thus, the formula was simple: Up tension equaled distress and anxiety; down tension equaled relief and pleasure.

As time went on, this concept led to many problems, and it has been challenged repeatedly. Within the province of infancy, for example, it is evident that far from eschewing excitement, the infant avidly seeks and needs stimulation. Furthermore, it is easy to document that under the proper circumstances (such as participation in a game), the build-up of excitement is evidently pleasurable for the baby, that he expresses ever greater delight as tension increases, and that he manifests quite striking degrees of upset and disappointment if the game is prematurely interrupted.

SROUFE'S FORMULATION. Sroufe (quoted in Stern, 1977, pp. 65–66) has suggested four determinants of infantile emotional expression. Although state and developmental level clearly influence such expressions, the intensity of stimulation and the gradient (or rapidity) with which it rises and falls also affect such responses.

- *Neonate.* During the REM sleep of the newborn, rising and falling cycles of arousal appear, engendered by rhythmical brain stem discharge. Sroufe suggests that the periodic smiles of the sleeping infant are due to this inner discharge rising or falling above or below some presumed threshold. Such smiling would be one instance of emotional expression in response to changing internal states.

- *The Awake State.* Once the infant is awake, he is less the victim of internal stimuli, and what is coming in from the outer world accounts for his affective displays. Sroufe asserts that the suddenness with which stimulation occurs, or its contour of modulation, is critical for affective experience, that is, the abruptness of the increase or decrease of stimulation begets emotion on baby's part. Any sudden switch leads to what Berlyne (quoted in Stern, 1977, p. 65) calls an *arousal jag.* It is the sort of thing that happens when baby is thrown up in the air and caught; there is a sudden change, to which the baby may react with either laughter or wails, but in any case, with feeling.

- *Cognitive Arousal.* Fluctuations in what might be termed *cognitive arousal* provide yet another trigger of affective display. When a partially novel, or *discrepant,* stimulus is presented, and the baby experiences a mismatch between the schemata already in mind and the current stimulus, it poses the infant a very real challenge. Given a situation that is potentially within his capacity to grasp, the baby "works at it" with increasing tension until he "gets it." When he solves the problem, there is a distinct reaction: The tension dissipates, and the baby smiles. Thus, at an appropriate level of development, stimulus-schema mismatch becomes a potent source of cognitive arousal. Inability to master a discrepancy can also be a source of upset as is evident when the baby tries unsuccessfully to fit a piece into a form board. Some developmental theorists have interpreted *stranger anxiety* to be the child's "active comparison of present experience with a stored schema" (Kagan et al., 1978, p. 85).

- *Overstimulation.* Where the shift in tension is too rapid or too extreme, no mastery is possible and the baby will cry. This is readily demonstrated by producing a sound that is too sudden and too loud; the attentive baby will not be able to cope with so great a volume delivered at so rapid a rate and will simply begin to demonstrate distress. Such overstimulation can come from a variety of interpersonal experiences and is an important source of infant learning about people.

Chapter 7

Personality Takes Form
The Second Half of the First Year

INTRODUCTION

Given the rapid rate of growth during this period, the totally new organization of developmental elements in the second half of the first year of life merits careful consideration.

It seems useful at this point to look at the baby overall, much as a pediatrician might, and to observe the process of development. The term *landmark* is the official designation for a specific level of achievement that measures developmental progress. Percentiles provide the conventional mode of studying and reporting landmarks, that is, where does the baby stand in comparison with a large population of children of that age who have already been studied along that particular axis?

Thus, the investigator might choose to measure head circumference by putting a tape measure around the heads of a thousand babies of exactly the same age brought consecutively to a well baby clinic. The emerging data would distribute in a way that allowed for a few babies with larger heads, most babies with head measurements pretty close together, and a few babies with smaller heads. Further investigation might demonstrate that where the head is above a certain size, the likelihood of hydrocephalus becomes more and more probable. Contrariwise, the more extreme examples of small head size might reflect a failure in brain development with an increased possibility of later intellectual problems. However, the investigator would also find that sometimes the extremes have no pathological significance but are merely normal variants. The cautious pediatrician then notes that the baby falls within the upper or lower range of likelihood and therefore merits further investigation. In this way, the several landmarks have come to be associated with percentile values asserting that, with respect to a given measure, the baby falls within a specified range or subgroup of the population. Such a landmark is important if falling within this range on the distribution curve tends to increase or decrease the baby's vulnerability for eventual pathological outcome. The Denver Developmental Scale is a commonly employed compilation of normative developmental data. Widely used for infant evaluation, it provides information on the age at which various percentiles of the population will have mastered various behavioral attainments (e.g., standing on one foot, drawing a diamond, etc.).

LANDMARKS

Motor Activity

A number of motor landmarks are associated with the second half of the first year. By 6 months the average baby can support himself in a sitting position (when pulled up to it). Prior to that he would just flop back, but now his strength and muscular integration are such that he can hold this posture.

Motor development progresses rapidly, and by 7 months the baby can pull himself up to a standing posture and maintain it if he holds on. This allows the infant to survey the world from a very different vantage point and with quite a different sense of mastery.

Within another month the average infant is crawling, and for the first time is self-propelling. Thus if he is on the floor and something looks interesting, the baby does not have to wail for it or try to get someone to fetch it; he can crawl over and explore. This is a tremendous change in capacity; in effect, the baby has been given wheels, and the acquisition is undoubtedly fraught with enormous meaning and excitement. This is another "first"; the infant is no longer merely a babe in arms. Crawling provides a genuine measure of autonomy.

Vocal Activity

Meanwhile, landmarks are emerging on other fronts as well. During this interval the vocal apparatus is maturing: The vocal chords, glottis, pharynx, and uvula are all coming into play as instruments of manipulation. The baby learns that he can make sounds, and this becomes another realm for mastery.

At about 6 months of age, the baby tends to make a tremendous variety of noises. The sounds of every known language have been recorded from babies who are learning to manipulate the vocal muscles; they make the sounds used in French, Chinese, German, Arabic, and all the other tongues (de Villiers & de Villiers, 1979, p. 21). But that stage is transient; within a couple of months the infants are as noisy as ever, but the sounds recorded are only those common to the languages that the baby hears; all the others drop out. At this point the babies' verbigerations sound familiar, like some odd simulacrum of recognizable speech, except that it is gibberish. This kind of verbalization is called *babbling*. Albeit expressive, it is not communicative; it is still a form of play at sound making. On the other hand, it is precisely at this time that the baby begins to display an unequivocal capacity to respond to discrete words with appropriate acts; he is beginning to understand spoken speech.

A factor that plays a role in this developmental sequence and that should not be overlooked is the maturation of the underlying neurological structures that bring the auditory system of the brain into full function; this process progresses actively during the first year, although it is not completed until the end of the second. Nonetheless, as growth proceeds, the baby can process auditory stimuli more and more efficiently. In the second half of the first year baby can begin to respond to his name and to many simple nouns and commands. He may speak his first recognizable word as early as 10 months (in rare instances even earlier) or as late as 14 months; these are the extremes of the average range.

Cognitive Abilities

As noted, the baby's discrimination and responsiveness to new stimuli progresses rapidly in the early weeks of life. Initially, the most interesting items are associated with the caretaker; the face, voice, touch, anything signaling the presence of the caretaker excites immediate and intense attention. As the baby becomes more adept at predicting and sensing the caretaker's presence and responsiveness, the intensity of interest shifts to things. By 6 months the objects of the world, especially new and different objects, become the prime claimants for scrutiny and attention. Between 7 and 10 months, however, the interest in novelty falls off to some extent; a mask or a new face no longer excites the same response as before. The baby appears to go through a period of uncertainty and withdraws some of his interest from an ever-changing world, whose complexity he is first beginning to appreciate.

A certain capacity for inhibition of behavior begins to become manifest at 7 months or so; phylogenetically, this may well have to do with survival and self-protective capacities. The child is becoming mobile; from a genetic view it may well be that those children who had a greater capacity to inhibit were able to avoid impulsive approach toward fascinating but potentially lethal situations, and their progeny survived. Thus, as the 8- or 9-month-old baby begins to crawl over a surface with a sudden fall-off, he stops at the edge and will not go forward. A bit later on, at 11 months, the infant demonstrates a concern with newness, even at the level of exploring or reaching for a new object that comes into the field of awareness; unlike his earlier excited pleasure with the appearance of a new plaything, the baby now hesitates a bit before reaching for it (Kagan et al., 1978). By 12 months of age the introduction of a new baby into the infant's presence will cause him to stop any action in which he may be engaged and to study the situation.

As for the baby's reactions toward adults, several new elements have been present since about 7 months (sometimes somewhat earlier). At this point the baby first shows signs of distress at the presence of a stranger, and this will continue to increase until the end of the first year; after that it declines. When Spitz (1965) first described this phenomenon, it was thought that anxiety was the universal and inevitable form for this kind of stranger-reaction (indeed, for a time it was called *eight-month anxiety*). Later, Mahler and colleagues (1975) were able to demonstrate a much wider range of responses than had been supposed, and they noted that although some reaction to strangers was usually present, it did not necessarily take the form of full stranger anxiety; more often the baby engaged in a kind of intense scrutiny or anxious exploration of the stranger. Both temperamental and environmental factors have been shown to influence the form and intensity of a given baby's response to strangers. Even at this early time, paradoxical patterns can be observed. That is to say, some babies are already manifesting a tendency toward counterphobic behavior; any potentially threatening situation, such as a stranger, immediately attracts them. Strangers excite their approach behavior; for them, this is probably the preferred means of undoing the flare of anxiety that would otherwise persist.

Separation Awareness

A similar set of variables appears to influence another major dimension of relationship and attachment, the reaction of a baby to the experience of separation from his caretaker. During the first half of the first year, the baby can usually manage the disappearance of the caretaker with a good measure of equanimity. Mahler speculated that the certitude of the mother's omnipresence is apparently enough to make her actual physical availability unnecessary. At any rate, up to a point, the baby's willingness to be picked up by other caretakers and even strangers is quite striking; many younger infants are relatively comfortable with being passed from hand to hand, although they brighten appreciably and respond in unique ways to the ministrations of the primary one, the loved one.

In the second half of this first year, however, the baby becomes far more choosy about with whom he will consort. The meaning of the disappearance of the mothering figure also undergoes a decided transformation. Distress at the mother's departure is common at 8 months, rises to a peak at 13 to 15 months (Kagan, 1971), and then declines gradually. This sequence is subject to considerable variation; within different environmental sets, different babies will show highly diverse patterns of behavior. Nonetheless, some form of stranger reaction and separation anxiety is ubiquitous; it has been recorded among human environments as diverse as U.S. suburbs, Guatemalan barrios, and !Kung bands in the Kalahari (Kagan et al., 1978). By the same token, the total absence of these behaviors in an infant suggests that in some way development is pursuing an unusual course. For example, one of the authors of this book (J.D.N.) has the clinical impression that many anorexic children are described as having displayed none of the usual discomfort related to these developmental challenges during infancy. They were "no trouble at all" as babies. Conceivably, the lack of these familiar developmental landmarks may in some way be associated with a predisposition to later problems.

Fraiberg (1977) further observed that these sequences are not much different for blind children; such youngsters too display both stranger reaction and separation distress in a form and sequence similar to those of the sighted child.

In this connection it is useful to recall the concept of *attachment*. Attachment was defined as an affectively charged tie between the infant and the caregiver, along with a flexible behavioral system that leads to its formation and maintenance according to instinctually set goals. This behavior is mediated by feelings and interacts with other behavioral systems; in this sense it is influenced by context.

Historically, Bowlby was the principal figure to focus on the role of attachment of infant to caretaker as a primary dynamic in development (Bowlby, 1958). Ainsworth, however, took Bowlby's general proposition and translated it into the language of a quantifiable laboratory procedure. She developed the *Strange Situation* paradigm, which has been widely followed and extensively explored. The procedure is relatively simple but consists of a number of steps. A parent and a 1-year-old are first introduced into a laboratory situation. They spend 3 minutes together during which the parent (normally the mother) is instructed to be inactive and to allow the baby to explore. At this point a stranger (to the child) enters and lingers for 3 minutes. The stranger converses with the mother during this interval, and, at the end of the time, the mother leaves unobtrusively. The stranger and child remain together for the next 3 minutes (or less if the child becomes excessively distressed). The mother then returns, the stranger leaves, and the mother and child are together for 3 minutes (during which interval the mother comforts the child if necessary). The mother then leaves again, and the child is left alone for 3 minutes (or less). The stranger reenters and stays with the child for 3 minutes; the mother then rejoins the child, and the stranger leaves. The mother and child finally remain together with no one else present for the last 3 minutes.

By observing the infant closely throughout, Ainsworth was able to describe how the child organized his attachment behavior around the important caretaker. In particular, the focus of the observations came to be directed toward the 1-year-old's response to reunion with the mother during and after the two separations. From the outset three patterns of response emerged that were originally classified as *securely attached, avoidant,* and *resistant.* These latter two categories are currently called "anxiously attached," so that the compound terms *anxious/avoidant* and *anxious/ambivalent* (or anxious/resistant) are commonly employed. They are also referred to by letter so that *Type A* = anxious/avoidant; *Type B* = securely attached, and *Type C* = anxious/ambivalent (or resistant).

At the outset, the securely attached (Type B) children used the parent as a base for exploration, and, after the parent had left and returned, as a source of comfort and contact. The avoidant (Type A) child would initially use the parent in much the same way, as a basis for exploration. Once the parent left, however, such a child would respond to the parent's return by shunning her and resorting to distancing behavior. In contrast, the ambivalent (resistant) (Type C) child responded to reunion with anger, at once seeking contact and rejecting the attempts to comfort him.

Originally it was thought that these patterns represented stable configur- ations that endured over time (Waters, 1978), but subsequent investigations have cast considerable doubt on this assumption (Thompson et al., 1982; Vaugh et al., 1979). There is much to suggest that under favorable condi- tions, that is, when no major factors have stressed the mother–infant interaction, then the attachment pattern does remain stable for an extended period. Where major vicissitudes do arise, however, they affect the state of the attachment bond.

This experimental paradigm has permitted an empirical approach to the concept of attachment that has excited keen interest among researchers and students of development. For example, they have made serious attempts to correlate the A, B, and C types with patterns of biological reactivity. Studies of maternal behavior have also emerged, as well as correlations between the infant's attachment type, his play competence in other contexts, and his capacity for social relations. Finally, the child's pattern of attachment at 12 months has even been correlated with a host of measures in the early school years (Sroufe et al., 1983).

Object Permanence

This term was coined by Piaget (1954) to describe the way a baby forms images within his mind. There is little evidence that the very young infant can retain images at all. Out of sight is out of mind. If the 6-month-old baby is shown an interesting object that is then covered, as far as the baby is concerned that object has ceased to exist. He may recall it well enough to cry for it briefly but shows no awareness that it continues to exist somewhere. From 6 months on, however, as we noted earlier, the infant begins to seek briefly after a disappeared object, and by 8 months, most children will reliably pull a handkerchief or a pillow aside if they see the object disappear behind it. Piaget believed that this advance is due to a maturation of the cognitive ability to maintain an intact internal image so that even when the object is concealed, the baby can still visualize it behind the interposed barrier and seek it out.

In effect, the baby has formed a mental map, a schema related to present experience, that he can now retrieve. Long before the infant develops such a capacity with inanimate objects, he appears able to retain an image of intensely valued schemata such as the mother's face or voice, and the baby will smile the moment he encounters them (Brossard & DeCarie, 1968). By the second half of the first year, however, this begins to happen with *minimal incentive stimuli*. The baby is beginning to maintain and to retain workable images within his thinking. He can keep both old and new schemata in active memory and can thus compare them. By 9 months, this new capacity has a most important consequence. The baby now becomes able to predict and anticipate future events because he remembers how such sequences have played themselves out before. He is thus far better at adapting to situations, even if they are to some extent discrepant. The infant has a body of experience to draw on, and with it he can begin to think ahead about the meaning of things. Because the baby can predict what it portends when he sees his mother reaching for her coat, he may forthwith begin to wail; however, if she also picks up the baby's hat and coat, it means that she is taking him along, so the wailing stops, and the baby waits, perhaps a trifle anxiously, but expectantly.

As is true with each new addition, however, this ability has problematic aspects as well, such as when a stranger appears for whom there is no existing schema, which makes it accordingly difficult to predict how this unknown individual will behave. In the face of this and other novel experiences, a new kind of distress gradually develops—the cognitive experience of uncertainty—and at least for a while it looms large on baby's emotional horizon. Presently, the observer sees again and again that when the baby can predict, he laughs; and when he is uncertain, he becomes troubled and may very well begin to cry. (For more on the evolution of anxiety, see Volume 2, Chapter 7.)

Investigators have also noted that the presence of a familiar person can cushion the appearance of this distress at the sight of a stranger. Whether this is strictly a matter of context is still to be determined; the baby might behave differently in an unfamiliar setting such as a laboratory than he would at home, and it is possible too that the presence of the familiar person provides the baby with an "opportunity for response" that is otherwise lacking. Thus, the child whose mother has left but whose father is still present, perceives the father's nearness as an opportunity to continue to engage in familiar behavior. This may be enough to offer a buffer for the baby's uncertainty; he may be worried but he is not overwhelmed. Accordingly, the accompanying distress, albeit present, does not become manifest.

Imaging Capacity—The Discovery of the Self

It is noteworthy that the child is unlikely to be very imaginative at this age. Although the baby is able to retain images with ever-increasing competence, he is not yet up to creating them to any great extent. Thus, when alone in the dark, the infant is not "generating possibilites"; if he cries, it is because the baby misses his mother directly or because he is hungry, and not because he has imagined some scary creation. That kind of imaginative behavior does not usually appear until the child is about 3 years old. At 2 years a more concrete kind of cognitive uncertainty makes for the associated stress.

From the 9th to the 12th month the infant begins to communicate an ever more differentiated set of signals to indicate his needs. Thus, the baby begins to use his finger to point, and his demands on his mother to meet his needs increase in intensity and specificity.

According to Piaget, the construction of a stable inner image probably begins when the infant can discern the continued existence of an object even when he no longer sees it. But the baby's attempts to recover the hidden item are still egocentrically dominated by the centrality of self-reference. The baby at this stage seemingly cannot think past his own action schema; *his* movement, *his* action, makes the invisible item reappear.

At 10 months however, the baby's capacity to track an object perceptually has grown considerably. And somewhere after the beginning of his 2nd year, a day comes when the caretaker can hide an object behind two or more handkerchiefs or pillows, and the child will track right along, go unerringly to the proper hiding place, and retrieve the toy. By this time the internalized image of the object (which goes on existing even though the object itself is out of sight), rather than the action schema, determines baby's behavior. The capacity to retain the image of an object intact within the mind, whether that object is in view or not, defines what is called *object constancy*. It is a considerable achievement, and it is the beginning of what we usually consider to be "thought."

Generally speaking, the child perceives the covering of the object as an invitation to a game sequence of hide and seek. Thus, the early use of images is related to problem-solving play, where things have to be figured out as part of a game. Initially, there is a joyous response to novelty, and the baby experiences the process of discovery as fun. As time goes on, new problems begin to evoke a more pensive, even a wary, quality of response. It parallels, perhaps, the shift from excitement at the novelty of a stranger's face to the wariness of stranger reaction.

This is a time when the discovery of the self becomes evident. The first-person pronoun, *I*, will appear when the child is about 22 months of age; *you* and *he/she* will follow about 2 months later. But visual recognition of the self occurs much earlier, and the use of images that the baby can control (such as mirror reflections or simultaneous video screenings) along with images that the baby cannot control (such as movies or still photos of the self) provide a way to evaluate both the emergence of self-recognition and the quality of the ensuing response.

There are now a great many reports about what happens when a baby is placed in front of a mirror (Brooks-Gunn & Lewis, 1984). At 5 months, babies already respond with smiles when they can watch their own reflections. From 9 to 12 months of age, they respond to such a situation with laughter, cooing, and excitement, and about a third of babies will begin to play up to the mirror to get the response from the image. By 15 to 18 months, most babies are doing that; more than that, however, they will turn toward an object that appears behind them when they see it first in the mirror. Clearly, the child now possesses the cognitive ability to sort out that there is an image, that it is an image of himself, that he must take certain spatial considerations into account, and that there is a phenomenon of reflection. By about 20 months, self-conscious behavior is the rule, that is, once the baby perceives his own image, he becomes coy and acts "silly." This is specially true if a smudge or dab of color is placed on the child's face; by about 15 months he will give this special attention. Before 9 months, if the mirror is changed to a distorting reflective surface (typical of the fun house at a fair), the baby responds with pleasurable interest. Or if the investigator places a smudge on the infant's nose or a label on his brow and allows him to look in the mirror, again the child shows no behavioral change. Evidently, at this early time, the baby responds to the quality of novelty rather than to the specificity of the experience.

From the 13th through the 15th month the infant's imaging processes undergo an evident transformation. As the child studies his own image, he becomes sober and pensive. Left to his own devices, the baby might well undertake to make something of a show before the glass. Adding a label to his brow or a smudge on his nose leads to study and an attempt to touch the new addition but, characteristically, at first only in the mirror. Where the investigator substitutes a distorting surface for the mirror, the baby's reaction is likely to become even more intense and betrays no evidence of pleasure.

In brief, the observer can see the evolution of the baby's self-perception from an experience of novelty without evident self-reference to the dawning awareness that the image has some important connection with himself. Along with this goes a wish, and an attempt, to master this phenomenon. In a sense this probably parallels the emergence of a primitive sense of self as an objective presence in the world.

Similarly with videotapes or still photos: At 9 to 12 months, the baby smiles more at images of himself than of others. By 18 to 20 months the identification is clear and is often verbalized. In brief, self-recognition is a process that takes place slowly but progresses steadily over time.

This type of self-recognition is particularly noteworthy because it probably underlies the emergence of important sets of social emotions. Brooks-Gunn and Lewis offer several examples; for one thing, the experience of empathy that characterizes this developmental moment can only occur if the baby is able to sort out his selfhood. In effect, for the child to be empathic he must experience something of what another person feels as though he felt it himself. To do this he must have a sense of a separate self. For another, gender feelings too will depend on being able to feel the self as a separate entity with the appropriate gender quality. Yet another illustration is the ability to practice deceit; this too hinges on the child's sensing himself as one kind of person and then acting as though he were someone else. Many of the more advanced social roles and feeling states depend on the appropriate and adequate development of a sense of self. It is of interest that when a group of infants who had been observed to be insecurely attached were tested for self-recognition, they were unusually early in achieving this capacity. Presumably their precocity had a defensive character.

Chapter 8

The Dynamic Perspective

PSYCHOANALYTIC DATA

As noted at the outset, two sources of data are employed in constructing developmental concepts. One is essentially the direct observation of young children and of mother–child interactions in the laboratory or under natural conditions. The other, however, comes about in quite a different way. Historically, it arose from clinical rather than laboratory observation and was the product of work with sick patients. Not only that, the patients were, in the main, fully grown adults who chanced to receive treatment from a man who used the information they provided to construct a theory of child development. Remarkably enough, the ensuing conceptual structure has in broad outline remained intact through some 80 years of exploration and is only now undergoing major transformation and overhaul. The clinician, of course, was Sigmund Freud.

When Freud was working, relatively little was known about personality development. He was a neurologist, and as such, he encountered many puzzling cases that were just then beginning to be explored. These were the so-called hysterics—patients who presented with apparent neurological disorders, but whose bizarre symptoms defied rational neurological explanation. Worse still, it had been discovered that they responded to treatments such as suggestion and hypnosis that smacked rather more of the scorned and discredited medieval humbug than of the newer scientific methods just then achieving eminence.

Freud plunged into work with this group of patients and devised a method for exploring their illness that he called *free association*. He had the patient speak aloud all the thoughts that crossed his or her mind. The injunction was to verbalize everything, leaving out nothing, telling it all.

This turned out to be very difficult for the patient to do. In trying to find out why it was so hard, Freud discovered many of the laws that govern human mentation. More to the point, as his patients managed to achieve something approaching free association, their thoughts repeatedly carried them back to childhood and to the reliving of emotion-laden, often traumatic, events, which they thus recaptured in memory. Occasionally, during this process, profound alterations occurred in their symptom picture. As a result, Freud came to believe that these memory sequences represented formative experiences that had meaningfully altered his patients' personalities and character formation; the consequences of these traumatic events, in turn, gave rise to the patients' maladaptive behavior and failed coping. Freud drew much of the material for his theories from this body of data.

At the time, Freud was seeing his patients six times a week for hour-long sessions, and was dealing with immense volumes of information. His conceptual power was equal to the task, however, and he was presently able to superimpose on this flood of turbulent and sometimes chaotic communication a set of conceptual principles. The resulting theoretical constructs proved capable of ordering this information into a more or less coherent structure.

One product of Freud's work was a theory of psychosexual development. In brief, this asserted that human development proceeds through a series of stages, each dominated by a particular instinctual set, each associated with a specific form of lust that was the sexual pleasure of that time, and each regulated by a limited array of coping devices (which Freud called the *mechanisms of defense*) that contributed to the formation and color of character.

The theory was by no means neat and concise. It developed gradually, had many loose threads that dangled every which way, and had few methods for application that were simple, straightforward, and readily reproducible. Stranger yet for a theory of *child* development, not until a number of years later was this developmental schema, reconstructed from the recollections of *adults*, checked against actual child observation. Nonetheless the theory's overall structure held together remarkably well and, indeed, has not been altogether superseded, although, to be sure, much as been changed. To this day, certain kinds of information are best understood in Freudian terms, in particular, certain characteristics of the stages of psychosexual development (Freud, 1905/1953). These are called the *oral, anal, phallic, oedipal,* and *latency* stages, and it seems safe to say that as terms, they have moved from the constraints of technical usage into the larger social realm; they are now part of the vocabulary of every educated person. Nonetheless, the terms have considerable technical depth, and starting with the oral stage, below, this chapter will explore that aspect of their meaning.

The Oral Stage

To clarify what the term *oral* means, imagine a 2- or 3-month-old infant. The baby has been in a state of alert attention but is now beginning to get hungry. As the moments pass and hunger mounts, the child shows a heightened restlessness in the form of increasing diffuse general activity. But the food does not come. Presently, the baby begins to whimper; he is beginning to feel the hunger keenly and his distress is mounting. The restlessness is becoming intense, the baby's head is turning from side to side, and a fretful quality permeates his behavior. Still the food does not come. Soon the infant's arms and legs are moving more actively, and the restlessness is taking on a quality of agitation. More than that, the whimpering intensifies and gives way to crying. Despite this, however, the food still does not appear. Now the feeling of hunger really starts to press, and within a short while the crying mounts in intensity, the baby's arms begin to windmill and his legs to bicycle. Moreover, the autonomic nervous system kicks in so that his skin becomes flushed or blotchy, with patches that are alternately suffused and pale. In addition, the volume of the crying gets progressively louder, until the baby is literally howling in his distress. And still the food is not there. Whereupon the howling gives way to screaming: the baby is profoundly upset, every muscle is straining and tensing, the infant's passion is so intense and so consuming that it permeates every fiber of his being. He is overwhelmed, totally beside himself, almost literally "screaming his head off."

Never again in life do humans feel things as totally as they do in those early moments of becoming. Later on people develop affective bulkheads, learn to compartmentalize feelings, and find ways to rank order their emotions. Only in certain pathological states such as profound psychotic regression or perhaps catatonic excitement might an individual go through something akin to what the baby feels; but those are the rare extremes. It might be argued that such an experience as orgasm generates passions of equal intensity and generality—even then, however, most people can still answer the telephone if they have to. In short, even under such unusual circumstances, later emotional states do not have so total a character.

But for the hungry baby it is another matter. He howls, screams, and thrashes about; he is altogether pervaded and, indeed, overwhelmed by his emotions, until—along comes mother with breast or bottle and thrusts the nipple into baby's mouth. And then, after the brief moment it takes to identify what has happened, what a change takes place! The lips close down, the sucking rhythm begins, the milk flows, and a beatific expression spreads over the baby's face. What joy, what bliss, what transcendent ecstasy he feels! The baby sucks, pulls, and chomps at the nipple and takes in his milk avidly with every evidence of being transported by the sheer hedonistic rapture of it all.

It seems reasonable to think that there are two dimensions to the baby's satisfaction. One is relief from the feeling of inner tension and from the pain and frustration of unrequited yearning for nurturance. The other is the experience of pleasure, the pleasure of mouthing, sucking, suckling, tasting, swallowing, along with the warm inner glow, the goodness, the fullness that presently ensue—in brief, the pleasure of enjoying the mouth as an organ of primary delight.

This powerful experience, in some version or another, will repeat, day after day, perhaps several times daily, over and over again, for months. It would be surprising if such an intense relief and delightful reward arising from the mouth did not etch in and become a significant and persistent presence in life thereafter. Indeed, there is much to suggest that something of this sort does happen. Thus, the commonest of all human addictions is not morphine, heroin, cocaine, alcohol, tobacco, or marijuana; it is simply food. This is especially true in the developed countries, where food is plentiful and relatively easy to get. Consider the problems that otherwise well-functioning persons frequently encounter when they try to diet. Many physicians, for example, with a disciplined turn of mind, a history of mastery in so many sectors of their lives, and unusual capacities to make long-term commitments and to delay gratification may do no better than average (i.e., do poorly at best and frequently fail) when it comes to dieting. And this despite an extraordinary level of understanding about the implications of their excess weight for health. Concern to the point of preoccupation with food, dieting, and weight is a striking characteristic of current American society. Among other things, slimness has become a much-emphasized ideal. For example, during the years 1960 to 1980, beauty contest winners and magazine models have become progressively and significantly thinner, yet during the same period and within the same social context, the average weight of women in all height categories has actually *increased.* Indeed, a logo portraying the essential dilemma of our times might very well visualize the 20th-century human poised vis-à-vis the refrigerator door. If this is hyperbole, it is not extreme.

The Syndromes of Orality. Orality plays a role in life in many ways, on many levels. In particular, it gives rise to a number of syndromes that are, not surprisingly, peculiarly difficult to treat. Obesity, anorexia, bulimia, alcoholism, and addiction are as discouraging an array as a doctor could confront. It is not that these conditions are untreatable; it is rather that patients often resist help, many must be treated under duress, and the level of recidivism is high. Within the framework of Freudian developmental theory this is easy to understand. Considering that the origins of these conditions are rooted so early in life and that the major symptoms deal with so primitive a set of need satisfactions, the difficulty in their management is all too logical. Orality has such fundamental and immediate rewards that the vulnerable individual is often helpless in the face of the inner clamoring for satisfaction.

As a matter of fact, resorting to the mouth to cope with stress, lower tension, obtain relief, or find release is a remarkably common form of behavior. A college professor speaking to a group of students, for example, can observe that during the lecture many of them will be handling their mouths: Here is someone chewing a pencil; there someone else has a finger or a hand to his mouth; elsewhere a lip chewer is at work; and yonder a sufferer is dreaming of getting out of the lecture hall and having a drink or a smoke. Sucking in itself is immensely pleasurable to the infant, even when no food is taken in. (The efficacy of the pacifier is evidence of the importance of such nonnutritive sucking.) Moreover, ingested food is a powerful modifier of mood and state. Beyond the relief from visceral tension caused by satiation, the absorption of nutrients leads to profound alterations in blood chemistry, levels of neurotransmitter precursors, and consequent brain neurophysiology. Investigators are only beginning to understand the complex influences of different food constituents on attention, wakefulness, and mood (Conners, 1980; Wurtman, 1983).

Similarly, in later life, many oral forms of gratification and self-soothing depend on more than physical activity that stimulates the oral cavity (as with gum chewing). In the case of alcohol and tobacco, the physiological effects of ingesting alcohol and tobacco further reinforce the already pleasurable engagement of the mouth and lips. Smoking is a particularly good example of this sort of thing; despite the Surgeon-General's warnings on cigarette packages that assert the dangers of their contents, approximately 25% of Americans continue to smoke, and tobacco companies remain a lucrative investment. The pleasures of sucking and occupying the mouth coupled with the psychophysiological effects of the ingested nicotine enslave many people. The resort to the mouth for tension relief is too fundamental to be readily altered by regulations and laws. The story of Prohibition is a classic illustration, and the frustration experienced by those who would regulate many illegal drugs is only the current extension of the same conflict. The enforcement authorities rightfully complain that there is little they can do as long as an intense demand persists. And the demand persists.

Thus, on one level, the term *oral* speaks for a current in human affairs that deals with a uniquely powerful human experience. It goes all the way back to the very beginnings of growth and continues to have enormous force all through development.

Orality: The Pleasure Component.   For the very young (1st year of life) baby, oral pleasure is probably the highest level of sensuous experience. Some psychoanalytic observations suggest that at this time of life it stands in the pleasure hierarchy where orgasm will stand at a later stage of maturity. From this theoretical view, oral pleasure is the kind of sexual pinnacle of tension, excitement, and then gratification to which the baby can rise, and as such has a prime role in organizing all infantile experience. Nor is the pleasure component entirely lost in later sexual development. All sorts of oral behaviors are part of subsequent erotic sequences from nuzzling, biting, sucking, nibbling, and licking through kissing and tongue kissing, to various forms of oral–genital interaction. In some people, the maximum sexual gratification remains in that realm, and nothing is so satisfying to them as some form of oral sex. In such instances, the psychoanalyst speaks of fixation, a failure to abandon an earlier developmental position, a *hung-up* state. This means that in this one aspect of the person's life, he or she continues to fulfill the mandates of earlier epochs, even though the individual may have successfully advanced to more mature levels in other spheres.

The assertion that children had a kind of infantile sexuality was advanced by Freud in seminal work (Freud, 1905/1953). When the idea was first made public, it aroused a storm of opposition. At the time, children were regarded as innocent and free from carnal wish or thought; assigning any kind of sexuality to them was repugnant to the then right-thinking person. Once people began to look at children from a Freudian standpoint, however, it became evident that whatever else they might be, children are by no means innocent in any pristine sense. Children are avid pleasure seekers, and many of their primary pleasure experiences derive directly from body sensations. In particular, the mouth plays a powerful, sensuous role in the very young child's life.

Orality thus exemplified two vital dimensions of classical psychoanalytic theory. First, the mouth and its longings provide the primary passion and motive force that bring the child into affective contact with his mother, and, by extension, the world of people. Freud referred to this as the anaclitic theory of object clinging, meaning that the infant's first human relatedness or sexual satisfaction arises from his self-preservative (or, in this case, nurturant) needs. As such, it is the prototype for intensive relatedness. As Freud put it, children learn to feel for other people who help them in their helplessness and who satisfy their needs. Such a love is on the model of, and a continuation of, their relationship as sucklings to their nursing mothers. In Klein's view (1937), the infant's bliss in being suckled is not only the prototype and basis for sexual gratification, but of all later happiness. It is this bliss that makes possible the feelings of unity with another person (Shor & Sanville, 1978).

Secondly, the infant's oral activities in feeding, that is, sucking, biting, taking in, spitting out, become the paradigms for modes of interaction with the world (such as the taking in of knowledge, sensation, and identifications with others). For example, Erikson (1950) saw the *organ modes* associated with feeding as the basis for crucial adaptations to the social and physical world. In his view, these concern first of all the activities of taking in, getting what is given, and getting somebody to give. All these are aspects of the sucking mode.

The feeding infant develops a more active-incorporative mode, organized around biting on and through things and biting bits off them. In Erikson's view, this "active-incorporative" mode also characterizes the development of other sensory organs. The eye and ear group discern and take in sight and sound. Hungering for sensations, the infant "feeds" his eyes and ears. Later neutral and social patterns will also reflect these early oral organ modes, which are presumed to underlie apprehension and receptivity.

This powerful, inclusive vision of the impact of early oral experience has been subjected to criticism from a variety of quarters, even by developmentalists working within the psychoanalytic tradition (Bowlby, 1969, 1973, 1980; Stern, 1985). Drawing on both theoretical considerations and empirical work with human and monkey infants, these authors have challenged the notion that oral needs and experience provide the prime motive force or critical interactive locus for the development of the infant's interpersonal relatedness.

In particular, Harlow, a gifted psychologist, provided a thoughtful and considered critique of the role of orality in personality development

(Harlow & Harlow, 1965). In his series of brilliant experiments with baby monkeys, Harlow separated infant monkeys from their mothers and put them alone into a setting that contained a wire frame figure about the size of the mother monkey. In one set of experiments, the wire frame was covered with terry cloth. In another, the frame was bare, but a bottle of milk was mounted so that its nipple protruded from the frame. The baby monkeys were then frightened by a moving toy, whereupon they withdrew immediately to the "shelter" of the terry cloth "mother" to whom they could cling. In contrast to this, they sought little interaction with the wire frame "mother" who merely fed them. By inference, orality seemed less important than other aspects of mother–infant interaction, in particular, the possibility of attachment.

There are two dimensions to this. On the one hand, anyone who studies monkey behavior is aware that infant monkeys survive by clinging to the mother monkey's fur. Initially, they attach to the mother's chest and often have a nipple in their mouths; later they move to the dorsal position and cling to her from that vantage point. For the arboreal monkey, after the initial weeks when the mother holds it, survival of the infant involves the ability to hold on while the mother makes its way through the trees; the infant who fails in its clinging has a long fall to the forest floor and is unlikely to survive. Among humans, probably the only remnant of this primitive pattern is the grasp reflex, the involuntary closing and clenching of the infant's hand whenever the palm is stroked. In any case, the immediate transferability of Harlow's experiment to illuminate the human condition is not altogether self-evident.

However, it is also true that although human infants surely need the pleasure and relief of nurturance, that is not all they need. The catalog of their additional requirements has given rise to an alternative theory of attachment and forms a fascinating research study. To recognize the sensuous aspects of orality, however, is only to begin to appreciate its implications for orality has meaning on many levels.

Orality: The Fantasy Component. Orality involves a characteristic fantasy that permeates affectional life. The fantasy is unexpected but oddly logical nonetheless. It is that of cannibalism, the ingestion of another's substance. In brief, according to this view, all humans start life as little cannibals who lust to devour the ones they love. To the extent that the child suckles at the breast, he does some of that directly. But beyond that, the child loves with his mouth and wants to take in his love objects in that way, to engulf them whole. By the same token, he also considers his mother's mouth and thinks about being engulfed. It is important to recognize that these ideas are associated with intense emotion and will tend to recur later in life in contexts and at moments of powerful impulse. The imprint of these concerns is not hard to document. Thus, if a young man were to fall head over heels in love with a young woman, he might call her all sorts of affectionate names, such as honey, sweety, sweety pie, and lambchop. The oral quality of this array is no accident; on the contrary, it profoundly expresses his feelings. A few decades later in the life cycle, the grandmother encountering her new grandchild for the first time may look at the infant adoringly, cradle him in her arms, and exclaim, "You precious thing, I love you so much I could eat you up!" And with that she buries her face in baby's body so that her open mouth presses against his midriff. Meanwhile, the young parents look on with delight and are neither surprised nor nonplussed by the cannibalistic assertion; on the contrary, it seems altogether grandmotherly—and very loving.

The fear of being devoured is also easy to document. The terrors expressed by many young children show this with special vividness; there is a bear under the bed, a tiger is in the closet, some creature is present that will eat them up. Such children do not need to have been exposed to any stories or encounters with the theme of being devoured; their ideas seem to come from within. It is no accident that the stories designed for children have so frequently included this theme, from the *fee, fi fo, fum* of the fairy tale ogre to such relatively modern stories as that of Pinocchio and the whale. The devouring theme persists because of its deep psychological roots, and its erotic and aggressive dimensions play an important role in relationship life.

Orality: The Cognitive Component. On quite a different level, orality is basic to some abstract functions as well. In particular, it has much to do with the capacity to learn. In a certain sense, all learning experience is a kind of oral taking in. Piaget, for example, used the term *assimilation* to speak about the aspect of knowledge that involves the taking-in component of experience. For some psychoanalysts, every significant encounter with external experience involves, among other things, a measure of ingestion. To learn means to take in something from out there and to convert it into a part of the self. When people learn, they are changed and are, to some extent, different from the way they were before the learning took place. Perhaps they have greater understanding or greater competence, a new skill or more information to bring to bear on a problem, or now know what to avoid—however it may finally express itself, they are changed, different. Such a person has internalized the subject matter, and, in a real sense, assimilated it, metabolized it, made it part of the self. But this is not merely an analogy; if this particular variety of psychoanalytic thinking is correct, then underlying the cognitive work of learning is an instinctual act of oral devouring that is primal and essential. A purely cognitive kind of learning with little or no oral component might be the sort of thing students do when they *cram* the night before an examination and forget most of the content immediately thereafter. The material does not really become part of them because it has not been truly assimilated. But when an individual becomes deeply interested in a subject, then language itself begins to speak for the process (e.g., I love math, I just eat that stuff up; or, I devoured the book in one sitting) (cf. Stern, 1985, pp. 235–237).

In the areas of values, ethics, ideals—areas of great emotional charge—the oral quality becomes dominant. Thus, memorial services for the dead are often followed by a funeral feast. (In truly primitive societies the body, or a part of the body, of the deceased would itself be ceremoniously eaten. This was the basis for the discovery of the slow virus that produced kuru among a tribal group in New Guinea.) Thus, too, within many Christian churches, the moment of highest emotional intensity during a worship service is communion—when the members of the congregation take in the "body" and the "blood" of Jesus by literally eating bread and drinking wine. Wars have been fought over whether this is a symbolic act or an actual ingestion of the real Christ; more to the point, this ritual is a reaffirmation, a taking in of the values, the tenets, and the principles of the faith, an ultimate act of identification. It is noteworthy that the Eucharist derived historically from the earlier Jewish Passover feast, which is a special rit-ualistic meal commemorating the origin of the Jews as a nation, their enslavement and liberation from Egypt, and their journey through the desert to the Promised Land. Again, it is not by accident that such customs originate or are retained by different human groups; in each instance the founders of the religion reach for the most profound expressions of the feelings of that people, the acts that will confirm the taking in and mainte-nance of its teachings for them, and come up with one form or another of oral practice. It is simply the best way to learn.

Oral Vulnerability

As mentioned earlier, there are a number of oral syndromes, and they are difficult to treat. In the very nature of the theory, presumably everyone undergoes an oral stage, and the chances are that no one has had the perfect parenting to get through it without any stress or difficulty; why then do some individuals remain troubled by oral symptoms and others grow up without evident problems in this realm? What, in fact, makes for this kind of vulnerability? The answer is again complex and must be considered on multiple levels. In some instances, the oral needs of a baby may be innately and constitutionally more powerful than those of the average infant. Young babies can vary widely in the degree of need they show for a pacifier, with some infants eschewing it altogether, and others needing one almost contin-uously. On a more pathological level (see Chapter 1) certain families seem to have a high proneness for alcoholism, and the condition appears at an early age in generation after generation. This tendency has also been alleged to be more prevalent in certain population groups, such as the Amerindians and the Irish. Although such general assertions can be assailed on many grounds and firm data are still lacking, in any given case constitutional factors should be carefully considered. Indeed, there are symptomatic constellations such as the Prader-Willi (Prader *et al.*, 1956) syndrome, in which pathological oral behavior in the form of morbid appetite is a central part of the condition. Hence, disturbances of orality clearly can have biological roots.

A second level of etiology may best be configured in behavioral terms. Clinically, professionals know that many mothers respond to their child's every wail or attentional bid by feeding him. Such caretakers appear to lack any other resources for interaction, and they thus train the child from earliest life to ease every tension and to cope with every stress by oral stimulation. The caretaker may herself be heir to such an upbringing, may have a low tolerance for frustration, and may resort readily to oral gratification and consolation. When her infant is frustrated, she may be quick to attribute to him her own poor tolerance for discomfort. For the infant, the resort to oral gratification then becomes a learned pattern of response, a fixed, habitual automatic coping action that he carries out without thought or plan; it is simply this person's "natural" way of reacting to frustration.

Yet another level of explanation involves two alternative dynamic sequences: overstimulation and deprivation. The overstimulated child is used to a very high level of sensory input of all kinds. He is handled, thrown up and caught, tickled, massaged, yelled at, hit, fed a great deal, hugged, kissed, licked, handled, and all in all flooded frequently with great gouts of affect and sensuous arousal. These can arise either from directly invading the baby's person or from involving him secondarily in a noisy, riotous, eruptive environment where he is a passive and helpless audience and sometimes a victimized participant. Such children will later tend to cope in characteristic ways. They will either inhibit their emotional reactivity, constrict down their available attention, and adopt a stance of self-numbing compliance and passivity to avoid the storm. Or they will take an opposite tack and become overly reactive, hyperkinetic, voracious, and sensation hungry in an attempt to adapt to their overwhelming environments through identification. Sometimes the passive withdrawers will later seek the sedative effects of alcohol or other "downer" drugs to help them retreat and to deaden their reactivity; the hyperresponders may turn to stimulant drugs (including alcohol for its disinhibiting effects) to achieve the opposite outcome.

In contrast to this group are the emotionally and attentionally deprived children, who have never received the right kind or the right amount of maternal care. They are by and large a hurt and desolate group, at once profoundly sad and aggrievedly angry, who simultaneously manifest varying degrees of depression, chronic rage, and difficulties in attachment. They will often turn to oral means, both as a substitute for the longed for but unavailable relationship experience and as an anodyne for their pain, whether in the form of food or substance abuse.

More than this, when the deprivation is specifically in the oral realm, then reactions may follow that deepen the strains in that specific zone (Lourie & Nover, 1980). Some young infants respond to a failure in achieving oral connectedness by refusing to eat, by ruminating (regurgitating, masticating, and reswallowing their feedings), or by spitting up and vomiting much of what is offered them. Refusal to eat may result in a failure to grow and to gain weight (the failure-to-thrive syndrome) with dire effects on health and a serious threat of stunted later development. As noted, in the ensuing years, such individuals may show many difficulties in attachment behavior.

Along with the factors noted above, other dimensions of early experience also act powerfully to heighten vulnerability. Children identify with the significant adults about them from a very early age and if these adults smoke, are alcoholic, or gorge themselves on food, this behavior becomes part of the primary modeling system that the child uses to construct his early inner templates for behavior. Thus, the presence of oral disturbances in some important person within the child's immediate milieu is of critical importance; in effect, these disturbances can serve as a model for the emerging sense of identity and expose the youngster to the likelihood of absorbing some version of the symptoms he sees. In short, whether the professional approaches this area from the view of behavioral theory, social learning theory, or psychoanalysis, the outcome is much the same: Early models are important.

In summary, vulnerabilities have multiple origins and may arise in connection with various childhood constellations. Biological factors clearly play a role, although the details of the specific genetic and constitutional elements for many oral syndromes are largely unknown. Disturbance in parenting can be of major importance, particularly if the parents model disturbed nuncupative behavior, continuously reinforce conditioning, or overstimulate, deprive, or fail to set adequate limits on their children's various bids for gratification.

THE BEGINNINGS OF THE SELF

Only now are researchers beginning to unravel how the sense of self first comes into being; several developmental schemata have been put forward. For clinicians, such models have singular value in giving a measure of coherence to the often confusing and complex clinical picture presented by self-pathology. The following material will illustrate one such approach.

An early formulation involved the powerful message of physical sensations. According to this notion, the baby learns to distinguish between inner and outer reality by touching the pillow or the sheet and then touching his skin or mouth. Almost immediately the baby becomes aware of two kinds of sensation: one provides two feelings and the other, only one. This does not tell the baby a great deal about the world, but it does draw a distinction, and it divides experience up in a predictable way. To be able to make this distinction at so young an age is no small feat.

On quite a different level, many theoreticians added another assumption. They supposed that at an early age, the baby starts to piece together the world in quite a special fashion. Because of his relatively undeveloped state, the baby's fund of knowledge is thought to consist of two major classes of experience, the things that he enjoys and the things that he avoids, in effect, pleasure and pain. This in turn translates into the next theoretical assumption, that the baby would like to maintain the pleasurable experiences and keep them as part of himself, whereas he seeks to extrude unpleasurable things. The pleasurable items might include a full stomach, the taste of milk, the mother's smile, the mother's voice when it is soft and loving, the way the skin feels when it is dry and warm, the mother's hands when they are soft and gentle, the sound of a bell or rattle, and so forth for the many experiences that the infant knows only as his own. These are initially experienced as part of himself and are tinged with the dawning emergence of a sense of self.

By the same token, the infant relegates all the unpleasant feelings to the limbo that he perceives to lie outside the self-feeling. Such feelings, which are excluded from belonging to the self-world, include the sensations associated with hurt: an open safety pin, milk that is too hot, hunger pangs, the mother's voice when she is angry or upset, the mother's hands when they are rough and punitive, a sudden loud noise, a cold and clammy diaper. All these experiences are likely to have much the same valence for baby, they are unpleasant and hence are the nonself, the part that does not belong.

According to this view, the baby thus gives his experiential world an initial structure. The infant knows who he is (everything pleasant) and who he isn't (everything unpleasant). To the extent that such a structure occurs, for a while it is probably a satisfying state of affairs. Vestiges of this kind of thinking are likely to persist throughout the rest of the life span. For many people such an ordering of events tinges much of their thinking and forms the basis for many deeply felt attitudes of considerable importance. In particular, this way of thinking underlies such configurations as prejudice, bigotry, and social exclusion. It allows the individual to arrogate all positive qualities to his or her own side of the line and to assign all negative qualities to the other side. Thus, a European and an American discussing the relative merits of their respective cultures presently might each define two realms, positive and negative. And, mirabile dictu, all the positives would belong to the self, and the negatives would attach to the other. This is the psychological basis of xenophobia, the state of mind in which the stranger, the outsider, is the bearer of the dark burden of all our lurking rage, envy, lust, venery, guilt, and hatred, whereas, we are, as we perceive ourselves, virtue and sweet reasonableness. Perhaps somewhere in the phylogenetic dawning of human consciousness this may have had survival value, and groups who regarded strangers as enemies tended to survive better than did their trusting and peace-loving cousins. Whatever its origins, this tendency to externalize the bad and take title to the good seems to be an early presence in human development and a persistent theme as personality unfolds.

This would explain the curiously sticky quality of so much prejudice. Many people find themselves possessed of hostile attitudes toward other ethnic groups, toward other religions, toward other races, toward people from certain cities or regions, in short, toward all manner of human variations. When the authors of these sentiments "learn better" and try to free themselves of these attitudes, they find this difficult to do. Somehow the old outlook stays on, just under the surface, ready to appear in the face of even minor stress. Many a would-be convert to a more humane, broader view has struggled with "discarded" positions even while acting on his or her new beliefs. The professional is at a loss to explain why these prejudicial viewpoints do not dissolve and disappear with new knowledge and heightened awareness, but they do seem to persist, despite the person's best efforts.

If, in fact, this developmental view is correct—if the structuring of the very earliest sense of self and sense of other takes place along this pleasure/unpleasure dimension, then such early organizations would set a profound and formative stamp on development. The subsequent readiness to respond to the world in this fashion would thus be understandable.

Symbiosis

This model has still other striking implications. The child has included parts of the mother in his view of self, the good, rewarding, pleasure-yielding parts to be sure, but all within the boundary of *self*. This is a curious idea, the notion that an individual's boundaries can contain another person; it defies logic. And that is certainly true; within this theoretical framework these early attempts at forming a sense of self are unrealistic and illogical. Nor is this any great surprise. Coherent thought and applied reasoning are minimal in the first 6 months of life; the only question is, What kind of thinking and what kind of relationship do, in fact, exist?

This question reflects one of the great concepts of modern child development as well as one of its great controversies. Do babies go through a stage of symbiosis, or do they not? Is there a necessary experience of fusion and blending with the significant other, or are babies aware of themselves as separate entities from the outset? The model of symbiosis and fusion described in the ensuing material is maintained principally by the clinicians. The researchers in child development largely disagree with it. The following account first describes the concept of symbiosis and then looks at it from the two points of view.

Briefly, the model (as articulated by Mahler, 1967) states that somewhere around the 8th week of life, the child has become aware of the pleasurable and the unpleasurable as distinct and definable sensations. The baby is now addressing a true social smile to the appropriate face and is beginning to build some primitive form of a sense of self. Only the *self* that the child constructs contains many percepts of parts of the mother; her face, voice, hands, breast, body are all included in this image of self.

The weeks and months pass, and this entire developmental organization progresses. The child's capacity to distinguish among the items of his experience grows apace, he learns to push and to reach for things, he comes to recognize people and objects, and his sense of form is obviously advancing. Only in one area does the baby seem to remain static, and this is in his insistence on blending the self and the mother into a single entity. To understand this, it is necessary to consider the psychological, indeed the existential, position of the infant.

To a baby, the mother is very big. This is hard to put in its proper proportions; the baby's neediness and emotional dependence are such that she is not merely big, she is BIG. Enormous. Tremendous. Stupendous. Colossal. Gigantic. Titanic. Vast. Mammoth. Brobdingnagian. (It is therefore no surprise to find that mythologies of cultures as diverse as that of the Mycenaean Greeks and the Australian aborigines include accounts of the Titans of yore, or of a Dreamtime when the gigantic Rainbow people trod the earth.) The mother is an awesome presence in the baby's life, who can bring total happiness and fulfillment or overwhelming pain and frustration. She can pick the baby up in the air, throw him about, carry him under her arm to any and everywhere; she knows when he is hungry or cold or distressed; she is truly omniscient and truly omnipotent as well.

If the language employed here begins to sound theological, it is not altogether accidental. This kind of infantile experience may rather resemble the later encounter of the more mature mind with the concept of deity; indeed, this early experience may well be the psychological precursor for the later emergent. To the extent that this is true, it helps explain why the infant clings so tightly to the sense of fusion with the mothering person. In effect the baby is one with "god," and that is a powerful experience, not something to be readily yielded up.

For the baby, then, according to this model, he and his mother are a single entity bounded by a continuous perimeter. The baby's advancing perception and organization of his world proceed in all but this one respect—despite the self-evident quality of their apartness, the baby keeps the link to his mother intact.

This sense of fusion is thought to be a blissful state, rich with rewards. There is a sense of partaking of greatness, of being one with something grand and mighty that is vastly superior to what the child could be alone. After all, on his own, a baby of that age is totally vulnerable and utterly unable to fend for himself. The mother can do anything with and to him; no greater security is possible than to be part of her.

Mahler calls this state of mind *symbiosis* and considers it to be an essential step in the eventual achievement of a true sense of relationship and individuality. According to this view, the child who is not allowed to form an adequate symbiotic bond remains in a highly vulnerable state that may later find expression in serious symptomatology. Such a youngster has never formed the initial bridge to another person that underlays all subsequent relationships; there will always be a great inner gap between him and the people about him. This may take the form of a lost withdrawn state, an isolated autistic position, or a schizoid stance from which the person can later emerge only with the greatest difficulty. Or the failure of symbiosis may be a precursor to some form of depression or to the kind of violent psychopathy associated with the inability to form object relationships. The rare child may escape unscathed, but generally speaking, the absence, loss, or failure of early object attachment (without adequate replacement) is a very serious matter indeed.

By the same line of reasoning, a child who enters this state of psychological symbiosis but who then fails to emerge from it is also in peril—less severe, perhaps, different in kind, but nonetheless potentially seriously disabling. The outcome here is more likely to be a severe borderline or narcissistic condition with or without an associated propensity for violence or depression. A sense of self as incomplete or damaged, feelings of emptiness, loss, and fragmentation, terrible reactions in the face of separation, and pathological kinds of dependency are among the likely sequelae. To be sure, temperament and the vicissitudes of environment will have a profound effect on how a given personality takes form; at best, however, symbiotic fixation is a tremendous hurdle for the developmental course.

The residual effects of symbiosis are thought to shape later childhood and adult experience in many ways. For example, the behavior of many adolescents (and not a few adults) who join cults suggests this earlier form of adjustment. Parents who have been able to visit with such a youngster at cult headquarters will often say something to the effect that they did not know their own child. The youngster was somehow not there for them; the youth's face wore a "thousand-mile-away" expression. If the teen-ager offered any description of what it meant to be part of the group, the account suggested that he had given up his identity, lost his outlines, merged in some unfathomable way into the group, or into the compelling presence of the group-and-leader. The youngster would speak of being part of something larger than himself that was totally gratifying, smoothed away all care, and eased all hurt. Within the magic circle of the group lay all love, harmony, truth, and beauty. Outside the group lay a desolate world filled with evil, ignorance, oppression, or strife. And so on and on the panegyrics would continue. (Cults vary in how much evil and confronting hatred they projectively attribute to the world around them.) The profoundly regressive character of cult participation thus resembles early symbiotic experience.

Another less disturbing example of awakened symbiotic experience is the state of being in love. Someone in the throes of an intense love affair may say that it feels as though the object of his or her affections "is right beside me," or, even more intensely, that "the two of us are one, blissfully joined together, a single being, united." In such ecstatic states couples find themselves in seeming total accord, feeling each other's feelings, thinking each other's thoughts, finishing each other's sentences. Beginning with the biblical injunction that man and wife "shall be one flesh" (Genesis 2:23) and the myth of Aristophanes in Plato's *Symposium,* Western literature concerning love repeatedly returns to these metaphors. Freud (1961, p. 64) spoke of the "oceanic sense" and Michael Balint (1966) of the supreme happiness of the illusory regression to "primary love" in which there is "complete harmony," "a harmonious mix-up" of wishes and satisfactions.

Nor is this sort of symbiosis confined only to people. Things too can have a like claim on the emotional life of predisposed individuals. Assume, for example, that a young man has fallen in love with a particular sports car. This car is mostly hood, it seems to extend forward endlessly in faultlessly streamlined silhouette, and to that individual it is intoxicating, overpowering, totally captivating. It is also too expensive, and so he can only stare longingly at it in the showroom window.

Then one day the youth comes into an inheritance, the funds are suddenly available, and he buys the car. The youngster gets behind the wheel, guns the engine (auditory bliss), and drives around town in a circuit that passes the homes of all his friends. At length the boy goes home and parks the car in front of the house, steps out, perhaps gives the car an additional lascivious stroke, and then goes into the house. He closes the front door, goes through the house, and out on the back porch. He is now 150 feet and two closed doors away from the car, but somehow—it is still with him. There is a link, an ectoplasmic rope, that extends from his person, passes through all the intervening barriers, reaches across the distance, and connects to the car. The point of this discussion is that precisely the same feeling of connectedness (in theory) forms the basis of the baby's sense of security. A built-in tie to the mother simply defies reason and transcends the limits of reality; the love affair is total, and the two are one.

Differentiation

If the rewards of symbiotic fusion are so great, why then do humans ever leave it? It it is that good, why does not the child simply stay there permanently? The answer Mahler offers is simple; the pressure of development is an immense force that carries the infant forward and presses ever ahead. His very growth, the cognitive and perceptual strengths that increase every day with the brain's elaboration make it impossible to maintain the fiction of fusion. At some point the baby must give it up and embrace the new competencies and capacities that life is thrusting at him pell-mell.

At 6 months, the baby can sit up without support, and within another month he is pulling himself erect while holding on to the bars of the crib. By 8 months the baby is likely to be crawling or somehow making his way about. His abilities to reach for things, figure things out, remember things, recognize things, as well as all sorts of additional intellectual competencies, are increasing apace. All these achievements are exciting, gratifying, and beguiling. The normal baby is eager to engage and to attack problems that are even remotely within his grasp, and so the blissful state of symbiotic attachment gives way to a constantly increasing interest in the world of objects and reality.

In particular, the mother's face, hands, breast, and voice are coming together in progressively clearer fashion; her outlines are taking form, as are the child's own; and the sense of differentiation from the symbiotic unity begins to grow and to advance. As Mahler et al. (1975) describe it, the process is gradual. At first the feeling of separateness is likely to come only when the baby is particularly secure and feeling particularly good about himself. At this time, any hint of stress causes baby immediately to want to be picked up so that he can regain the sense of fusion and reunite with the grandiose mother of yore. But as he grows, the moments of separation are longer, and the periods of regressive reunion are less protracted; in time they occur only when baby is really upset and specially needy.

All this happens during what Mahler called the *differentiation phase,* the time of "hatching," the period of emergence from symbiosis. It starts at 5 or 6 months of age, continues until 10 to 12 months or thereabouts, and is, by its nature a time of special vulnerability. After all, the child is leaving the protected state of being "one with god" and, for the first time, is venturing into the world as a nascent individual. That is inevitably a challenging and potentially stressful state. Just to be a crawler already betokens the capacity to leave the orbit of the protecting adult and to set forth on some kind of voyage of discovery. It is a fascinating world out there, to be sure, and it calls to the baby with a siren voice. But the presence of the mother (along with the promise of reassuring symbiotic reattachment) is also a powerful lure, and all sorts of compromises and alternating patterns emerge.

The very ability to begin to be independent (in however larval a sense) awakens as well a need to restructure the mother–infant relationship. Things cannot be the same, but how are they to be different? For one thing, the baby begins to regard the mothering person as a separate but distinct individual; she becomes important, not just for her caretaking, but as a very specific individual. When feeling needy, the child wants her and not a substitute. The function of feeding, changing, or soothing will no longer suffice; the presence and the ministrations of the one particular loved and unique personage is critical.

Stranger Anxiety.   As already observed, many children 6 to 11 months old find the appearance of a stranger something of a challenge. Now that the baby has made a commitment as it were to a specific mother, what is he to do with another motherlike person who does not fill the necessary specifications? For some children it conveys a quality of threat, and they become stressed and show evidence of fear or begin to cry. This is not the usual response, but it is familiar enough to have received the name "stranger anxiety" (Spitz & Wolf, 1946a). Although for most children, such an encounter represents a cause for concern, it does not amount to so massive a threat, and instead, they show a considerable degree of interest in and exploration of the nonmother. In such situations, once the infant has detected the stranger's presence, he often looks to the mother as though searching for a cue as to whether the stranger is safe to explore (a process termed *social referencing*). How the mother responds is important in determining the infant's balance between anxious inhibition and curious exploration. A few children show paradoxical reactions; they are drawn to strangers, are excited by their appearance, and offer every evidence of pleasure and interest.

Counterphobic Reactions.   One of the threads that binds these reactions together may be the readiness with which a given child tends to resort to such mechanisms as splitting and counterphobic reactions. The readiness of more vulnerable youngsters to split their relationship world into all good and all bad (with the mother regarded as all good and the stranger as all bad) may underlie the stranger anxiety. Instead of the dawning understanding that the mother is sometimes kind and sometimes angry, which the more secure child now begins to perceive, these more fragile youngsters have to maintain a sort of idealized and purified image of the mother. There are thus two separate figures in the child's life: One is an angelic mother, the idealized image of the remembered moments of blissful exchange; and the other is a demonic presence, constructed from the accumulated rage, frustration, and pain that the child has episodically experienced. Where the child's defensive organization takes a projective form, then the stranger receives the valence of the bad presence and embodies the split-off anger and hurt, which the child now experiences as coming from the *outside* and hence as terrifying.

Where the mechanism takes a counterphobic form, then it is precisely this more frightening presence that becomes attractive, and the child is drawn to strangers because they are scary. The great need is to reverse the feeling of anxiety and to turn it into a pleasurable and thrilling attraction. This need has considerable drawing power; thrill seeking and playing with danger are no great rarities in human behavior, and this may be their first expression.

Separation and Anaclitic Depression. Another aspect of development that characterizes this time of life is some children's vulnerability to depression. Here the professional can see the clinical utility of the symbiotic connectedness model and the presumed consequences of beginning to separate from it. With the giving up of this singular sense of fused oneness, the child must replace the symbiotic bond with a more mature kind of object attachment. Once such an attachment emerges, the child begins to experience an enormous need for the chosen object. This is not surprising; at this point the symbiotic mother is lost as a part of the self; now she is a separate person with whom the child has to negotiate rather than being able to take for granted (as the symbiotic child used to do). This is much scarier: How is he to be sure of her, how is he to keep her steadfast? She thus becomes "the mother of separation," a presence from whom the baby can separate only with difficulty. A variety of separation reactions may now begin to make themselves felt, but the most serious is that associated with *anaclitic depression*. This term was coined by Spitz (Spitz & Wolf (1946a)) to describe the responses that he observed in some of the babies he followed during his research. An enforced separation from the primary caretaker resulted initially in protest behavior, but, when the mother figure failed to return, presently the more fragile babies fell into a state of withdrawal and manifest depression. Their food intake fell, they stopped growing, they refused eye contact, they became relatively unresponsive, some of them resorted to self-stimulation, and they appeared woebegone and bereft. In a few cases the depression was so profound as to be life-threatening. A best, without adequate replacement of the missing caretaker, this behavior would go on for an extended period seriously affecting the child's development. These youngsters acted as though the basic prop to their emotional security had been pulled away—whereupon they crumpled inwardly and collapsed. If the mother returned within a few days or even a couple of weeks, the condition would rapidly reverse itself. Where no such reunion was possible, the use of substitute caretakers who were consistently there was essential.

Many children have multiple caretakers, and the research is not yet in concerning the implications of this approach. The chances are that among those persons available to him, the baby will usually direct his primary attachment to one individual but will accept substitute presences—at least for a time. These will include the other parent, grandparents, babysitters, siblings, and a variety of other presences whom the babies learn to depend on and with whom they may relate well. Although the ideal model is certainly that of a single, central, organizing, caretaking presence, many babies do have multiple caretakers, with their care fractionally distributed among several individuals. The implications of such rearing patterns are at present uncertain.

The Practicing Phase

As development proceeds, the baby approaches the end of the first year of life, and a crescendo of new experiences culminates in one of the great revolutionary epochs in the life cycle. Almost simultaneously the baby begins to walk and to talk. His development takes a great leap forward, and in effect, he joins the human race.

Up to now, the baby has been a crawler or a cruiser, not able to be truly like the people about him who stand erect and proceed about their business in the world on their two hind legs. At this developmental moment the baby, for the first time, can begin to navigate free and upright, and his pride and elation often know no bounds. The baby begins to toddle about in the hurried and precarious way of the early walker; he falls over readily and picks himself up to go forward once more; and it is all exciting and exhilarating. At about the same time, the baby is beginning to say under-standable words and to receive the rewarding responsiveness of his captivated parents. It is a great time all around, a true change of phase and of state. The babe in arms, who relies on the magic of maternal intuition for the satisfaction of his needs, makes the transition to being a walker and a talker, who can go after what he wants and ask in words for the things he cannot reach by himself. The mastery implied in this is enormous. The baby has crossed a phase barrier of considerable importance and has entered a wholly new state of adaptation—and in a very real sense he knows it. Above all, the baby's emotional state reflects this progress by taking on the quality of a prolonged "high." Things are upbeat now, and each day means more interesting experiences and greater competence in so many areas. Greenacre (1960) has called this the time of the baby's "love affair with the world."

Inevitably, this new, overall state alters the baby's relationship with the mother in significant ways. In particular, the infant's newfound capacity to toddle about makes it ever more possible for him to follow his mother everywhere—except of course when she goes out, whereupon his recently acquired verbal capacity adds force to his protests. But shadowing mother is likely to be the baby's typical behavior around the house until some fascina-ting diversion comes into view and off he darts to explore. This might claim him for several minutes but the separation from mother soon makes itself felt, and baby looks about (Where is she?), takes a bearing on her, and comes toddling back to charge up and be reassured (a process Furer, and then Mahler, called *emotional refueling*) (Mahler & Furer, 1963). The baby is then ready for the next foray into novelty and adventure.

This, then, is how the development of the infant and the young toddler looks from the theoretical perspective of separation–individuation theory. As noted earlier in the chapter, the whole concept of symbiosis has come under strenuous attack in recent years (Horner, 1985; Stern, 1985). The next chapter examines this critique and the alternative theory of development on which it is based.

Chapter 9

The Self: Stern's Theory of Development

THE EMERGENT SELF

In a recent volume, Daniel Stern (1985) has proposed a theory about the development stages of the sense of self. The realm of study he selected is the emergence of the sense of self during the first 30 months of life, with a special emphasis on the events of the first year. As a researcher, Stern has built his concepts on direct observations and has culled from the ongoing investigations in the field. Hence, the data arising from a number of the experimental and research approaches described earlier form the basis of many of his ideas.

Using such data, Stern regards the first 2 months of extrauterine life as the time when the infant begins to experience the process of *emerging* organization. Things come together for the baby in novel ways, and the baby is aware of this happening, as well as ready to use the new organizations that are beginning to crystallize. As Stern interprets the experimental findings, there is no primordial subjective sense of undifferentiation; there is only the recurrent experience of achieving this bit of organization or that. Sequences of sensory encounter begin to fit together. The feel of the nipple in the mouth and the intake of milk become connected; they go together. Being held in a certain position presages feeding; the holding and the feeding go together. Bit by bit some predictables emerge; bit by bit a sense of the organization of experience begins to build up. As the baby learns, each clicking together of bits of such organization kindles a spark of self-feeling, and slowly but incrementally a sense of self starts to take form.

The key term here is *organization*. In some ways this is analogous to Piaget's use of the term *schema:* It is an internal construction in the mind that connects up some elements of experience; this construct then becomes available to the baby for subsequent use in mastering and ordering experience. Each time the baby achieves an additional bit of such inner organization, he is also aware, on some level, that he has done something. For Stern, this earliest sense of being and doing is basic to the sense of the emerging self.

What processes are already present in the baby to create such organization? Stern's answer includes some rather unexpected capacities. First is *amodal perception,* called by some authors *transmodal,* or *cross modal,* perception. To understand this concept, it is necessary to know that learning is usually assumed to involve a principal mode, that is, a person learns through the visual mode, the auditory mode, the tactile mode, the kinesthetic mode, or through some other sensual pathway. A person learns Braille, for example, through the tactile mode and cooking, in large measure, with the help of gustatory (taste) activity. Amodal perception goes beyond this. It involves encoding perception in some unknown form of representation so that what the baby learns in one mode (e.g., touching or tasting) he can recognize in another. A nipple with bumps on it is put into the infant's mouth without him seeing it; he knows it only by touch, taste, and feel. Nonetheless, if the baby is then allowed to look at an array of nipples, his eyes will fix immediately on the one with the bumps; he will recognize it among other nipples the first time he sees it. Presumably, somewhere inside, the baby has formed a notion of the nipple (achieved through touch) that translates readily into another sensory modality (sight). For Stern, such yoking of visual and tactile sensations suggests the presence of a single, higher order image or schema of the nipple, an amodal perception. Similarly, the infant develops a unitary image or schema of the breast whether he apprehends it visually, smells it, or suckles it. Nor does this inner construction emerge merely from accumulating repeated experiences; the infant is predesigned to form such unified higher order perceptions. Stern believes that this linking up of sensory experiences has a sort of déjà vu quality for the infant. When the baby first views something that previously he has only touched or tasted, he does not quite have a feeling of discovery but rather its precursor, the sense of the familiar in the encounter with a new experience.

The organization of experience, however, involves not only cognitive (perceptual) factors but emotional elements as well. In this connection Stern introduced another group of unfamiliar and theoretically novel presences, the *vitality affects.* This indicates states of change in emotion and in experience generally; it involves such dynamic qualities as rising, falling, increasing, diminishing, surging, fleeting, bursting, quieting, intensifying, and the like. These descriptors can apply to any changes in motivational states and tensions; they are *forms of feeling.* A person may experience a feeling of rage or happiness, but this is seldom a steady and continuous state of feeling. Instead the emotion is likely to rise and to fall, to come in gusts or waves with crescendos and diminuendos, to be experienced in pulses or surges, and, in short, to have a shifting, changing character that is very much a part of the experienced feeling. These shifts and changes, then, are the vitality affects; they are immediate presences in the stimulus qualities the infant experiences, from both the outside world and within the self. These vitality affects stand in contrast to the categorical affects (such as happiness, sadness, fear, anger, disgust, surprise, interest, and shame). For example, the vitality affects are the main tools of the puppeteer whose characters show no facial expression but whose qualities of movement alone communicate, quite precisely, the puppet's "state of mind." They are the basic means for evoking the effects of abstract dance and music. And they are probably the first affects to which the infant responds. What impinges on the baby is not the feeling itself so much as how it is expressed. It is the activation contour, the rate of change of intensity over time, that is central here, and the infant apparently has an inborn capacity to perceive these rushes or diminuendos of experience, to abstract them in amodal form, and to link them together with remembered elements of experience. This linking together organizes the nascent perceptual and interpersonal world, and the organization will presently give rise to a sense of other as well as a sense of self. Thus, whether the mother soothes by words or wordless stroking, the infant apprehends her calming diminuendo in similar fashion, and the organization of a sense of a discrete other takes form despite the variations in specific behavior. This kind of experience then forms one part of the emergent self of the infant.

The other pathway is through efforts in construction. Considerable research in the perception of infants suggests that very young babies construct perceptual unities, such as the mother's face, mother's voice, and mother's combined face and voice, according to a regular and predictable pattern. These constructions proceed literally from birth; they are based on assimilation, accommodation, association, and the identification of invariants. Together with amodal perception (of both the abstract qualities of experience and the vitality affects), they create a sense of inner organization, an awareness of the linking together of the various domains of perception, affect, and experience.

Heretofore, different theoreticians have focused on specific aspects of infantile life to account for organization. (Piaget emphasized actions; Freud stressed the feeling tones of pleasure and unpleasure; others designated discrete categories of affect or states of consciousness, affects, or cognitions.) Stern states, however, that infantile experience is more global as well as more unified than each of these accounts implies. As they grow, babies gradually and systematically keep putting together the elements of their experience to identify self-invariant and other-invariant presences, and they thus begin the *construction of organization*. This global subjective world becomes and remains the "fundamental domain of human subjectivity" (Stern, 1985, p. 67). It is the unconscious or the preconscious matrix from which conscious experience will later arise, and, in particular, from which all creative efforts will subsequently emerge. It is the world of the emerging self.

THE CORE SELF

The second stage, extending roughly from ages 2 or 3 months to 7 to 9 months, is when the sense of a *core self* takes form. This construction is the product of a rather special set of experiences: (1) *self-agency* (the child's feeling of being the author of his own actions and of *not* being author of the actions of others), (2) *self-coherence* (the child's feeling of being whole, with boundaries and with a central locus of action, and recognizing that others are similarly constituted), (3) *self-affectivity* (the child's awareness of patterned inner qualities of feeling as well as the perception of affective states in the significant people about him), and (4) *self-history* (a sense of continuity over time, the child's feeling that along with those about him, he "goes-on being" (Stern, 1985, p. 90; Winnicott, 1958). From these crucial self-invariants, or islands of consistency, the infant constitutes a sense of the core self and the core other. These are not cognitive constructs so much as they are experiential integrations taken completely for granted and operating outside of awareness. They are the self-experiences necessary for psychic health; their absence in whole or in part will result in a sense of fragmentation, experiences of fusion, inthrusts of depersonalization, or dissociative states.

Stern's term *invariants* requires some introductory explanation. Underlying each of the four categories of self-experience noted above are a number of such invariants. For example, first among the components is the sense of *self-agency*. This includes a sense of volition and the formation of a *motor plan* for any action. When a person wants to do something, a sort of map of the behavior forms in the mind, and the individual proceeds then to enact it. (Although the sense of volitionality has been much scrutinized by philosophers (Anscombe, 1961), the neurophysiological correlates of the motor plans that precede intentional movement can now be studied (Georgopoulos et al., 1986).

The second invariant contributing to the sense of an organized self is *proprioceptive feedback,* the pressure, tension, and kinetic sensations from skin, tendon, and muscle that guide infant motor acts from the outset. Thus, while playing pata-cake, the infant has a different sense of self and other if he moves his own hand to hit his mother's hand than if the mother takes his hand and moves it.

The third invariant specifying agency is *consequence of action.* Because all self-initiated action produces some kind of change in the child's experiential world, there is a constant schedule of reinforcement in response to such actions. (Motions always give rise to proprioceptive sensations.) But action on others produces highly variable responses, and the infant has a considerable ability to discriminate such different reinforcement patterns. These three invariants confirm the sense of agency.

Five invariants underlie the sense of self-coherence including *unity of locus, coherence of motion, coherence of temporal structure, coherence of intensity structure,* and *coherence of form.* A sense of place is innate; at birth infants will orient their gaze toward the source of a sound, and at 3 weeks they are upset if the mother's face and voice are in different loci. More than that, when in motion, the mother tends to move as a unit; all the sensory experiences that define her (the visual images that arise from her, the sounds she makes, the tactile experience she proffers, the taste of her body when it is mouthed) change place together. But most important of all is that all parts of the mother (as well as her voice) move in synchrony, and they do so at a different rate and rhythm from the baby's self. This temporal ordering and the contrast of the mother's temporal (and spatial) structures with those of the baby give each individual—both individuals—unity and coherence.

The various behaviors that emanate from another person usually share a common intensity profile, an invariance that Stern terms *coherence of intensity structure*. For example, the intensity structure of an angry mother involves a congruence in the modulation of her voice and the tempo and vigor of her bodily movements, just as the mounting distress of the infant's crying, hungry self involves congruent behaviors and stimuli of comparable intensity emanating from the self.

Finally, an individual has a recognizable and enduring form. By 2 to 3 months, infants can recognize the mother's still picture, and they know the mother's face whether she smiles or frowns.

Self-affectivity is constituted from a number of invariants: (1) the *proprioceptive feedback* from the affect-associated motor behaviors, (2) the inner sensations of *affective arousal* and its autonomous accompaniments, and (3) the specific qualities of the *affective feeling*. This applies to both categorical and vitality affects; the subjective quality of the feeling provides the invariant presence.

The sense of *self-history* (continuity over time) depends on memory. Can the infant recall the experiences of agency, coherence, and affect? Newborns can, in fact, remember sounds that they heard in utero, and cued-recall of motor acts is readily demonstrated at 3 months. Experimental work such as that of Nachman and Stern (1983, p. 93) suggests that the infant has good recall of earlier affective experiences. Moreover, such empirical studies give credence to the working assumption of clinical psychoanalysts that an affective core to the self persists all during development and into adult life. Regardless of the vicissitudes of such memories, they make for a sense of personal continuity, a self-history.

The role of memory is thus particularly crucial. How does it work? Stern suggests that recurrent interpersonal events, such as feeding, each leave a memory trace. The infant then combines or averages these traces to distill a generalized form for the event. In effect, this is an affect-invested model of a succession of similar events, which Stern calls a *representation of interactions that have been generalized* or, more succinctly, a *RIG*. Such RIGs are the basic units for representing the core self in interaction with a core other. These "islands of consistency" that form and coalesce out of the welter of infantile experience allow for a shifting dynamic construction of the sense of both a core self and a core other.

Early on, infants learn that the regulation of their affective state is very much in the hands of others. An exciting game filled with intensity and arousal is the product of mutual play; the infant cannot achieve these feelings alone. The degree of arousal, the intensity of the affect, the sense of attachment (mutual cuddling, mutual holding, mutual eye contact), are all self-experiences that cannot exist without a significant other. Somatic states, such as sleep and hunger, are to a great extent similarly regulated.

For Stern, all of this argues against any experience of fusion, merging, or symbiosis. Indeed, he regards the concept of symbiosis as a "pathomorphic, retrospective, secondary conceptualization" (Stern, 1985, footnote p. 105) that does not hold up under direct scrutiny. The self-experiences of the infant may indeed depend on the interventions of the other, but they belong entirely to the (infant's) self. From Stern's view this does not imply a loss of boundaries or sense of fusion. In each play exchange there is a certain variety; from one time to the other the game is never exactly the same. Similarly, during moments of feeding or somatic care, each participant follows a distinct, albeit sometimes parallel, pattern of movement, intensity, and rhythm; no sense of merger is present. The parent serves an important role as an instigator and modulator of the infant's level of arousal and affective state. Thus, in the presence of the regulating parent, the child's self-experience undergoes change. But is it not in the form of merging. The change is felt as part of the core self, whereas the other, although essential to the change, remains distinctly the other. The remembrance of both self and other in interaction is kept in the memory trace of the episode and forms a constituent of the RIGs. Whenever the infant encounters previously experienced feelings, the appropriate RIG is activated. As part of the generalized experience thus recalled to the child, the past presence of the significant other (the averaged memories of the other) is now experienced as an *evoked companion,* one who participates in the current experience. If the current interaction differs in some detail from the previous exchange, the RIG is modified and then stored awaiting the next cuing. Such a RIG acts as a standard for experience. (Referring to the infant's accumulated experiences with attachment to and separation from mother, Bowlby (1980) spoke of the child's internal "working model" of the mother interacting with himself.) By offering a context for experience, the RIG provides stability and continuity, and it thus helps evaluate new interactions as they occur.

Stern believes such RIGs come into being by the 3rd month of life, if not even earlier. They form a part of the infant's world thereafter; as a result, from the first 6 months on, there is a continual recall of social interactions so that whether alone or with another, the infant is almost constantly engaged in social experience. The infant's sense of being with the other can extend to things as well; the mother's play with the baby's things allows these objects to be temporarily personified for him. Self- representations thus do not exist in a vacuum; to a very large extent they consist of the self in interaction with others. In this way the experience of *being-with* is pervasive; it is a permanent, healthy part of the internal landscape of the mind. Under favorable circumstances, the preponderances of these internal images of the self in interaction with others will be harmonious or, at any rate, positively tinged. Under such conditions the infant's expectations will be generally hopeful and confident, a state of affairs that Erikson (1950) termed *basic trust.* Under less favorable circumstances the working model that the infant elaborates is less benign or reliable; this, in turn, will have ominous implications for future development. In short, the press of those social reminiscences and corresponding expectations serves ultimately to shape and guide behavior.

The RIGs that the infant comes to elaborate about his mother will simultaneously be affected by the mother's RIGs of her own developmental experiences with *her* mother; these early experiences will determine how the mother perceives the infant—as lovable, fragile, annoying, vulnerable, intrusive—and whether she views him as a super-toy, a predator, a competitor, or a companion.

THE SUBJECTIVE SELF

Building on the sense of core self, the next major developmental advance is the formation of a sense of a *subjective* self. According to Stern, between 7 and 9 months, the infant grasps that not only is he a locus of feelings, intentions, and interests, but that others are too. (As Stern puts it, the infant discovers that he has a mind and that other people have minds as well.) Furthermore, it is possible to share and exchange such inner experiences. This discovery opens the infant up to the domain of *intersubjective relatedness;* the baby becomes aware of an empathic process bridging the two minds and can, for the first time, experience a sense of intimacy. Indeed, in Stern's perspective, just at this juncture (Mahler's practicing phase), as the infant is forming a more elaborate sense of self, he first becomes capable of something akin to merger experiences. Thus, from Stern's view, merger is not an original given. Rather, to the extent that something approaching merger is possible in the form of intimacy or attunement, it results from various developmental accomplishments.

What subjective experiences do infants share? Stern offers three kinds: joint attention, intention, and affective states. From early on, the infant follows the mother's line of gaze when she turns her head to look at something. By 9 months, however, the infant goes beyond that. He can point with his finger and then check back to his mother's face to see if she shares his focus of attention. The infant can signal his wants by gesture and can check to see if the mother has grasped his intention to communicate. If she has not, the baby can also modify his form of communication. The baby becomes able to tease, implicitly declaring his awareness of the other's state of mind and manipulating it. And finally, through social referencing, the baby can resolve emotional uncertainty or mild anxiety by looking toward the mother to get a cue about how *she* feels in order to determine how *he* should feel. At this point affective exchange is both the predominant mode and the chief subject of communication with the mother.

The organizing subjective perspective that now appears is a maturational emergent; that is, once it has appeared, it employs the existing means (rule structures, action formats, and discovery procedures) to implement itself, and it works within a context of mutually created interpersonal meanings (often in the form of reciprocal fantasy interaction).

Intersubjective successes can enhance feelings of security; indeed, intersubjectivity has enormous survival value.

How does a person share affective states? How does a parent mirror back to a baby what that baby feels? The parent must "read" a baby's state and do something to let the baby know that his feelings have been understood, and the baby must be able to receive the message. During the infant's first 9 months of life, the mother is reflecting and imitating the baby's behavior, with variations. At around this 9-month point, however, a new element appears; the mother begins to express affect attunement in a novel fashion that has not heretofore occurred. She resonates with the baby's affective state. She might sing along with the baby's acts or do a little dance mimicking the baby's excitement when he masters something. Or she can give special stress to her verbal response in order to convey her attunement. One way or another, by vocal inflection, facial expression, or whole body tempo and posture, she conveys the sense of sharing the baby's feelings. At this stage, the attunements match the baby's behavior without actually imitating it; in fact, they match the baby's feelings in the form of metaphor or analogue. This is not mirroring, which is a more inclusive term, nor is it empathy, which involves a conscious, cognitive dimension. Indeed, most attunements occur largely automatically and out of the mother's awareness. Upon careful inquiry, about two-thirds of the time, mothers were unaware, or only partially aware, of their attunement behavior (Stern et al., 1985).

What is it about another person's affect that can be matched to convey attunement? Stern distinguishes three elements: intensity (in the form of absolute intensity and intensity contour), timing (as temporal beat, rhythm, and duration), and shape.

As studied in the laboratory, most attunements are cross modal in whole or in part, and they are usually performed because of the mother's desire for interpersonal communion. Sometimes mothers over- or underrespond to tune the baby to a higher or a lower pitch of response; at other times mothers misattune because they cannot help themselves.

It is noteworthy that when the mother's attunement behavior was appropriate, infants apparently took no notice of it and merely continued to do what they were doing; but if the mother acted in a misattuned way, the baby would stop his activity and look at his mother as if to inquire, What goes on?

The key underlying mechanism for attunement is amodal perception, whereby such abstract properties as intensity, time, and shape allow matching patterns of behavior across modes. Although mothers attune to both categorical and vitality affects, most such maternal resonance occurs with the vitality affects. Unlike categorical affects, these are present on an almost continuous basis, and they allow for states of maintained attunement.

THE VERBAL SELF

During the 2nd year of life, language emerges, and the sense of a verbal self comes into being. Signs and symbols become possible by about 15 months; these give rise to language and to symbolic play. Deferred imitation appears by 18 months; the children must be able to create mental images, recall them, and perform the acts the youngsters seek to imitate. They must, in addition, be able to go back and forth between the mental image and the motor performance (to judge whether they are getting it right), and they must be able to imagine themselves in the role of the one they are imitating. This implies an objective view of the self that is evidenced by a number of different observations: Before 18 months of age, children whose faces have been marked and who are looking in a mirror point to the image; after 18 months they point to themselves. They see themselves as objects, a *categorical* rather than an *existential* self. They begin to use pronouns, *I*, *me*, *mine*, and to fix on their gender identity: They belong to the category of boys or girls. Empathic behavior also appears in this period; the child will seek to comfort a distressed other.

Infants can now transcend experience and work on themes in play or imagination. They can objectify themselves as part of the play and then coordinate various action schemas (those recalled, those currently experienced, and those wished for). All this the child can render in words.

Language becomes a set of meanings negotiated between child and adult; there is a process of continual movement back and forth between word and thought. As the child starts to talk, he is pressured to maintain a new order, social rather than merely personal. The child uses language to recapture the special sense of being-with that exists between himself and the adult; they share a mutual world of meanings. Thus, language serves both for separation–individuation and for togetherness. The mother offers the word that the infant borrows to attach to his experience; the word is thus a shared transitional phenomenon. Ultimately, language gives the child the ability to narrate, to tell his own life story, or to create stories.

Global experience of a core self is not verbal, although later on language can claim some parts of it and make it an experience separate from the global sensations. The child now encounters the persistent life issues of attachment, autonomy, separation, and intimacy on the basis of shared meaning of personal knowledge. These issues lead two lives, the original felt one, and now, a verbalized version. Sometimes the language expresses it all; often a lot of the meaning is not made verbal.

In the nature of things, language separates out "official" versions of perceptual experiences for social communication. Inherently, however, the global quality is thereupon fragmented, and the amodal properties of experience then go underground. The infant gains entrance into a wider cultural membership but loses the wholeness of primary experience.

Words apply to classes of things, RIGs. To speak about specific events takes a good deal of maturity. The child learns that gradually; at the outset he must struggle to convey meaning. It is not that the infant expects the mother to be omniscient; it is merely that initially the baby has not learned to specify.

There are many points of slippage between inner experience and language. Language specifies modality and misses the amodal; it refers to general episodes instead of specific instances; and it is inadequate for describing internal states, such as affects. Language readily depicts categories of information but does not lend itself as easily to shadings or gradients—and it is the gradient that may be most important. In many instances, where a certain social response is expected, people devote a good deal of interpretation to any difference between the performed response and the awaited inner image. Similarly, there can be a difference between what is said and what is meant; the extreme case produces lying or the double bind.

On a more subtle level, language is less deniable than intonation or attitude; hence, by not being verbalized, major aspects of experience can be denied and slip into the unconscious. In addition, many aspects of self, such as continuity, remain in the background and do not usually get verbalized. Thus language fragments the self. The same is true for many of the vitality affects that arise during interpersonal interaction. In effect, language forces a space between the inner world of interpersonal experience and the representation of such experience. And it is within this space that neurotic constructions form.

Finally, as language and symbolic thinking develop, children can begin to distort reality, to imagine and wish for the impossible; they can create unreal and exaggerated images of self or other and thus elaborate fantasies and neurotic constructs.

SUMMARY

These then are Stern's views about the stages of development of the sense of self during infancy. As Stern conceives it, such stages can serve as basic templates for the emergence of important character traits and can offer illuminating explanatory concepts to account for certain forms of psychopathology. It is as yet too early to offer a judgment about the fate of these ideas; they do represent an important new approach to understanding personality development.

PART III

The Preschool Years

Chapter 10

Early Toddlerhood

INTRODUCTION

Within the Freudian system, each successive stage of growth is conceived as developing under the influence of a particular erogenous zone, and in this sense the second major epoch is designated the anal stage. A critical time for personality unfolding, it deals with that period of growth when the infant becomes a toddler and begins to engage his world with a vastly improved motoric and cognitive competence. Roughly speaking, this epoch extends from the 12th to 36th month of age. During this interval of elementary civilizing, the sense of an interpersonal and verbal self, the acquisition of speech, the beginnings of impulse control, and the sharpening of boundaries all flower at once and intertwine to establish the nascent personality. Attachment and separation issues take on new dimensions, and the struggle for power and control, with the attendant manifestations of sadism and masochism, come to dominate the shape of relationships. More than that, the beginnings of anal sensuousness and of phallic and clitoral interest appear, and thrust their many new and clamorous demands into the already intricate mix of developmental emergents.

This chapter considers this epoch first from the viewpoint of toddlers' general interests, overt patterns of behavior, and characteristic problems.

The focus then shifts to the Freudian view—an era dominated by an erogenous zone involving anal erotism, the power struggle, and anal sadism.

Following this, the discussion turns to narcissistic development during this interval and the further vicissitudes of those first-year-of-life experiences that emphasize grandiosity and narcissistic vulnerability. Ego growth in general is the next topic, with impulse control and object attachment forming the nucleus of the discussion. Within that context there is a reconsideration of negativism and the developmental epochs described by Mahler as the *practicing* and *rapprochement* phases. Separation issues, toilet training, transitional objects and possessions, and the character of thought processes during the passage through these years will in turn be reviewed.

CHARACTERISTIC INTERESTS AND BEHAVIOR

Three great interests dominate the behavior of the young toddler (White, 1975). The first is a continuing preoccupation with the whereabouts and activities of the caretaker. The youngster spends about 15% of his time shadowing his mother, following her about, clinging to her, or watching her. Hence, despite the evident emotional importance of this behavior component, it does not consume a large percentage of the toddler's time. The toddler's second major interest is exploring his world, which fills much more of his day and, during early toddlerhood, is a major preoccupation. The third great claimant for the toddler's attention and energy is the practicing of new motor skills. During later toddlerhood this is perhaps the quantitatively most important single activity, with the time devoted to it increasing as the months advance. The actual behaviors are diverse, and a complete list is impossible; much depends on the opportunities available within any particular cultural environment. Activities may, however, include the following (White, 1975):

1. Dropping and throwing objects.
2. Swinging hinged items.
3. Opening and closing drawers and doors.
4. Standing things up and knocking them down.
5. Putting items together and taking them apart.
6. Putting objects through openings.
7. Pouring spillable materials into and out of containers.
8. Manipulating switches to get effects.
9. Manipulating simple locks.
10. Spinning round objects or pedals.
11. Climbing.
12. Engaging in various kinds of ball play.

In addition, the child devotes a significant amount of time to nontask behavior, when he simply stands and stares; in effect, the toddler is idling. No apparent goals are associated with this behavior; for a time the youngster merely does nothing. Finally, what White calls "passing time" is rather common in the life of toddlers; they are put into some kind of confining surround, a playpen, a highchair, a crib, or an autoseat, where they must stay until released. For the most part the children seem to do very little during such intervals, often not even using the materials provided for play; they simply pass time. An observer has a sense that this state of mind is more passive and less functional than the idling noted above. The idling child seems to be thinking or recharging; the confined child passing time appears to be blanker and merely waiting.

Most of the time, however, the toddler appears to be in a state of constant investigation and discovery. At the start of this period the child is much committed to exploring. He is endlessly busy studying his living area, looking, touching, feeling, handling everything he can reach. He is likely to spend a great deal of time looking out the window. He climbs whatever stairs he can get to and is fascinated by toilet bowls. If allowed to, he will splash in the water within the bowl at length and may try to drink it.

The mouth continues to be a major organ for all kinds of exploration. These youngsters may put anything they find into their mouths. Because they do not respond to tastes and odors in the same fashion as adults, they mouth or swallow whatever they can reach regardless of taste or odor making this a common age for accidental poisonings.

By and large, such youngsters love to play outside. There is much for them to discover, and they particularly enjoy playground experiences, such as swinging in a swing or playing in water.

Younger toddlers spend little time watching television. They might attend to a children's program briefly, but as a rule these do not hold their attention. The capacity to stay with such programs as "Sesame Street" increases only gradually during these toddler years and does not ordinarily become a major preoccupation until later.

Toddlers are fascinated by language and listen avidly both to the expressions uttered by the people about them and, in time, to the words they hear through the radio and television. The growth in their ability to understand language is prodigious. At 12 months they may understand perhaps a dozen words; by 24 months they can react appropriately to several hundred. In particular, by the 2nd birthday they can comprehend and respond to simple prohibitions and warnings. By age 36 months the child can carry on a good conversation and will often talk with adults as though they were peers.

Somewhere between 13 and 16 months a pattern of negativism appears. The child begins to say "No" repeatedly and often seeks to do precisely what has been forbidden. This kind of behavior is quite predictable, and almost all children show it. Its duration is variable and might be as short as 4 to 6 months; for the most part it endures well beyond the second birthday and, in some instances, never disappears at all. As the toddler's representational play becomes more elaborate, scolding or saying "No!" forbiddingly to a doll or stuffed animal (in imitation of the caretaker) is a common occurrence.

For optimal development, there must be a balance between the several major interests of this time. The preoccupation with the caretaker, the interest in exploration, and the desire to practice motor skills can be profoundly affected by the style of child rearing. Some families foster the attachment to the caretaker at the expense of other aspects of development; other families fail to provide the child with enough of the necessary person-to-person interaction. In some milieux the child will be blocked from adequate freedom to explore; in others there may be insufficient protection from the hazards implicit in such activity. The quantity and quality of environmental responsiveness can affect survival; it is certainly a key factor in personality formation and cognitive development.

PSYCHOSEXUAL THEORY: THE ANAL PHASE

Earlier chapters have explored some of the implications of the oral stage and the attributes that classical psychoanalytic theory ascribes to orality as a governing principle. Within the framework of this Freudian approach, the next stage of development is connected with elimination, in particular, the infantile encounter with anal sensation and the management of anal functioning. In Freudian theory, urethral functioning too is considered a powerful begetter of fantasies and various emotional reactions, but it falls short of anal experience as a site of pivotal, personality-shaping events. In addition to the direct sensuous responses attending elimination and anal/urethral stimulation in general, psychoanalysis has traditionally associated a number of personality traits with this phase.

This survey will first consider how psychoanalysis views the more primitive drive aspects of anality. It includes an exploration of the nature of anal pleasure, the evidences for this phenomenon, and its possible role in personality functioning. Then there is an explanation of the aggressive aspects of anality and the theory of anal sadism. Within psychoanalysis the drives are generally considered to be either erotic or aggressive in character. Each developmental stage has its own complement of each, and the specific configuration of sexual and aggressive drives is regarded as being central to the developmental implications of that stage of growth.

Anal Erotism

During the first year, the infant achieves the pinnacle of oral erotic pleasures. The baby has faced the world as a suckling-nursing entity, and has experienced the joys and satisfactions that may be achieved through the mouth. Now, at the end of this phase, many babies wean themselves and put away the use of sucking as a primary technique for ingestion. The intensity of the oral pleasure seems to diminish, and the chief recourse to mouthing behavior occurs when tension relief is needed. As a result, the baby may keep mouth activity alive and may resort to the bottle from time to time, but the oral role is now peripheral. For the most part mouth behavior serves as a comforter, a refuge for moments of tiredness, a way station on the path toward sleep. Some infants will retain the thumb tenaciously as anodyne for the pain of existence, and thumbsucking may persist well into the succeeding years. Most children, however, confine themselves to a nighttime bottle as the major overt vestige of this oral stage.

A new center of pleasure begins to claim the youngster's attention. The focus of sensuous reward shifts, and the perineal structures come to the fore as the prime site of gratification. Both the eliminative and the genital apparatuses become the focus of concern and exploration. However their respective patterns of psychological unfolding, albeit simultaneous in time and in many ways parallel, are nonetheless different one from the other and require separate study.

It is not easy to discuss the anus as an organ of pleasure. Social training generally turns people away from ready or natural conversation about anal issues and allows it scope only as a property of childhood or within the context of humor. Yet in the Freudian scheme, this childhood pleasure component is an all-important compass that points development very clearly in a given direction. How do investigators know that children do, in fact, take pleasure in anal sensations?

Direct Observation. On the basis of direct observations of normal children, Galenson (1979) reports that during the opening months of the 2nd year of life, these children began to show a great awareness of and response to defecation. Prior to that, emptying the bowel had happened as it might, after meals or while the child was in his crib, without notable associated behavioral changes other than some straining and reddening of the face. Somewhere around 14 months, however, the toddlers began to show increasing awareness of bowel action. As they built up toward an episode of defecation, they might begin to squat and strain, they grunted and pulled at their diapers, and then, as defecation proceeded, they withdrew their attention from whatever they were doing at the time, their gaze turned inward, and they appeared deeply preoccupied with the subjective component of the experience. Not infrequently they hid behind furniture, went off into a corner, or disappeared into a different room. Emotionally, their behavior suggested excitement, sometimes pleasure, and on occasion fearfulness.

After defecation, they sometimes played with the stool. Some children would signal for a diaper change; others would actively resist changing. Frequently the infants could be observed feeling and touching the anal area. In the study population (which included 70 infants equally divided as to gender), this sequence of behaviors tended to cluster around the 12th to the 14th month and appeared independently of toilet-training efforts.

During the children's everyday activity, they showed an evident interest in toilets and toilet behavior. They often followed adults into the toilet, and they would attempt to investigate the anal area of animals, siblings, or parents. A great deal of play focused on dump trucks and garbage cans; toy toilets were flushed and dolls were used repeatedly to enact diapering and eliminating. The toddlers frequently piled up and amassed objects engaged in games involving messing and scattering materials, and enjoyed filling and emptying various containers. Patterns such as obsessive arranging, compulsive neatness, and hoarding (often interpreted as defenses against impulses to mess) were also much in evidence. As the months went by and the children moved more deeply into this stage, certain accompanying affects became more prominent. In particular these included the fear of loss of rectal contents or loss of control. Disturbances in bowel function, either as diarrhea or constipation, were not unusual.

Urinary behavior shows a similar primacy in the children's interest and attention. The toddlers tended to play with the urinary stream, their attention turned inward during the act, and they usually signaled for a diaper change afterward. During urination, the youngsters tended to react emotionally with excitement, shame, and anxiety. Play patterns commonly involved water and puddles, and much interest was expressed in hydrants, hoses, faucets, and the like. All this usually came in the train of the interest in anal activity.

Anal Smells. Certain behaviors of small children are certainly suggestive enough of anal pleasure. Quite often parents walk into the baby's room when he is about 12 months old and make the rather distressing discovery that the baby has been playing with the contents of his diaper. The parental response is usually at once dramatic and persuasive; most youngsters get the message and do not persist in such patterns. Indeed, the continued practice of fecal play and fecal smearing suggests the kind of serious psychopathology associated with brain injury or a very troubled parent–child relationship. Nonetheless, hints of the pleasure component of this phase often persist and continue into later life. This is a rarely spoken of part of everyone's awareness.

Thus, from early on most people experience a sense of revulsion at fecal smells. If an adult should happen to step into a toilet that has recently been used, he or she might be repelled by the heavy aroma of excrement that hovers there; it seems foul, even disgusting. Yet when we defecate ourselves, the smell may be far less disturbing to us; indeed, the act of defecation is often experienced as pleasant, and the associated odors are not at all offensive. They may even have a certain measure of reward associated with them.

Nor does this ambivalent attitude necessarily stop with the odors emitted by a person's own body. Young mothers report that when their own baby soils his diapers, there is nothing especially troublesome about cleaning and changing him. But if such a mother babysits for a neighbor and that baby needs changing, the smell seems awful. Thus, even in this vicarious fashion, the quality of anal experience betrays a vein of pleasure, however limited in degree. In fact, a moment's thought suggests numerous commonplace evidences of the anus as the site of pleasure. Anal masturbation is no great rarity, and anal stimulation as foreplay is a common part of the sexual pattern of many heterosexual people. Moreover, many homosexual men use their own or their partner's anus and rectum, or both alternately, as the principal mode of sexual interaction and gratification. Evidently, the inclusion of this part of the body under the rubric of the sexual is by no means stretching a point. For many people it *is* the point, or at least a desirable part of the point.

Anal Impulse and Language. Some of the evidence for the role of anal pleasure in human affairs is less direct, although no less impressive. Thus, in the matter of language usage, probably no part of the body has as many descriptive terms or euphemisms as the general region of the buttocks. If, for example, an instructor of a group of medical students starts the exercise of having the group call off all the words they know for that part of the body, even a "slow" class will quickly come up with 12 to 15 terms. Groups with larger vocabularies at their beck will produce 19 or 20. A few outstanding populations with access to regional or ethnic variants may think of as many as 25. That is a great many synonyms for anything.

More than that, as the naming process proceeds and each term is called out for the instructor to write on the board, another phenomenon quickly intrudes: The group begins to laugh with each call, and a curious drollery ensues.

Why so many words, and why the laughter? What, after all, is so funny about merely naming a body part? Obviously it *is* funny and the laughter is predictable and general—but why? What is the joke, exactly? The key is likely to be found in an illustration offered long ago by a Dr. Davidson of New Jersey (personal communication, 1949). He observed that our culture never seems satisfied in naming the bathroom. Indeed, the word *bathroom* is itself a euphemism; literally, it means a room in which a person bathes. Alternatively, Americans may call it the *lavatory,* where a person laves, or the *washroom,* where he or she washes. Or the namer might prefer the *rest room,* where the occupant rests, or the *lounge,* where presumably someone lounges. Yet another alternative is the *powder room,* where a woman powders, or, cunningly, the *little girl's room*—on the premise, no doubt, that big girls do not do such things. "Why," asked Davidson, "do people keep up this shifting, changing pattern?" And the interpretation he offered went something like this: No matter what the euphemism may be, as people continue to use that term, sooner or later the smell breaks through (perhaps not unlike a process Freud referred to in another context as the return of the repressed). Once that happens, it is necessary to abandon that usage and seek something else. I would add one term to Davidson's list: currently, Americans often utilize a man's name, *John* (the room is designated as *the john*), presumably to get as far away from the involved function as possible.

A way of verifying that concept is to resurrect a term that has fallen into disuse and to study its impact. It is of interest that an earlier term was also a man's name, allegedly the name of the inventor of the flush toilet. His name was Crapper, and for a long time the common usage was to go to the *crapper.* Few people indeed will use that language today; it is far too crude and almost shockingly suggestive of the immediate experience of defecation. Because it reveals rather than conceals and the smell has broken through too flagrantly, the term has been largely abandoned in ordinary speech.

The laughter unmasks the profundity of the emotion associated with this part of the body, with this set of functions; and it exposes the conflict between the pleasure and the need to keep it all out of sight and out of mind. It is the nervous laughter of anxiety; it expresses the need to make something endurable by turning it into a joke. It tells of concealed imagery, concealed emotional pressure, hidden instinctual thrusts. It is precisely here that the anxiety becomes manifest, for the laughter betokens the fear of loss of control, the panicky realization that something may escape that is supposed to be contained, something may become public that is supposed to be private. In particular, the forbidden pleasurable play of infancy that the individual's rearing, training, and socializing have taught him or her to forget may suddenly emerge, creating confusion and humiliation. Once again the person would be back in the nursery, having had an "accident" and facing parental opprobrium. So people make a joke about any reference at all to this array of experiences and keep feeling uncomfortable about what word to use. (In a well-known television series the hero is shot in the buttocks, and no report of this wound is filed with the insurance company because ". . . we couldn't think of any way to tell them where you'd gotten hit [audience laughs] . . . ")

For many people, bathroom jokes are an endlessly rewarding form of staple humor. Unconsciously, it allows for a continuous effort at mastering themes about which these raconteurs have never become altogether comfortable. Some people seek to add a dimension of virility and evident power to their expression by lacing their language with all sorts of forbidden "dirty" words; in effect, they are telling their world: "You may think you have trained me, but I still make all over the place any time I want to, so there!"

But it is unnecessary to seek the extreme cases; indeed, the extent to which excremental language is part of the vernacular is remarkable. Shit, bullshit, horseshit, ass, asshole, shitass, horse's ass, to be pissed, or pissed off—these are not the excessive crudities of the great unwashed, these are everyday usages designed to lend pungency and pith to the expressive style of many average people. It is noteworthy that there is a sort of political dimension as well; such terminology is a form of expressing defiance against whatever is perceived as constituted authority. Again, it is a way of saying: I defy your toilet training and I thus defy your authority. I do what you have forbidden; I handle my excrement and smear it around; I enjoy myself in a way you have said is wrong. Aren't you shocked?

In sum, the reason there are so many words for that part of the body and the reason people laugh at any reference to the anatomy or the physiology of elimination is the fear of loss of control. It creates anxiety, and to overcome the anxiety, people make it all into a joke—and then try to find a new, as yet uncontaminated word to use for a shield.

Muscular Pleasures: The Joy of Action.   Quite apart from the zonal pleasures, there are other sources of gratification at this toddler stage. Muscular activity as such, the excitement of ambulation, the joy of climbing, the thrill of successful manipulation, all the many rewards of pulling, pushing, tugging, and handling the immediate world are plentiful in the life of the toddler. Direct sensuous pleasure accompanies the performance of muscular acts, and the evident beginnings of this experience are to be found during this epoch.

Anal Aggression

The anal apparatus is a source of pleasure; for some people it is the sexual organ of first choice and the site of maximal erogenous gratification, and for all people it is a highly sensuous part of the body with many attendant emotional overtones. The aggressive aspect of this phase, however, is less evidently connected to anality as such. It is not self-evident that the anus contributes directly to expressing the associated anger and aggression. The psychoanalytic experience is, however, that the two themes, anality and sadism, appear together so regularly in patients' associations that the tie-in is considered to be direct and immediate. Indeed, it is common in psychoanalytic parlance to refer to this era as the anal-sadistic stage of psychosexual development.

The toddler's burgeoning powers of locomotion and exploratory zeal not only expand his horizons but also bring him into new areas of potential conflict and prohibition with his parents. In addition, his growing verbal comprehension and capacity for delay lead to increased parental expectations for self-control (Horner, 1986). Thus, the toddler finds himself in a struggle for autonomy and control played out in many arenas—where he can go, what he can eat, what he can play with, throw, or break. At the same time he remains almost completely dependent for all his needs on his parents, who continue to be his principal objects of security and attachment.

The Power Struggle.   For such a child, the need to cope with this crisis of *autonomy versus dependence* pervades life and colors many, indeed most, of his interactions. He wants to cling, and he wants to explore; he wants to be close to the powerful and reassuring mother, and he wants to be free and unfettered in acting on his curiosity and realizing his exploratory interests. Accordingly, he is agreeable, compliant, and loving at some moments, and imperious, demanding, and tyrannical at others. In particular, at times the toddler will insist that the adults carry out his wishes forthwith. In addition to coloring the quality of his interpersonal relations, all these factors are elements in the pattern of his important inner work, the effort to sort out a coherent—and increasingly separate—sense of self.

This is a complex time, and various theoreticians have emphasized different aspects of the child's developmental efforts in their model building and theoretical understanding. Thus, Freud saw one arena as overshadowing all others in importance—the battle over toilet training. In Freud's view, the perineal area and the processes surrounding defecation were major sources of pleasure for the infant. How such a toddler negotiated the task of bringing his eliminations under control in response to his parents' demands involved fateful issues that Freud believed would permanently shape his character and style of relating. During toilet training, the toddler takes control of his own body yet also offers the mother his compliantly delivered excretions as a gift of love and request for approval (Abraham, 1921/1966, Freud, 1905/1953).

In this view, conflicts between activity and passivity, sadism and masochism, obedience and oppositionality—indeed, the very issue of ambivalence itself—find definitive expression and partial resolution in the arena of anal concerns. Furthermore, the toddler's struggles for control and autonomy sharpen the boundaries between the child and his parents and introduce concerns about the loss of the mother's love and approval. It is because of Freud's emphasis on the centrality of the anal zone and its vicissitudes that this period is known as the anal phase.

Within this Freudian framework, the central relationship issue that preoccupies both parent and child at this developmental moment is the struggle for control. In this context, the toddler and parent are often in conflict about various wishes of the child or limits imposed by the parent. However, the struggle at times seems to be about the question of control itself: Who is in charge, who can force the other to give in? At times, it seems as if the child wishes totally to dominate the parent. The actual means that such a toddler has at hand for forcing the adult to comply with his wishes and for achieving control are limited at best. He can cry, whine, cling, or demand. He can tug, push, or pull at the parent. When frustration persists, he is likely to have a particularly difficult time, and the theory asserts that at this point the toddler will try to obtain compliance in the simplest and most natural way: He will inflict pain on the significant other. He will bite or pull hair, he will hit out or scream, he will find some way to hurt, and he will continue to torture the other until that person gives in. In effect, the child has become a little sadist, and seeks—at least at moments—to achieve dominance through inflicting suffering.

Sadism.   The concern with pain, the experiencing of pain, and the inflicting of pain are so characteristic of this time of life that (as noted earlier) within psychoanalytic writings the epoch is often given a hyphenated title: the anal-sadistic phase. For the child, how the pain is engendered is less important than that it achieves the sense of dominance of the one and submission by the other. The essence of the sadistic experience is to rule over someone who grovels before the master. A favorite form of sadistic behavior is thus to humiliate (there is much evidence of this in later schoolyard teasing or in the way certain siblings incessantly demean one another), but it can take many other forms. Among adults, sadistic impulses are often expressed in sarcasm and cruel, highly personal confrontative thrusts; but they can find physical expression as well in blows, abuse, and beatings. Or they can become sexualized requiring one person to bind or chain the other and to engage in whipping or other physical torture for one or both participants to achieve sexual pleasure. The forcing of the person's will on an unwilling other offers the desired reward to the individual with this mindset; the act of rape is perhaps the prototypic example. But whatever sadism's specific mode of enactment, its essential content is always the assertion of power. One person dominates and the other submits, one tyrannizes and the other yields and abases him- or herself; this seems to be the instinctual core. The variety of the styles of expression of this tendency are without end.

Evidently this theme of dominance and submission does not disappear with the passing of the anal phase. It is the rare person who can resolve these issues once and for all in childhood; most people have to work at containing such impulses much later into their life-spans. But at this early epoch these concerns flower luxuriantly and are often in the forefront of relationship issues.

It is important to understand the nature of the sadistic wish. In its extreme guise, sadism is manifested in a form of sexual perversion where the achievement of sexual pleasure requires that one of the participants assume the position of victim, either actually or symbolically, and the other play the role of oppressor. This can be dramatized (in children's games or in adult foreplay) in relatively innocuous ways, such as teacher–student, in somewhat more ponderously playful ways, such as royalty–subject, or in more troublesome fashion, such as master–slave or conqueror–captive. In its most extreme varieties (where the full perversion is present), sadism demands the enactment of roles such as punisher and punished, or torturer and tortured. In such cases, actual infliction of physical pain is an important prerequisite for orgasm. However, the basic purpose of the pain is implicit in the curious apparatus that accompanies such practices, the black leather boots, the belts, and the rest of the bizarre regalia. The point of the behavior is once again to show who is dominant.

The word *sadism* comes from the name of the Marquis de Sade, who was a well-known author of tracts and novels that are read to this day. His most famous work is probably *Justine*, the story of a French girl who travels the countryside seeking care and protection and encounters instead various rebuffs, disappointments, and outrages, many of which involve torture and humiliation. Much of Sade's writing is overtly pornographic and obviously suffers from the author's pathological preoccupation with this area of psychosexuality. Yet paradoxically, he was also an intellectual supporter of the French Revolution and engaged in many forms of protest against what he considered to be social injustices of the *ancien régime*.

Masochism. This term, too, is derived from a man's name, in this case that of Sacher-Masoch, an Austrian intellectual and author whose works featured many passages portraying the search for suffering as a part of erotic pleasure. So notorious were these descriptions that the condition wherein the attainment of orgasm requires the experience of pain or humiliation became synonymous with his writing and eventually came to bear his name.

Dynamically, masochism is a cognate experience that parallels sadism. When the toddler's attempts at sadistic dominance meet the limits, threats, reproofs, and the acts of punishment and retaliation of the surrounding adults, the youngster faces grave issues. Either the child persists in his quest for dominance and continues the associated negativistic, provocative, and demanding behavior, or he seeks some other outlet for the feelings. The adults are saying, in effect: "Any more of this and we won't love you any more; if you keep it up you will be physically dealt with." Nonetheless, the inner pressure to hurt, to attack, to prevail is there; what is the child to do?

The answer that certain children (perhaps the constitutionally predisposed) find is to turn the feelings against the self. They quite literally attack themselves. Pfeffer (1985) quotes the work of Shintoub and Soulirac (1961) who observed that 15% of all normal toddlers between 9 and 18 months of age engage in some form of self-injurious behavior; as development progresses this gradually diminishes so that by 5 years, such behavior is no longer evident. It is a rather common sight to see an angry, frustrated 2-year-old react to some moment of towering vexation by screaming and slapping his own face or banging his head. Some children habitually pull out their hair. An occasional child will hold his breath. In one way or another such a youngster will take out his frustration on his own body, as though deflecting the powerful sadistic wish from its primary target back onto himself.

In the Freudian view, this is what happens. The child directs against himself the blows that he fears to visit on the caretakers. His rage is great, but the dangers that its expression invites are greater still; the compromise is to become his own target. In the predisposed child, this self-inflicted pain serves as a powerful safeguard of the parents; the turning against the self wards off from them the child's rather terrifying excesses of rage. In a sense, the child's pain is reassuring; it confirms that the youngster is thus protecting his relationship to his parents. Eventually the pain itself becomes a source of pleasure and hence a habitual practice. Sometimes this self-injury is fully overt, in the form of actually striking the self; sometimes it is less direct and takes shape as an "accident," an apparently happenstance event that results in knocks, bruises, and, in more serious cases, stitches and casts. A parent may open the account of the child's problems by a statement such as: "Somehow, all his life, he has always had accidents." Indeed, the investigator has but to observe some of these children briefly to note that they recurrently thrust themselves into all sorts of dubious or hazardous positions; they are forever teetering on the edge of one catastrophe or another.

To be sure, there are a variety of routes to accident proneness. Some involve the impulsiveness and inattentiveness found in children with attentional deficits. Others involve a preoccupied and neglectful caretaker; in the face of this the child is unable to internalize a caring, protective vigilance over himself. More closely related to the phenomenon of masochism, abused children direct a high degree of hurtful, even violent behavior toward themselves (see Volume 2, Chapter 21).

Unfortunately this tendency does not confine itself to childhood, and adults can live out a host of masochistic patterns. Beyond the toddler period, masochism often takes nonphysical forms. The child may sabotage himself in a variety of ways: "forgetting" to study for an important test; "losing" his books, gloves, or other possessions; presenting himself as a butt for teasing or attack by peers; and so forth. Moreover, even in childhood the youngster's discovery of the enormous social power of a tendency toward self-injury may vastly complicate the situation; the classic strategy of "I'll hold my breath until you give me what I want!" is but one minor variant on this theme. To the extent that the child seeks to control his environment, the assumption of the sufferer's role is a major ploy. For some adults the basic theme of their relationship life is to "suffer at" people. In effect, there is an exhibitionistic component to the masochistic disposition that can have different meanings under different developmental circumstances but that always has an impact on people. Thus for one kind of masochistic personality, the response of the audience shores up a failing sense of self. For another, the suffering is in the service of evoking an admiring or a sympathetic response from those who perceive it. Yet another dynamic may be to punish the observer(s) by making the viewer(s) feel guilty. Or the person might intend for the behavior to evoke yet more punishment from the social surround.

It is, in a way, surprising to find that suffering can serve as a self-enhancing factor in certain people's lives. For these very vulnerable individuals, the awareness of an audience's reaction (even a fantasied audience) affirms the sufferers' reality, presence, and significance. The ability to coerce others into noticing and reacting to them (and if they suffer obviously enough, others will indeed react) reassures them that they are indeed someone, they have made a difference, they matter (Stolorow & Lachman, 1980).

A particularly troublesome form of this tendency occurs where the individual accomplishes the suffering through provoking the environment to act as punisher. The person controls, not so much by inflicting the suffering directly on the self, but by needling and irritating people until they respond with the sought-for abusive, humiliating, or physically injurious reactions. Among children, this can occur at the level of peer interaction as well as with grown-ups. In a study built upon the use of Ainsworth's Strange Situation, Troy and Sroufe (1987) described the interactions of three types of children, ages 4 and 5 years. Earlier in their lives (when they had been 12 and 18 months of age), they had been assessed by means of the Ainsworth criteria and divided into three groups: securely attached, anxious/avoidant, and anxious/resistant. The authors divided the children into twosomes and put each pair in a viewing room. Under these conditions, the avoidant children attempted regularly to tease and dominate whomever they were with. If paired with another avoidant child, however, one or the other might take the role of victim (whipping boy), or the two might exchange roles, so that at different moments a given one of the pair might be either whipping boy or victimizer. On the other hand, if an avoidant child were paired with a resistant child, the latter would seek out the victim role as avidly as the avoidant child would try to become the victimizer. The secure children, however, would lend themselves to neither role; faced with a peer who was trying to establish such a state of affairs (a victimizer/whipping boy relationship), the securely attached youngster would either defend himself or would withdraw. In short, for the predisposed children the sadomasochistic style was their natural way to relate.

The authors of this study noted that the children who displayed avoidant attachment came from abusive and rejecting backgrounds and were reenacting some version of the relationship patterns that had dominated their experience. Similarly, children in the resistant group were from unpredictable environments that were felt to contribute to their insecure relationship style.

Similar patterns have been seen clinically in the way children (predisposed by child rearing or constitutional factors) orient themselves toward the significant adults in their lives. Some of these youngsters become singularly provocative; they are adept at "pushing the button" on the concerned adults, so much so that the grown-ups presently stand in constant fear of losing control. It is among the greatest paradoxes of child rearing that the very efforts to set limits on the provocativeness of certain children become converted by these youngsters into a form of perverse satisfaction, and the parents end up feeling helpless and in danger of being overwhelmed by their own sadistic impulses.

The likelihood is that the tendency to turn against the self derives from at least some constitutional elements. As such predisposed children thread their way through the complexities of early toddlerhood, this inborn tendency may incline them toward masochistic deportment. They may become extraordinarily difficult management problems at home, live out their home life as a chronic running battle, and later, when brought to professional attention, earn such sobriquets as oppositional disorder or conduct disorder. It seems likely that such youngsters, during their subsequent development, may become the scapegoats in school, and years later, in their marriages, they will find partners who abuse or exploit them.

Sadism and masochism are basic to a number of important interpersonal configurations. In childhood, teasing and being teased are highly charged experiences that can strongly color children's interchanges with their peers (Brenman, 1954). In many marital interactions such behavioral patterns are an everyday presence, taking the disguised form of "ribbing," needling, or practical jokes, or coming through more directly as criticizing, nagging, berating, bullying, or beating. Many an unlikely relationship characteried by gross and continuing mistreatment of one spouse by the other stands firm because the sadistic impulses of the one partner match and satisfy the masochistic needs of the other. There is pleasure in this for each; rewards are available to both; and crazy though it may look to the outsider, the necessary rapport, built on need satisfaction, is there.

Albee's play *Who's Afraid of Virginia Woolf?* is a brilliant literary example of such a relationship. The epicenter of this intense drama is the ingeniously sadomasochistic interplay by a middle-aged couple who exhaust themselves in a repetitious pattern of mutual torment to ward off the even greater pain of loss.

Sadistic elements are pervasive throughout the culture. Torture scenes are featured on many magazine covers and are included in many movies because people are drawn to them; they sell. Television violence is a continuing problem. And among the commonest fantasies that children carry forward into later life are images of beating, whipping, or punishing someone (who may be the child himself).

The Narcissistic Component

A number of authors have written about the early emergence of the sense of self in this epoch (Lichtenberg, 1983; Stern, 1985). During this period several important strands of narcissistic development begin to spin out, including omnipotence, bodily self-love, and self-esteem. In particular, a sense of the child's own territory now comes forward to claim his attention. It is a time marked by the beginning use of the word *mine*. The self has a geography, a quality of extension in space that allows for things inside—mine, and for things outside—not mine. The perimeter of the self need not stop at the body outlines; it can extend far beyond. If the child likes something, he takes it into his territory and it becomes "mine." In terms of Mahler's theory, the youngster can carry forward into this era the remembered grandiosity of symbiosis and seek to join this to his growing wish to be the dominating force in his world. His territory spreads, and it embraces the caretakers—they too must obey him. And in some homes, in fact, they do; the parents fail to set limits, and the child's sense of power and entitlement persists far beyond the usual time frame. In most households, however, a more sensible response prevails, and the parents set limits to the child's dominion. The child gradually contains his grandiosity and diverts the pretensions to omnipotence from the forbidden to the permitted. The numerous small frustrations that the parents visit on the youngster in response to his demands, and the gradual pattern of limits and controls that they institute, serve to establish the child's appropriate territory.

Everyone, when growing up, must endure such vicissitudes. During their early years all children cling to pretensions of grandeur and, in time, must yield up grandiose images of self, give up on demandingness, give up the sense of entitlement, and bit by bit learn better. Reality experience provides painful lessons of punctured vanities; all children must embark on the lifelong task of containing (at least partially) their narcissism. Much of this work gets under way during early toddlerhood. It will take years to complete the task and to arrive at a mature level of realistic self-regard and self-confidence, but the beginnings are here.

If these lessons fail because the caretakers omit the necessary work of setting limits, of putting bounds to grandiose pretensions, of curbing the excessive yearnings and the prodigious demands that typify this phase, then the narcissistic position is reinforced, and children become little tyrants. A 2-year-old can be a peculiarly difficult person, and without limit setting and redirection of energies, unfortunate traits can become fixed parts of character and, in time, continuing sources of stress.

The overdemanding child is, after all, not a happy person; the very excesses to which he is habituated guarantee a state of morbid instability that will eventually cause both him and his caretaker(s) much pain. At the time, however, it is difficult for child and parent to perceive the outcome of their behavior; both are gratified by the child's pleasure in living out his larger-than-life scenarios, and neither can see anything wrong in letting the child have his way. As a result the child's growth is slowly but inevitably warped in a narcissistic direction.

Overgratification, however, is not the only cause of such a symptomatic stance. Narcissistic grandiosity can arise not merely from the fostering of certain self-aggrandizing potentialities but also from the child's defensive response to inordinate neediness and stress. Many children suffer emotional deprivation or encounter overwhelming traumata during their growing up. From birth they are rejected, neglected, handed from one grudging caretaker to another, and/or abused. One recourse open to them is to seize on and cling to a compensatory narcissistic position; they can thus defensively ward off the terrifying sense of helplessness and worthlessness by holding fast to whatever shreds of grandiose feeling they can retain. Presently they are asserting angrily that no one can tell them what to do, that they are in complete charge of their lives, and that they can take whatever they want when they want it. This attitude is characteristic of certain serious delinquents who come from very stressful backgrounds, and who act in this peculiarly arrogant way for fairly extended periods during their troubled careers.

In such instances, the grandiosity flares up initially during early childhood; it acts as a cushion against the intolerable reality of being tiny, helpless, vulnerable, and unloved; the assertions of grandeur buffer the inner certainty of inadequacy and emptiness, and the insistence on entitlement wards off the profound feeling of worthlessness and of having no lovability whatsoever. The healthy child has no need for such adaptations because he has a great, loving, gratifying other to help him past the stresses of growing up. Where this is lacking, the child invokes all sorts of compensatory devices; survival demands them.

Under certain particularly unfavorable conditions, the deprivation of neglect and the damage of abuse are accompanied by a lack of limits, whose effects may in turn be compounded by the caretakers' implicitly or explicitly encouraging the child to take whatever he wants. The child's bitter sense of grievance exacerbates the existing feelings of angry entitlement. In effect, both sources of narcissistic disturbance operate at once, and the ensuing syndromic forms are peculiarly difficult to cope with, either in daily living or in therapy.

A key factor here is the nature of narcissistic rage. To the extent that an injury is experienced as part of the child's narcissistic organization, the pain is likely to be particularly keen and of a special quality. It is the pain of "hurt feelings," wounded pride, public shaming, or humiliation. People often speak of this kind of pain as an unforgivable insult, a slur on their honor that they will remember forever. This emotional stance generates enormous rage, a sort of unrelenting and continuing pressure for vengeance and retaliation, which can have fateful consequences. This kind of injury to a family's honor or good name provides the breeding ground for feuds and vendettas that may endure for generations. As a rule, the only anodyne is revenge, the feeling of having paid back in kind. Children can be extremely sensitive to such slights and injuries from an early age, and they can be all too active in inflicting such injuries. Teasing is a classic means that children employ to find the narcissistically vulnerable spots in one another's psychic armor. They seek to generate as much pain as possible by wounding their victim where it hurts the most. Coupled with a pernicious identification with the aggressor, such pain and the associated rage that it engenders exert a powerful shaping impact of personality development (Kohut, 1972).

THE EGO

The anal phase is truly an extraordinary time for elaborating ego mechanisms. The child starts this epoch by weaning, walking, saying his first words, and moving toward a new level of thought. The transformation from supine infant to crawling, walking toddler is dramatic and exhilarating; among other things, it feeds the child's normal grandiosity.

Many important character traits now come sharply into focus. These are amalgams of the earlier temperamental tendencies plus the new emergents that development brings with it. Thus, one child is cautious, reluctant to try anything new, hesitant to explore, and careful to avoid anything risky. Another is headstrong, impulsive, always on the go, always pushing. Here a child is stubborn, willful, resistant; there is one who seems relatively content, tends to cling, and does not oppose in nearly so active a way. All of them will be touched to varying degrees by the typical toddler negativism, power struggle, and search for autonomy, but the blend will be different in each case, and the intensity of these themes will vary widely.

The Mastery of Impulse

This is a critical moment for major advances in the regulation of impulse, because this is a time when an impulse is far likelier to trigger action than to beget thought. Youngsters at this age probably engage in very little fantasy; they are inherently action-oriented, and much more inclined to respond to a wish by doing than by daydreaming. Indeed, the matter of impulse control becomes one of the major issues in their rearing. All of this makes for significant difficulties in their management. They are quick and into everything, and parents must be very alert to keep them out of trouble. They are prone to break things, to swallow things, to wander off, to have accidents, and, in general, to do the forbidden. These factors are some of what makes this time the "terrible twos." In response to this set of determinants, many parents simply shift whatever is movable or breakable up onto some high shelves in the hope of keeping these young marauders out of the more likely kinds of trouble. Even a transient lapse of watchfulness can mean a hot pot pulled over, a cut on broken glass, or a nasty fall. A high-energy level, the age-determined need to be oppositional, a primary pleasure in movement, and an insufficiently developed sense of caution can make for considerable vulnerability. As noted, the 2-year-old is a creature very much given to rapid and intense expression of drives. The inhibition of yearnings is not his long suit, and it is a signal moment in the child's growth as a civil being when a capacity to delay and a readiness to control first make themselves evident. To some extent, the forerunners of these attainments begin to manifest themselves very early in life. For example, the nursling may look into his mother's eyes when taken away from the breast and thus hold back, however briefly, from crying. But it is not until the 2nd year of life that a word, a look, indeed, the mere presence of a caretaker can instill a sense of limit. The child learns which activities and objects are "no-no's." He hears that injunction, the doggerel of containment, over and over again, many times a day. But it is not just a matter of what the toddler hears. The wise parent knows that albeit the appropriate words are essential, in reality the toddler often needs the active presence of an adult and the physical removal or redirection of his body. Toddlers need the act of control along with the words of control; the lessons may have to be repeated endlessly, until finally the act is no longer required and the word is enough. At this point, the child becomes habituated to a firm statement as a sufficient intervention and has taken a great step forward.

Thus, words alone are often not the answer; when they are not, their useless repetition can do more harm than good. Indeed, the continuous repetition of unenforced injunctions that the youngster blithely disregards is a mordant eroder of the control apparatuses. It eats away their strength and steals from them all their pith and substance. In time, the controls languish, grow flaccid, and wither; and when the child then tries to cope with the still greater surges of rivalrous rage and oedipal yearning in the subsequent years, they are of little use.

The tuned-in parent knows that the need to set limits is as vital to the child's integrity as the supplying of vitamins; no one can grow straight without these things. The parental intervention, the necessary limit, the protection from self-impulses, the training in elementary restraint—all these must be sedulously provided. But in themselves these controls are still only part of what is necessary. For there is another essential dimension of limit setting that caretakers must also offer, and that is the supplying of alternatives. This encourages the child to develop sublimatory possibilities. If parents limit an impulse, the child may withhold it from the forbidden time and place but then proceed to express it elsewhere. If, however, the parents provide some object he can handle instead of one he cannot, some toy he can pull or hammer on instead of the fragile household item he has found, or some surface he can crayon or smear instead of the forbidden wall, then the alternative or the replacement serves to train and redirect impulse from troublesome outlets to acceptable ones. It does not forbid aggression; it merely civilizes it. This is an essential feature of early toddlerhood, and teaching children the use of substitute gratifications and alternative paths toward discharge renders them an extraordinarily valuable service.

The language of limitation or, more precisely, language as part of limit setting deserves special attention. The role of words as organizers of the control apparatus is crucial. A child must learn to identify feelings and yearnings and to ask for what he wants. He needs experience in receiving permission or refusal, and he must learn to cope with both. When he is refused something, he is entitled both to an explanation and to an alternative. As noted, in the beginning, mixed patterns of words and action are the rule. The child is held, his hand is blocked, or he is picked up bodily and transported elsewhere. Meanwhile, the verbal limit setting goes on: "No no, you may not do so and so, not now, not here; you may instead do something else, not with another's possession, only with your own possession."

Where things go well, gradually the words alone come to have force, the need for holding the child diminishes or arises only sporadically, and a new level of regulation slowly becomes established. Evidence of the toddler's beginning internalization of parental controls may be seen in his play when he scolds a doll or spanks a stuffed animal. (Many a parent will admit with embarrassment how accurately the toddler has caught a chiding note or cutting edge in the parent's tone or gesture.) Occasionally a late toddler will stare at some tempting but forbidden object, hesitating and even repeating half-aloud to himself a previously voiced admonition ("We look but we don't touch").

In addition, the use of punishment has an appropriate place in the training of children. There are youngsters who are particularly exigent and insistent on having their way, and some pattern of aversive stimuli may be necessary. The behavioral psychologists who have studied this area suggest such interventions as sitting the child in a chair facing a corner for a brief interval (for 2 minutes at 2 years; 3 minutes at 3 years, etc.) as a limit-setting act. According to their research some element of punishment is a necessary aspect of child rearing; as with other measures of intervention the goal is to avoid both too little and too much (Forehand & McMahon, 1981).

The story of children who get too much punishment is a cultural tragedy. Aside from the overt instances of the more flagrant kinds of abuse, a host of children are reared in essentially punitive environments. For example, many children are raised under circumstances where they receive violent behavioral cues with little verbal backup. Thus, the parent might regularly curse at a child, strike him, or push him roughly away from the forbidden item. This then becomes the paradigm of all regulation. Such a form of intervention might indeed inhibit undesired behaviors but eventually is likely to have an unhappy outcome. Because the child is repeatedly flooded by anxiety, his response will tend to be more total and more primitive; as he grows, he may become fearful, inarticulate, and inhibited, so that generalized massive constriction ensues. Or he can take the opposite tack, follow the model thus offered him, and become a violent person in his turn. Under stress, he will then feel pressed to do to others what has been done to him. Such controls as he develops will be fragile and brittle. The tightly contained impulses will all too readily be externalized, and because he has known physical violence he will tend to act out physically and violently.

Here, too, identification with the parent is a powerful force; only in this case it is the angry and aggressive as well as the prohibiting aspects of the parent that serve as the model.

The Parent as External Control.   At this toddler level of development the key factor in impulse control is the presence of the parent. This in itself acts as a great modulator of eruptiveness and miscreance; in effect, the child is good as long as the policeman is about. Indeed, as long as the smell of authority is in the air, the child can be at rest; there is no question of misbehavior. It is here that the child begins to make the great transition from power to authority, the necessary step that ultimately keeps any civilization in order. It is one thing for the child always to be calculating the contest of strengths and to do whatever he can get away with whenever he feels an impulse. It comes down to a simple matter of brute confrontation: If the child is stronger or can run faster than those who would stop him or apprehend him, then he commits the misdemeanor in broad daylight and fights or runs. Why not? It is quite another thing to accept the presence of the adult as a symbolic forbidding of any violation; when the authority is there, the child behaves. Then the child has gone beyond the immediacy of mere contest and accepted the necessary meaning that underlies all real social control: the sense of authority. It is not so much a question of the policeman's power; it is the aura of his presence that counts. It is awe rather than fear that keeps people in a state of social compliance. Lacking that, there are always more people than there are police, and more opportunities than can be policed. Crime is most rampant in those urban areas where all sense of legal or community authority has broken down and only the contest of power remains.

During this time the child must move away from needing literally to be held or physically removed from temptation or punished for nis insistence on doing the forbidden; he must advance to containing his own impulses at the mere sight or presence of the caretaker. This is the beginning—the passage from responding to the primary power of the caretaker to the attribution of an aura of authority. The power is there, concretely; it resides in the mother's size, muscles, voice, and energy. The authority is the child's own creation, which he lends the mother; in effect, it is a sort of myth the youngster creates about her response that he then uses to help himself do as he is supposed to. (Later on teenagers will say of their quite gentle parents, "My parents would kill me if I did that!")

The role of the father begins to emerge here in rather special form. Within the traditional two-parent family (when both parents are figures in the home), the father is usually less of an immediate presence for the child(ren) than is the mother. Even when he is home, typically the mother provides primary child care. Father is thus somewhat remote and mythical. This is probably less true in today's younger families than it has been in the past; cultural values have shifted, and young fathers are encouraged to participate more in child rearing than was formerly the case. Nonetheless, even under those circumstances the likelihood is that the input of the two parents is qualitatively different, and that in subtle ways the father's remoteness and the mother's intimacy are still material influences on child development.

Traditionally, this two-tier structure made for a hierarchy of control, an authority behind the immediate front line of interaction, a sense of a more abstract paternal presence whose power was greater than the usual maternal authority. It is reflected in the partially jocose line, "Wait till your father gets home!" Father offers the more massive physical presence, but underlying this is the concept of ultimate justice, unforgiving principle, the final source of rewards and punishments. This emerging view of the father leads a child toward a sense of authority in the external world that paves the way for much of the construction of social conscience and self-regulation that lies ahead. For the younger toddler, authority is still external, still a particular person who must be present. However, a transmutation is already under way; the early steps toward idealizing that person presage new things to come. It is surely basic to all the learning that must be done at this time around impulse control.

Currently, something on the order of half of American families are single-parent households. This does not mean that no other parenting person is available; for example, in a divorced family where the children live with one parent, the other may well continue to be an important participant in their rearing, or a grandparent who does not reside in the home may nonetheless play an active part in the lives of the children. In fact, there are many variables of unknown importance. The child of a working mother may spend most of his day within the framework of some kind of day care or baby-sitting arrangement; the mother herself may then serve as the more remote and abstract presence who is the final authority behind the immediate hands-on management of the day care staff. The impact of the single-parent style of child rearing is still a matter of great uncertainty that requires further research (Adams et al., 1984).

Shame. A particularly critical and sensitive mode of social regulation involves the dimension of *shame*. This is peculiarly a part of anal-stage psychology and exemplifies, to some extent, the nature of both regulation and control at this time of life.

What is shame? What would be a synonym for it? A common association is *guilt*, but in fact, that is quite a different idea, with a different history and a very different function. A closer synonym would be embarrassment. What do people feel at a moment of intense embarrassment? The usual experience is to wish to be out of sight. People who have been through it describe it in such terms as these: I wished that I could have sunk through the floor; I wished that I could have shrunk down so that I was tiny; I wished that I was a million miles away; I wished that I could have become suddenly invisible!

The general thrust of their feelings is the key wish not to be seen. The great threat consists of the eyes of the significant other(s). The profound sense of humiliation arises from having been observed in a compromising way or of having been seen participating in dubious behavior. It is of the essence here that the behavior itself is not in question; there is often no discomfort at all with that, and indeed it may even be highly rewarding in a variety of ways. The problem is simply to have been seen doing it.

Perhaps the most meaningful example of just that sort of experience is the emotional flare that ignites when an individual is sitting on the toilet and someone unfamiliar, in particular someone of the opposite gender, opens the door by mistake. Their eyes meet, and each is shocked, but especially the person using the toilet at the time. As a rule, there is a quick "Excuse me," and the intruder immediately closes the door. If the individuals should happen to meet presently, most likely they will never again mention this incident. Nonetheless, this is by no means a trivial experience; it is excruciatingly humiliating. As a rule there is a brief surge of emotion, and then the "observed" quickly talks him- or herself down: "What difference does it make, nothing could really be seen, it is perfectly natural, everybody goes to the toilet, so what!" All true, and all helpful at the time, but the point is that for a moment this was a shaken person who had experienced powerful stress. The individual had been seen, not in doing something about which he or she felt guilty, not in the commission of a misdeed, but in doing something that is not supposed to be observed. (The one who opened the door is often equally disturbed at having seen something that is not supposed to be seen.) The key, again, is the seeing.

That sort of reaction (to being seen in a way that begets humiliation) is particularly important for doctors to be aware of. For example, a doctor has a patient in for an examination. They meet in the doctor's office, the doctor inquires about the reasons for the visit, and takes an appropriate history. Next, the doctor ushers the patient into the examining room, telling the patient to please undress and sit up on the examining table in preparation for the examination. With that the physician leaves for a few minutes. Presently, the doctor comes back, taps on the door, and opens it. While the door is still ajar, a nurse happens by and says: "Oh doctor, those lab reports you were waiting for just came in," and proceeds to show the doctor the report. They confer briefly, people pass in the corridor, and it takes half a minute until the doctor finally enters the room, closes the door, and proceeds with the exam. Meanwhile, the patient has been sitting there, naked, helpless, and exposed, dying a thousand deaths, and perhaps too embarrassed even to ask for the door to be closed.

That night when the patient goes home, it is not the good examination, the thorough study, and the thoughtful treatment program he or she is likely to recall; it is instead that awful moment of humiliation.

In a more subtle way, this sort of thing happens in other contexts, for example, a night club where a stand-up comic is doing his act. As he is going through his patter, someone in the audience gets up and heads for the back of the room. At once the comic starts to clap his hands and chant, "We know where you're going, we know where you're going," and waves to the audience to join in the chant. The person who is leaving is momentarily covered with confusion; somehow he or she has been caught at something. It is embarrassing.

The situation suggests the question: "So what if people know where someone is going, why is that anything to be remarked on?" In this case the answer turns out to be rather complex. It has to do with the fact that instinctual drives tend to be expressed in the form of fantasies. Every time men and women approach the gratification of each of the major instincts, they create an image of themselves (or of others) actually engaging in whatever action is necessary to satisfy the instinct. If, prior to dinner being served, they glimpse the food, or even the set table, they have a brief picture of themselves actually eating. If they approach a sexual encounter, numerous erotic fantasies come to mind. And elimination is no exception to the rule; a person moving in the direction of that activity thinks momentarily of being engaged in that process.

So when the stand-up comic says, "We know where you're going," he is evoking in the minds of all those present the image of that person eliminating; in effect, he has opened the bathroom door on the other, and the victim is covered with the predictable embarrassment.

Shame is a powerful presence in people's lives. Entire cultures are regulated primarily by shaming. The notion of exposure to society's gaze can be devastating; sometimes a person may resort to suicide rather than face this pain. Indeed, in some cultures, ritual suicide is prescribed as the only means of undoing the possibility of shame. In American tradition, Nathaniel Hawthorne's novel *The Scarlet Letter* tells the story of Hester Prynne, who had to wear the letter *A* (for adultress) sewn onto her garments over her heart. As a central feature of her punishment, each day, for a certain time, she had to stand in the pillory, the place of public punishment, and expose herself to the scorn and derision of the populace. Pillories have disappeared, but gossip columnists (and, for that matter, straight news stories) serve very much the same function today. Ultimately, what *is* shameful is essentially an expression of culture. For example, in some societies public defecation is quite acceptable, but public eating is not. All in all, shame seems to be a powerful instrument for molding social norms and maintaining social values.

Shame is the ultimate regulation from without. It reflects the experience of the small child who is engaged in some form of miscreance, such as tearing pages from a book or dismembering a sibling's doll, and who then looks up to meet the critical parent's disapproving gaze. As their eyes lock, a great stab of emotion lances through the child, compounded at once of a fear of loss of the parent's love along with a less clearly formulated terror of potential destruction, total crushing obliteration. This kind of reaction establishes the pathway for shaming as control.

In their personal ethical development many individuals never advance further than this point (Kohlberg, 1969). In circumstances where they think that they can be observed, they behave as well as they should. Where they think that they can get away with something, they do so—to the extent that they have a natural bent to take a chance. Where other elements of personality make-up incline them to take many chances, as with counterphobic teenagers, then the way is open for delinquent behavior. Many delinquents are, in fact, unreconstructed 2-year-olds with many impulses, few inner constraints, and controls only from without.

Self-Regulation and Attachment. A major aspect of self-regulation is organized around the child's sense of attachment. During these months, the need for parents' love and availability is an omnipresent and powerful yearning, and understandably so. In the time when our species was young—and today as well for that matter—such parental involvement was, and is, basic to survival. Given the many stresses and frustrations that arise during child rearing, it would be natural for all children to be battered were it not for the emergence of an intervening factor during the phylogenetic advance of our species that has tended to protect the small, helpless, and yet troublesome and provocative young. And that something is the affection our species feels for its cubs. The infant is aware of this and, where elements of uncertainty have been introduced, seeks for reassurance that the affection is still there. During this toddler phase in particular, the less secure youngster tests parental affection to the limit. The child challenges it, denies it, contradicts it, sets himself against it, seeks to undo it in every way possible, and watches attentively to measure the results of his depredations. "Will Mother still love me if I do this? Will Father destroy me if I disobey? Will they abandon me if I assert myself against them?" Where the fit has been problematic and the relationship stressed, a host of such tests and trials and challenges to parental affection occur during this epoch. In a sense, the child never ceases to work on these issues; the need is urgent, the youngster must know that he is loved, despite everything.

Inevitably, and necessarily, he learns the limits. He discovers the point at which parental affection is replaced by parental rage, parental poise by parental outburst, parental attention by parental rejection. In this murky land of conflicting motives and feelings much of the labor of child rearing and much structuring of the child's character takes place. Clearly, the parent whose affection is resilient and whose own self-esteem and impulse-control are stable has a decided advantage in coping with a miscreant 2-year-old, but these are not conditions that the adult can juggle at will. These parental states of mind are themselves the residue of a lifetime of growth, experience, and interaction; in particular, they tell the story of the parents' own early years. The parent raises a child with what he or she was offered as a child; the parent's own past and his or her own parents are the ghosts that haunt the nursery (Fraiberg et al., 1975). Such ghosts are not readily banished. The best the person can do is strive against them with the knowledge and the understanding offered by subsequent life experience.

The Power Struggle and Object Relations

Early toddlerhood involves a power struggle that the child defines for his parents and that the parents, in turn, formulate for the child. The key issue for the baby is the emerging sense of autonomy, the progressive consolidation of a sense of self. It is a portentous event, a genuine birth process that follows the original biological emergence by many months. It is a time of great change, great challenge, and great hazards. As described in the previous chapter, Mahler designated the original step away from symbiosis during the second half of the first year as *hatching*. Within her theoretical framework it is the beginning differentiation of a separate self, the opening experiment in pulling free, a first breaking out of a presumed merged and satisfying state of unity. It is a true venture into the unknown. It is in this state of mind that the child confronts the issues of separation.

The Power Struggle. An aggressive component appears at the same time as the immediate, pleasurable erotic dimension of anality. It is a complex presence and takes a variety of forms, but in its simplest outlines it comes down to a desire for total domination. In a way it is easy to understand.

By 18 months or so the child has come through a tremendously varied set of psychological experiences. (These will be characterized differently depending on the theoretical position assumed; in any case they are of considerable import.) From Mahler's view (one currently adhered to by many clinicians), early on the child experienced a symbiotic phase, with an accompanying sense of fusion with the highly valued caretaker; associated with this experience was an extraordinary sense of grandiosity. Then came the separation from mother, the hatching, the beginning emergence of the sense of self as an autonomous individual. As a result, the child must presently face the reality of being a small, vulnerable, helpless being in a world where the important people are so much bigger. This flies in the face of the newly emerging feelings of autonomy and self-direction. With this realization, the child becomes torn; he wants to be close and dependent as before, and at the same time, he wants to assert his difference and his newfound mastery. Once the child felt great and powerful because he was so closely attached to the powerful one; now he feels separate from her but must confront the problem: How can he get his wishes fulfilled? How to get the caretaker to act as he, the baby, wishes? In his immature way the child feels at moments that he does not want to be controlled, he wants to control; he will not be dominated, he will dominate. With this, he seeks to regain the sense of power and superiority that once he knew. When such feelings mount, he begins to try to bring the significant others in his world to submit to his will. He would control them; he would make them behave as he desires; he would dominate them utterly. And if they do not comply, he will force them to do his bidding and compel them to act as he wishes. It is important to recognize that this is a figurative account; the child does not yet have the verbal maturity to formulate things in this way. These yearnings are most likely experienced in primitive image symbols or in some other nonverbal fashion. Nonetheless, within the Mahlerian framework, this is the gist of the child's thoughts.

This extraordinary state of mind instigates some equally remarkable behavioral patterns. For many 2-year-olds, negativism, intense demandingness, refusal to comply with routines, defiance of limits, and eruptive tantrums are common elements of behavior. More severe reactions appear occasionally and include prolonged screaming episodes, running away, refusal to eat, refusal to accept toilet training, cruelty to pets, destructiveness, and other disturbing behaviors. In these extreme cases the caretaker comes to feel tormented and may become intensely provoked because everything is so negative; everything is a battle.

The youngster's inner drive is straightforward: "I will fight you until you give in. I will dominate you by hurting, needling, and upsetting you so that you can't resist any more and will yield to my demands. I will cause you so much pain that you can't stand it any longer, and so I will win!"

In brief, the child has come to a developmental crisis in the balance between his efforts at self-assertion and his fear of the loss of attachment. Mahler and colleagues (1975) called it the *rapprochement crisis;* it is a normal developmental outgrowth of the child's ever-increasing competence and mastery plus his age-appropriate yearnings for dominance and control; the toddler really can do many things for himself, and he has surges of grandiosity that lead him to moments of tempestuous and imperious assertiveness. But he is withal, still small and relatively weak; he cannot fend for himself in the world, and he knows this. Indeed, with the advances in his cognition and understanding, he knows it better than ever before. The child is at once terrified of losing the presence and the affectionate care of his parents and of losing a sense of control over their comings and goings. Once he has really differentiated himself from the feeling of fusion and *primary attachment,* then it seems to the baby that the only safe state of being is to have the parents right there, under his control. Otherwise, if they leave for a moment, how can he be sure they will return? The baby has now matured enough to begin to entertain the idea that they might just go away and stay away.

For the most part, children who are not inherently vulnerable and who have had a reasonably secure 1st year of life, with the consequent achievement of an adequate level of basic trust (Erikson, 1950), are not overmuch preoccupied with such concerns. They worry at the time of the parents' actual leave taking, but their capacities for self-consolation are good, and these, plus the presence of a familiar supportive adult along with attractive distractions, offer sturdy reassurance, and the children settle down quickly. Should there be a real separation for any reason—should the mother or the father leave home, fall ill, or simply withdraw from the child—then the youngster is likely to suffer greatly and to show ill effects for a long time thereafter. Such an unforeseen separation can constitute a genuine traumatic event and play a meaningful role in later symptom-expression and/or character formation. Thus, later patterns of chronic rage or chronic depression can have their inception at such a point in development.

The way the child copes with separation is a two-sided problem. A great deal depends on the mother and on her management of these separation needs. She can act to facilitate the child's efforts to achieve a measure of autonomy, or she can move to block these strivings. Excesses are possible in both directions. The healthy orientation would be for the mother to allow the child to try new things, to wander off a little and to explore, to experiment with his world and attempt to make discoveries while at the same time keeping an eye on him to protect him from handling what is dangerous or from getting too far away. An anxious mother, however, tormented by her own separation fears, will not allow the child to leave her side or explore on his own. Implicitly, and often enough explicitly, her message will be: "If you separate from me, you will die."

In contrast to this, the narcissistic mother will be largely blind to the child's needs because her own needs are so obtrusive; she will require the child to function as her adorer, instrument, extension, and ornament. She might, for example, push the child to achieve far beyond what is natural or comfortable for him so that she can display his accomplishments. The child is merely her means of achieving her goal of self-aggrandizement. In any case, she will give scant support to the child's own wish for some realm of independent functioning. The encouragement he does receive to function as a separate individual will arise only because many times the mother is too busy with her own concerns or, more likely still (and ultimately of more destructive character), the mother is the one who needs the care or admiration, and it is the baby's responsibility to do whatever is necessary to keep his mother happy.

On the other hand, the other kind of excess is also common: rejecting the child or prematurely thrusting on him all manner of unrealistic expectations. "Go away, I can't stand you; you're just like your [divorced] father." "If you don't like what I'm serving you, then don't eat anything." "I'm too tired tonight, you're old enough already, go to the refrigerator and make your own dinner."

Negativism and Boundaries. A child can control his body and destiny with a number of techniques; to some extent, all children utilize all of these methods. One of the best boundary definers is surely negativism. This is an extraordinarily effective tactic and is almost a universal presence at some time during the early toddler phase.

The toddler is aware of his mother's wishes, and generally speaking, he wants to go along with them. At the same time each act of compliance also confirms the child's attachment and dependency, or, within the framework of Mahler's theory, his oneness with the mother. From this standpoint, when the child agrees, submits, or obeys, he feels as though he is, in fact, assenting in the reality of fusion, of belonging to mother. By complying, he accepts being merged with her again. The toddler's struggles to find and define his own boundaries clearly dominate this developmental moment. To distinguish himself as his own person, the child must define a difference, indicate a boundary, draw a line. The easiest way to assert nondependence is to be noncompliant, to do the opposite of what someone else expects. Hence, whatever the mother may ask of the child, he says: "No!" In negativism there is a declaration of selfhood, which is what the child seeks with his defiance. It is the easiest way for the child to declare his separateness and assert a modicum of independence.

When the toddler defies his mother, he trumpets his autonomy; such automatic opposition is efficient. The negative response builds a kind of identity—it says at least what the child is *not,* and this allows a sense of feeling that he is no longer merely a part of something, but is now distinct from that something. Perhaps there is as yet no fully defined self, but at least the baby is not merely an extension of his mother.

Such a position is a great step forward. Once the child discovers his own initiative, he begins to treasure this ability; it is heady stuff, and the youngster may revel in it. For a time the child may seek out all the forbidden areas and actively pursue each of them. As noted earlier, this is a time when accidents occur, when poisonous ingestions take place, and when the ubiquitous negativism may incite vulnerable parents to batter their uncooperative children. The negativism can be very pervasive; sometimes it becomes almost routinized and automatic. The mother asks, "Do you want a piece of cake?" and the child answers, "No," even as he extends his hand for the cake. In effect, the child is trying to construct a boundary around an area that does not belong to others and that he will presently experience as his "self." This effort is of signal moment for later development and will, in some measure, concern him for the rest of his life, because the experience and the preservation of boundaries are vital to subsequent mental health. The possible invasion or penetration of the child's boundaries will become a new hazard and a source of stress that will henceforth require protection and defense. By the same token, the loss of boundaries, with a slipping back into fusion, will be among the more threatening experiences in later life.

Progression and Regression. The child's development, however, is not a straightforward progression toward greater autonomy. It is not as easy as all that because two processes proceed at once that are intimately related to one another. On the one hand is the newly minted concern with differentiation and the hard labor of drawing distinctions and achieving distance; on the other hand is the toddler's natural regressive tendency to slip back into a state of infantile dependency. Within Mahler's framework, this regression is into the marsupial pouch of fusion, the return to symbiosis. The infant does not depart so gratifying a wholeness easily; the desire for dependence, passivity, protection, nurturance, and resignation may influence the attitudes of a lifetime. It is possible that genetic factors determine the balance between these two inclinations and load one child toward autonomy and another toward passive dependency. If such genetic influences exist, their character is unknown (although their effects are perhaps discernible in such terms as the balance of activity vs. passivity, externalizing tendencies vs. internalizing, shyness vs. assertiveness, confident exploration vs. anxious inhibition). It may well be that one child clings where another explores or that one is compliant where another is assertive because such inherited givens underlie the form and expression of these attributes (see, e.g., Marks, 1987, on the genetics of fearfulness). As is always true, the environment will foster or inhibit the expression of latent tendencies, and the child's behavior will emerge as the resultant of these internal and external vectors.

The Transitional Object

Much of the current knowledge regarding this transitional period of life is associated with the work of Donald Winnicott, who lived from 1896 to 1971. An extraordinary British pediatrician turned child therapist and theorist, Winnicott was intrigued by the problem of how the child came to be his own person. How did someone become an autonomous human being while still retaining the capacity for intimacy? At times, Winnicott posed this question paradoxically: How does the infant develop a "capacity to be alone" in the mother's presence? For Winnicott, this was a hard-won developmental accomplishment. In a classic paper, Winnicott noted that somewhere toward the end of the first year of life and the beginning of the second, many children become attached to an object that they carry around with them wherever they go (Winnicott, 1953). In particular, they seem to need it when they go to bed at night. This object is often a blanket, but it can also be a stuffed toy, a pillow, a diaper, a bottle, or indeed almost anything to which the child takes a fancy. Whatever its form, it characteristically has a very special meaning for the particular child, and its presence appears to be necessary to avoid anxiety, tears, and apprehension. American readers typically associate the image of the cartoon character Linus with the blanket-carrying child. The anxiety that Linus suffers when his blanket is in the washing machine captures something of the emotional import of the object.

When Winnicott's study first appeared, professionals widely recognized its general validity. Subsequently, numerous papers were published extending the idea of a transitional object into the realm of separation theory, object-relations theory, borderline psychopathology, and creativity. From the perspective of theories that postulated an early subjective state of merger between infant and mother, the transitional object was seen as the child's replacement for the symbiotic mother. From this theoretical view, the infant going through the phase of differentition was, in fact, defining his boundaries, setting himself up as a separate individual, and distinguishing himself definitively from the great, affectively charged mass of mother. Evidently this is not an easy step to take. It involves coming out from under the eaves of the sheltering, protecting other into the uncertain climate of nature in the raw. One way to ease the transition was for the infant to resort to a compensatory device—the newly available capacity to symbolize—and to attribute to the chosen object something of the mother's qualities. In effect, the object became a talisman, magically imbued with the essential power of the baby's ur-mother of yore. So long as the child kept his mother's symbol close by, he was not altogether alone and exposed to the world. The talisman provided the sense of shelter, attachment, and the feeling of the mother's presence; the baby thus could keep loneliness and anxiety at bay. In effect, most youngsters could not merely renounce the sense of being a babe in arms, more or less continually connected to the mother. Although physically they were walking now and climbing, psychologically, they still had to wean themselves away. This they could do only in a gradual, stepwise fashion.

The transitional object provided a marvelous stepping-stone; it created the essence of an object attachment out of a piece of cloth. Through projection, displacement, condensation, and symbolization, the physical substance of the object became imbued with companionable and reassuring affects. Herein lay the link to creativity, here the sense of attachment was reasserted, and here the work of separation and differentiation could be further pursued. Thus students of these areas saw in the transitional attachments a mid-stage in the several processes of separation–individuation.

In Winnicott's view, the transitional object was more than a simple substitute attachment object (although it served that function as well). Instead, he emphasized that in a crucial sense this object was the baby's creation. The parents might provide the actual toy or blanket or diaper, but only the baby himself could imbue it with its magical qualities of being both mother and not-mother. The object thus retained, in part, the mother's powers of comfort and security, yet, unlike the mother and most important to the infant, it was under *baby's* control.

Looked at from a somewhat different angle, to the extent that a child carried about a transitional object, the youngster had not yet completed his work of delineating clear boundaries between himself and the important other (Rolphe, 1979). Such a toddler was partially separated and partially attached. He had not yet fully distinguished inside from outside; he had gone some of the distance, but the journey had not yet ended. The child was a person in transiton. It would still take months of such separation work for the child to conclude the process successfully and define and toughen his outlines so that they would need neither negativism nor transitional assists to keep them intact.

Some investigators also regarded this transitional position as a site for potential pathological fixation. Such theorists (e.g. Masterson, 1972; Rinsely, 1980) considered certain borderline personalities to be arrested in their development at this point. These theorists then ascribed the psychopathology of these patients to the psychological characteristics of the epoch and described the pathology within that framework, that is, the patients' patterns of angry, anxious attachment to the important people in their lives were thought to have much in common with the emotions displayed by the toddler in his relationship with his object (Modell, 1963, quoted in Gunderson, 1984). Frijling-Schreuder (1969) described such patients as feeling like toddlers whose mothers are permanently out of the room.

Such a diagnosis can be made in childhood. There are borderline youngsters who seem arrested in their interpersonal development at a stage betwixt and between self and other, where inner musing overlaps with outer perception (see Volume 2, Chapter 5). For such a child, things blur and almost lose outline; their own identity appears to waver and to want to blend in with that of significant others, ego boundaries seem about to give way, gender is confounded, and there are moments when fantasy gets confused with reality. This symptomatic picture prompted the suggestion that perhaps these characteristics represent the echo of a developmental epoch where just such a state of affairs prevailed. According to this hypothesis, should the genetic and environmental circumstances of the child's life cause fixation at this level, then the borderline syndrome would appear.

The many careful studies with adults now suggest, however, that the borderline state does not relate back easily to any single level of ego or libidinal fixation. The various findings these patients display derive from a much wider spread of possible sites of trauma, overindulgence, or arrest, and no neat formulation as to epoch of origin will fit the clinical pictures that emerge (Gunderson, 1984).

Walking Erect—The Practicing Phase

In addition to the concerns with boundaries and negativism, there are other dimensions to the strivings for autonomy. One of the most obvious is the achievement of body mastery involving such functions as gait, movement, and eliminative self-regulation.

Probably one great initial surge toward the sense of self as an independent entity derives from the assumption of an erect posture. The practicing phase with its joy in locomotion is characterized by the stimulation and the excitement of going at the world from the new position. Indeed, in a sense, it is the vertical posture and upright locomotion that create the conditions for the emergence of boundary concerns—the child's perimeter is after all in some measure a function of his posture.

The anal-stage child's exploration by climbing, handling, destroying, and "getting into things" serves to fulfill many needs. Among them is the child's search for the limits to his reach, strength, and capacity to do. Ultimately, these become woven into the child's sense of outline, the outer reaches of the self. They become part of the image the child is gradually composing of his own who-ness, a deeply felt experience of self-identity. Along with these the accompanying delimiter of identity sets forth the boundaries of who the child is *not* with special clarity and pungency. Part of this is achieved by the experience of limits, and the child who receives clear and unambiguous messages about his limits is in an infinitely better position to demarcate himself from his world than is his age-mate who receives no such supports and who, all too often, can arrive at no such resolution.

A lack of limits, a vagueness of outline at this time of life, can initiate a host of ills. Grandiosity or low self-esteem—or both—can follow where the caretakers never state forthrightly what the child cannot do (because the parents do not care, because the babysitters fear to upset the child, or because the adoring caretaker cannot bear to frustrate baby or to tolerate his protests). Any hint of wavering in the border between the self and the outside world can weaken reality testing. Where the caretakers do not help with limit setting, the fantasy of what the child wishes to do and the real boundaries to what the child, in fact, can do remain forever soft and changeable—and so he never achieves the definitive clarity that draws a sharp line between these two modes of perception/cognition.

Separation

These conflicting tendencies find their most overt expression around the issue of separation. Again and again, in a variety of contexts, the management of separation issues arises as a critical site for the child's attempts at mastery and for parental intervention. As already noted, some of the most cogent research in the field has been structured around the creation of brief separations of standardized form and duration. In addition, however, a host of natural events illustrate all too clearly the powerful meaning of separation in the lives of both child and family.

Babysitters.   Somewhere in the 2nd year of life it is not unusual for a toddler who heretofore did well with his baby-sitter to develop acute distress every time the parents seek to leave. Prior to this point, the child might have seemed quite content with the pattern of his care. Then, usually between 16 and 20 months, when the baby-sitter arrives and the parents make ready to go out, the child sets up a storm of protest. Although his words may be few, his message comes across with exquisite clarity: "Don't go, I don't want you to go. Stay here!" The wails go on and on, over and over again, with weeping, clinging, and every evidence of distress. The astonished and dismayed parents try to comfort the weepy toddler but to no avail. Eventually they depart with his cries dinning in their ears. Later they call back anxiously only to find out that after they had departed, the child had settled down immediately to a pleasant evening. Nonetheless, next time around the same thing happens: a major display of anxiety and protest at the moment of separation.

Bedtime.   A similar pattern of bedtime behavior is characteristic of many 2-year-olds: a complex sequence of resistances to falling asleep. The parent prepares the child for bed, they go through bath, pajamas, storytelling, and tucking in, and now the moment has come for the parent to depart. At this point the requests begin (again not quite in these words but with some such message): "Tell me another story, I'm thirsty, I want my Teddy, the curtain is too high, now it's too low, the closet door should be open, there's something under the bed, I want my shoes by the bed, where's my toy soldier—put it on the dresser—no, right in the middle," and so on. Even where the child's level of speech development limits him to two-word sentences, this routine can go on for a long time.

Obviously the child is inventing pretexts to keep the parent in thrall, to cling to the parent's presence, to maintain the attachment. But an associated phenomenon is also likely to appear. The child insists on ritual, a patterned sequence of repetitious behaviors. Certain moves must be repeated exactly: the bedtime story and litany recited in precise order, the arrangement of the night table or the position of the doors reestablished down to the last detail, with anxiety and protest at any hint of deviation. Clearly the child is striving to ward off something with all this, and many a weary parent has felt a curious mixture of empathy with the youngster's obvious distress and irritation at this endless manipulative behavior.

Nor is this ritualistic and anxious bedtime pattern altogether easy to understand. What seems to play a role is the child's concern with loss. For one thing, going to sleep means loss of consciousness, loss of all the stimulation, achievements, and acquisitions of that day. At 2 years, simply being awake and alert can be exciting; so much is going on and so much is interesting that the child hates to give it up. In particular, it is rewarding to have the parents present and to have their attention; it is even more rewarding to have their obedience and to realize fantasies of mastery and dominance. Going to sleep is a renunciation of proximity and control; it is a slipping away, a letting go. No great wonder then that many children fight sleep for a time and hold fast to their sense of control.

Rapprochement

In many ways, this aspect of the separation experience is part of a larger struggle that characterizes early toddlerhood. It is a time when the conflict heightens between the child's push for greater independence and his wish to retain his old closeness and intimacy with the mother. As noted earlier, this stressful developmental moment has been called the *rapprochement* phase by Margaret Mahler. Within her theoretical approach, it betokens the opposing tugs on the toddler toward symbiosis on the one hand and toward autonomy and further maturational advance on the other. Each of these offers pleasures, and each is accompanied by fears. The pleasure component of symbiosis needs little description; it speaks for being close to the powerful and adored other to the point of melting into her. It means being held, protected, and cared for in passive and infantile ways so that the child loses his outlines and joins entirely with the mother's selfhood in a perfect union. At the same time, however, this longing provides a source of the major fears. For the melting experience of symbiosis means the loss of all the autonomy, competencies, and achieved boundaries that have come with growth and development. In effect, the child fantasies being orally devoured by mother and becoming part of her at the expense of all the feelings of selfhood that have thus far been achieved. This is indeed frightening.

The other side of the ambivalence of the epoch is the lure of growth and advance, which is where development naturally takes a child. But this pattern implies that he must meet more and more requirements, accomplish more and more tasks, master more and more competencies, endure more and more aloneness, achieve more and more independence from the reassuring caretaker, and maintain more and more self-regulation. At the end of it all, despite the many pleasures of mastery and autonomy, these advances, too, can be problematic. The result is likely to be a youngster who clings to his mother with one hand and pushes her away with the other, and who behaves at some moments as though nothing will satisfy him. Mahler's work suggests that the child's internal image of the mother apparently fluctuates dramatically as well. At any given time, the child's longings for the mother make her alternately the object of yearning or a dangerously tempting, engulfing presence. At other moments, the mother's expectations that the child display greater independence, autonomy, and self-control are experienced by the toddler as withholding, rejecting, or hateful (especially when colored by the projection of the baby's own angry, frustrated feelings). From the theoretical perspective, how to integrate these highly charged images of the angry *mother-of-separation* and the longed-for or tempting *mother-of-symbiosis* is the major challenge of this phase. Under reasonably good conditions, the child is presently able to separate with a prevailing air of confidence; he gives up on the more regressive wishes and behaviors and opts for the progressive course. In effect, he makes up with the caretaker and moves ahead into the next developmental phase. This component of the experience then gives the epoch its name: *rapprochement.*

Not all students of development are in agreement about the character of these events. No one challenges the idea that this is a time when the toddler struggles mightily with conflicting pulls, but a number of investigators (Horner, 1986; Stern, 1985) have questioned whether these relate to symbiosis as such. They have asserted that the struggle for autonomy need not require that the child be concerned with fusion or engulfment; it is enough that the youngster be caught up at once in the wish to cling as against the wish to be independent and autonomous. Horner (1985), for example, sees the core conflicts of this epoch as stemming from the clash between the toddler's greater capacity for willful assertiveness and potentially dangerous exploration on the one hand and the parents' developmentally determined, increased expectations for cooperative obedience and self-regulation on the other. As Horner puts it:

> The central organizing features of this developmental period are not loss of symbiotic union and fear of its self- and autonomy-destroying re-attainment per se, but rather the dynamic of individually-distributed and separately-felt interests and needs on the part of the infant and caregiver that are in varying states of conflict and resolution. . . . Rapprochement, then is not a process of dealing with lost symbiotic bliss but a process of restoring positive equilibrium following perturbations, a process of re-attaining basic love and security when frustrations and resistance/opposition, and their correlated affects, have been effectively dealt with. (1985, pp. 9, 21)

Hence the existence of symbiosis and the corresponding rapprochement phase in Mahler's sense of the term are by no means universally accepted, and the field awaits the outcome of further research.

Toilet Training

The beginnings of self-assertion are markedly influenced by many body-related developments, such as the erect posture and toilet training. This latter experience is a part of every child-rearing sequence and deserves separate consideration.

Toilet training is important because it involves one of the elementary acts of socialization, the avoidance of dirty messes and bad smells. This seems to be a banal observation, but in the phenomenon of childhood encopresis, despite the teasing and rejection of his classmates, the affected school-age youngster seems to be indifferent or uncaring about this aspect of his behavior. Clearly, toilet training can either fail to be acquired or, once learned, can then be unlearned (see Volume 2, Chapter 18). Under very primitive conditions, for example, where the mother is profoundly deprived, disorganized, retarded, or psychotic, the child may never be toilet trained, and the outcome is ". . . a dirty child in a dirty family" (Anthony, 1957). Under more usual conditions, the majority of parents tend to toilet train children some time during the 2nd or 3rd year. A notable minority will train their youngsters early, often before 1 year of age. These infants can indeed be made to be clean and dry by 1 year, but this is largely accomplished by reflex conditioning rather than through acquiescence. Under these conditions later struggles may all too easily bring about a period of regression, and the early training can break down. This produces the more complex phenomenon of wetting or soiling in a formerly controlled child, but now with additional resistances and defensiveness set in place.

The Time of Training. For the most part authorities have recommended conducting toilet training when the child is between 18 and 30 months of age, with the weight of suggestion falling toward the later rather than the earlier part of that interval. There are several reasons for selecting this as the optimum time (Brazelton, 1962). For one thing the child's motor control allows him a more dependable mastery of all the necessary adjunct behaviors: He can sit up well and can control his sphincters consciously and specifically. For another, he can communicate more effectively in words and can better understand the parents' wishes and expectations. However, there is also the period of normal negativism to contend with (roughly between 14 and 24 months). White makes the point very forcefully (1975) that it is probably best to await the waning of this uncooperative period before initiating training. If at all possible, it is important not to involve this key aspect of socialization in the battle for control that is so common during early toddlerhood.

Patterns of Training. As is true for so many of the phenomena of childhood, toilet training is subject to a great deal of individual variation. Factors such as health, temperament, rate of maturation, parental personality organization, family structure, social circumstance, and other external influences will all play major roles in what happens at this time. An American father who raised his children in a poor town in South America observed that his young son more or less trained himself; the character of their domicile brought the child into a great deal of contact with many rural children; there were many opportunities to see them eliminating; and presently the child simply copied their patterns. Indeed, in many homes a slightly older sibling offers a prime model and stimulus for a given child who wants to be like or to vie with the older brother or sister.

The usual story for more resistant children is some such account as this: "I put Johnny on the potty and he stays there for an hour or longer—and nothing. Then as soon as I put the diaper back on, he crawls behind the sofa and has a B.M." Children may resist the training for a variety of reasons. Medical conditions such as constipation or painful anal fissures may interfere with training. Or the youngsters may cling to the sheer pleasure of eliminating as they wish, which, together with all the associated sensuous experiences, they enjoy too much to give up readily. Under still other circumstances, this question of compliance can fall athwart the youngster's power struggle and be caught up in this as another counter in the game. In the quest to dominate, the child's negativism rules the day, and he opposes his parents' toilet training demands, just as he may say "No" to so many other things. Sometimes the failure to respond to a request for control of this function has more to do with the child's immaturity. The youngster whose development lags simply is not ready to take control; the parents need to wait until a certain amount of additional maturation has taken place. This is particularly true for nighttime enuresis. By age 6 years, about 25% of white males still wet at night, whereas by age 10 years this has fallen to 12.8% (the figures are lower for white females).

Along with these individual determinants, however, many interpersonal factors can influence a child's readiness for toilet training. A common situation occurs when the mother of a 2-year-old is well into a second pregnancy and decides to train the toddler quickly so that she does not have to cope with two children in diapers when the new baby arrives. Although the mother's motive is certainly understandable, from the child's view it is probably a bad time to begin training. Pregnancy inevitably draws the mother's interest and emotion into herself; the 2-year-old is already experiencing some sense of loss or deprivation. Futhermore, when the new baby comes, things will get worse. The mother will be far more preoccupied than she is right now; the child's deprivation will be real, and for a while at least, painful. The new infant's prerogatives will seem enviable, whereas the 2-year-old's rewards for being older are less self-evident. This is not the time to heap the added demand of renouncing bladder and bowel pleasures on the existing stresses. In general, it is wise to defer such training in the face of any other conflicting demand, such as a move, a new marriage, the mother's taking a job outside the home, or some other major transformation that will test the youngster's adaptive capacities. It is not impossible to train a child under such circumstances; it is merely more stressful, and the vulnerable child will encounter more serious difficulties (e.g., failure to achieve control, tantrums, withdrawal, regression to more infantile patterns).

Accelerated training is also possible with intensive behavioral methods. Thus, the parent can set aside a certain day for this special occasion, prepare the way by a detailed account of what is to come, provide the child with a doll that the youngster can toilet train, and give the child special attention, active rewards, and a flood of encouragement. This can be made into a daylong, full-time, ceremonious effort. The proponents of this method allege that toilet training can thus be accomplished in 24 hours (Azrin & Foxx, 1974). For most children, however, it is probably best to allow the process to take a little longer. A gentle, patient, unswerving indication to the child that this is what the parents desire and expect best serves to bring a youngster to a full and relatively voluntary decision to accept the social rules and to conform. And this acceptance and identification with the mother's attitudes toward cleanliness are a major dimension of the process.

LATER DERIVATIVES OF ANALITY

According to Freudian theory, the anal pleasures as well as the inhibitions of these pleasures tend to persist as lifelong traits. Freud asserted that in almost every life it is possible to find a variety of expressions of these impulses as well as the defenses that contain them. That is to say, the desire to soil may find direct expression or may be evidenced paradoxically in the form of excessive neatness. For example, consider the pleasure in messing, making a mess, and maintaining a messy state. In Western society most adults keep a certain amount of cleanliness and order in their lives, both as an aspect of their personal body care and as part of the way they manage their immediate environment. But, in a great many instances, somewhere in their lives, even very neat people are likely to preserve an island of mess that is peculiarly their own. They might have a drawer that stays unaccountably chaotic, or it may be a desktop. Sometimes it is a closet, a bathroom, a bedroom, or perhaps a garage. Wherever it is, this island of chaos is likely to stand in marked contrast to the person's usual demeanor and to have a quality of special importance; no one is supposed to arrange it or to interfere with it, "Every time you clean up my desktop I can't find anything for a week." The master of the mess is almost ready to do battle to preserve it; it is curiously precious and intractable. Even the person's own repeated resolutions to clean up the desk or closet somehow never quite succeed—or stay successful.

The same residue is evident in certain habitual practices of many people. There the pipe smoker is digging out the remaining ashes, scraping out the inner surface of his pipe, running a furry wire through its inside, tapping out the scrapings into a receptable and then going back for more. Or a cigarette smoker is leaving butts behind, with ashes spilling this way and that. Or a nonsmoker may find it necessary to clean her fingernails during social occasions, or sweep invisible bits of dust off the desktop—one way or another many people keep up an involvement with mess or dirt throughout their lives. Nor should it be overlooked that, along with the play with ashes, the tobacco user is also producing smells. There are many other examples— everything from a liking for "stinky" cheeses to the common use of scatological language.

Withal, it is the mastery of these issues that Freudian theory regards as the source of uniquely important character traits. Thus, the anal phase sets in train many tendencies, such as neatness, orderliness, meticulousness, and cleanliness, that are so basic to an organized life, indeed to a civilized life (Abraham, 1921/1966). The defenses against the ready expression of anal impulses are in part internalizations of and identifications with parental attitudes (and the later values of other adults and of society in general), and in part early conditionings that have received continuous reinforcement and have accordingly persisted. Over time, the child learns to abhor feces, to dislike dirt and mess, to avoid bad smells—and to feel embarrassed at exhibiting any such preferences. The result, Freud believed, is the forma- tion of character traits that embody some of the "lessons" of the child's early encounter with anality and that begin to build up a set of attitudes and stable response patterns basic to later living. Freud believed that some of the most useful and fundamental elements in personality organization origi- nate here. An individual is clean, clean-cut, neat, fragrant, trim, orderly, punctual, frugal, proper, seemly, and so on for a long list of rather comfort- able-sounding characteristics, all arising as defenses against anality.

By the same token, where things go awry and there is too much or too little of such inhibition, then difficult symptoms may emerge. Neatness becomes obsession; punctuality, punctiliousness; orderliness, compulsion; correctness, rigidity; conscientiousness, scrupulosity. Or, in the case of too little, traits such as tardiness, sloppiness, dirtiness, unkemptness, disarray, and disorganization prevail. Even if the professional accepts Freud's hy- pothesis that all these traits are indeed derived from anal phase experience, the extent to which they are connected directly with toilet training is still a matter of debate. On the one hand, the importance of the positive con- structs can be seen by assuming that proper toilet behavior involves time, place, and practice. Thus, the child's appropriate use of the toilet engages such basic capacities as punctuality and the ability to act expeditiously and in a timely way in other areas. In general, the child who learns to be responsi- ble for his body and for his own needs can be regarded as having made a truly important step toward mastering responsibility in any dimension. From this theoretical standpoint, toilet training is the nidus around which the crystal of adult civility will form and grow.

This entire approach has been challenged by such authors as Chess and Thomas (1984), who have emphasized that so universal and natural a process as toilet training could scarcely have the portentous implications ascribed to it by psychoanalytic theory. Furthermore, they have taken issue with emphasis on toilet training as a renunciation of instinctual satisfaction. Rather, they argue, it can also be seen as an advance in task mastery and social competence, yielding skills that are a source of pride and satisfaction to the child. In their longitudinal study, they noted little evidence of disturbance in relation to toilet training, save in a few cases of rigid or inconsistent parental attitudes. In an empirical study, Sears et al. (1957) found that the optimal ages for initiating training were either between 6 and 12 months or after 20 months. That is to say, training begun during those intervals seems to go forward with relatively little difficulty; the older-than-20-month infants were able to accomplish the feat in the briefest period. A key factor in diminishing the degree of associated upset was the amount of maternal warmth that was present, an element that appeared to be more important than the degree of maternal strictness per se. These investigators' work illustrates the point that toilet training is but one of the many socializing interactions that are embedded in the overall context of an ongoing parent–child relationship. This critical human matrix is in turn colored by the participants' style, temperament, and so on. It is thus extremely difficult, if not impossible, to isolate the effects of toilet training from other associated variables such as the mother's general child-rearing style and temperamental goodness of fit. The investigators, however, were not able to shed light on the long-range characteriological impact of the time or the way children were trained. Hetherington and Brackbill (1963) could find no correlation in 5-year-olds between toilet-training experience and empirical measures or orderliness, parsimony, and obstinacy. These investigators also reviewed their own and others' inability to find consistent correlations between these traits, which, according to classical psychoanalytic theory, should covary with each other (because they are the common product of the subjects' early experience).

Whatever its potential long-term impact on personality development, this achievement of self-care is of special importance. Toilet training is one of the moments in which a caretaker gives over a major aspect of body management into the hands of the child. It is no longer the mother who cares for this important set of functions; it is the toddler. He is no longer dependent; he is autonomous. The child's body is not an extension of or a possession of someone else; his body is his own. An inner signal is no mere prompting for a bodily response; it is a reminder of a need to make a social decision—and then to act on that decision. Moreover, the responsibility for all that is the toddler's own. At the same time (as noted), this taking over of a regulatory function that was previously the mother's involves an acceptance of and identification with her attitudes. It is a real step. In short order this new-found sense of responsibility and autonomy will extend to clothes, choice of colors and items to wear (and not wear), and presently to styles and combinations, and so on.

This assumption of body care is thus one of the great breakthrough events that combines synergistically with the many other expanding dimensions of cognitive advance, visual-motor coordination, organization of fine-motor control, and definition of identity; in their aggregate they give the toddler an ever-increasing sense of his own separateness and uniqueness. This involves not only mastery of neutral capacities to learn and to acquire skills but the taming of pleasurable (and aggressive) impulses as well; it is thus peculiarly central to such realms as self-esteem, self-control, and the feeling of growth and advance. The child's body is more than ever his own, and everything from hairdo to choice of shoe styles begins to move into the orbit of self-concern.

Disturbances of rearing style can compromise this development in a variety of ways. Thus, the overanxious parent may never really release the child from constant care and scrutiny. The youngster has instructions that on no account is he to flush the toilet before the parent has conducted an inspection, and any hint of a stomachache, or such a symptom as constipation, sends the parent into a flurry of concern. Sometimes parents will say— and only half playfully: "It's not your body, it's my body, I have to take care of it, I have to know whatever you feel, whatever happens!"

The very compulsive mother may be constantly concerned about cleanliness and may insist on being the one who wipes the child's behind after each bowel movement; such a pattern may persist until well into the grade-school years. In effect, the child never achieves full control of his body; at best it is a shared responsibility, and child's sense of identity is correspondingly never allowed to sharpen and mature. This type of distortion is even more marked in the case of the narcissistic parent who sends out the message: "You are clean because of *me*, *my* training, *my* teaching; you are *my* contrivance, and your mission is to fulfill *my* dream and do *my* bidding."

In each instance the child's separation–individuation work is made more difficult, and the vulnerable child will fail in the necessary stage-accomplishment appropriate to this epoch. Autonomy has many dimensions and involves numerous sites of developmental advance. The body-care area takes in the matter of self-feeding, deciding about food preferences and avoidances, and nighttime bottles; it includes the management of toileting issues, clothes preferences, and aversions; and it involves as well the gradual defining of which areas the child is to control and which are the province of the mother—and under what conditions. For example, sickness may change the rules, radically and abruptly, and such lessons may also come early.

Possessions

As this work goes on, it is paralleled by a series of advances in the adjacent areas of attachment to physical objects. The role of possessions and territory as emergents of this stage has already been noted; this now translates into the child's many special feelings about having his own things. Once again this process starts with the child's body. Early on, the things the child possesses are his own parts, including the feces he produces. These are peculiarly his own and signify for the child some of that transitional world he is just beginning to understand; how a thing can be owned and yet not be part of the body. Some children go through a phase during which they will sit on whatever they play with, for example, a simple jigsaw puzzle, before actually beginning the play (Noshpitz, unpublished observation). In effect, they make it into part of their own body, like feces, before they can use it for the intended game purpose.

Under certain circumstances, children may be reluctant to give up their feces. They become constipated and hold them in; they treasure and retain them, clinging to these products of their bodies as though they were precious possessions. Later in life there are people who accumulate possessions; they are hoarders and amassers rather than collectors, whose relationship to things has a simple retentive quality. They may never use, sort, or label the materials they collect; they just pile them up—but their need to keep on gathering in more and more can be a persistent—and even a ruling—passion. Eventually, what they end up with is a huge mess, and someone usually throws the whole thing out.

There are more mature and sublimated derivatives of this same tendency so that collections can become arrays of great scientific, historical, or aesthetic value, precisely identified, meticulously described, and carefully arranged to produce a powerful sense of order, purpose, and achievement. Albeit such a collection offers a radical contrast to the amasser's scruffy mess, the chances are that the underlying impulse derives from the same developmental epoch. The maturity and the sophistication of the child's ego in working with this impulse can be radically different from child to child and will determine the final outcome.

Some individuals will manifest a certain colitis of behavior; they will alternately have a constipation and a diarrhea of possessions. They will hoard protectively and then spend indiscriminately, manifesting a basic instability of attitude that, in fact, demonstrates the infantile nature of their regulatory apparatus. They have never finished the early work of evolving a sense of what is *mine,* and their uncertain and wavering outlines become translated into very self-detrimental behavior.

For many individuals, possession is a source of a great deal of gratification. For the true collector, obtaining a desired item provides intense pleasure as well as relief of a certain measure of tension.

Gender Identity

Recent research suggests that the awareness of gender differences is achieved by most children during this toddler period, probably by 18 months of age. This awareness is a momentous emergent and underlies the great sequence of developmental unfolding that initiates the later construction of gender identity. Technically it constitutes the true beginning of what was formerly thought of as the phallic phase of development; this period will be discussed in the following chapter.

At the same time, significant dimensions of gender identity are defined in anal terms. In particular, attitudes toward dirt are significantly entwined with the traditional profile of gender organization: women are dainty and sweet smelling; men are dirty and smell of sweat. Men protest their virility with "dirty" words; for women such terms are considered unfeminine. The traditional homemaker role involved much contact with dirt—but typically in the service of removing it: The woman changed the baby, cared for the sick, and cleaned house. The man was the creator of mess, and the woman cleaned up after him. Even the balance of submission–domination elements in the roles of males and females reflects the influence of anal influences in determining gender patterns. One of the curious qualities of the more recent shifts in the definition of gender roles has been to eliminate the differences between the relationship of anal factors to gender behavioral assignment (both genders change the baby and share the housework).

Thought

As the child begins to speak, he communicates an ever clearer image of his thought processes. The early forms of thinking constitute a complex entity that this volume cannot explore in depth. However, some of the salient findings follow.

Freud (1911/1958) delineated two major forms of thought. The one is the kind of rational activity commonly associated with using logical rules to reach sensible conclusions. This includes reasoning from cause to effect, from premise to conclusion, from assumption to demonstration. There is a quality of coherence, consistency, and predictability about the thought sequence; it is rational, orderly, and it makes sense. It is embedded in the rules of logic or of mathematics, and it has given rise to what we call the scientific method; many great human achievements express this kind of thinking capacity.

On the other hand, another kind of thinking, in a sense, violates much of what is basic to the principles of logical thought. To understand that, consider, for a moment, Aristotle's Laws of Thought. In his *Metaphysics*, Aristotle sought to define the most elementary principles that underlie all logic and all rational thought. He came up with three such laws, of which two will perhaps be enough to illustrate the point. The first states merely that for any given entity *A*, *A* is, in fact, *A*. In other words, a thing is itself. This fairly elementary assertion is called the *law of identity*. It speaks for the conservation of definition, for the stability of the essence of things, and it states simply that for rational purposes, once you have made an assumption that something is, you have to go on assuming it continues to be the same thing throughout your subsequent line of reasoning.

Another principle is that associated with *contradiction*. Given a universe that contains two different entities, *A* and *B*, for any given element in that world, if it is *A*, it is not *B*, and if it is *B*, it is not *A*. In brief, within the framework of logical discourse there can be no contradictions; if a thing is itself, it cannot at the same time be something that is not itself. Again, a fairly obvious and self-evident assertion.

The key point, however, is that Freud's second mode of thinking violates these principles point by point. For example, suppose I were to say, "Last night I had a dream, and in my dream I stood on a hill and held in my hand a bright red apple. As I gazed at the apple, it turned into a bird and flew away. That is all of the dream I can recall."

"Well," you might answer, "that's the way it is in dreams, that's the way it happens." But if we apply the laws of thought, what about the conservation of identity? First an apple, then a bird? "No," you would say, "in dreams it is different." And of course you would be right. In dreams it *is* different; the nature of the thought processes involved is not at all the same as in rational thought, and different rules prevail. In dreams thought is ruled by similarities (even of obscure and trivial character) and by the intensity of the feelings surrounding ideas and things, rather than by logical relationships. Things are linked emotionally rather than rationally, on the basis of some unexpected similarity instead of logical equivalence, and there is thus a constant sliding of cognitive meaning. Apparently insignificant ideas or percepts come to be invested with all of the intensity, meaning, or affect originally attributed to a totally different entity (e.g., an original wish to go upstairs and destroy or violate a parent might get translated into an unaccountable fear of heights, a process that Freud called *displacement*).

Nor is this the only characteristic of dream thinking. Another principle of such thought stipulates that all of the meanings of a chain of associations may converge on a common idea, a process called *condensation* or symbolization (Laplanche & Pontalis, 1973). A flag or an icon may thus command great quantities of emotion, and any element of a dream may be crowded with significance.

Primary Process Thinking. Dream thinking is often called magical thinking or, in the Freudian system, *primary process* thinking. According to that mode of classification, the more rational, logical forms of thought are collectively designated as *secondary process.* Although both kinds of thought are present from the outset, the primary process forms are probably dominant during the earlier years. Freud believed, however, that primary process thinking persists throughout life in the realm of the unconscious (whose activities are ruled by this form of thought). The relationship between the two kinds of thinking can be illustrated by taking as an analogy the interaction between a canoe and a lake, where the secondary process canoe floats on the primary process lake. When the wind is fair, when no deep upwelling disturbs the tranquility of the surface, when no powerful current sweeps across the lake, when, in short, the water is calm, then the canoe is exquisitely maneuverable. At the beck of the paddler it darts, skips, and gyrates, whirls about, stands on end, and enacts tricks of all sorts. Its performance is limited only by the paddler's strength, skill, and talent. If a strong wind blows up, however, or a powerful current comes snaking through the lake, waves and turbulence will make the canoe difficult to manage. It tends to go out of control, and more than that, it is in constant danger of capsizing altogether.

This then is the situation with the different kinds of thinking. Humans are logical reasoning beings as long as they are not under the sway of some powerful emotion. If a major challenge confronts a person, however, or a great surge of feelings rises up within, it threatens the capacity for rational thought, other forces take over, and the logical self is confounded, sometimes totally swept away for a time.

Indeed, Freud once commented that the important decisions are always made by the unconscious, which is, in a way, a restatement of that same idea. When people choose a lover, a mate, a career, or even a place to live, in many instances the determiner of choice turns out to have been something other than a thought-through, logical process. One person may have had an impulse, an instinct; another may have listened to his or her heart, to intuition, or to inner fears; there are many ways of formulating the commonplace that in the final analysis humans are in large measure ruled by primary process. It therefore becomes all the more important to understand something of the nature of this kind of thinking.

A related form of thought is what Piaget called *preoperational* thought. It has a number of important characteristics. For one thing, similarity is of crucial importance, particularly if the similarity allows for enlargement of the idea. This is the basis of all simile and all metaphor; it is at the heart of much that is called poetic. For example, in his famous poem, "The Highwayman," Noyes wrote, "The moon was a ghostly galleon tossed upon cloudy seas," and readers resonate in sympathy to the beauty and the power of the imagery. They catch the similarity and are at the same time lifted up and moved to higher sensitivity. At no time are they troubled because the moon is not a ship, galleon or otherwise; that is irrelevant. Within the framework of magical thinking, things similar to each other are equal to one another. It is important to recognize that much of what is called *symptom choice* is based on such thinking.

Thus, if a person develops a phobia because of some complex interpersonal interaction, the phobic object represents an attempt at a solution of the relationship stress, some symbolic substitute based on an element of similarity. When little Hans grew afraid of horses, Freud (1905/1953) systematically elaborated the ways in which the notion of the horse condensed feelings about father, mother, and the host of fantasies and relationships that prevailed in the child's life—because in little Hans's mind, the noise, the size, or the smell associated with horses was somehow like that of his father.

The rules that govern this form of thought are very much of a piece with what Freud once called the *dream work,* a mode of thought within which certain rules prevail. In particular, certain agglomerations of meaning tend to take place during condensation so that a particular element in the thinking has not one but many connotations and can include affective as well as cognitive components. Thus, for a small child, the parent may point to a stick, and the child will burst into tears. The stick is not merely the threat of punishment, it is a reminder of prior exchanges, it means the threatened loss of the parent's love, it suggests rejection, it is humiliating, and perhaps it stirs some masochistic wish as well. This massing together of multiple associations, rich in emotional content and united by their attachment to a single referent, makes for the creation of symbols and for their formidable impact. Such symbol formation is the natural consequence of this process, and such early thought is especially rich in symbols. For the adult, many powerful symbols are an everyday part of life—a pattern or a set of initials scrawled on the side of a house, a flag, some memento from the past—the symbols are countless. This characteristic allows for dream interpretation, a process of trying to dissect out the various denotative elements from within an agglomerated mass of associationally clustered, connotative meanings.

Magical thinking has other characteristics as well. Thus, a typical aspect of this form of thought is that it is animistic. The belief system called *animism* holds that all things are alive. Rocks, furniture, the book a person is reading—all are sentient and imbued with life. Animism is evident in the beliefs of the ancient Greeks, who perceived naiads in the streams, tritons in the waves, and dryads in the trees. In Shakespeare's idealized *green world* there were "tongues in trees, books in the running brooks, sermons in stones, and good in everything" (*As You Like It,* Act II, Sc. 1). Generally speaking, 2-year-olds take this for granted, and various tales in which the objects of the world come alive and speak or think seem quite understandable to them.

This can be helpful in terms of their management. Thus, for example, when the nursemaid is leading the toddler up the steps and the child stumbles and barks his shin, he will begin to wail. The nursemaid, who has never heard the word *animism*, immediately slaps the step saying, "Bad step, you hurt my Johnny!" and the child is mollified. The life, the intentionality of the step, is taken for granted; the caretaker knows intuitively how children think and rectifies the situation forthwith.

In many ways adults fully give up this way of thinking. Still, on a cold winter morning when the car won't start, the threats, pleadings, and reproaches that a great many people make to their recalcitrant vehicles at that moment of intense frustration will sound an awful lot like animism to an outside observer.

Another aspect of magical thinking that has considerable impact is the way it construes the nature of the body and body parts. For the toddler, body parts seem alive and capable of moving about. Many of the child's concerns and attitudes toward toilet training may be colored by the belief that the feces may be alive and capable of feeling (Anthony, 1957; Erikson, 1950). Body parts attached in one way do not have to stay that way; then can just as easily be placed in some other arrangement if a person knows how to go about it. There are all sorts of evidences of this belief in mythology, particularly in the roster of mythical beasts. Pegasus has the body of a horse and the wings of an eagle. The Sphinx has a woman's head and the body of a lioness (and perhaps the claws or tail of yet another creature). The centaur, the Minotaur, the mermaid, the hippogryff, the griffin, and the chimera are all founded solidly on the conviction that body parts can move about or that body shapes may change. People in fairy tales are forever being changed into frogs or toads, unicorns become maidens, and fluid elastic body boundaries are constantly giving rise to new and promising, or terrifying, possibilities. Later in childhood, Superman will use a phone booth, Wonder Woman will whirl around, and Captain Marvel will say *Shazam!*—but the basic principle of the mutability of the body will remain throughout.

Laboratory Studies in Metaphorical Thinking. The development of the capacity to think in symbolic and metaphorical terms is currently under active investigation. Piaget has described the development of play as advancing along several axes. There is an action component that includes an ever-increasing array of actions in sequence. There is a self–other dimension characterized by a progressive shift from self to other as the focus of the play; ultimately, this finds expression in the form of a complex role structure within the play sequence. There is a movement away from the concrete quality of the depicted events toward a readiness to use ever more imaginary elements in the play construction. And finally there is the planful organization of pretense events around a goal.

Working out of a Piagetian framework, Lucariello (1987) studied the play of 10 such mother–child dyads. It is noteworthy that at very young ages (e.g., between 24 and 29 months), children will engage in symbolic play with their mothers. When the play was based on items within the child's experience—such as preparing tea or serving a meal—the child would initiate the play sequence more often than the mother. When the play was based on some theme that was altogether imaginary or with which the child was relatively or totally unfamiliar, the mother always started the play.

In fact, children are quite likely to engage in symbolic play with their mothers, and mothers often initiate the pretense. At this age, children tend to elaborate event-based fantasies; within that perimeter, however, they achieve quite high levels of symbolic activity. This capacity underlies the effectiveness of play therapy.

Metaphorical thinking itself as a developmental phenomenon is increasingly the focus of study. DeLoache, for example, started with the assumption that the ability to think in a symbolic way required that the subject be able to think about a concrete object in two different ways at the same time. The object must be perceived as the thing in itself, and the object must also be recognized as standing for something else. DeLoache regards the ability to do this as "a crucial aspect of mature, flexible thought" (1987, p. 1556).

Children between 2 and 3 years of age (16 subjects with a mean age of 31 months; 16 with a mean age of 38 months) were shown a scale model of a room (actually the room where the study was taking place). The researcher explained the connection between the model and the room to the child. Then, as the child watched, an object (e.g., a tiny stuffed dog) was hidden in the model room, and the child was asked to retrieve the full-sized toy that had been hidden in the equivalent place in the real room. Half the children were posed the opposite task; the toy was hidden in the real room, and the children were asked to find it in the scale model.

There was a dramatic difference between the performances of the two age groups. The older children (the 3-year-olds) did very well on the retrieval task between model and real room, whereas the younger children (at $2\frac{1}{2}$ years) seemed unable to make the connection between the model and the real situation. The transition was quite striking and suggested that some kind of maturational step had been taken during the second half of the year between the 2nd and 3rd birthdays. On the other hand, if asked to start with a photograph of the room rather than a three-dimensional representation, the younger children did better. The investigator assumes that this is because the photograph is already a symbolic representation; when the child is shown where the dog is hidden in the photograph, the youngster is already in the symbolic mode; accordingly, the transition from the perception of a concrete object to thinking in a symbolic mode does not have to be made.

The acquisition of the ability to regard objects as both symbol and thing-in-itself is a developmental emergent that occurs somewhere between $2\frac{1}{2}$ and 3 years of age.

The experiment utilizing photographs does underline another aspect of the development of metaphorical thinking. Vosniadou (1987) makes the point that in studying children's speech, it is evident that from the time they first begin to speak, children make statements that sound metaphorical. The youngsters are not capable of explaining even simple metaphors, however, until about age 4. The ability to utilize metaphor rests on a basic competence, namely, the capacity of children to perceive similarities among the objects and events of their world. It is not enough, however, to stop with the mere recognition of similarity. Metaphors reflect transfer to knowledge from one domain to another, with the added quality that to be a true metaphor, there must be a conscious violation of an established category. (For the moon to be queen of the night, the thinker must violate the usual limits of both social hierarchies and astronomical objects.) The ability to form such constructions is manifest at quite an early age. But it is a development that continues to ripen and mature all through the years of childhood and adolescence and is not fully achieved until the individual has attained psychological adulthood.

The theories of metaphor have included (1) the notion that a metaphor is simply a substitution of one category for another; (2) the idea that a metaphor implies a comparison between categories; (3) the concept that a metaphor is an interaction between terms that allows them to be seen from different points of view simultaneously (viz., DeLoache's assumption above); and (4) the suggestion that the formation of metaphors is, in each instance, a utilization of the similarities within different categories in the service of creating a new and more abstract category. This new formation would include the intersection of whatever is similar within the two original categories. The essential element seems to be that items showing some degree of similarity and arising from conventional categories of a necessary degree of remoteness from one another must be juxtaposed in a meaning-ful way. Piaget (1962) did not think that preschoolers could form the necessary conventional categories that are basic to metaphor, but subse-quent investigations have demonstrated that such capacities exist from a very early age.

There are evident methodological problems with studying children's metaphors, for example, when does a child with a very limited vocabulary simply employ a known word to designate something he does not know? When does a child merely pretend that one thing is another with no sense of any similarity between them, no wish to transcend categories, nor any intent to make this a metaphorical comparison or expression (a child picks up a block, says it is a cup, and pretends to drink from it). Despite these difficulties certain conclusions can now be stated with some assurance. Three-year-olds can distinguish statements that make sense from those that do not; 4-year-olds know when items are from the same conventional category and when they are from different categories. In particular, 4-year-olds can use toys in quite metaphorical fashion.

Metaphorical thinking is particularly important in helping the child acquire new knowledge. Indeed, from a very early age children are forever relating new experiences to what they already know; as a result, a continuing transfer of knowledge takes place with metaphorical thinking. For example, conveying the notion that the body is like a machine can be a powerful way to begin molding a child's thoughts about biological functioning. If the adult offers the child an analogy with sufficiently familiar terms, even early preschoolers seem to be able to think in a fashion that would correctly be understood as metaphorical.

Chapter 11

The Later Preschool Years
Phallic Phase

INTRODUCTION

The 3-year-old is quite different from the anal-stage child. Under optimal conditions, some of the negativism is beginning to fade, the power struggle is less intense, and toilet training has been accomplished. The child experiences a beginning sense of mastery in respect to his body and has taken on a partial but very real responsibility for its management. Some of these children are still vulnerable to occasional toilet "accidents," and they often experience great distress and humiliation at this failure of mastery.

The interpersonal capacities of the time are striking. The child is working through the rapprochement phase of separation/individuation and no longer needs to shadow his mother everywhere and to "refuel" emotionally if he should go off for a time playing or exploring at a distance. He is far more independent in his capacity to entertain himself, and the way he relates himself to the caretaker now might entail an occasional visit to bring some striking new discovery to her and deposit it on her lap. In terms of behavioral management, far more negotiation is possible, and the child is increasingly receptive to explanation and reassurance. Altogether, the 3-year-old is likely to be a far more tractable and reasonable person than he was just a year ago.

The separation issues of this epoch take on a new character. The youngster has usually accommodated himself to familiar baby-sitters and can allow the parents to leave without the storm of protest that might once have been typical. Extended separations from important objects are still matters of considerable gravity, but the child responds to them with less of the massive reactivity of the earlier epoch. If development has proceeded well and the environment maintains its stability, the child is less concerned about the presence or absence of the object of his attachment and more interested in the quality of their relationship.

When with other children, the child evidences much growth in interpersonal competence, and he can now join in a cooperative enterprise. The parallel play of the 2-year-old (where the child "did his own thing" next to another youngster of the same developmental status who was similarly engaged) now gives way to the ability to share and cooperate, and the 3-year-old demonstrates a good capacity to join another child or children in building a house or playing a game. Altruistic feelings are also more commonly expressed; if another child is crying or distressed, the 3-year-old may extend active and sometimes very effective gestures of comfort, reassurance, and consolation. Side by side with this new capacity for cooperation and altruism arises an ability to compete and to share in simple contests of one kind or another. If the preschool teacher says, "Let's see who can clean up faster, Table A or Table B," the scurrying is intense.

One of the most striking emergents of the epoch is the use of play as a vehicle for expressing inner concerns and interests. For the first time the child is able to participate fully in fantasy play, so that the sensuous aspects of the toys do not take precedence nor does the child's ability to master certain muscle patterns (as is so typical for the 2-year-old with his pull-toys); instead, the meaning of the plaything—the doll or the fire truck or the toy soldier—is central to the child's selection and use of that item. He uses the toys to tell a story, and it is usually a story of some import to his inner life.

Other aspects of ego growth are also remarkable during this interval, especially those associated with language usage. The 3-year-old can understand about 1000 words, can follow fairly complex directions, and can engage in real conversations with an interested adult. Such a youngster, with his more tractable disposition and more engaging style, is often considered "good company" and evokes quite a different response from adults than he did just a year ago. Usually this rapport works to the child's developmental advantage, but sometimes it is too much of a good thing. For example, a mother whose husband has left her at this juncture in the child's life sometimes turns for comfort to her little boy and uses him as replacement and consoler for her absent spouse. Or the little girl's winsome and beguiling ways presently net her an unlooked-for sexual advance from her teenage male baby-sitter.

The phallic phase is marked by an increase in the child's genital interests, which come to play a dominant role in his behavior. This heightened genital interest includes a preoccupation with the genital anatomy (both the child's own and that of others), an upsurge in genital masturbation, and a new erotic attitude toward the parents (Parens, 1980). With time, as the child moves into the oedipal phase proper, this erotic interest comes to be focused primarily on the parent of the opposite sex, with the same-sex parent now seen as rival. For boys, and, to a more mixed extent, girls, intrusive modes of behavior dominate much of this epoch (Erikson, 1950). Thus, boys' play is dominated by vigorous locomotion, both with their own bodies (running, leaping, hitting, thrusting, pushing) and with suggestive toys (cars that dash, planes that soar, guns that shoot, sticks that zoom, rockets that fly, and swords that penetrate). Along with this comes an increasingly erotized possessiveness to love objects, chief of whom is the mother. For little girls, the inner logic of this phase is more complex. Although she may equal the little boy in her locomotor and social advances, the anatomical and sensate focus of her early genital experience, the clitoris, is less visible and comprehensible than the boy's penis. At the same time, many aspects of the girl's burgeoning sense of herself as female, such as a new interest in having babies, entail less palpable and less easily grasped notions of inner space.

THE FREUDIAN VIEW

Within the Freudian developmental tradition, the phallic phase was thought to begin at the end of the anal stage, roughly at about 36 months of age. This is when the hallmark of phallic interest, genital masturbation, was expected to appear, and it was presumed that the characteristic fantasies of the epoch were also likely to emerge. More recent investigations have altered these views considerably.

The Emergence of the Phallic Phase

The child usually becomes aware of sexual differences between 12 and 18 months of age. By the time they are 18 months old, most children have already perceived that there are two kinds of bodies. This information resonates with what they are learning in encounters with boys and girls about whom they think and with whom they cope on a variety of fronts. In time, these many observations and the fantasies they generate provide part of the basic groundwork for the later development of masculinity and femininity.

The Freudian outlook assumed that the child's early attention to the differences between male and female bodies tends to focus on the presence or absence of the penis; for the young child, this is the most prominent and salient evidence of gender difference. This belief led Freud to dub this era the *phallic phase*. However, Freud based his formulations on a reconstruction of events recalled by adults during analysis. Later investigations have radically altered the time frame within which these phallic-phase events are expected to emerge.

As a result of a variety of observations, Roiphe and Galenson concluded that sometime between 15 and 21 months, the toddler begins to manifest a heightened and affect-laden interest in the genital region (his own as well as that of others). Thus, the awareness of body differences comes much earlier than Freud had assumed. For example, investigators observed youngsters 12 to 18 months old in a situation where they could watch a new baby being changed. The toddlers were obviously intrigued by the body of the younger child, and, more to the point, they actively compared their own genital region to what they saw of the other's. The little boys were reportedly elated and the little girls somewhat crestfallen by what they observed. These reactions, however, were apparently not of extreme character nor did they last for extended periods (Galenson, 1980).

Subsequent psychoanalytic observations have tended to confirm these direct observations, and as psychoanalysts have continued to report their more recent findings, they have been able to recover memories and to reconstruct attitudes suggestive of such earlier sexual awareness. As a result, the picture is changing overall, and it is becoming clear that the awareness of sexual differences is perceived much earlier than had for so long been assumed.

The Erotic Component: Masturbation.

What does seem to happen is that starting in the 2nd year of life, children take an increasing interest in genital sensation. This area apparently becomes more alive for them now, more sensuous, and more rewarding. They begin to masturbate more at this time, repeatedly touching, manipulating, or rubbing the penis or the clitoris. When engaged in such activity, a rapt expression is likely to dwell on the child's countenance, and often a sense of internal communion, of inner fantasy elaboration, accompanies the behavior. Little boys tend to become very conscious of their erections at this point; they have known all their lives that this happens, but the phenomenon now appears to take on new interest for them. Little girls, on the other hand, although they are as fully involved with their clitoris, may or may not discover the vagina as such. On the other hand, the sensuous awareness of warm and pleasurable inside feelings is recalled by many women as a phase-specific experience. (Not infrequently adults expedite little girls' discovery of the vagina either through attempts to wash and douche it, or through efforts to seduce the children and use them for the adult's sexual pleasure.) In any case, once the little girl realizes its existence, vaginal masturbation will typically appear. Much masturbation is indirect by means of straddling or rocking on objects or through the use of thigh pressure; more typically the child employs her fingers. Occasionally foreign bodies will be introduced into this space and can even get lodged there, necessitating a trip to the emergency room.

Speaking generally, it is both normal and universal for children to handle their genitals. It is also quite difficult for adults in our culture to observe this behavior with equanimity. Many adults become rather tense in the presence of a masturbating child and, if not schooled to the contrary, will interfere with the child's behavior. The adults tend to do this either in terms of reproof or by seeking to distract the youngster, perhaps by inducing the child to engage in some other activity. The Victorians considered masturbation to be self-abuse, a pernicious, health-threatening, physically dangerous and morally wicked form of behavior that they had to force the child to give up as soon as they observed its presence. Professionals repeatedly declared that genital stimulation was a major threat to physical, mental, and moral well-being, and parents made every effort to scotch this destructive habit from the outset by never allowing it to take root in the vulnerable child's behavioral pattern.

Left to his own devices, however, the average child will engage in this kind of self-stimulation at frequent intervals and with a certain evident satisfaction. Many children masturbate at bedtime before going to sleep, or when bored and otherwise not occupied. For others, it is an intercurrent behavior that might appear at any time and that will take place in the presence of adults unless the child has received a message forbidding it. Yet another pattern exists wherein a child, usually a boy, touches himself repeatedly for reassurance, in order to be comforted, to know that all is well with him.

During this phase, an increasing interest in and preoccupation with genital sensation becomes manifest. Why this should be so is unknown; the researcher may readily speculate that from an evolutionary point of view, the species counts and not the individual; accordingly, all members of a species are likely to develop those behaviors that make for species survival. An interest in genital sensation has obvious advantages from such a reproductive point of view, and it is possible that those members of a species who develop an active interest in this kind of feeling and who do so early will tend more actively to perpetuate their kind. Hence, to find that children seek such sensory experience is very much in keeping with an evolutionary perspective.

The biological events accompanying this shift of interest are unknown. Myelination and central nervous system maturation may bring a child to a state of phallic-phase readiness at this developmental moment. In any case, this is the interval when such patterns are most likely to appear.

In addition to the touching, other aspects of phallic-phase interest also become prominent at this time, in particular, those associated with looking and showing. Both the viewing and the displaying of erotic images are ancient and traditional forms of sexual stimulation, but it was not until Freud (1905/1953) reported his findings that the universality of these factors as elements of childhood adaptation became well known. The sexual pleasures of scopophilia and of exhibitionism, are, in fact, prominent presences all throughout childhood, and their importance should not be underestimated.

LOOKING.   A definite quantum of erotic excitement is commonly associated with looking at sexual images. Travel through any large city in America, and somewhere in town a cluster of "adult book stores" offer their wares to the potentially interested public. The entire income of these establishments derives from the premise that looking can be so rewarding that customers will pay rather large sums of money for the opportunity to do just that.

This species-specific reaction to sexual images profoundly influences many realms of human endeavor, for example, the content of laws (about obscenity, pornography, voyeurs, indecent exposure, flashers, etc.), the design of clothes (as reflected in hemlines, necklines, hot pants, bikinis, etc.), the structuring of advertising, and numerous aspects of entertainment (soft porn and hard porn on TV, X-rated movies and videos, scatological phone messages, etc.) to mention but a few. This continues into the most personal details of adult erotic engagements, such as arguments that couples have about leaving the light on or off during their sexual encounters.

All this is already evident in childhood when youngsters want to go into the bathroom with parents, to shower with parents, to watch babies being changed, or to engage each other in playing "doctor" with mutual exposure and visual exploration. To be sure, this is also one dimension of the more general quality of curiosity that characterizes this time of life. Nonetheless, the direct interest in visual stimulation by looking at nakedness and genitals is already in evidence.

SHOWING.   Many people experience a powerful urge to show themselves sexually that parallels the gratification afforded by looking. The pleasures of display are readily evident in many aspects of human adjustment—the show-off, the natty dresser, the flashy car. An affluent society offers many opportunities for conspicuous displays. All these provide the sensuously rewarding thrill of being looked at and the associated gratification of having the power to arouse emotion in the significant other, especially to arouse erotic longings of sexual envy. Again, whole industries are built on the need for display and the pleasure in fulfilling the promptings of this need; it is a core aspect of human experience.

The Aggressive Component.   Thus, the immediately sensuous rewards of genital contact—touching, looking, showing—constitute the essence of the erotic side of phallic phase experience. There is, however, an aggressive side as well.

COMPETITIVENESS.   Within the Freudian schema, the phallic phase gives rise to the drive to compete. This is when children learn both to cooperate and to vie with one another; in particular they come to know the pleasures and the urgent drive to best the other at some activity. At this developmental level, such competition is often connected directly with bodily functions or appearance. For example, little boys may have a contest to see who can reach further with his stream of urine, or who can more accurately hit a target; and little girls may be very concerned about who is the prettiest, or who has the prettiest dress. Most 2-year-olds are too self-centered to compete; they simply want it all for themselves (just as they are too self-centered to engage in a cooperative project). But as the 3rd birthday comes up, there is a decided shift in the engagement with others. It takes form as an increased capacity to participate in a shared undertaking, and a parallel desire to outdo the other, to be first, to be best. The notions of winning and overcoming competition have their roots here and have obvious implications for later social development.

THE WISH TO CASTRATE.   There is another side to the aggressive components of this stage, however, that needs some explication. The discussion of magical thinking in the previous chapter noted that this is a time when all children maintain a curious belief that body parts are not permanently in place, that, in fact, the child could move them about, if he but knew how to do this. This kind of thinking is enshrined in a great many legends and fairy tales.

The 3-year-old thinks in this way, and, intuitively, adults know this. A characteristic game that adults initiate quite spontaneously with such little ones is "I've got your nose!" In effect, the adult is saying to the child: "I know how you think, and I will participate with you in a game you will find very interesting; it's right where you live."

Given such a belief system, such a child goes through considerable internal stress in negotiating the developmental labyrinth. This is a time with great rewards and great dangers; children need both help and luck to come through the developmental challenges of this stage without emotional mishap.

Take, for example, the situation of a little boy who arises early and wanders into his parents' bedroom. He may be just in time to see his father, who has only partially awakened from REM sleep, get out of bed and go stumbling off toward the bathroom. The father's penis is erect or at least partially engorged, the little boy catches sight of this, and the thought crosses his mind: "Oh, how I wish I had that! [after all, he has already had the experience of fondling his own penis, and he knows how good it feels] Now just look at what Daddy has there. Daddy's is so much bigger; he has so much more."

Psychoanalytic experience suggests that under such circumstances, the average little boy experiences an intense pang of greed and yearning. He wants what he sees, and, as part of this wish, he is likely to think of taking it away from his father. Often enough, this stirs up archaic memories of how to get things, primitive impulses from an earlier epoch, so that the wish takes the form of perhaps biting it off, swallowing it down, and thus making it really his own. This kind of psychological possessing is typical of oral-stage thinking, and the child will resort to it at moments of great emotional stress. Such thinking is atavistic, but perhaps all the more powerful for that. It leaves a deep trace on the child's inner life, and is, in a way, prototypical of the aggressive thoughts of the time; the wish to cut off the other's genital is a basic part of phallic-phase aggressivity.

Along with this come a series of fantasies of phallic prowess, many of which entail triumph over and destruction of a rival. Inevitably, the competitive (besting the other) and the envious (taking possession of what the other has) themes flow together, and the youngsters dream of demonstrating phallic prowess through guns, knives, and swords, and all manner of thrusting, killing, and shooting. In its own way it is quite a violent time.

Further Development of Gender Identity

The increased interest in genital concerns brings a child closer to the core experiences of gender determination, and the children begin to sort out this aspect of their identity on a variety of fronts. Because the work of each gender is necessarily different, each will be treated separately in the following sections.

The Boy. The great discovery of early childhood is that there are two kinds of people in the world, those with a penis and those without. This is seen by the children rather differently from the way they will eventually apprehend such information as adults. In fact, most children do not readily subscribe to the "two kinds of people" theory; as far as they are concerned, there is only one kind, people to whom a penis is issued. After that, some of them are allowed to retain the organ, and some have their penis taken away. Or, possibly, some of them were issued a penis, and some of them were not. This means that a penis is a vulnerable and contingent thing; indeed, to have one also implies the possibility of losing one. After all, the little girls have obviously lost theirs, so it is evident that it can happen.

Within this universe of discourse, the notion of losing the penis is called *castration* (an inaccurate use of the term, but accepted usage), and, for many reasons, it has emerged as a central theme in this age group's developmental experience. The most obvious reason is the pleasure that the male child experiences in touching and manipulating his penis. At this time in his development the penis is a source of the most intense feelings of gratification, a very valuable and exciting presence in his life. More than that, it has a curious life of its own; it stands up sometimes without his being able to control it, and at such times the sensuous reward is even greater. In a variety of ways it is really quite unique.

Beyond all that, there is the powerful social reaction to this part of the body. Children readily recognize the enormous concern that society places on concealing, revealing, joking about, laughing about, or otherwise reacting to this organ. It is important to parents, to baby-sitters, to teachers—to all the important people. By concealment, innuendo, hints, and humor, they all make much of it, so that its importance, albeit somewhat mysterious, is nonetheless self-evident.

But perhaps the most critical factor of all making for the importance of the penis is one about which investigators can only speculate because there is neither basis nor data. It simply seems plausible that an organ concerned with species survival would have a strong phylogenetic hook associated with it, a tendency to overvaluation and conservation that would have been bred in through many generations. In any case, concerns about the penis are very prevalent in boys of this age, and these concerns persist throughout adult life.

Each gender must account for gender difference in some way. It is likely that all children form some kind of theory to try to explain what they see, that is, all children have something between their legs that feels good, but some children do and some do not have a penis. Little boys' theories tend to follow a certain model and to lead to rather typical conclusions. The boy thinks:

> I have pictured Daddy's penis to myself and wished to take it away; what if Daddy could read my mind? What if he knew what I was thinking? What would happen then? And the answer follows quickly: Daddy would be very angry, he would punish me, he would do to me what I was thinking of doing to him, he would turn me into a girl.

With that thought comes a tremendous pang of fear and concern; the child begins to worry. And to worry, and to worry. To be sure, some youngsters are more concerned, and some are less so. Many factors play a role in determining just how much a given child does, in fact, react to this idea; for certain more vulnerable children it becomes the center of their existence. For a long time thereafter, they devote the entire organization of their personality to coping with the anxiety this idea has engendered. For most children it remains a background thought, not without impact, but without the commanding presence it attains in the child fated to become neurotic.

By and large, however, the thought of castration continues to be disturbing, and the little boy will manifest his concern in many ways. Thus, the I've-got-your-nose game alluded to earlier has considerable meaning for such youngsters. When the adult sets up this kind of play, the child typically wants to do it again and again. Often there is mounting excitement during the game, with the child appearing more and more delighted with each repetition. That is to say, he is laughing more loudly and insisting more intensely on repeating the sequence. If the observer steps away from the play idea for a moment, it is apparent that the little boy is dealing with anxiety, that the laughter is a defensive maneuver to convert what is frightening into what is funny and exciting (the classic psychological mechanism underlying thrill-seeking behavior). Fundamentally, the child is seeking to master a threatening and potentially very frightening experience; even though it scares him, he can find a real quality of reassurance in the game quality of the play. He can play as though castration happens, but in reality he is always in control, and it does not happen. (Needless to say, the quality of the adult's behavior is critical.)

This then is a cue to understanding so many of the events of this time. All children have a host of built-in means for coping with the stress arising out of their inner vulnerabilities, and these coping mechanisms are a saving grace. The child seeks to accommodate himself to the challenges that development brings; hence, the naked emotions are not as visible as their processed and disguised versions. Difficulties occur when the coping devices themselves become foci for adaptive troubles. Thus, for example, a little boy who seeks to overcompensate for his fears may repeatedly seek out sources of anxiety to prove to himself and to his world that he is not afraid: He takes risks, climbs up on wobbly high places, clings to insecure perches, holds on with one hand when two seem scarcely sufficient, and needs again and again to demonstrate his indifference to danger. Another child who is wracked by fear of body damage gives up on assertiveness, refuses to fight, won't even defend himself, and becomes target, scapegoat, and victim in the schoolyard. Thus, as the child develops, the phase-specific issues encountered have many overtones for behavior in general and for that youngster's security system in particular.

Little boys, then, must cope with the themes associated with castration and find some way to engage these issues and to master them. In a sense, the problem is one of self-mastery; the boy's fears are largely a product of his own creation. He projects onto the parent his inner assumptions of rage and retaliation, and he becomes the victim of his own aggression. To be sure, a fair number of little boys are, in fact, subjected to quite literal castration threats. Upon seeing the child masturbate, some parents give him all sorts of terrifying warnings: "If you touch yourself, your pee-pee will fall off! You will be damaged for life." These threats reinforce the fears that are already imminent, but the reinforcement is not even necessary. Even with the kindest and gentlest of parents the child may find reason to fear; the roots are after all within himself.

Although the evidence for castration concerns is commonplace, the true character of this anxiety is usually sufficiently disguised so that it is not recognized as such. Little boys will manifest all sorts of fears and behavioral ripples that will be taken for granted as some of the natural nonsense of childhood, the sort of thing parents live with until the child "grows out of it." For example, one of the authors (JDN) visited his sister when her son, Bobby, was 3 years old. As brother and sister were chatting, the sister mentioned that she was having the worst time keeping shoes and socks on Bobby; no sooner would she put them on and tie the laces than he would untie them and pull off both shoes and socks. This was a regular thing; it would keep happening throughout the day. A bit later in the visit, the author chanced to be alone in a room with his nephew who was seated on the floor and assiduously pulling a sock onto his foot and then quickly taking it off. Then once again he donned it and then removed it immediately. The author said, "You know, Bobby, even when the stocking covers your foot and you can't see it, your foot's still there. It doesn't go away." The youngster looked up at him in a startled fashion and said: "You mean now? When it's covered like this, it's still there?" "Yes," he was told, "It's always there; you don't lose it." With mounting excitement the child began to pull the sock on and off, over and over again, calling out delightedly: "Now? And this time too? And now too?" He had to repeat this a number of times to become sufficiently reassured; clearly, it had been a tormenting problem: Where does the body part go when you can't see it?

Again, the intensity of the emotion and the repetitiousness of the behavior indicate the considerable concern that such issues characteristically occasion in a child's life. A great many of the "habits" of childhood are more or less disguised attempts to cope with the anxieties emanating from these haunting castration themes. For example, masturbatory behavior sometimes becomes more and more frequent and may reach a point where it is practically constant. In effect, it appears to take on a compulsive form. In such instances it is not the pursuit of sensation that drives the boy's behavior; it is the endless need for reassurance that he is indeed all right, that his body is intact, that castration has not taken place.

Occasionally the child may choose some other part of the body as a symbolic substitute for the penis and will engage, for example, in head rubbing or hair pulling, which then becomes a habit disorder of childhood.

Although castration anxiety is a universal presence during development, it is not necessarily a precursor to later difficulties. All little boys go through it and, presumably, master it, more or less. Without adequate parental support, however, during the early growing-up years it can become a troublesome and tormenting presence; more than that, in many serious ways it can disturb the onward flow of experience and growth. The implications of castration anxiety for later pathological outcomes should not be underestimated. Traces of this experience persist in certain forms of homosexuality, for example, where the person is capable of sexually loving only people with a penis. The very thought of a body without this organ is dismaying to the individual, sometimes even disgusting. The ideal love object in such cases is often a very muscular, highly athletic male who is the very antithesis of a "castrated" person. (It should be noted that this is only one variety of homosexuality; this complex adaptive mode has many forms and varieties of expression.) A great many problems of heterosexual men may also stem from castration concerns; these include psychogenic impotence, ejaculatio praecox, male frigidity, and many others. The compulsive masturbation of childhood can be mirrored by an equally compulsive heterosexual philandering in adulthood, wherein the need to maintain a sense of security as an adequate male requires endless redemonstrations of the capacity to engage women sexually.

The Girl. The little girl has an even more complex equation to solve than does the boy. She has to account for appearing to lack something that he has. To understand the thinking of the child under these circumstances, it is essential to try to reason like a 3-year-old; this is not easy or natural, but it is necessary in order to grasp something of the child's experience.

The key variable is the girl's sense of pleasure in manipulating her clitoris. This is a highly gratifying experience and, just as is true for the boy, this part of the body becomes very special and rewarding. The social valuation of the groin is no less obvious to the girl than it is to the boy, and thus both inner and outer experience conspire to make this region a very intriguing part of the self. Given all that, the little girl can see that whatever she has, the boy has more. It is a bit like being served a piece of cake; more is better. Whoever has gotten a bigger piece is preferred, better loved, or more fortunate. It may all too easily appear to the girl that someone else is preferred.

Having encountered this mystery, she has to sort out what this means. She may conclude that it is all a matter of timing and of being good. If she is a very good girl and waits patiently, someday she will get a penis; she just has not received hers yet. Or, she may feel that she did get one but that for some reason it was taken away. In any case, many little girls, at some point during development, acquire the sense of not having gotten their due. There are, however, a great many ways to come to grips with this.

To begin with, there may well be strong biological reinforcement for the girl's acceptance of her gender position. That is to say, Stoller's proposal (alluded to previously) that there exists an innate sense of *primary femininity* may well be valid. In effect, this would imply that the little girl's sense of self as feminine is a biological given and as such, may play a role here. Although possibly true, the evidence for this is elusive.

In terms of child rearing, however, a number of femininity-enhancing statements consonant with primary femininity are often tendered to little girls, and these move in quickly and smoothly to compensate for any sense of deprivation or mistreatment. Thus, from a very early age little girls are told that they can have babies, whereas little boys cannot. Much or little may be made of this within a given home, but it is always a factor in the girl's awareness.

For many girls this is a considerable reward. Whether there are genetically patterned aspects to this, researchers do not know; socially, it is obvious that a goodly number of little girls take readily to doll play and baby play, and they devote many hours of each day and much creative energy to elaborating fantasies about having babies and caring for them. For some little girls the baby doll is the paramount presence in their lives for a long time. More than that, many a mother feels that this is the "right" kind of play for her little daughter and sees to it that this kind of play material is readily available. Sometimes it is all that is available.

Another form of support can be condensed to the word *pretty*. Again and again the little girl hears about how pretty she looks, how pretty her dress is, or her hair ribbon, or her outfit—or, for that matter, her hair, her hands, her whole body, every part of her. This is no small boon; for the rapt young child these compliments can become a vital presence in her thinking and self-valuation. Again, whether or how much biological preconditioning there may be is unknown; the social reinforcers, however, are plain to see. Nothing could be more commonplace than for little girls to be complimented on their appearance. As with the idea of having a baby, probably for most such children, the accent on their prettiness is immensely rewarding and does a great deal to compensate them for any injury engendered by concerns about genital differences. They proceed to grow within a framework of intense interest in their appearance, and their attention is directed in large measure to clothes, style, hairdos, and other factors that might affect that appearance.

Not infrequently, all this stress on appearance is likely to be associated with the notion of being attractive, of evoking interest and excitement in the male. (In most instances, although varying in degree, this will in part be an expression of an earlier identification with the mother. The initial target is usually the father, but there might be a rapid generalization to all men or to some particular visitor to the home—even little boys who are playmates can be the objects of such efforts.) Many a child of this age becomes overtly—even dramatically—coquettish. She is not only concerned with being pretty; she tries to the best of her ability to *use* her good looks, to thrust her charms on the attention of the onlooker. The whole panoply of what would later be considered bold or seductive behavior can now be played out; at this age such behavior is usually considered "cute." It is evident as well that such patterns could challenge or frighten the mother, or perhaps serve as a vehicle for the expression of the mother's own more or less suppressed impulses. In any case they set up some form of responsive vibrations within the mother's own feminine organization. This will have considerable meaning for the character of the ensuing mother–daughter fit.

Finally, parents communicate to children a whole range of attitudes about appropriate gender-role behavior. Should they cross gender lines, both boys and girls are likely to hear in so many words that they are not supposed to act that way, such behavior is for the other gender; they are prompted to act in whatever manner the parent considers correct for a boy or a girl. Some of these attitudes become enshrined in poems such as: "What Are Little Boys Made Of?" Other attitudes are implied rather than stated. Then there are some that are learned only through derision and critique of what is regarded as off-gender behavior. (The patterns of gender-related teasing will be carried forward by peers later in latency, but many parents initiate such attacks much earlier in development.) The direct instruction in gender-appropriate response and performance begins at birth, is conveyed both consciously and unconsciously, and is a continuous presence all through early development.

In so complex a form of adaptation as the organization of gender identity, children are likely to explore all sorts of variations and blind alleys. For example, probably every little girl tries at least once to urinate like a boy; the outcome is predictably unsuccessful and often humiliating, and the behavior quickly disappears. As one adult woman ruefully recalled, "I wet my socks." Another common pattern is exemplified in the following anecdote. A mother had sent Susie, her 3½-year-old daughter, out to play in the yard with some visiting neighbor children. Suddenly one of the playmates, a little boy, came running in to announce that Susie had taken off all her clothes and was running around naked. Mother dashed out and, indeed, her naked daughter was prancing happily about. Mother immediately pulled up the panties, pulled the dress over Susie's head, delivered an admonition, and returned within. A few minutes later the helpful little boy was back: "Susie did it again!" Again the mother dashed out, again she reclothed the child, delivered a few stern words, and left all apparently once more in order. But then it happened a third time, and a fourth, and it finally took almost force majeur before the child would behave.

What was happening? Some of the following issues were working themselves out: Within the mixed play group Susie was asserting that she did not feel any sense of lack about her body—"I am pretty all over, see, look at how pretty my body is, who cares if I do not have a penis, every bit of me is pretty!" Again, the peculiar insistence of her behavior betrays its overcompensatory quality; under these conditions the need to assert and to display was even greater than the wish of this usually well-behaved little girl to be in the mother's good graces. It would take some time and some inner work before the child could accommodate both to her mother's dicta and to her own needs, and the growth of her feminine identity could proceed comfortably.

For both genders the vicissitudes can be many, and few children pass through so turbulent a time completely unscathed. On the other hand, it is likely that the combination of primary gender endowment and adequate social support will see most children through to achieving a sufficient level of comfortable gender identity.

The Phallic Fantasies

Numerous fantasies characterize this period, so many, indeed, that no attempt will be made to render an exhaustive list. These imagic creations are of special significance because within the framework of psychoanalytic theory, this is the moment in development when the resort to fantasy as a coping device reaches its highest peak. The child first learns how to manipulate inner images during the 2nd year of life; by age 3 years this is a well-mastered competence, and the child begins to rely on fantasies to solve the hard problems of existence.

Now is the moment in growing up when the belief that wishing can change reality reaches its apogee; for the phallic-phase child the lesson of Tinker Bell—that if you believe hard enough, it will happen—truly strikes home. Children's songs are consonant with this kind of thinking: "Wishing will make it so, just keep on wishing, . . . " Adults, with a native awareness of where these youngsters are psychologically, create fantasy entities, such as Santa Claus, and then debate hotly whether or not to tell the child that they are but myths. The fantasy component of children's' lives merits special attention because these fantasies have enduring resonances into the future and will influence many essential developmental constructions. In effect, some of these fantasies become structural parts of personality and give form and direction to many essential aspects of interpersonal attitude and style. Seductiveness, shyness, and a variety of other personality traits may involve important underlying images of this sort.

However, in later life, where such fantasies continue to be functionally operative, they are usually (but not always) unconscious. Some of the earliest and most striking psychoanalytic discoveries consisted of uncovering these disturbing ideas by patients who had been altogether unaware that these sequences existed in their minds. In effect, the images had persisted as templates for behavior and had given the patients a model for their own functioning that they were compelled to repeat over and over again without understanding why they did so. All they knew was that they felt tempted (perhaps *driven* would be more accurate) to act in particular ways or felt anxious if they did not act in these ways, or both.

The Phallic Mother. One of the commonest thoughts of children at this time of life is that the mother, whom they have probably seen naked either by plan or by accident, cannot be without a penis; she is too big and powerful for that. They are convinced that somewhere she has one, and if they could but spy on her or were allowed to look, they would surely find it. (One 3-year-old boy informed his father, "Mommy doesn't have a penis; she has a *giant!*") Although by no means universal, this is not an uncommon idea. When increasing maturity and insight correct some of the distortions of the earlier years, this particular notion is usually given up. In occasional cases, however, the myth persists as an active presence within a child's personality organization; in such instances it can seriously affect the erotic dimension of development. Thus, one of the commonest fixed ideas in cases of fetishism is this belief. For the fetishist, the idea of castration, of the mother lacking a penis, is so disturbing, that it warps reality itself, and the patient clings to some physical object that becomes the substitute (maternal) penis. As long as he has the shoe, the cane, or whatever the object to which he has become attached, he does not need to fear castration, and he can be potent and loving. Without that, however, he is lost—anxious, empty, and impotent; or at least he is deprived—something essential is missing. In occasional instances, various forms of character pathology such as stealing have also been known to derive from this source. Such a person is disposed toward secrecy and seeks in hidden ways to recapture that which has been concealed or withheld. In certain lives such fantasies can have a remarkably tenacious quality. (In the light of what researchers are learning about the heritability of character traits, it is also possible that the unconscious selection and retention of such fantasies is part of a genetically determined orientation of personality.)

The Independently Mobile Penis.   The curious sense of the transferability of body parts noted above gives rise to a general conception of the penis as being able to move about independently. In fact, for the little boy, this part of his body has a life of its own; every so often it stands up "all by itself." It is not like the rest of him; he cannot altogether control it. In fantasy, it becomes a kind of messenger; it is capable of ascending to great heights or flying through the air; it can be detached and sent out, as it were, to do errands or accomplish missions. It is the genie coming out of the bottle. In certain contexts this imagined entity takes on grandiose dimensions associated with speed, power, and sometimes destructiveness. Children, when playing, can represent many such ideas with cars, planes, trains, daggers, swords, pistols, bullets, rockets, missiles, ray guns, and the like. Sometimes interests that originate as phallic-phase concerns can, in later life, contribute to the formation of powerful inner motives, that drive an individual to a particular career, such as crane operator or pilot, or, under less fortunate circumstances, press him to engage in high-speed driving or other dangerous patterns of movement (e.g., piloting stunt planes, performing high wire feats).

Pregnancy Fantasies.   All little children encounter the phenomenon of pregnancy and must find a way to fit that in with what they understand about the human body. Such youngsters usually have no very clear concepts of the insides of people; as they see it, what is inside their bodies is likely to be first food, then feces and urine, and finally perhaps blood. The notion of internal genitalia, for example, has little meaning at this age unless the child is imagining a hidden penis. The little girl may have a feeling of inner sensuous glow that spreads diffusely over her lower body and seems to come from the inside, but this scarcely brings with it a picture of any definite presence within (Kestenberg, 1961). Hence, when the child encounters a pregnant woman the commonest theory he entertains is likely to be the notion of some special result of eating. After all, the youngster has firsthand knowledge of such experiences; after he has eaten a lot, his tummy becomes big and full, so it is no great mystery to unravel that something of the sort has happened to the pregnant woman. Again, a personal observation of one of the authors (JDN) may illuminate the point.

One time the author was invited to the home of a psychiatrist friend and his wife for dinner. The couple had two sons, and the wife was pregnant. The two little boys, Johnny and Tommy, were 5 years old and 2 years old, respectively. They were seated at table next to their mother, who had prepared a steak dinner for the several guests. The mother had served the guests, she had placed a steak on her own plate, and she was beginning to cut up some meat for the boys. Suddenly Johnny, the older child, reached across with his fork to his mother's plate and pulled her steak onto his plate. Mother immediately restored her meat to its proper place, admonishing Johnny: "Now you just wait a minute, mister, I'm getting yours ready; leave Mommy's steak alone." She resumed cutting the children's' portions into bits, whereupon Johnny reached across with his fork and did it again. Once more, the mother took her steak back onto her plate and spoke to Johnny a bit more severely: "Stop that, young man, or you will not be able to sit at table. That's Mommy's portion; yours is right here and will be ready in a moment." But it didn't help; within a few seconds once again Johnnie had his fork in his mother's steak. This time his father became involved, "Stop that at once, or there will be trouble." But the youngster did not stop, and in a short time there was a miniature eruption. Finally, kicking and screaming, Johnny was removed in disgrace and put in his room.

The author was a helpless spectator to all this. He was agonizing all the while whether to intrude, or whether it would be best just to keep out of what was after all not his affair. For better or for worse, he did keep out of it, but it was not easy. It seemed to him that the child already had one sibling and was none too pleased with that one. Here was Mommy busily at work, eating, eating, eating, making him yet another one. He did not want it and was prepared to do everything in his power to stop it. That included despoiling the mother of her most likely source of siblings, the meat she ate. Having reached this (for him) not illogical conclusion, he proceeded to act on it with grit and determination. Alas!

Other Fantasies.   The above is not an unusual story; the fantasies of this time of life provide intense, imagic constructions. In their own way they are coherent, and all too often, they are profoundly unreal. When they become enshrined in personality disturbances, they can precipitate a host of hard-to-treat symptomatic behaviors. Many of the so-called perversions represent such developmental snags (e.g., the fetishism noted earlier), and a number of anxiety-driven behaviors, such as voyeurism, exhibitionism, Don Juanism, and certain forms of promiscuity, are in part rooted in the child's phallic-stage fantasies about how to cope with the issues posed by castration anxiety, reproduction, and the like.

Many of these themes have found their way into human myths. For example, in Greek mythology the Gorgon Medusa had been a beautiful woman who had angered the goddess Athene. The goddess thereupon turned Medusa into a monster of surpassing ugliness, with a dreadful face, glaring eyes, and live snakes for hair. So horrible was her visage that whoever looked at her turned into stone.

The hero, Perseus, was enjoined to bring her head back to the king of Seriphos. Perseus obtained all manner of magical aids, including a shield with a polished reflecting surface; he was thus able to cut off the monster's head by avoiding direct confrontation and seeing her only as an image mirrored in the shield.

The story is of interest because the theme of Medusa occasionally comes up during psychoanalysis. When it does, the patient characteristically brings back associations of having seen the genitals of an adult woman. The "castration" (as the observer perceived it) is the genital area without a penis; the curly pubic hair is snakelike. It seems to the patient a terrifying sight. Indeed the image is so disturbing that he (it is usually a man who recounts this particular association) freezes with anxiety—and is at the same time aroused sexually so that he has an erection (turns to stone).

Polymorphic Perverse Fantasies. One group of fantasies is of striking importance in this connection. The time sequence of the phallic phase causes it to overlap the anal epoch to a considerable extent (Parens, 1980). Moreover, the echoes of the oral stage are still reverberating and have by no means disappeared. Hence, depending on their individual developmental patterns, at this juncture certain children can find themselves in the midst of a maelstrom of turbulent ideation. At some moments images from any one of these stages can predominate; at others, the images overlap and oral, anal, and phallic fantasies tumble about simultaneously inside their heads. When erotically excited (e.g., during masturbation), such a child entertains many primitive ideas and fantasies: of feces in contact with mouths; of anuses in contact with each other or with clitorises; of the penis juxtaposed with the mouth, the clitoris, or the anus; or, indeed, of any of these sensuous sites or their products in contact with any other in all kinds of mixed-up combinations. Ordinarily, this is a transient condition and the child will presently achieve phallic-phase dominance. The preoccupation with yearnings or images from earlier developmental levels will drop out, and the primary content of fantasy will be versions of clitoral or penile sensation and mind-pictures connected with these organs. For some people, however, unfortunate combinations of traumatic and temperamental factors cause the confusion of levels and fantasies to become a point of developmental arrest. The individual thus fixated will envisage sex as a welter, a potpourri of arousing admixtures where everything goes on at once. Indeed, when such an individual grows older, he or she will seek to arrange for such experiences as best life allows. The preferred patterns of sexuality may ultimately involve several individuals of both genders in the same bed, with a need for each person's every orifice to have contacted each other person's every orifice, along with multiple changes of partner and position before the session is over. Not infrequently such individuals regard themselves as the exemplifiers of liberated and avant-garde sexuality; the psychoanalyst sees them as driven to live out the fantasies of the troubled 3-year-old.

As is true of all these fantasy patterns, the awareness that such a developmental sequence may exist comes from the analysis of people who are possessed by and who live out such early images. Usually they do not come to analysis because of sexual problems; they appear because they are suffering from depression, have developed a phobia, or are otherwise symptomatic. Their particular sexual orientation comes up incidentally, although it may presently become the focus of analytic attention. The psychological orientation of the early phallic phase has been called the "polymorphic perverse" position.

Primal Scene Fantasies. There is a very special group of images that adult patients bring up during psychoanalysis, relating to early memories of childhood exposure to adult sexuality. These recollections are so ubiquitous and so emotionally laden that they have been given a specific designation—the fantasies of the *primal scene*. It is not altogether clear why this group of associations has the emotional power that it seems to have; theoretically it entails the archetypical quality of what psychoanalysts mean by *trauma*.

In the average home, adult sexual behavior is a frequent and regular event. According to the strictures of our culture, it is definitely off-limits to children, and most adults take some pains to safeguard their children from exposure to grown-up sexual activities. Nonetheless, such activity is not inherently silent, and it also carries the kind of emotional force that may render an adult temporarily unaware of some aspects of his or her environment. These factors provide possibilities for naturally curious children to be exposed to at least some aspects of what the adults are doing, and psychoanalytic experience suggests that most children are, in fact, so exposed.

A great many factors influence the way such things take place. Thus, socioeconomic realities are major determinants. Poor people tend to live under crowded conditions, and the only safeguard for the adults (if they are to have any sex life at all) is to "wait till the children are asleep." Although not so intentioned, the children gradually obtain quite a graphic rendition of what sexuality is all about (at least as practiced within their home). It is a truism that alcoholism and poverty often go hand in hand, and alcoholism is one of the circumstances that can profoundly influence parental caution as far as this particular form of discretion is concerned. Under such conditions, exhibitionistic sex is no rarity.

In middle-class homes, soundproofing is often abysmal and children at least hear if they cannot see; 3-year-olds also wander around the house at night and find their way into the parental bedroom, and, for that matter, the parental bed. Some adults enjoy sex during the day, when the possibility of discovery is greater; there are summer trips to the mountains or the seashore where privacy barriers are inherently harder to maintain; a variety of commonplace conditions, in short, can provide children with some glimpse, or more than a glimpse of adults interacting sexually. There are also parents who, for their own neurotic reasons, often linked to early childhood experiences, more or less deliberately (albeit sometimes unconsciously) flaunt sexual activity before the child. Baby sitters may offer another opportunity for children to view such activity. Teenagers are at the height of sexual excitability; after the children have been put to bed, the sitter may find it a golden opportunity to invite in his or her partner for a private evening together. If the children should happen to wake up, they are presently afforded the views about which they are so curious.

The chances are that such encounters are well-nigh universal, and, like castration anxiety, they pose the child a challenge that, in most instances, is met and mastered without impeding development. Under some circumstances, however, primal scene experience can apparently play quite a role in shaping an individual's attitudes toward sex, gender, and the management of anxiety. This may come about from special circumstances of exposure, from accumulated stresses of which this is but one, or from some inherent or acquired vulnerability that renders a given child inordinately susceptible to the impact of these events. Thus on the one hand, a child may have inherited a susceptibility to panic attacks; and on the other, the child may be the target of teenage or adult sexual acts (or other forms of sexual overstimulation) that will certainly affect his vulnerability. Disturbances during the previous anal stage or a genetic predisposition to anal stage fixation may have left a child with a strong sadomasochistic tendency; this too will color how that child perceives and interprets the phallic-stage experiences when he encounters them (i.e., sexual excitement may be strongly associated with dominating or submitting, with hurting or being hurt). Whatever the reason, there is little doubt that for certain children, the effort to cope with exposure to the primal scene takes them to the extremes of their adaptive capacities, and, all too often, beyond. At such times symptoms may appear, or, even when no direct evidence of dysfunction is manifest at the time, sites of fragility may become established that, under the impact of subsequent stresses, will later give way and lead to disturbing problems.

The usual psychoanalytic explanation advanced to account for the powerful effect of this kind of experience involves the concept of *flooding*. In brief, this view asserts that the organism can contain a certain level of stimulation, as it were, and still maintain homeostasis. If the amount of stimulation rises above this threshold, then the higher levels lead to overload. This is always a serious threat to basic organismic equilibrium; the individual cannot metabolize the amount of stimulation flooding in, and in some measure the system breaks down. Thus, a child watching adults engaged in sexual exchange might have a tremendous sense of inner excitement, arousal, fear, or anxiety that he cannot discharge in any way. The tension continues to build up, and there is nothing the youngster can do. A profound sense of strain and helplessness ensues, a feeling of not being able to stand any more, and yet more keeps coming. Ultimately, something must give way; the child must implode inward or explode outward. Most children view coitus as a fight of some kind; they tend to make it into a dreadful but enormously exciting sadistic exchange. (Later they may want to see movies with dinosaur battles, over and over again.) In any case, if the particular child's tendency is to internalize, he might become anxious and frightened, and for a time be inconsolable. Along with this, he might have a sense of great wrongdoing in merely having seen what he knows is forbidden to look upon, and he may begin to complain of headaches or stomach pain. The implosion might take a neurotic direction, and he might then develop a blinking tic, where, symbolically, he keeps trying to turn off the forbidden image.

Or the child might be an externalizer who handles tension through action; he might now become combative and attack other children in nursery school or engage them in predatory sexual play, seemingly driven to relive the "battle" over and over again. Or the child might act provocatively toward adults and seek to "fight" with them as he has seen the adults "fighting"; or at least he can use his provocativeness to control their excitement and reaction instead of being the passive and helpless victim, who is overwhelmed. In any case what has happened to such a youngster is best understood as *trauma.* The child has been exposed to more stimulus demand than he could master and has, in effect, cracked under the strain. It is this sense of emotional avalanche, when the child can endure no more yet is forced to experience more, that gives trauma its special character.

As development proceeds, the professional can see some of the residual effects of this problem in the way some children come to regard sex as the final form of dirtiness. (When asked if he thought sex was dirty, Woody Allen is said to have replied: "It is if you do it right.") And this attitude develops despite the most heartfelt efforts by enlightened parents to demystify sexuality and to make it a positive value in the children's lives. Some of the complexities of this issue can be seen in the values that attach to the commonest sexual word in our language, *fuck.*

Superficially, this word is the crude term for sexual intercourse. It is usually employed as a transitive verb, *to fuck,* and immediately conveys images of copulation. However, people commonly use it with quite a different connotation in mind: It means "to play a dirty trick on, to abuse, to take advantage of, to extort, or to cheat." This is particularly true when expressed in the passive voice: "I was fucked." Thus, the same term that portrays sexuality in its most graphic form offers one of the most trenchant means for expressing dismay and rage. It implies assault and victimization. And this, indeed, is what many a child perceives sexual congress to be, the victimizing of one partner by the other. The man stabs the woman with his penis and beats her with his body. The woman castrates the man; she takes his erection into her, devours it, and destroys it.

An example from recent literature gives a sense of what this primal scene experience is like for a child. One episode from the first volume of the great fantasy novel *The Lord of the Rings* (Tolkien, 1956) will illustrate the point.

The story involves the quest of a small band of heroic figures led by an old wizard. They are trying to find their way across a hostile countryside where they are constantly beset by a virulent enemy. They are at length driven to enter a vast cavern where they must brave the hazards of crossing an underground city, Moria, built many years ago by the Dwarves, who had carved their city out of stone under a mountain range. According to the story, they had delved too deeply and had released a dreadful entity imprisoned in these depths that had destroyed them and devastated their city. Hence, the heroes are fleeing through a place of total darkness, a huge, empty deserted cavern with no living thing about, and with their way lit only by the glow from the magician's staff.

During their advance, they begin to hear the enemy from whom they have been trying to escape; it comes to them at first in the form of a great drum beating, which grows louder as they go forward. They stop in a room and bar the door, but to no avail; the enemy breaks through and they must fly once again. Once more they try to bar a door, and once again the enemy bursts the hinges in hot pursuit. They cut across a plain and come to a great crevasse in the earth, a bottomless pit spanned by a tiny bridge across which they run at full speed—but the enemy is now upon them so they have no choice but to turn and meet the foe.

To their horror, the ranks of the opposing forces are led by the same monstrous being that had destroyed Moria. It is a huge winged figure of shadow and fire; its outlines are indistinct, but it is fearsome and bears in one hand a whip and in the other a sword. The wizard engages it in a fierce battle on the bridge. At one moment the combatants draw apart, and the wizard uses the respite to strike the bridge in front of the monster with his staff so that the span fragments and precipitates the creature into the depths. It tumbles downward but as it falls, the monster swings its whip and catches the wizard by the foot. Down he goes with it, and both disappear into the chasm. The bridge has been destroyed, however, and the remaining heroes escape.

This then is the frightening and exciting episode, a magical tale of a dark, underground encounter between powerful, chthonic forces. Seen from a psychodynamic perspective, it is also, perhaps, the story of a little boy about 3 years old who wanders about the house at night when all is in darkness, frightened and seeking his parents' presence. He comes to the door of their bedroom, and he hears a rhythmic beating that gets louder and louder as he comes closer. He hesitates at the door; there is a certain dread at the thought of opening it, but his need is great (and perhaps also his curiosity), and finally he turns the knob and lets it swing open—and there he sees two figures struggling in the darkness. One has a staff, the other is less distinctly outlined but is full of passion and movement. As the child watches, their combat reaches some kind of a climax, and both seem to collapse and to fall into a state of immobility.

In the case of a master storyteller such as Tolkien, such an early traumatic moment can be retained in memory and later converted into a profoundly moving and exciting episode within a larger tale. For many children, however, this experience is filled with catastrophic meaning; they are suffused with emotion that they cannot discharge or even articulate, they are at once terrified and erotically aroused, they want to repeat the experience and they want to forget it, and for a time they may become fretful and difficult "for no reason." Frequently such children have nightmares, and they will indeed return to the parental bed, this time with a bad dream.

Derivative Attitudes

The vicissitudes of the phallic phase are many, and the consequences are often experienced in more or less subtle attitudinal sets that later remain with the child as part of his emotional equipment. Often this is a feeling about the youngster's body or overall appearance; sometimes it takes on a more general cast such as feelings about his likability.

For the boy, a feeling may emerge that his penis is too small, or that there is something wrong with it. It may seem to him later that the erection has a curve that should not be there or is deformed in some way. He may feel vulnerable, inadequate, or lacking in some fundamental quality of masculinity; he isn't tough as a man should be, he isn't attractive to girls, and he just doesn't measure up to the full dimensions of what he senses masculinity to require. Later he may tell his doctor that for some reason he cannot void in a public urinal; if there is another man anywhere nearby, he simply blocks and cannot initiate a stream.

Or, the clinician may encounter the defensive adaptations to such attitudes, their reversal or denial. Under certain circumstances a youth may experience feelings of grandiose invulnerability or of cocky, self-laudatory sexual attractiveness. He may harbor a conviction that no one could resist his charms; he can have any girl he wants. There may be a need for a Don Juan promiscuity or for sexual exhibitionism dictating certain kinds of dress (with pants too tight and shirt buttons undone) to assert the young person's lack of fear of castration. Or the individual may have a driven (and equally unconscious) need to engage in some form of hazardous behavior to make a similar point.

The girl, too, may show many traces of the rocky course of phallic-stage development and emerge from this epoch with feelings of being deprived in some unnameable way; something about her is lacking; something is wrong with her; way down deep she feels unlovable. Or, like the boy, she may seek to overcompensate for these feelings and develop attitudes of seductiveness and coquettishness designed to reassure herself that she is indeed loved and lovable, is indeed desirable, and has conquests that she can turn to and think about (and perhaps tell about). Various patterns of teasing or promiscuous behavior may be part of such a picture when the youngsters seek to sort out the complex emotions arising at this time.

Chapter 12

The Later Preschool Years

Oedipal Phase

INTRODUCTION

The little child inevitably experiences everything important that happens as coming from or attaching to the parents. The parents stand in the center of the emotional world, and all significant feelings sooner or later swirl about and are caught up with these primary figures. Whether it be love, hate, fear, or sexual allure, the parental presence is entwined with the causes, the effects, and the experience of these emotions. During the phallic phase this has very special consequences for development.

The Erotic Component

As phallic-phase sensuousness sweeps over the child, the youngster turns to the bodies of both father and mother to seek at once the arousal he craves so much and the solace from tension that becomes so necessary. There is a good deal of questing for embraces, holding, rubbing up against, tickling with, and attempts to engage parents in mutual physical explorations. Some of this takes place when children get into the parental bed to cuddle; some occurs during "horseplay"; bathing offers a ready opportunity; the sensitized child and the unaware parent can even turn dressing and undressing into a kind of sexualized game. Parents often do not recognize the degree to which the child's libidinal developmental needs may influence everyday behavior.

The average person rearing a child will act intuitively to set limits on the possible excesses of physical interplay. The parent senses that something is getting out of hand; the child is getting a little too excited. The adult thereupon finds a more neutral activity and sends a message: "That is enough, let's do something else." The child will usually go along without difficulty, and nothing really registers on consciousness; the child has simply quit one game in favor of another. At the same time, within the inner world of the child there is room for a welter of nuances. The child may experience the limit setting as frustrating, threatening, rejecting, or unloving; alternatively, the youngster may find it a relief, a source of reassurance, a help with his efforts to control and to sublimate, and/or a reason to feel even more secure with the parent. Or there may be (and probably is) a mixture of these feelings.

Some parents, however, have had unfortunate experiences of their own during this moment in their growing up and are ill equipped to meet the demands of the phase. Such parents fall into patterns of too little or too much; they forbid all intimacy or insist on precocious modesty; or they seduce the child more or less overtly, and the pathology is transmitted forward for yet another generation (see Appendix 12–1 for a discussion of the pathological derivatives of the oedipal phase).

During this epoch, the children offer the full panoply of phallic-phase demonstrativeness. They exhibit themselves so that the little boy's penis may be much in evidence and the little girl's panties on almost continuous display. They are curious and want to see. They might ask to go into the toilet with the parents or may wish to shower or to bathe with them. There might be all kinds of bids to wrestle together or to have Daddy carry the child piggy-back, and the little girl, in particular, might enjoy knee riding a great deal.

At the outset the bodies of both parents are poles of powerful attraction; the children of either gender might alternate between homosexual and heterosexual interest. Under the combined tutelage of biology (their innate tendencies) and society (the parental injunctions, precepts, models, and stories; the media they encounter in the form of movies, TV, children's books and magazines, etc.) children presently tend to be drawn to the body of the parent of the opposite sex. This is the chosen one who becomes the target of their passions and fantasies, and they go through a time of deep love and erotic attraction to that parent. This reaches such proportions that the child wants to have that adult all to himself. It is not unusual at such a moment to hear of children proposing marriage to the father or the mother.

The necessary implication of this state of affairs is, however, that the child must do something about the other parent (of the same sex as the child). This parent is now the rival, and however well loved that parent might be (and usually is), at the time, the need to eliminate or at least exclude this rival is paramount.

The Aggressive Component

The child is thus caught in a truly difficult situation. On the one hand, the youngster loves both Daddy and Mommy, and on the other, one of them stands as rival to a new and powerful element in life that is not easily denied. This conflict begets many fantasies, among them thoughts about how to eliminate the rival, perhaps by destroying the competition, by outwitting the adult, by driving that person away, by running away with the other partner.

Occasionally the tangle and the frustration of all this get to be too much; the child becomes disobedient and starts to act provocatively, as if seeking punishment. Such a youngster has irritable moments when he cannot be mollified or comforted, has tantrums "for no good reason," has inexplicable headaches or stomachaches, and otherwise evidences strain and tension. This may be episodic, fluctuating according to some internal rhythm whose causes may not be readily apparent. Occasionally a child will seek to dominate things at home in some stubborn, driven, repetitious fashion that everyone finds very wearing; behavior like that of little Johnnie at dinner (related in the previous chapter) is relatively common, and its origins remain closed to the parents; they regard the child as simply being cranky and impossible. Periodic outbursts and tantrums occur in response to some punishment or frustration, and the child may scream at the parent, "I wish you were dead."

The Oedipal Constellation

As traditionally described (Freud, 1905/1953), the Oedipus complex provides a somewhat oversimplified picture of a very complex state of mind. To be sure, the child is caught up in these more or less conscious wishes to attract the parent of the opposite sex and to eliminate the rivalry of the same-sex parent. But the child still has a great need and love for both parents. The erotic attraction swings back and forth from the one possible partner to the other; the child wobbles between the homosexual and heterosexual positions, often only half aware of the inner musings and yearnings, and buffeted by changing and shifting affiliations and rivalries. Eventually he settles down to a steadier course, usually of heterosexual character, with the oedipal yearnings remaining largely in shadow and in dreams. In terms of their later influence on choice and form of love relationships, they can resonate for a lifetime.

Later Derivatives

The impress of the oedipal experience on character formation should not be underestimated. What transpires during this epoch affects the style, quality, depth, and overall form of later interpersonal patterning. The ability to love deeply, to feel the more sublimated urges of tenderness and protectiveness toward the loved one, to experience a mature, sexually enriched, and deeply caring affection for another person are all products of a successfully mastered developmental encounter at this time.

By the same token, various arrests or fixations at the oedipal level make their presence known in no uncertain fashion as development proceeds. Thus, some men and women forever move into one triangular relationship after another. No sooner have they emerged from one complex, entrapping, and difficult embroilment, than they "find themselves" entangled in some other equally complex affair. Often enough these relationships are as destructive to their own lives as to the lives of the others in the situation.

The Don Juanism noted in the discussion of the phallic phase can be shaped by oedipal considerations; the involved individual must not only have many women; they must all be women whom he takes away from other men. It is the triangle that is the target as much as the sexual conquest; this gives it its oedipal tinge. This can affect both genders; there are women who compulsively seek only men who already "belong" to someone else. In their interpersonal relationships, such men and women function as permanent oedipal children (although the consequences of their depredations are by no means child's play).

INTELLECTUAL DEVELOPMENT

A review of the cognitive dimensions of this phase shows that the child has now acquired a great many competencies. The elementary civilizing of the anal phase has been accomplished, and a whole new world of mastery and achievement lies ahead.

Language

The growth of language in the 3rd year of life is simply phenomenal. The 3-year-old can often converse reasonably well in complex sentences; indeed, an adult can exchange ideas with some of these children, which is seldom the case a year earlier. Sentences are now many worded and are couched in essentially accurate grammatical form; the earlier infantile constructions ("me good") have largely been replaced with more conventional syntax.

Thought

The child is into the stage of thought that Piaget denoted as prelogical or preoperational. In effect, much of what such a youngster thinks about is the wish fulfillment, fantasy-dominated type of magical thought. The beginnings of abstract thinking are already present but are not as yet prominent. The youngster is likely to have a special affinity for stories with magical themes and magical solutions to problems. Symbolic thinking has recently appeared, and the notion that one item can stand for and represent another is soon taken for granted. More than that, the child masters role playing and it becomes important in dealing with both fantasy and relationship. The readiness for social play patterns is at hand, and games of playing war, playing house, or fulfilling heroic, caretaking, or otherwise appealing roles occupy a good deal of the youngster's time.

Curiosity

A characteristic phallic-oedipal phase emergent is the appearance of a great deal of curiosity. This trait continues the exploratory interests of the toddler, but it can become fully manifest only when some of the urgencies of anal-phase demandingness, the imperative quality of the 2-year-old, have come to rest. At 18 months and 2 years the child is fascinated by the novelty of the world he is discovering. There is a hunger for contact with the new, for touching, handling, and encountering—and for bringing much of it back to show the caretaker. As the child gains mastery and the inner pressures abate, then the youngster's innate capacities to think, observe, and seek to understand his world become ever more evident. With this, the question "Why?" can become an omnipresent aspect of his interactions with caretakers. There are so many fascinating and incomprehensible things out there; the child wants to find out about all of them. The impulse-bound 2-year-old is still busy for the most part with inner imperatives; the concerns with body mastery, the power struggle, the work of separation–individuation, the rapprochement crisis—such a child may be too preoc-cupied with these vital issues to have time and energy for wondering, "Why does a watch tick?" But by 3 years, and in the ensuing years, many earlier issues have come to rest, and the child's attention turns outward toward trying to understand his environment. Or sometimes the curiosity turns inward; there are, after all, many fascinating inner fantasies to keep the child busy as well, and often these provide an even greater lure than external phenomena. Thus, many things, both inner and outer, intrigue the child; not surprisingly, 3-year-olds will pelt the adults caring for them with seemingly endless repetitions of "Why?" which is a request not only for information, but also an exploration of the form, syntax, and ground of explanation.

The pressing queries may be, to some extent, fueled by the sexual curiosity concerning the great mysteries of this time of life; the covert and unconscious basis for some of the inquiries may amount to "What are you doing behind the closed bedroom door? Where is Mommy's penis? Why are bodies of boys and girls different?" and the like.

During psychoanalysis, it is sometimes possible to link the emergence of later investigative interests to earlier sexual curiosity. This has led to the aphorism that the scientific researcher is a person who is forever peering up under the skirts of Mother Nature.

Play

The child is likely to attempt to resolve some of the tensions of this phallic-oedipal stage, with the newly acquired developmental emergent, represen-tational enacting through play. Through this prime means of personal expression, the child can control the reexperiencing of all the strain, hurt, humiliation, and panic that have beset him. Within the framework of make-believe, the youngster becomes doer rather than victim. The child regulates the amount of feeling and not the adult; the child determines the outcome and not the painful or frustrating reality (in effect, the child converts a passive position into an active one—a mechanism that serves as a major defensive maneuver). Moreover through play, the child can pit a wished-for version of events against an array of fantasied, and feared, possibilities.

To be sure, this mastery is all in displaced form; it is all make-believe. Nonetheless, many children who can play the matter out experience a definite improvement in self-feeling and relief from at least some tension. For this reason play is used extensively in helping to prepare a child for surgery or to assist him in coping with a loss. More generally, the entire process of play therapy depends to an appreciable extent, on just such factors; when skillfully managed, it can allow a child to titrate his pain, to cope with many vicissitudes in a symbolic, once-removed fashion, and to do so without having to come to grips with the full impact of the situation all at once.

Role Play

The developmental achievement of the ability to create, maintain, and manipulate inner images coincides with the emerging interest in looking and showing; this combination creates the conditions for a whole new level of integrated accomplishment, the ability to play a role. This is the moment when truly dramatic play—the make-believe that is so much a part of childhood—first appears.

Dramatic role play has been studied by many investigators, who have found it to be rich in implications for development and for problem solving on many levels. It is a powerful means of socialization, and through its use, the child practices how to deal with gender, aggression, intimacy, dominance, submission, and a host of similar accomplishments of critical import for future adjustment.

For some children it fits in with other elements of personality unfolding, for example, a narcissistic bent, and can thus become not merely a passing adaptive mode but a dominating and continuing presence within their pattern of daily functioning. Such children are dramatic to the point of being histrionic and are forever donning one costume or another and strutting about as they declare, with deadly seriousness, that they are some grandiose character. At their current level of personality functioning, the behavior is very earnest and very real. They are not out of touch with reality; they simply find it relatively easy to put reality aside and to feel that what a person wishes for is what is.

Later character traits that a child derives from this time of life include the following: striking dramatic attitudes; elaborating on everyday experiences to achieve a dramatic impact; experiencing the world in a sort of resonance with great figures in history, literature, or show business, and responding accordingly; or seeing himself and his circumstances in histrionic terms. This sort of posturing is frequently a powerful factor in peer relationships and general social adaptation. Given one set of developmental circumstances, peers will regard such an individual as colorful, fun, or interesting; given another, they will see such a youngster as a vain, pompous, egotistical, attention-grabbing show-off. No single outcome follows invariably from such a fixation, and the meaning of this, as well as of other personality factors, can be gleaned only by attending to the full range of constitutional and historic elements as well as the current stresses and adaptations present in a given life.

Body Image Consolidation

As the interest in bodies and in gender differences comes to a head, the child begins to acquire an ever more realistic sense of his body outlines. The concern with body parts moving around implies a good deal of attention to the details and lineaments of the body; the children's interest in looking impels them to study bodies, their own and those of others (when they can catch a glimpse). For example, the doctor game, which 4-year-olds tend to play in private, has among its many other meanings the continued exploring and learning about how bodies look, move, and feel. Children's curiosity concerning adult bodies accompanies the sensuous interests so typical of this time of life (the insistence on going with the adult into the bathroom, pressing to bathe with the father or mother, or simply asking many questions about the human body). But the child's own body also becomes an object of study. There is always the mirror, the experience of looking at pictures, the child's fantasies of how he would like his body to be; all of these contribute to an ever more intense preoccupation with and attention to body outlines. Nonetheless, in some ways the body outline remains essentially primitive during this epoch, and if the child tries to draw a person, the figure usually resembles a potato.

Emotional Development

The 3- to 5-year-olds do not explode into emotionally driven action as readily as 2-year-olds, but their range of affects is considerably wider, and the depth of their feelings is as great as that of the younger child. The capacity to regulate emotion is growing apace, and the child can experience a great many more discriminated feeling responses to the stresses and achievements of his life. Of particular importance is the ability to name feelings and to distinguish among them. The youngster can say that he is a little happy, a lot happy, or several stages in between; sadness too can now shade from feeling blue to a sense of profound grief, and it can find expression in words. The child's ability to differentiate among feelings and to give some account of degree is a considerable accomplishment at this early time, and the capacity to identify, to modulate, and to grade affective response is the great precursor to the much broader and deeper range of emotions that will come into being at puberty.

Coping Patterns

In considering the mastery component of play, it is of some interest to look at children's playthings and at the import of such activities.

Boys. This is an era of play with guns and rockets, of pretend killing and returning to life, of make-believe involving motion and speed. The little boy will often pretend to shoot and then assert, "Bang, you're dead." He will delight in having planes or rockets that presently become platforms for more shooting and mayhem, and he will move these craft rapidly about to simulate great flying speed. Sometimes these youngsters are great builders and put up all sorts of towers and other structures, the taller the better. But power and speed are the hallmark of their efforts, and they are masters of make-believe. Costumes are important; boys like to dress up in a cowboy suit, a gladiator's armor, a Superman outfit, or G.I. Joe regalia. For a little while they can escape being 3 or 4 years old and correspondingly small and helpless; instead they shift into the never-never land of being whoever or whatever they prefer.

Girls. The 3- or 4-year-old girl may choose many different kinds of playthings. One subgroup of girls tends to play with dolls and various facsimiles of living arrangements. A favorite game is "playing house," wherein the child reproduces her world in microcosm and then peoples it with characters who represent the important people in her life. Some girls take to baby doll play with enormous avidity and may also show an intense interest in clothes and physical appearance. (Rather than focusing solely on caretaking dramas, doll play may emphasize fashion and beauty contests.) Other girls, however, prefer more active, physical games and play with their male peers on equal terms. Indeed, the girls have a developmental advantage and are ahead of many of the boys in their physical skills. For the little girl, too, dress-up is often a favorite game, and many a family photo album is adorned with such a little one in a mock wedding gown, a bikini, an evening dress of some sort, or elaborate furbelows that delight everyone—the child most of all.

NORMAL SOURCES OF ANXIETY

The average child will encounter many experiences that stir suggestions of frightening inner concerns. As a result, perfectly commonplace events may become invested with unexpected and undesirable negative charges.

Haircuts

Somewhere around this age, many children receive their first haircut. For most youngsters, this is no great event; for some, however, the approach of a stranger with scissors in hand is enough to stir their worst fears, and they burst into tears and refuse to cooperate. Nor can they explain what upsets them; all they know is that they are scared. Sometimes it takes considerable cajolery to get the child through the episode; sometimes the parents employ threats; and sometimes the mother must stand by and hold the child's hand to alleviate his fears. But whatever modality the participants eventually resort to, the haircut may still prove to be an ordeal for everyone (including, as a rule, the barber).

Injections

Shots for the prevention and/or the treatment of illness are a pediatric reality of the 20th century. The figure who approaches with what seems to be a huge needle is a childhood fear that is lived out daily at every child health center; there is no easy way to dispel the emotion or completely avoid the pain. The usual euphemism is to tell the child that he or she will feel "a little stick," "a little mosquito bite," or some similar metaphor; but for most children it does not wash. They know what is coming, and they do not like it.

Occasional children add fantasy burden to the unpleasantness of the reality experience; they see the needle as a punishment involving a kind of total body invasion or a form of castration. These youngsters are said to have a pathological fear of needles. And this describes it well; the fear in such cases is of a great deal more than needles. Nor is there any simple panacea for such panic reactions; the doctor or nurse may attempt to desensitize the child psychologically by letting him handle the instruments, by having the child give shots to a doll, by reviewing the experience with the child in advance and playing it out over and over again. All these make sense and should certainly be part of a sequence where shots are in store and there is time to prepare; receiving an injection, however, can be a truly traumatic experience for the boy or girl who is vulnerable to castration anxiety.

Physical Examinations

For most children, the age of modesty occurs well after the preschool years, and the issues that medical exams stir up do not stem primarily from the shame spectrum of emotions. For a given child, however, disrobing might mean the exposure to danger, the nearness of some procedure that all too suggestively approaches the stuff of nightmares. Where this is true, the tears and lamentations might begin from the outset of the examination.

Pediatricians are all too familiar with this syndrome and usually have a bag of tricks to ease the child's distress. In essence they say to the child, "The doctor will not harm you or even hurt you very much, the doctor knows and respects how you feel, and there is nothing to fear." Physicians can accomplish this in several ways. They can provide gifts and rewards, can allow the child to handle the stethoscope and otoscope and perhaps look into the doctor's ear or a doll's ear, or can permit the youngster listen to his own heart. Such techniques work well with most children; under optimal circumstances, physical exams can be a site for mastery where the child overcomes an initial fear and emerges with a sense of accomplishment and even triumph.

Again, however, for the vulnerable child, a visit to the doctor can be a considerable challenge and a source of real stress. The analogous experience is the dental exam with its sometimes demanding treatments; dentists who specialize in work with children also have to develop an array of methods to help the child past the hurdles of early fears and fantasy distortions. Children who are emotionally secure can tolerate a rather considerable degree of necessary discomfort if they have the support of someone close and familiar; a major source of difficulty for many such procedures is that the practitioner is a stranger. Given the potential for separation dread inherent in childhood, the presence of a totally strange environment is a major amplifier of childhood fears.

Caretaking adults often underestimate the readiness of children to translate everyday events into their own constellations of threat and danger. Few people consciously recall what it was like to be small and highly imaginative, and there is a ready tendency to criticize the child, to laugh at his fears, and to make light of what the child experiences as a heavy burden. This conveys to the child that if he is anything less than a resolute adult in the face of the threatening events, he is displaying a deplorable personal inadequacy. The other extreme is the position taken by many caretakers that the child is infinitely fragile and must not be exposed to any traumatic experience, that they must forever protect the child, and, indeed, that no matter how much protection they may offer, it is never sufficient. This state characterizes the overanxious mother and the overresponsive child. The parent conveys the message: "You are not supposed to have any discomfort in this life, and if you do, it is unfair and merits protest, yours or your caretaker's." Such children are deprived of experiences of mastery that could strengthen their sense of confidence. The result is the predictable whiny, insatiable child whose motto is "It's not fair!" and whose demands are exceeded only by the excessiveness of his protests. To find the middle ground between the Scylla of parental overprotectiveness and the Charybdis of insensitive parental demandingness is a major requirement of mature child rearing. It is not always achieved.

The Fears of Childhood

Of the frequently encountered phobic manifestations of this time of life, some are so commonplace that adults consider them to be the normal property of the 3-year-old; these include the fear of the dark, the fear of thunder and lightning, and not infrequently, the fear of some animal. For example, Freud's (1909/1962) famous case of Little Hans, the first child to be psychoanalyzed (by his own father under Freud's guidance), presented originally with a fear of horses.

There are also some less common fears, such as the child's concern that as water runs out of the tub, he will be swept away as well. The end of the bath can be an agonizing moment for such a youngster. Less common but no less frightening is the child's apprehension that some biting thing is in the toilet bowl—a dragon, a snake, or something equally fanged and horrid—and as he sits on the toilet, he is vulnerable to attack from beneath. In some instances the child does not verbalize these fears to the parents (or, having been laughed at once does not mention them again), and he gives little outward evidence of what he is coping with but recalls the experiences for years. (For a further discussion of the fears of childhood, see Volume 2, Chapter 7).

Traumatic Events

A number of characteristic situations arise that can provoke untoward responses in 3- and 4-year-olds and that, in the more vulnerable children, may cause serious reactions. Not all of these events are inevitable, but they are sufficiently common to affect many children, and they frequently lead to referrals of children for help.

The Arrival of a New Sibling.   There is no ideal or optimal time to have a next baby. Whenever a mother becomes pregnant or a new sibling arrives, the import for the child or children currently in the home is likely to be substantial; this is a developmental given. The meaning of the new arrival will vary radically depending on significant physical health, mental health, and social variables, such as the temperament of child and mother, the youngster's previous life experience, the age of the child (or more precisely, his stage of development), the kinds of alternative supports available to both child and mother, and the current socioeconomic status of the family.

For the oedipal child the arrival of the new baby tends to have a particular kind of traumatic content. Many children see it as clear evidence of betrayal; their beloved partner, the target of their oedipal loving, has turned instead to the feared and (ambivalently) hated rival. The baby is the overt evidence of this liaison, and the child is at once mortified and disappointed, sometimes to the point of being downright embittered. In one way the situation helps resolve the Oedipus complex; the child must recognize that the parental liaison holds firm and will not be broken up no matter how strong the child's wish. At the same time, the new baby must frequently bear the onus and may never be forgiven. The next sibling to come along may be better tolerated, but not the first baby to arrive during the oedipal period. A state of sibling tension may ensue that will not be resolved—if ever—until both the children are in their teens or into young adulthood.

Other grounds for complaint may have signal importance in particular contexts, for example, the oedipal child may also have been the baby of the family, and this position is now taken over by another. Or a gender issue can play a role, for the new baby may have a penis, which the oedipal child has not, or the new arrival may lack a penis, which evokes both scorn and fear.

It is important for parents to be keenly alive to the stress factor that accompanies such events and to work actively with the child around such feelings. The common tactic of telling the child how great it will be to have a new brother or sister is not necessarily bad if the parents allow room for feelings that in some ways it might not be altogether great, that the child has the right to feel a little jealous, hurt, angry, and resentful of the changes and the presence of this uninvited (by the child) guest. The parents must carefully preserve the freedom to express such negative feelings, although they must just as zealously reinforce the necessity of acting appropriately toward the new arrival. From the child's view, the fact of a new baby can hurt on a variety of levels.

The profundity of the reaction is sometimes visible in the strikingly regressive behavior that follows the baby's birth; the oedipal child may start to whine and cry a great deal, may become enuretic at night after many months of good control, or may start to have accidents or become destructive to objects around the house. In short, the 3- or four-year-old may once again become like a 1- or 2-year-old child. As a rule, this is a transient reaction, and most children recover equanimity after a while. But not all; sometimes this heralds in a whole new chapter of emotional upset that may eventually bring the child to therapy.

Surgery. Health problems may arise at any time to dog the child's progress, and these are often of powerful, indeed, of critical import to the whole course of personality unfolding. A fairly common problem is surgery. This can take many forms from relatively minor procedures, such as putting tubes in the middle ear, to massive interventions, such as correcting life-threatening cardiac lesions. The complicating presence in all of these procedures is the psychological impact of such events on the child's sense of security. Many youngsters are certain that the surgery is a punishment for wicked thoughts or wishes (the contents of masturbatory fantasies). Or the child may experience the surgery as a warning of what can happen if he continues to entertain such ideas. Nor is it always easy to disabuse the child of these misconceptions; as a rule their roots lie deep, they are only partially conscious, and they are thus not readily accessible to cognitive correction.

As a consequence, when it is possible to delay surgery until later without compromising health too badly, it is generally advisable to do so. The phallic-oedipal period is definitely an undesirable moment in development to undertake elective procedures.

When the surgery is essential, then the professionals and the parents must make a serious effort to help the child achieve an assay of the situation that is as realistic as possible. This entails a careful and factual explanation of the reason for the surgery and the events that will surround it, such as undressing, prepping, and anesthesia. If possible, the parents should arrange a visit to the hospital that can familiarize the child with the setting and the admitting procedure so that the situation will not be an altogether new one. At home the caretaker can help the child play out the experience of the surgery by encouraging him to take the role of surgeon, with a doll as patient, and repeating this as many times as necessary. (One pediatrician kept a surgeon's cap and mask and an anaesthesia mask in his desk drawer as props for explaining surgery to children. Many children's hospitals now provide a program to prepare children for surgery, including tours, puppet presentations, booklets for home use, etc.) In the hospital, the parents should accompany the child into the room where the anesthetic is given and join in the countdown, and they should be on hand when the youngster awakens or shortly thereafter. If the child must spend several nights in the hospital, it is of considerable importance to avoid heaping the burden of separation on all the other stresses implicit in the situation. Someone close should be beside the youngster during as much of the stay as possible, preferably sleeping in the same room.

The point of this account is to give some sense of the proportions of the stress that such a child must bear, and the quality of care that these needs mandate. At best, surgery and hospitalization are great stressors of young children. Skillfully handled they can be occasions for considerable expansion of coping skills and ego mastery; when badly managed, however, they can leave psychological scars that last a lifetime.

Divorce

Only in recent years has research begun to accumulate on how disturbing divorce is to the course of development (Wallerstein & Kelly, 1980). Its noxious effects are inversely proportional to age, that is, the younger the child, the worse the effects. To understand this, it is necessary to adopt a somewhat modified view of the meaning of parents to a child. The usual practice is to think in terms of the child's relationship to each parent as an individual. What gets lost in this formulation is the meaning to the child of the relationship between the parents. For the younger ones in particular, the bond between the parents is akin to the surface upon which the child walks; it is, in effect, the ground beneath his feet. When that relationship is disturbed, the child feels as though he is caught in an earthquake, the very basis on which he exists begins to shake, and everything in his world is at once insecure and trembling. For the average child divorce causes profound anxiety, and the youngster feels literally that his world is falling apart.

As though this were not enough, there are, in addition, several developmentally based problems of considerable import. In these preschool years, the tendency to think in egocentric, self-centered ways is altogether age-appropriate. When anything of great significance occurs, the child's first inclination is to consider himself to be the cause. Either the child did it, or someone else did it because of the child, or at best the events are somehow connected without him knowing exactly how. Perhaps the child entertained some wicked wish or had some bad idea. Perhaps it was something the child had failed to do that made all the difference. The child may not be certain how he influenced what has transpired; there is only a deep sense of being at fault. For the oedipal child, in particular, the feeling of responsibility and wrongdoing is likely to be a major factor; what happens is so consonant with his wishes and fears that is is hard for the youngster to escape the onus for whatever occurs. If the parents are at each other's throats and eventually do split up, the child is likely to display several signs of depression or anxiety, such as a tearfulness, nightmares, or phobias. Or the youngster may turn toward behavior disorder by beginning to make life miserable for those about him and provoking a great many punishments. In short, the child shows the general stress response noted earlier as a possible reaction to the birth of a new sibling. Somatic complaints, such as stomachaches and headaches, are fairly typical responses, as are regressive behaviors such as whining in a formerly composed youngster or nighttime wetting in a child who has been previously dry. The specific symptoms are variable; that there will be some symptoms is a virtual certainty.

In keeping with this formulation, the average child who suffers the breakup of his family will maintain a long-lasting wish for some happening that would reunite the two parents. It is as though breaking the marital relationship also sunders something within the child, and the youngster spends many years dreaming and wishing for some way to have it all repaired. In part this yearning reflects a desire to undo the child's sense of sin, in part to restore the former integrity of the family world.

Under these circumstances, children need a great deal of help. Unfortunately, when such events unfold, the involved adults are themselves not doing well, and often they can barely muster enough energy to deal with their own disastrous problems. However much they care about the child, they are simply too overburdened by what they are going through to give the youngster even the time and attention they were able to offer before the crisis. As a result, the child ends up twice deprived, and all the more distraught. It is a good time for mental health intervention.

DEFENSIVE ADAPTATIONS

The emotion aroused by oedipal wishes can create considerable stresses. The child is whipsawed by conflicting feelings. Automatically, such a youngster turns to the available adaptive tactics inherent in his temperament; the child has displayed long-standing preferences for particular adaptive styles and has had the benefit of exposure to the coping modes of the adults who are his primary models and regulators (as well as the objects of his present concerns). Now the child uses whatever resources he can marshal to cope with the demands of the epoch.

Masturbation as Defense

One of the most effective approaches that this developmental level encourages is to avoid potentially dangerous action by discharging the tensions into fantasy. Thus, the child need not *do* anything that will bring down the wrath of the caretakers; he need only *imagine* it. To the extent that he confines himself to such imagery, he will not attract the lightning and will survive. At the same time, the child can obtain at least some release from the inner pressures, some reward for the yearnings, some appeasement of unrequited desires by living out in imagination those events he wishes would happen. And there is in this particular case the added benefit of being able actually to feel some of the sensuous reward if, during the imagining, the child self-stimulates. Masturbation, along with its accompanying fantasies, thus becomes a prime source of comfort and relief; it serves at once to permit the inadmissible and to prevent the unthinkable. The youngster can both gratify the wish—for the moment at least—and be saved from its consequences.

In homes where masturbation is condemned, the youngsters may perform this in secret. Or they may give it up altogether and seek recourse in fantasy without the accompanying body manipulation. Flight into fantasy is common among children and is not necessarily a problem, unless the degree and depth of fantasy involvement achieved begin to interfere with everyday living. This is an unfortunate possibility with oedipal children and might mandate active therapeutic intervention.

Inhibition

Although no single or simple paradigm encompasses all the concerns of oedipal children, the most distressing emotions are likely to be the combined fears of castration and of loss of love. Although boys are more likely to suffer from the first and girls from the second, clinicians may encounter either or both in children regardless of gender. These fears can become haunting presences that dog the child at every turn. Children will adapt to these feelings in characteristic ways; internalizers, in particular, will seek solutions within themselves and will try to rework their own thinking and feeling life in some way. Thus are born the fantasy-oriented children described above; in some instances, however, even this mechanism is too threatening. More vulnerable youngsters become terrified at the very thought of oedipal conflict; even to imagine about it is too much. They must go beyond thought, and all too readily they inhibit both thought and action.

Such children become very good—too good. They set up internal barriers to imagining wrong things and to doing bad things so that masturbation disappears, assertiveness gives way to compliance, and anxiety about possible imperfections replaces spontaneity and direct expression of feelings. The children become quiet, anxious, and perfectionistic, and sometimes they may even move into the realm of the compulsive; other children show strong evidence of depression. Most characteristic, however, is the child's obedience. There is a total commitment to being compliant, avoiding misdeeds, and keeping initiative in check.

The final clinical picture depends on the degree of the constriction. In many instances what emerges is a quiet, somewhat withdrawn, perhaps a moderately constricted, but not an overtly pathological child. There are plenty of people of this sort in society who wonder why they cannot be more free with their feelings and who suffer a sort of internal bondage with a more or less chronic limitation of their capacity to have pleasure. To outward appearances they get along quite well, become good workers, and are good citizens (again, perhaps a little too good). However, they often remain limited in their ambitions, competitive strivings, and capacity for pleasure (especially sexual pleasure within the context of an intimate relationship). They are also more likely to be vulnerable to emotional disturbance of the depressive variety.

Passivity

Another dimension is the potential development of attitudes that forbid self-assertion or even self-protection in the face of threat. The child adapts to the menacing quality of oedipal concerns by giving up initiative and enterprise. The youngster adopts an attitude of simply waiting and allowing the significant other to take action; he fears the consequences of self-activity and feels safer as the victim of someone else's initiative. In short, the child adopts a passive stance in the important areas of life and attempts to regulate his behavior around a central core of waiting for others' cues and commands. Left to his own devices, the child just sits.

This is an undesirable developmental position that becomes particularly serious if the child actually will not defend himself when attacked by other children; it signals a state of heightened vulnerability that does not bode well for developmental progress. Worse still, a strong admixture of guilt may lead to an additional masochistic element that actually invites pain and humiliation. The child's position will affect many realms such as his self-esteem, self-assertion, independence, and readiness to take charge of his life in a variety of ways (let alone the direct consequences of failing to protect himself when attacked). Minor degrees of passivity may be tolerable, but if this is present to any significant extent, active therapeutic intervention is indicated.

Counterphobic Behavior

When children, by natural bent (perhaps augmented by the availability of a familial or a culturally significant model), tend to turn to the outside world and take action, that is, externalize their coping efforts, a variety of patterns may emerge, but the most notable is the *counterphobic defense.*

This term describes a behavior pattern that entails doing dangerous things (e.g., children who deal with stranger anxiety by seeking out strangers). Functionally it is a way of dealing with anxiety. Ordinarily, anxiety initiates avoidance behavior; counterphobic behavior reverses the sign so that anxiety becomes a lure, a beckoning attraction. The individual says, in effect, "Afraid? I'm not afraid. Or if I am, I like it. I enjoy that sort of thing; it is the spice of life. See, I go out of my way to court danger, to seek it out!"

The counterphobic defense is effective because it has all the reinforcement of allowing for bold, adventurous, eye-catching behavior, often with considerable social impact. Moreover, it provides a kind of elation; the individual rises above his fears, feels larger than life, is indifferent to the weaknesses of the flesh. This trait is often present in those who undertake hazardous sports or who engage in thrill-seeking activities. Many heroes accomplish their feats because of having this factor in their makeup. It also makes for many accidents.

From the oedipal view it is important because it does ease the pain of castration anxiety. It sometimes gets the little child into trouble by driving him to climb up on high places or to take inappropriate risks in crossing streets. The parents will report that such a child is "fearless." When coupled with aggressive tendencies (often based on an identification with the aggressor), counterphobic behavior may also be responsible for many fights. Occasionally, too, it leads the child to act provocatively toward the feared castrator. A similar mechanism may underlie the public disrobing in little girls, or the exhibitionistic urinating, masturbating, or penis display of little boys.

Sleep Disturbance

A characteristic aspect of the Oedipus complex is that, in many ways, its expression tends to be covert. The children are dealing with global, massive surges of affect that they do not understand and that can be at once overwhelming in their sweetness and terrifying in their menacing import. The youngster tends to reserve these thoughts for when he is alone or, at any rate, for the inner world of fantasy; moreover, he may be so busy with playground and nursery school that during the day he has little time for these preoccupations. At night, however, such images surge to the forefront; they can be going-to-sleep musings, or they can fill the sleeping hours with terrifying dreams that might awaken the child in a state of near-panic. This is when running to the parental bed because of bad dreams becomes a common part of many children's adaptive repertoire.

Oedipal dreams tend to have a punitive or a retaliatory character. Their scenario is often one of attempting to run away from some great danger that is coming from behind and getting closer and closer. The danger mounts until it is unendurable, and the child wakes up. Or some dreadful visage appears, a terrifying mask of sorts that promises horrendous body damage of unthinkable character. The mask is, of course, the guise for the retaliating oedipal parent. It must be underlined that the reality of the parent's actual style and behavioral pattern does not dictate the kind of images that form; the child is casting his parent in the mold of his own aggressive creations.

Some degree of sleep disturbance is common at this time of life. The child might fear dreams so much that he balks at going to sleep. Such a youngster might be unable to drift off unless a reassuring someone is at the bedside and in physical contact until sleep truly comes. In addition to the night-mares, night terrors, sleepwalking, sleep talking, or enuresis may appear as part of a preschooler's sleep behavior. Children with retained transitional objects must religiously take the preferred toy, stuffed animal, or blanket to bed for such help and protection as it may offer. Even children who have given up their object may show a renewed interest in having some toy in bed with them "for company." Bedtime rituals can take on renewed importance or increased elaboration. For example, one 4-year-old boy began to insist on wearing yellow socks to bed to protect against the dangerous alligators of his dreams.

APPENDIX 12-1:
PATHOLOGICAL DERIVATIVES

A number of conditions in later life have been associated with fixation at the oedipal stage of psychosexual development. To associate anything as complex and multidetermined as a neurotic syndrome or a particular form of personality organization with the conflicts deriving from a single level of development is dubious; upon examination, elements of several developmental levels are invariably present and lend their particular hue to the condition. To regard a given syndrome as a phallic-phase or oedipal condition is really a shorthand way of stating where the emphasis lies in its manifestations. It certainly does not describe the totality of its origins. Withal, however, certain predominant forms can be discerned.

Hysteria

This term is complex: It has popular usage, historical meaning, and a current technical status. Popularly, it has meant—and often continues to mean—emotional excess, a state of being overcome by feelings to the point of temporary irrationality or inability to be "reached." The traditional response to "hysterics" has been to slap the victim smartly in the face, to throw cold water into the individual's face, or, in short, to shake or shock the person back to his or her senses. A proneness to this form of behavior is usually assumed to characterize women; indeed, the term, as used, is sometimes almost synonymous with femininity.

Parallel with this popular usage, hysteria retained a rather different technical meaning. It was essentially a neurological term that applied to a diverse array of symptom pictures. This group of conditions caught Freud's interest, and for many years the hysterical disorders served as the primary site for psychoanalytic investigation. Currently, however, the place of hysteria within the technical lexicon is undergoing radical revaluation (all references to hysteria have been dropped from the DSM-III-R), and the earlier status of this group of conditions is now largely of historical interest. However, the inertia of knowledge is such that the reader is likely to encounter this term for some time to come. Hence, it is worth reviewing briefly what hysteria came to mean within psychoanalytic framework.

Generally speaking, hysterical manifestations were thought to take two forms: character disorder and neurosis. The term *hysterical character disorder* was applied to a style of interaction with other people, a way for the individual to relate to his or her world. This involved using everyday experience to repeatedly (sometimes continually) enact inner oedipal fantasies. Unconsciously, the individual with a hysterical character disorder superimposed on the various people in his or her current life the persona of the original oedipal characters. In effect, the person continued to reenact childhood relationship patterns and to live out the earlier experiences over and over again. Thus, such an individual might level accusations of infidelity where no infidelity had occurred. A need to break up someone else's marriage or liaison might lead to all sorts of elaborate machinations; then, if the person achieved the rivalrous triumph, he or she would rapidly lose interest in the new partner. Alternatively, the person with hysterical character disorder might choose to love only unavailable or unsuitable persons, thus ensuring frustration and failure in love. As Freud put it, such individuals had "preconditions for loving" that inevitably caused them grief. For example, one young woman pursued men, who, in their age and ethnic background, were as unlike her father as possible; whereas the father was much older than she, the objects of her interest were always much younger; whereas the father was white, she was drawn to men who were black. In time, however, she came to discover that each of her boyfriends bore a remarkable resemblance to her father in terms of his irresponsible but irascible charm. In essence, the problem was a characteriological disturbance; the individual with a hysterical character disorder would repetitively act out some version of the inner drama of childhood on the stage of current real-life relationships.

Typically, such a patient displayed a dramatic, even a histrionic, style in interpersonal relations. The individual might be rather charming and engaging, often was quite attractive and immediately likable, and was likely to be considered "colorful." There was a characteristic flavor of sexuality in the person's garb, posture, gesture, jokes, verbal allusions, interests, boasting, teasing, and other elements of personal expression.

Under relatively benign conditions, coyness, archness, seductiveness, self-conscious cuteness, teasing references to the sexuality of the self or the other, a strong tendency toward sexual rivalry, the wearing of suggestive and revealing clothes (and then a shocked and highly offended reaction if confronted about such attire by parent, teacher, employer, or spouse), and other such emphases upon erotic conquest and achievement would be the order of the day. In more severe cases, promiscuity and bisexuality were part of the picture. If disturbed, such an individual would do dramatic things, such as swoon (near a couch), have a screaming fit, adopt a theatrical stance (e.g., sweep out of the door declaring that he or she would never be seen there again), or make some symbolic self-destructive gesture.

If, on the other hand, the condition expressed itself as a circumscribed neurosis rather than a character disorder, quite a different kind of picture would emerge.

In contrast to the characteriological disorder, the hysterical neurosis was a pattern of somewhat uncertain definition, but it suggested that the individual had turned the core oedipal problem inward on his or her own mind or body rather than outward on the world. In contrast to the externalization of the character disorder, the neurotic tended to show inhibition, constricted expression, and some form of dysfunction and limitation in body or mind, including motor disturbances, sensory aberrations, or alterations of consciousness. The presence of these symptoms established the diagnosis; and many symptoms indeed have been gathered under the rubric of manifestations of hysteria. The illness was likely to have an equally dramatic quality, but instead of enacting their fixations in the interpersonal realm, the hysterics' own bodies would become the sites for coital reenactments or the dramatization of castration themes. A host of odd behaviors called *conversion symptoms* could then follow, including anesthesias, paralyses, disturbances of gait, tics, seizures, perceptual aberrations, and other impairments to function of voice, limb, or body. When they occurred together in a shifting kaleidoscope of symptoms, they were referred to by the French term *grande hystérie*.

During an earlier, pre-Freudian epoch, quite a different group of problems was thought to be allied to these conversion syndromes; these were called the *dissociative reactions*. The great French neurologists, such as Janet and Charcot, thought the symptoms represented a splitting of consciousness, an abrupt division between sectors of mind, so that the contents of thought and feeling became sequestered into isolated compartments. Here they lumped the cases of multiple personality, hysterical amnesia, fugue, and perhaps certain forms of depersonalization.

Why one individual would take the path of character disorder as opposed to neurosis, or vice versa, has never been settled. Presumably it represented once again a matter of constitution, some unknown factor in genetic makeup, plus the specific environmental reinforcement necessary to bring that particular symptom complex to full expression. In both instances, however, the fixation point was considered to be the same, namely, at the oedipal level.

Perversion

The classical psychoanalytic definition of perversion was a state of personality organization that allowed the attainment of maximal sexual gratification only by some practice other than genital heterosexual union. The accent falls strongly on the word *maximal;* the capacity to achieve erotic titillation through almost any part of the body and with a very wide variety of partners is apparently inherent in the human biological makeup. What provides the optimal and most rewarding erotic experience is, however, another matter. That preference has roots that ramify through the entire column of sexual development; the individual chooses a final pathway after a long, complex process of sorting out possible routes for the discharge of sexual tensions. He or she must mass fantasies, avoid dangers, and search among alternative avenues before reaching an unconscious but definitive decision as to the safest route with the highest sensual yield. Where there has been a defensive flight from a more mature pathway to a more primitive outlet, then a chronic underlying conflict remains that, often enough, never gets resolved. To keep all this at bay, the person is driven to over-compensate. As a result, the chosen sexual mode may, and often does, have about it a driven, urgent quality that compels the individual with immense, sometimes with irresistible force.

The nagging, relentless character of many such sexual configurations, the need to repeat the same sequence of acts over and over again, some-times in spite of the most intense inner repugnance or in the face of almost suicidal guilt afterward, bears mute testimony to the character of pathologi-cal fixation that underlies the behavior. At the heart of many perversions (in the psychoanalytic view) is the individual's efforts to avoid castration; to do so, the person strikes some sort of inner compromise between the forbidden yearning and the imagined castrative threat. The individual then proceeds to live out the "solution" to the terrifying oedipal problem. For example, under one set of conditions the dynamic might be to say, in effect: "I do not hate you, Father, even though you abused me I love you; I don't want to bite your penis off, I want to bring you pleasure; I'm not a true competitor, I'm a child; I will set things right between us by avoiding your spouse, by avoiding your body; indeed, I will do such things only with other children"—and a pattern of seducing children into performing fellatio becomes a compulsive need, a driven component of the person's sexual practice.

In response to the stimulus sets evoked by different situational encoun-ters, people are capable of a wide variety of sexual styles and choices. Ultimately, however, some preferred mode of sexual behavior usually reflects the specific configuration of that individual's inner life. Sometimes an individual may resort to a particular sexual pattern only in the face of considerable stress; it is a fallback position, the reward the individual must have when he or she has given too much, when resources are depleted beyond the point of tolerance. In other instances it has the character of a recurrent obsession, a growing, itching, relentless need that requires con-summation of the act for dissipation or relief. Most often, however, it is simply the scenario the individual visualizes when thinking of sex at all. It is the leading image, the basic organization and reality of that person's sexual life.

Psychosexual development is a long and tortuous process, with many hazards along the way, and a great many sites for possible arrest and distortion. So it is not remarkable that the elements that come to be carried forward into adolescence, or into adulthood for that matter, bear the imprint of where the person has been during this journey and, often enough, involve some unresolved elements from the past. Much of this is captured in the individual's foreplay pattern or characteristic masturbatory fantasies; there may be all kinds of oral elements in the initial sexual arousal pattern. Or the person may require anal stimulation, sadistic or masochistic play, or the use of foul language. The resort to erotic images to titillate is a commonplace; that, or some other form of phallic voyeurism, is for many people an essential component of an enjoyable sexual engagement. In effect, the person's whole psychosexual history is repeated during a typical and comfortable sexual encounter. None of this is within the framework of the classical definition of the perverse so long as the ultimate high point of the erotic engagement is heterosexual genital intercourse. When that element gives way or becomes an afterthought in the wake of extended and complicated foreplay (e.g., lengthy and elaborate cross-dressing or bondage), then the assumption is that a fixation has occurred somewhere in the past, complete psychosexual maturity has not been achieved, and the individual suffers from a perversion.

Many challenges have been extended to this position. Perhaps the most ideological and controversial concern is whether variation in sexual orientations and needs arises exclusively from pathological disturbances of development or is biologically determined (biological variations on the theme, as it were, without attending conflict or disturbance). Because of the lack of confirming evidence, there is no definitive answer to this question at present. Gender development and vulnerability will provide a major field for research during the next decades.

Anxiety

Childhood fears come from many sites along the developmental sequence. In particular, they reflect the early experience of needing the caretaker and lacking her (usually, but not necessarily, her) presence at some crucial juncture. The early fear of loss or absence of the needed one underlies the more catastrophic kind of anxiety that children experience; under optimal circumstances, it will subside as development advances. In time, the child can muster a powerful array of cognitive operations that permit maintaining a mental image of the desired other in fantasy terms, or still later, that provide some rational explanation for the delay in the needed one's appearance.

During the anal phase, concern about loss of the caretaker's love and protective interest is central to the child. Perhaps his rage or badness has finally caused the beloved other to turn against him, to abandon him, to give him away. Perhaps, as punishment, a bad someone will come and take the child away. Parents know those feelings all too well and may threaten a youngster that if deportment does not improve, a bad man will come—perhaps a robber or a kidnapper—and carry the child off, never to see the parents again. Many a child has awakened at night screaming in the throes of a dream that played out such a sequence.

With the advent of the phallic-oedipal stage, the threat shifts to the great drama of castration. The child is imbued with all the yearnings of rivalry and all the fears of retaliation, and the endless permutations and combinations play themselves out. There are themes of conquest and retribution, of joining and then betraying, of seducing and then frustrating; accompanying them are all the attendant emotions of amorous passion, bitter disappointment, exciting conquest, venomous revenge, masterful triumph, and terrifying pursuit.

The child faces a considerable level of stress and turmoil and must learn to deal with his bouts of anxiety. Given the advantage of successful experiences at earlier stages of development plus good parental support, as they face oedipal challenges, the youngsters will usually manage well. Where such support is not forthcoming, a rather large, but nonetheless limited, number of possibilities are open to the child. The first is simply to endure it in the form of an anxiety attack. This occurs, but it is seldom present as such in early childhood. It is too unendurable; the child is organismically unready to tolerate that much stress; in some way he must transform it. Severely troubled children may be unable to cope; because they can find no way to make an adequate adaptation of this kind, they will experience a crippling disorganization and will "fall apart" from the anxiety. Sometimes they will have what looks like a tantrum, except that it is a terror tantrum and not a temper tantrum. Sometimes they will resort to mechanisms such as somatization, counterphobic maneuvers, sleep disturbances, and phobias. In short, all too many children find that it is not easy to be an oedipal child, and the traces of the ensuing conflicts can last a lifetime.

Somatization. Relatively less disturbed children will cope by somatizing the anxiety; they will develop physical complaints and may even become seriously ill. Vomiting or pain, typically in the head or stomach, is a common reaction. Some of the stomachaches of childhood are, in fact, the equivalents of anxiety reactions.

Sleep Disturbances. Another favorite site for expressing such feelings is during sleep, which is a vulnerable time because it involves the weakening of some of the controls of consciousness. There is an alteration of thresholds, and material that is ordinarily kept within the strict bounds of unconsciousness now comes nearer to awareness. The result is a frequent account of sleep difficulties that may take the form of night terrors during which the child does not awaken although he may show every other evidence of being terrified. Nor can the parents awaken the child even though they shake him, call him by name, pick him up and carry him, or even dash cold water in his face. The child continues to scream and to thrash about in the extremity of his panic and cannot be quieted or solaced. Sometimes this sort of thing goes on for 10 to 20 minutes before the child quiets down and resumes a more normal pattern of sleep. It is as though some dissociative state supervenes and must run its course within the sleep cycle before the child returns to normal. Presumably some biological substrate renders a child vulnerable to this form of reaction, but thus far its nature is unknown.

Another almost universal form of sleep disturbance is the nightmare. This phenomenon has been much studied by numerous authors; it represents an attempt on the child's part to wall off many of the dangerous oedipal concerns behind the parapet of unawareness. He knows about them (or thinks about them) only in sleep. Because sleep is not a time of good regulation of consciousness, it is all too easy for the intensity of the fantasies and the yearnings to rise above threshold and to pour over into at least semiawareness. The chief mechanisms then available are those of disguise, and so the angry face of the punishing father becomes a fearsome and horrid mask with dreadful fangs and glaring eyes. It is a blood-chilling and altogether terrifying visage filled with portents of dreadful things to come. This becomes so unendurable that sleep itself is disrupted so that the child can marshal the reality perception of conscious awareness against the fear. Frequently even consciousness is not enough, and the child actively seeks out the presence of the parent as reassurance against the fantasied menace.

Phobia.   Another means for coping with anxiety is displacement. The core mass of concern wells up and is rapidly and unconsciously shifted away from its proper source, the feared (albeit fantasied) parent, to some innocent bystander. The feared object may become a shadow in the bedroom; an ominous noise, such as thunder (sometimes younger children become frightened of noises from machines, such as the vacuum cleaner); an animal, such as a dog or a horse; a uniform, such as that of the mail carrier or the priest; or even a particular doll. The object of phobic transformation may be anything within the child's experience that now becomes imbued with the special feelings the youngster is trying to ward off. After all, it is far better for the child to be afraid of a dog than to be afraid of his father. The youngster can avoid dogs, not without some trouble to be sure, but he can avoid them; but his father? The child accrues a very real advantage by displacing the anxiety to dogs, so the compromise is struck, and the phobia appears.

As noted, all this takes place unconsciously by a sort of internal rearrangement of priorities and symbols, but, in effect, the language of compromise states the case reasonably well. The child substitutes an uneasy equilibrium for a potential catastrophe and goes on from there.

Some children, by dint of constitutional makeup, tend to externalize. When they encounter anxiety, they resort to what is essentially the same mechanism, except that it gets turned around in the counterphobic fashion already reviewed.

Chapter 13

The Beginnings of Conscience

INTRODUCTION

Why does the child ever give up on the oedipal wishes? Most people do abandon these ideas and, indeed, come presently to consider such thoughts (concerning sexual interaction or sexual rivalry with a parent) as alien and immoral. The question remains, however: Why does such a change in outlook take place? Why do not these yearnings and strivings simply persist and continue as exigent presences throughout life?

As a matter of fact, in many a life they do just that. (Technically, clinicians say that the individual enters adulthood with persistent oedipal fixations.) When this happens, a variety of unfortunate results can ensue. For example, the person may never successfully leave the parental home and will then stay on as caretaker and permanent child literally until the parents die. Or the individual so fixated may seek as spouse an obvious father- or mother-substitute and thereafter maintain a kind of child role within the marriage. (Such outcomes can also be the product of pregenital fixations, such as separation difficulties; oedipal stresses are only one, albeit a significant one, among several possible origins for such patterns of adaptation.) Or, as noted earlier, a strong tendency toward repeated involvement in triangular relationships can ensue, with much accompanying turmoil. In the normal situation, however, the child does give up on his oedipal position and moves to the next stage in development. Two groups of factors seem to make for such a healthy resolution.

Reality Pressures

The first of these is the sheer pressure of reality. The child is advancing from toddlerhood through the preschool years, and at 4 or 5 years the sense of his own body outlines, as well as those of his mother and father, are becoming ever more realistically perceived. The child is small, the adult is large, and no amount of wishing or imagining makes that difference go away. To be sure, Jack did cut down the beanstalk and slay the ogre; in the child's life, however, it is not working out quite that way. More than that, if a little boy is around when his father gets up in the morning from a state of REM sleep, the child may see the father's erect penis—and the comparison with his own proportions is devastating. Similarly, the little girl is all too aware of the differences between her own little body and her mother's opulence. Initially the child's longings and frustrations can be managed by wishes and daydreams, but as the months go by, the former illusions become increasingly difficult to maintain. The child has dreamed about having the power to entice and allure, to captivate and dominate, or for that matter, to exclude and destroy one parent or the other. But the dream grows less and less tenable in the face of the palpable awareness of the sheer differences in mass, size, strength, bulk, and material presence. After the first flood of denial and grandiose fantasy, the pressure of reality wears away at the wishes and the dreams—the child is simply no rival for the one parent and no mate for the other.

Another aspect of the attendant realities is the response of the parents themselves. One way or another, the child sends messages about his interests; he lets the parents know about his longings, and in turn the parents let the child know where they are. If they send the youngster realistic responses, these are enormously helpful to the child in strengthening his reality limits and boundaries and coming to terms with what is. However, a singular phenomenon encountered by child psychiatrists is the difficulty that some parents have in coping with this aspect of their children's development. For example, a physician's young son constantly pressed her to marry him. The woman told her son she was already married; she was the wife of his father. The youngster retorted that he had heard them argue a lot, and he knew that she and Daddy were constantly threatening each other with divorce. So why didn't she just divorce Daddy—and then the two of them, mother and son, could get married. The mother could think of no effective rejoinder and, in a kind of desperation, took an obstetrical text off the shelf, opened it to the chapter on teratomas and monster births, and showed him the malformed fetuses. "You see," she said, "I can't marry you because if a mother marries a son, that's the kind of babies they would have. So we can't get married!"

This may illustrate an extreme case, but it is not unusual in the sense of demonstrating the curious impediments parents encounter when they try to deal realistically with oedipal issues. The necessary factor is simply to say, "No, you may not marry me because it is forbidden, it is against our laws, our customs, and our values. Sons do not marry mothers, daughters do not marry fathers, sisters do not marry brothers. It is forbidden." That parents sometimes find this so hard to express is mute testimony to the sheer pain of their own early oedipal frustrations.

As the example also illustrates, the dynamics of the parental relationship also have a profound impact on the child's oedipal development. Under optimal conditions, the family's intergenerational boundaries are firm. That is to say, the parents' roles as each other's spouse are clearly delineated and not totally submerged in their role as parents. Under these conditions the parents do not turn to their children for the comfort, intimacy, solace, or sexual gratification (physical or psychological) more appropriate to a spouse; neither do they enlist the children as partisans in their marital tensions.

Optimally, the parents should never encourage or invite the child into seductive interactions that will inflame oedipal fantasy. Instead, parents will show their fondness and affection through talk, play, attentive care, and tenderness without engaging in excessive or inappropriate intimacy. The child's sexual feelings are easy to arouse; wise parents sense this and find that safe middle ground that extends love without titillation. Sometimes this is hard to do; external circumstances can place a parent under unusual stress. Thus, a young mother who has recently separated from her husband, or who has been deserted, may suffer pangs of intense need and loneliness. The little loving boy can become for a time her primary source of closeness, at once companion and comforter. She turns to him, clings to him, lavishes attention on him, and may even sleep with him; and he in turn is filled with excitement and delight at the arousing nearness of her body, the intimacy of her fondling, and the intensity of her attention. All his wishes, his grandiose fantasies, are at once fulfilled. In his daydreams, oedipal wishes have come true, wishing has made it so, he has ousted Daddy and taken Mommy all to himself.

In short, under optimal conditions the parent will not lead the child toward oedipal fulfillment but instead will provide a clear, firm message that this is not to be, that Mommy and Daddy care for each other and will not be seduced or destroyed by the child. And if they separate for any reason, this is their affair and not the child's; the child is not encouraged to feel that he is taking the place of the missing parent—or will ever do so. If properly managed, this parental message becomes part of the reality pressure that encourages the child to abandon the oedipal commitment.

Fantasy Pressures

However, not only realistic factors play a role here. Indeed, it is doubtful that reason alone can deal with such powerful feelings. An additional dynamic of cardinal importance comes into play at this juncture. For the youngsters create their own nemesis; as the oedipal fantasy plays itself out within their inner worlds, the thought of their triumph is very sweet, but then, what follows after? What if the ousted rival returns to take revenge, or should catch on early and is out to get the child? What then? The child begins to imagine all sorts of appalling consequences. It is the stuff of nightmares, and these little ones are quite likely to have nightmares. In particular, they fear genital injury. The boy thinks very simply that he will be made into a girl and is terrified at the thought. The little girl sees in this the danger of total loss, total destruction; surely, if she had any hope of getting a penis, now it will be lost. Of the two genders, she has the more complex task. All her life she has looked first to her mother for her care. Mother fed her in the oral stage, toilet trained her, managed her during the toddler period, and now is suddenly her rival during the phallic-oedipal period. The little boy has no such dilemma, he remains attached to his mother throughout; for a time, however, his father becomes the great rival. So little girls tend to compromise; for them, the process of shifting between the parents is less complete. The oedipal girl turns away from her mother to her father, but not completely as a rule; she tends to remain in an in-between state with strong links to both. Later some young married women may threaten to leave their husbands and "go back home to Mother"—and sometimes do so. Young men seldom make that threat.

The strength of the threatening fantasy—the demonized image of the angry retaliatory parent (seen in nightmares as a horrid slavering mask chasing the child over a surreal landscape)—is, in fact, more a measure of the intensity of the youngster's feelings than an index of parental hostility. Quite gentle, sensitive, and loving parents have been given fangs and claws by their dreaming 4-year-olds with complex behavioral results. It is indeed fortunate for all concerned that these issues tend to confine themselves to the world of dreams and daydreams; on the other hand, because these images are hidden inner creations, they are harder to correct and to translate into more realistic terms.

The gathering strength and the pressure of these frightening inner configurations act as another set of vectors moving the child away from oedipal fantasy indulgence. The thoughts and wishes simply become too dangerous, so the child begins to look for a way to avoid them. And presently a way opens up.

Thus, realistic self-appraisal and appropriate parental response plus fantasy threats that weave themselves about the original wishes bring the Oedipus complex to an end. This is a gradual but very real process; many a child goes through a difficult time as all this works out in his mind. But it is a quiet time of constriction and renunciation. It lacks dramatics and color and hence is little noted by parents and teachers. No one celebrates it in fictional accounts as is common, for example, with descriptions of puberty. There are no intriguing recitations of sexual adventure or dramatic interpersonal discoveries; on the contrary, if anything, the child's behavior smoothes out and becomes less troublesome. But in fact, the events at this epoch are fully as significant as they are at puberty, perhaps more so. The changes that occur now, albeit implosive rather than explosive and relatively silent rather than overtly expressive, are of fundamental importance for the formation of many vital character traits. These changes set the stage for *latency,* that period of relative calm and pliability that permits the child's immersion in school, peers, and practicalities.

SUPEREGO FORMATION

In particular, within the magma of personality a new organization crystallizes out; Freud referred to it as a *step (or gradient) in the ego.* All the prohibitions, injunctions, warnings, and teachings of the earlier years now seem to be pulled together into a new unity. In effect, another level of governance or organization is set up in the child's mind that will act henceforth as an inner regulatory agency. It will allow the child greater independence on the one hand (he is now self-regulating and hence potentially responsible) and will offer a closer link with family values and patterns on the other (the inner regulator speaks with all the accumulated messages about how to behave that the family has voiced during the developmental years).

This new emergent is the *superego*. It is not an organ of mind in the sense of having an identifiable anatomical or neurophysiological base. It is, rather, a functional entity that appears during the normal developmental sequence and consists of two essential elements, each with its own set of functions. These are the conscience and the ego-ideal.

The Conscience

A familiar term, employed in everyday usage, the *conscience* represents an inner presence that tends to be awakened by questions of right and wrong. In fact, it accomplishes several different tasks. Its first function is *to warn* and *to forbid*. Consider a woman who joins a queue at the bank waiting to be served by the teller. As she reaches the next place in line at the window, she may note that the man just ahead, who has had a large pile of bills counted out and placed before him, is now discussing something with the cashier. Suddenly, the thought trickles across the woman's consciousness, "Why not just grab that pile and run?" Immediately the thought is followed by a thunderous internal "No, that's wrong! You don't do that!" followed perhaps by a recognition of the impracticality of such behavior—"I would certainly be caught immediately"—and then perhaps by a feeling of disquietude at ever having had such a thought. The whole sequence may have taken only a few seconds, and nothing of it is visible to an external observer, but the conscience has made its presence felt. It deals with impulse; by warning and forbidding, it protects the individual from violating some social norm.

A second major function of conscience is *to inhibit*. This implies more than verbal content, it includes actual control of behavior. Suppose that a man returns home early one day, lets himself into the house, goes to the bedroom, and there sees his spouse in the arms of another—in flagrante delicto. Seized by rage, the man rushes to the dresser, pulls open the drawer where he keeps a gun, grasps it, wheels, and points it at the terrified couple. His finger tightens on the trigger and thereupon freezes. The man cannot move. Try as he might, he cannot pull the trigger. "Something" stops the action, "something" won't let it proceed, "something" inhibits the man. He cannot act.

This function of inhibition, of actually blocking unacceptable action, signifies the presence of the superego. To be sure, most examples of its operations are more mundane than the above and may not even be consciously experienced. In its nature as a regulatory agency, the superego exists well beyond consciousness; indeed, at times it operates in defiance of very powerful conscious wishes. Nonetheless it can determine behavior or, at any rate, influence is profoundly. Thus, with or without the person's awareness (more often than not unconsciously), the superego acts as an influential component of behavior. It can stop indulgence in forbidden pleasures or easy response to many enticing temptations. If it should become excessively powerful, it can stop the individual from engaging in even permitted pleasures and take much of the fun out of life. This is no rare state of affairs and, in some measure, bedevils the lives of many people. All in all, however, the superego is one of the great instruments of human socialization. It regulates interpersonal conduct and helps to maintain the integrity of community life. If the people in a given group have working consciences, then it is likely that a sense of trust, integrity, and predictability will be present; this in turn protects the security of people's possessions, the safety of their children, and the behavior of family members or neighbors. In short, life is very different than it would be if such conscience structures were not present.

All this is powerfully reinforced by the third function of the conscience— *punishment.* From the clinician's view, this is easily the most important dimension. Surely, it is one of the greatest sources of human pain.

The conscience has a peculiar capacity to hurt children. It acts as a part of the self that knows all the child's motives, has access to all his memories, reads and comments on all his fantasies, and judges all his actions. If the judgment is negative, if, for example, the child failed to heed an earlier warning about some forbidden act and has overridden the inner inhibition, then the conscience still has a final mechanism in reserve after the fact. It can critically attack, challenge, and devalue the child; it can heap abuse and demean and excoriate its victim. It sees all, knows all, cannot be evaded, and is not readily placated. Many a child finds out early in life that to be in trouble with his conscience is no minor matter, certainly not something to expose himself to lightly. More than that, the conscience can be so tormenting that, for a time at least, life is virtually unbearable. Either because the conscience dictates this as the only means of expiation or because the child seeks an escape from the intolerable inner tensions, the sufferer may well think of running away, of some act of self-punishment, or even of self-inflicted death. Sometimes he achieves this indirectly with a bad accident.

This self-punitive process may be more or less conscious; when it is outside of full awareness, it can be a prime predisposer to psychophysiological reactions. The child develops a stomachache, a headache, or some other complaint that the doctor cannot explain. The conscience has many ways to get at its victim and to induce suffering, and thus it serves as a prime reinforcer of its own precepts. It is a regulating agency with teeth and can profoundly affect the way the child grows.

In its organization the conscience includes a number of elements. This is perhaps easiest to understand from a genetic view—the conscience has roots in every stage of psychosexual development. So widespread are the arborizations and ramifications of its origins that a full exposition is impossible here; a few of the most paradigmatic themes can, however, illustrate the complexity of the matter.

In the oral stage, the child receives injunctions and limits from a very early age. When grandpa picks baby up and baby grabs his glasses, the *no-no's* appear immediately. They are not necessarily harsh or critical, but the infant knows affect when he hears it, and the message is there. Each developmental step brings new limits and concerns. From the infant's view, his world converts all too easily from the ecstatic and the angelic to the monstrous and the demonic. The baby tends very readily to be flooded by emotion, and his caretaker must protect him and regulate and modulate stimuli to maintain a prevailing quality of "good feeling." Once the baby starts to crawl, he requires a good deal of supervision and reaction by caretakers, and many injunctions are likely to be forthcoming about avoiding this and not doing that. The baby's own oral orientation will shape the manner of his emotion; faced with inevitable frustrations he will want to devour the world or will come to fear that he, in turn, will be the victim of some horrid toothed enemy. Oral rage and oral panic are poorly differentiated global feelings that at once express the immaturity of the control apparatuses of the time and the flooding quality of the emotion experienced during this early epoch.

As development proceeds, this flickering transient flare of oral destructiveness eventually becomes contained and deeply repressed. Although it will not normally reappear as such, it continues to remain a presence in the child's mind and can be keyed in by a particular stimulus set. Figuratively, the child has his own inner demon lying in wait, crouched to spring. Sometimes this will come back later in nightmares, sometimes it will form part of the fears of childhood, but for most people it never again becomes a conscious factor. Nonetheless, a small kernel will rest in the unconscious, and, if the individual should later fall into a depression, then such a presence may indeed make itself felt. It is common parlance to say, "He is eating himself up with guilt," and it is no far cry from the actual psychological phenomenon. (Middle English employs the same powerful metaphor for remorse: *ayenbyte of inurt,* the "again-bite" of "inner knowing.")

Anal-phase issues and experiences also lend their specific stamp to the development of conscience. The characteristic torture fantasies (often in the form of beating or whipping) of this time now become directed toward the self. Under the press of his conscience the child becomes his own torturer; he flagellates himself: "All is lost, no one will ever like me again, I will be left out of everything, my family will put me out of the house, . . . " The superego employs the pain of loss of love as a whip to lash the ego. But the imagery might be more brutal, or more sophisticated, depending on the child's total organization. Sometimes the anal component takes the form of shaming; the fantasy confrontation here is with the experience of humiliation, of public scorn and revulsion, of being the butt of ridicule and jeering. In any case, it is intensely painful.

The phallic phase makes its own contribution to conscience formation. Here the threat is typically that of castration: The little boy will be turned into a girl, the little girl will never be whole or complete or lovable. A child can go through the most agonizing pangs of terror, anticipating the dreadful things that will be visited on his or her body. Or the mind cannot think of the details, and a sense of formless, brooding, imminent doom pervades the inner world of the self. There is a powerful sense of personal wrongdoing, of error, of sin; the child has transgressed and is guilty, guilty, guilty; profound punishments of unnamable character await. The pain of such inner chastisements can reach exquisite intensity.

This then is the conscience component of superego, a potent and decisive presence. It plays a major role in personality formation and in the regulation of human conduct and contributes to many symptoms and syndromes.

The Ego Ideal

The other major component of the superego is the ego ideal. This term is a misnomer because it suggests a dimension of the ego rather than the superego, but this is its traditional designation.

The ego ideal has the task of regulating human self-esteem by holding before the child an image of what he ought to be, a model of a sort of ideal self. This becomes a leading presence in the individual's life, something that he strives to live up to. The feeling engendered is "How grand it would be if only I could be [act—be perceived by others as] that." If moments occur when the child does, in fact, live up to this ideal, there is a reward of considerable intensity. A warm glow suffuses the individual, a sense of inner acceptance, a feeling of positive inner oneness and unity, a knowledge of rightness about himself. The child has a quality of validity, and justification, of being where he yearns to be, where he should be. Life feels good.

Evidently, this is a matter of prime importance for the person, and feeling really good about the self is not a common state of mind. On the average, people spend much more of their lives seeking this kind of experience than they do possessing it. This kind of immense reward is transient, episodic, and in some lives, never achieved. People's reach exceeds their grasp; there is almost always a gap between what they perceive themselves to be and what they feel they should be. This can come about in a number of ways. Often the ego ideal is too inflated, too unrealistically proportioned. Thus, if a would-be author can feel worthwhile only if he or she turns out something that is as good as or better than Shakespeare's works; if the composer of songs has to best Schubert; if the psychiatrist must surpass Freud, then the likelihood of arriving at a sense of inner acceptance is vanishingly small. The result is likely to be a person who always feels less than he or she should be; the individual falls short, in brief, is a failure. Thus, some highly successful individuals continually and paradoxically demean themselves. They seem to set far less store by their own achievements than does the world around them; they are striving to follow the banner of their inner ideal, and in those terms they are, indeed, far less than they should be. So also a child with all *A pluses* on his grade card except for one mark that is "only" an *A* may therefore feel crushed and regard himself as a failure. Certain perfectionistic children illustrate this kind of behavior all too well; a sizable percentage of those who later become anorexic manifest some aspect of this trait. Part of the psychopathology in many anorexics involves clear deformation of the ego ideal, and in such instances, the pursuit of thinness becomes a hunt for an idealized body form, pathological though the wish may be.

Much of people's everyday experience of contentment or dissatisfaction with their lot, their sense of self-in-the-world, reflects the tension between the ego and the ego ideal. Even with a good conscience, with no sense of having done anything wrong, there can be a painful haunting feeling of not doing well, of not living up to the standard the person has accepted as his or her own. Because of this double nature of the superego, human beings must always answer to two masters and are allowed to feel good only when they have succeeded in placating both.

Developmentally, the ego ideal derives from a number of sources. The parents' conscious and unconscious attitudes exert a tremendous influence on what the child values and strives to attain, that is, whether to be pious, strong, brave, macho, submissive, seductive, handsome, beautiful, kind, smart, popular, accomplished, rich, powerful, sly, wily, prominent, smart, and so on. In a sense, the child internalizes some aspect of the parents' values and world view. In particular, the ethos and mores within the parental culture—or within the larger culture as interpreted and expressed in the parents' way of life—become part of the child's system of ideals.

In addition to these elements taken in from the outside, as it were, to help form the ego ideal, there is also another component, namely, the sense of grandiosity. It is in this aspect of superego formation that the derivative of the symbiotic unity-with-greatness comes to rest at last. As noted earlier, throughout development the initial feelings of fusion with the powerful parent bear a quality of immense power. Parallel with this, as the child grows, he gradually develops an array of inner ego structures; these involve motor, perceptual, and cognitive capacities. These in turn are presently enriched by accumulated memories, especially the impressions engendered by ongoing social experiences. As part of this growth, functions such as reality testing and social judgment emerge to temper and contain the sense of grandiosity, which becomes increasingly limited and ever more focused. It is not destroyed so much as it is tamed. It never really goes away, but under optimal circumstances it shrinks down and becomes part of the ego ideal, a functioning presence within the structure of normal personality that leads the person always to higher and better things. It does so by providing an inner model, an attainable ideal possibility to strive for, and where it is healthy, it allows the child a decent chance of living up to this ideal, at least occasionally. Unfortunately, in many instances, it is not healthy. Sometimes, the grandiosity will not have shrunk down very much, and the basic sense of self, the self-concept, is inflated and unreal. Under such circumstances, the child may later develop along narcissistic lines or, at any rate, will pursue a rich fantasy life filled with dreams of glory and of magical or science-fictional achievement. Or the child may oscillate between moods of grandiosity and feelings of worthlessness as he strives to cope with the inadequately regulated elements in his makeup.

Where the ideal is awry, it will make for major difficulties in self-esteem. It may be too low as is true of the spoiled and overgratified child, who feels himself to be already ideal, with no need to strive and who cannot understand why others fail to give him his due; it may be too high as in the case of the perfectionistic child; and it may be deformed and give the child a negative or "sick" model for a guide in his adaptation.

In terms of day-to-day happiness, the ego ideal is one of the most influential determinants of the person's inner feeling state.

THE SUPEREGO PROPER

Evolution of the Superego

The series of processes that create this agency of mind elaborate gradually, so that it takes form over time. Roughly speaking, its beginnings probably span the ages 4 to 6 years, but with considerable overlap on either side. In a sense, the anlagen of the superego form initially as islands, isolated experiences. Some of these are realistic memories: the multiple individual no-no's (which arose in response to specific prohibitions); the admonishings, warnings, and forbiddings; the recurrent moralizings; and the content of prayers and solemn injunctions about goodness and badness. Some of them are fantasy related and arise during the many moments of brooding disquiet when a fantasy of monstrous devouring, sadistic whipping, or remorseless castration flickers through consciousness. As these fantasies and memories mesh together, they carry with them the sound of the culture—its values and precepts, its forms and symbols, its solemn moments and ceremonies, the collective sense of the sacred and the awesome. These values, symbols, and ideals form a network and a new entity of mind that will function as a dynamic presence with all the many areas of performance noted above. Once the superego forms, the child is never again truly alone; he carries his culture within him. The voices of the parents and grandparents, the readings from Scripture, the rules of the nursery school teacher, the oration of the clergyman, the words of the police officer, the mail carrier, the storekeeper—all the authorities—are here embodied.

Usually, these memories are not experienced as discrete entities; they tend rather to form an amalgam. Out of it all emerge certain principles and limits that henceforth the child carries within. In particular, these limits bear on the most recent concerns, oedipal wishes and attitudes. At this point the child comes to know that incest is taboo, murder is taboo. Somewhere in all this the message is instilled: "Do not covet Mother's body, or Father's, or sister's or brother's; that is wrong, forbidden, bad." Along with this, the child knows of many other bad things, taboos from all the earlier periods. They range themselves alongside the oedipal taboos and carry with them many of the lessons of civilization. It is wrong for a person to eat human flesh, to expose his nakedness, to lose control of anal impulses, and so on and on. Later the child can never recall how he came to know these principles and practices. If asked, he will say that he always knew them. Everybody knows them; they are "self-evident."

Of course, for many of these injunctions, the process is incomplete. There is much more about civilization that the child needs to know and he continues to acquire this knowledge all through his life. And there is much that children do know that they tend to forget or to ignore. Indeed, the superego is phylogenetically probably a very recent acquisition; it is still a fragile entity needing much evolution and consolidation. Hence, self-governance is not easily achieved; in spite of "knowing better," people tend readily to fall into temptation—it is probably the usual rather than the exceptional state of affairs. In the face of this weakness, people set up many alternative supports for the superego; they create devices and institutions that strive to shore it up, to strengthen it, and to make up for its deficiencies. They join Weight Watchers clubs or Alcoholics Anonymous; they go to church every weekend to listen to sermons; they read inspirational literature and self-help pamphlets or ask newspaper columnists how to regulate their behavior; and most common of all, they turn to one another to ask advice, help, or direction when they are sorely tempted and feel that their controls and judgment are slipping. It is the rare person whose inner controls are truly completed in a wholesome, thoroughgoing, and comfortable fashion; the usual pattern is a patchwork creation of domains of excessive overcontrol alternating with sizable areas of insufficient development. As a result, people often fall prey to impulsive behavior and/or excessive inhibition, causing endless problems and travail.

Mechanisms of Superego Formation

Freud saw the formation of the superego as a crucial step not only in the child's renunciation of oedipal strivings but in the development of psychic structure. While preserving parental prohibitions, the formation of the superego made possible a new level of self-regulation, and hence autonomy. As Freud (1940) put it:

> A portion of the external world has, at least partially, been abandoned as an object and has instead, by identification, been taken into the ego and thus become an integral part of the internal world. This new psychical agency continues to carry on the functions which have hitherto been performed by the people . . . in the external world: it observes the ego, gives it orders, judges it and threatens it with punishments, exactly like the parents whose place it has taken. (p. 205)

Thus, the mechanism of identification or incorporation (or more broadly, internalization) plays a critical role in superego development. The child encounters a source of external regulation that he takes in and makes a part of himself. The external voice becomes an inner presence; the injunction received from outside becomes a fixed part of the inner equilibrium. But there are certain preconditions to such taking in of significant others, and these are not always met. Insufficient or distorted formation of superego structures may easily occur when the stability and solidity of early human relationships have been marred by discontinuities in caretaking or by major problems with caretakers. Thus, identification is likely if the child has a sustained affectionate relationship with someone who ministers to him and meets his needs on many levels. Under such conditions, the child values the caretaker, wants to please him or her, and seeks avidly to accomplish this. But an even more basic need system is also present. The child strives always to learn how to be, how to act, how to cope, how to adapt, how to solve problems. This is part of the very warp and weft of childhood and animates the majority of childhood activity. Much of this need system is unconscious, but it is, if anything, all the more compelling therefore. Offering a model who is sufficiently (if discontinuously) present and who interacts actively with the baby is one major way of giving the child the essential template he needs to accomplish this organismic learning.

On another level, a still more primitive set of forces deals with a child's needs to protect himself from his caretaker. All relationships have dangers; inherent in all closeness is the threat of distance. Attachment allows for loss, and to love another is automatically to be exposed to the possibility of rejection or abandonment. Indeed one of the major roles of internalization is to allow the youngster to maintain the image of the valued other when that other is away; it is separation, in particular, that fosters identification. But there is also the real danger that separation will not be intermittent;

sometimes children are permanently abandoned. Then complex distortions and mystifications of the remembered image may ensue, and the superego is altered accordingly.

Finally there is the phenomenon of child abuse—physical, sexual, and emotional. Such abuse has a powerful and grim impact on superego formation, which may go awry in any one of several ways. There may be a failure of internalization so that the youngster grows without adequate superego development (such an abusive conscience figure cannot be taken in); there may be distortion of internalization with a primitivization or deformation of superego structures (the figure is taken in with all its cruelty and abuse); or there may be a mixture of excess, distortion, and absence of adequate regulatory systems that gives rise to highly uneven superego formations and a consequent pattern of radically deviant behavior. Thus a given individual may be highly inhibited and overcontrolled in the sexual area so that he or she is impotent or frigid, and at the same time the person may be unable to control aggression so that he or she is violent and murderous.

THE END OF OEDIPUS

With the knitting together of the superego, the oedipal phase comes to an end. Before consideration of the next stage of growth, it is worth stopping a moment and studying what happens. What ends with oedipal adaptation? Perhaps it is easiest to grasp this by keeping in mind the concept of a *great renunciation*. Throughout development, at the close of each stage, the child must give up much in order to grow; at this point, however, the need is greater than at any time before.

The major renunciation is that of the bodies of the parents as the objects of childhood wish and fantasy. No more does the youngster dream of taking over the one parent or the other to have for his own, or of the elimination of the rival to allow this takeover to happen. Incest is forbidden, murder is forbidden, the child does not think of either parent as lover or rival. All of that must go into repression, into forgetfulness, into the realm of the unconscious. In a way, it is not a true renunciation; it is rather a banishment of these yearnings from the ongoing experience of daily life. But, in effect, they lose their hold on the child's interest; the child is freed both of their claim to his attention and their ubiquitous presence in his imagination. Thus liberated, the youngster can turn his energies elsewhere.

Along with this, there is an allied renunciation, also of tremendous import. For the child has now had his fill of wishful thinking. Wishing has all too clearly failed to make it so, fantasy does not solve life's problems, daydreams are gratifying but they just get the child into trouble, and all in all, that whole approach to dealing with the world has been a failure. So a giving up of fantasy now ensues; no longer is it the dominant or the preferred mode of address to the world. On the contrary, henceforth a lapse into daydreaming will be a slip, a backward step, a form of self-indulgence. A new kind of thinking must emerge that is more realistic, practical, and limited by genuine possibility.

Along with this goes yet a third renunciation, for what is now finally and definitively abandoned is the claim to grandiosity. The oedipal wishes are inherently unrealistic and bear the stamp of all the earlier infantile pretentiousness. Now, as the ego ideal forms, all this larger-than-life assumptiveness becomes consolidated within that agency, and the ego is freed up to look at self and other more conservatively, with a greater sense of reality, and with a relative freedom from the megalomanic expansiveness so typical of earlier thinking.

The freedom, to be sure, is a matter of degree. It is the nature of these processes always to be incomplete. There will always be ambiguous, partial solutions, with many unclear areas. Personality has no sharp edges, and the end of a phase is likely to be a shading off rather than a boundary. Thus, as he grows the average child carries forward a sizable titer of grandiose wish and thought; it is likely to appear mostly in daydreams and as an interest in superheroes, but it is there. Nonetheless, where development has done well, this becomes a minor and peripheral aspect of adjustment; functionally it has little to do with how the youngster thinks and lives. The closeout of Oedipus sets the bounds to this as well.

Finally, the child renounces most of the memories of earlier childhood. It is almost a kind of rebirth, a fresh beginning. As oedipal issues are repressed, so are most of the prevailing circumambient recollections. The child leaves behind the sense of self-as-toddler, self-as-preschooler; all that is forgotten. The child will build a new identity now, one compatible with the word *child* as distinct from *baby*, and to this end he abandons many of the wishes, dreams, and even the recollections of those earlier years. Later on, an adult who is asked to describe his early memories, can recapture only a small handful of images from preschool years—it is as though memory begins with age 6 or 7. In fact, it is the permitted memories that begin then; the rest are forbidden. They are too closely tied to oedipal events and woven about with associations that fall under the decree of banishment.

And so, with the help of the overarching dome of the superego, the child at last caps the great well of infantile drives and fantasy; contains the forces of magic, awe, and mystery; and curtails the freedom to roam in forbidden realms. The end result is that a whole new state of personality organization emerges, and the child moves into latency.

PART IV

The Grade-School Years (Latency)

Chapter 14

The Early Grade-School Child

DEFINITION

In psychoanalytic parlance the latency stage gets its name from the fate of the phallic-stage instincts, which, at the end of the oedipal phase, become quiescent. These passions and yearnings are by no means eradicated or destroyed; for that matter, they are not even totally neutralized. In a variety of ways they continue to signal their presence and activity. But the intensity of expression has fallen to a far lower level; under average conditions only hidden hints and oblique manifestations of these instincts will emerge, and the commanding interests and motivations of the time are elsewhere. Thus, from a behavioral view, the child becomes calmer, more pliable, less immediately involved with parents, and more immersed in the world of peers, activities, and school.

There has been much discussion in the literature as to whether the characteristic quality of latency is due to a weakening of the instincts, to a strengthening of the ego, or to both (Benson & Harrison, 1980; Sarnoff, 1976). Shapiro and Perry (1976) made a particularly interesting point in observing that quite aside from psychoanalytic theorizing, historical, cross-cultural, and neurospychiatric data combine to suggest that an important transformation takes place at 7 years. This change is based on biological maturational emergents and is expressed in the many alterations in cognitive and regulatory capacities that emerge during this epoch. Many societies begin formal education or apprenticeship for their young at this age, and various religions allow the 7-year-old to begin participating in the traditional ceremonies. The child's abilities to delay, to socialize, to master symbols, to concentrate for longer periods, and to perceive himself as part of a larger organization than the immediate family, all come into focus during this stage of growth. Latency is a product of the interplay of these developments with one another as they emerge simultaneously within the child.

Perhaps most striking of all is the relatively minimal attention that society has directed toward this great sequence of changes. No poems are written about the advent of latency; no novels or plays celebrate its arrival. Considering the magnitude of the changes that occur, this is startling. It may be because, in so many ways, this process involves a constricting down, a banking of the oedipal fires, and a quieting of the riotous fantasy of the preschool years. As a rule, the child becomes more attentive, better behaved, relatively tractable. This is the opposite of the explosion of puberty—it is an implosion, a containing of instinct and a toning down of the more tumultuous aspects of behavior. Although latency provides one of the greatest advances of the human life span, it is, after all, the mere acquisition of civility and the launching of learning that occur here; no dramatics, no eruptions, nothing colorful.

THE TRANSFORMATIONS OF LATENCY

A number of major shifts at the end of the oedipal period contribute to the emerging character of latency. Each change is a critical, powerful alteration in the way personality forms and adapts, and each signals a new departure for subsequent development.

Renunciation of Interest in the Bodies of the Parents

The first great transition, which involves the giving up of the bodies of the parents as objects of sexual and aggressive interest, begins during superego formation. This process is partial at best; as the "giving up" proceeds, it is more or less total, more or less complete. To a great extent it depends on the way the parents handle sexuality, in general, and the way they respond to that child's sexual interests, in particular. It varies as well with the form and level of aggression in the household, the modeling and stimulation that confront the child, and the kind and quality of protection the parent(s) offer(s) in the face of the danger of flooding and overwhelming stimuli. Inevitably, all these environmental givens are interacting with the many facets of the youngster's constitutional endowment; what overwhelms one child may not even trouble another; the alloplast will respond very differently from the autoplast. But the task is always present; as he enters this phase, the child should be actively withdrawing from thinking about parents as sexual objects or as rivals.

This shift away from body interests arises with the organizing of taboos. At this point, the parents' bodies become taboo. This will presently be paralleled by the child's concern with his own body as taboo; this is the age when modesty rather suddenly appears and previously uncaring children begin to assert their rights to body privacy. The original incest taboo appears to spread and to cover ever more territory.

Renunciation of Phallic-Phase Interests

The basic psychological mechanism that brings latency into being is the renunciation of phallic-phase interests. Indeed, under optimal circumstances the child gives up the whole universe of phallic-phase yearnings and imagery; the many scenarios of oedipal triumph and castrative retaliation, of having or begetting babies, of rivaling or being destroyed by the "other" parent; all the lurid yieldings and triumphs and flights that have danced through his imagination or found expression in his play. For the time being, the entire zone of genital pleasure seems too impossible to attain and too emotionally costly. For sheer peace of mind the child cannot persist in these interests; under the pressure of the superego he yields and moves away, choosing his path of retreat from among several possibilities.

Repression. One of the safest and surest of the defense mechanisms is repression. As is universally true of these mechanisms, it operates entirely in the unconscious. No one knows what he or she is repressing or when; the person can know only that somewhere along the line, this has happened. People usually detect repression by discovering a memory gap; they recognize that something that was there is no longer present, or, at least, they cannot find it when they seek it. They can recall the context, but some item—a word, a phrase, a name, an image—some part of it has been erased and can no longer be recaptured; it is forgotten.

When, however, repression is massive enough and sufficiently widespread, people are likely to lose a great deal more than merely some word or image. What gets repressed is the context itself, and an entire epoch in a person's life can disappear. It is a sort of psychological overkill in the service of defense. The very instincts and yearnings that originally gave rise to all the oedipal creations are now brought under the sway of superego. In effect, they are driven out of awareness into the outer darkness of forgetfulness and repression; now they can only return in well-disguised form. Because they are still present in the unconscious, however, they continue to be a threat; if the control system slips, they may once again surge into view. Hence, as this period progresses and the child continues to work on such issues, various defensive emergents appear to support the work of repression, and the youngster has recurrent (seemingly inexplicable) concerns about modesty and sexual teasing.

The closeout of the phallic-oedipal position is at best a partial affair; it leaves behind a delicate balance subject to all sorts of compromise accommodations. Thus, the withdrawal from the interest in the parents' bodies may not be quite complete; there may still be traces of the former state. One of the rituals of latency preserved through many generations can be discerned by watching a boy walking along a city street, repeatedly altering his gait and muttering to himself: "Step on a crack, break your mother's back." Albeit speculative, the professional can readily conjecture about the nature of the "crack" that the child "steps on" with so catastrophic an effect on mother. It seems not far removed from the oedipal fantasies of sexual possession that had filled the child's mind just a few years before. Nor, for that matter, does masturbation disappear during latency, although it may be less frequent and occasion more concern than during the preceding period.

Masturbation. In early latency the new-formed superego is still harsh and primitive, and the pressure to inhibit the masturbation of the previous phallic-oedipal stage may be intense and unrelenting. Along with the genital play, the child perceives the accompanying fantasies as forbidden and shameful, and makes a resolute effort to put them firmly out of mind. Indeed, the thrust of personality interests takes a step backward to prephallic-stage concerns. The youngster begins to wander in these more infantile realms of thought and feeling only to find that he has exchanged one danger for another, and now he must do something about this substitute set of images and yearnings. He strives to cope by repressing the objectionable elements and by turning his interests toward outside things rather than to inner concerns, toward being good rather than indulging in wicked thoughts. Alternatively he may become provocative in order to get punished by the outer environment rather than face the inner sins along with the remorseless inner retaliation.

Apart from occasional breakthroughs, most children succeed reasonably well in their flight from masturbation; from time to time enactments of this practice may occur in both boys and girls, but it is usually not a dominant aspect of their behavior. In the more vulnerable youngsters, some rather paradoxical symptomatic behaviors have been noted as the children struggle to bring all this under control. Thus, in certain instances, the very excess of castration anxiety can lead a child toward compulsive masturbation, in an effort to reassure himself that his body is intact.

As children move past early latency and into the middle years of the epoch (from the 5–7-year-old into the 8–10-year-old period), their competence and mastery increase steadily. This applies to the management of masturbatory behaviors as well. In many instances, the child successfully suppresses the overt behavior and transmutes it instead into various substitutes or equivalents.

Various authors have noted quite a few such masturbatory equivalents; thus, some children who were not previously much interested in fire play may now draw off to themselves and make little fires or just burn matches. These youngsters are not firesetters in the usual sense of antisocial behavior; often they are rather careful to avoid letting the fire get out of control. But they are still caught up in the passion play; they use the dancing flames as a site for forbidden fantasies. Other equivalents involve insomnia (or other sleep disturbances) or rituals of various kinds (nail-biting, scratching, and head banging) (Francis & Marcus, 1975). In an early discussion of delinquency, Anna Freud (1949) suggested that many of the antisocial acts of childhood were, in fact, the overt living out of such repressed (and hence unconscious) masturbatory fantasies.

Other Derivatives. These patterns of compromise can find expression in other kinds of interpersonal behavior. Thus, in spite of disdaining girls, a boy may be very conscious of their gaze and do cartwheels or otherwise show off his strength or agility where they can see it. Or two boys may engage in homosexual play together. The commonest form of such behavior is probably looking and touching, in effect, some version of mutual masturbation; but any form of oral or anal practice may occur. An isolated instance of such behavior is not of grave clinical significance; regular and/or repetitive patterns of this kind, however, probably mean that there is a disturbance in the unfolding of sexual object choice—and sometimes of gender identity.

By and large, latency sex play is tentative, exploratory, or experimental. It reenacts the lingering echoes of forgotten yearnings; sometimes there is a total repression of what the body of the opposite sex looks like, and the dominant sexual concern is curiosity, the desire to see. Much depends on how total the superego formation has been. Because this can range from the fragmentary, incomplete, "Swiss-cheese" superego structure of the overstimulated child (who does not have a true latency at all) to the constricted domination of the neurotically inhibiting superego of the overregulated child, many behavior patterns are possible. For the most part, where development has gone well, the accent falls far more heavily on the containment of these impulses than on their expression. Where the repressive superego strictures are particularly powerful, the youngsters have all sorts of uncomprehending and truly naïve conceptions of maleness, femaleness, and reproduction, let alone sexuality (e.g., boys have dirty minds and are interested in sex whereas girls have clean minds and are not; babies are conceived by kissing or by getting married; sperm are transmitted psychically, etc.).

Regression to the Anal Phase

Presently, the flinching away from oedipal things is so great that a sort of id regression takes place. The child literally moves backward along the instinctual sequence to the anal period and reconsolidates there (Bornstein, 1951). This change is apparent in many overt ways.

Jokes. It is at the age of 6 or 7 that the youngster is likely to bring home his first jokes. The 3- and 4-year-old may laugh a good deal, but by and large such a child does not tell jokes. Or if he does, the adult listener may be hard put to know when to laugh. The order of the account does not proceed quite as a joke should, and the point of the story is likely to be obscure (although the preschooler finds it hilarious). But the young latency child is sufficiently mature to recount a truly funny story and to keep the punch line where it should be. And many do, with gusto. The listener is, however, likely to be impressed with the anal character of the recounting. These jokes typically are, in fact, bathroom humor, as in the following examples:

> There was this lady who was sick and the doctor told her she couldn't eat green peas. Then after a while she got better and doctor said she could. "At last," she said, "I can have a pea again." Ha ha ha!

Or,

> Did you hear the one about the elephant who had diarrhea? It's all over town! Ha, ha, ha.

Of such stuff is (early) latency humor made. More to the point, of such stuff are latency-drive organization, interest, and relationship style constructed.

Obsessive Activities. These youngsters go back to the anal patterns in a host of ways. Once again they show the former joy in muscle activity, body movement, equilibrium, and coordination. Most latency children are actively involved in a wide and heterogeneous assortment of sports and hobbies. More than that, they will engage in many of the more derivative and defensive aspects of anality and will seek obsessive diversions, from needlepoint to jigsaw puzzles. Many are good at details, and they are prime candidates for what this culture (and, for that matter, most cultures) requires of them: to learn. Just as the anal stage was the time for learning language, the latency period is the developmental moment for initiating the child into society's formal educational practices. It is not by accident that youngsters start first grade at the beginning of this period, but rather reflects a consensual awareness of readiness. Children may attend play school or nursery school earlier, but these schools engage the children through their natural mode of adaptation: play and fantasy. With the advent of latency, however, children change; they are busy now not so much in expressing instinct as in controlling it. They are no longer, like phallic children, fantasy oriented; they have returned to the anal-phase emphasis on motor activity. Now they focus less on make-believe and more on how to do things in the real world. A similar drift is evident in their psychopathology; during these years clinicians see many elimination disorders, learning disorders, and conduct disorders, and relatively few sexual problems or hysterical symptoms.

Collecting. Another great anal-stage derivative is an interest in collecting, and latency youngsters are often passionate collectors. What is collected will vary widely with culture and opportunities, but the tendency to amass things is close to universal. Collections can extend from the trinkets in a boy's pocket—an Indian arrowhead, a bit of silver paper from a gum wrapper, a broken knife blade, two marbles, and so on—to an elaborate array of carefully pinned local butterflies, each with its appropriate designation clearly lettered on the accompanying label. Objects of little intrinsic worth and ready availability form the likeliest targets of the latency urge to amass, and bottle caps, matchbook covers, and beer cans, let alone seashells, minerals, and fossils (in appropriate neighborhoods) grace many a home with their profusion (if not always with their orderly arrangement). Commercial enterprises have made fortunes selling such items as chewing gum by including with each unit a latency collectible, for example, a card or sticker adorned with the image of a baseball player, rock star, space hero, classic automobile, or whatever else might appeal to this age group. There are doll collections, sticker collections, lead soldier collections, toy furniture collections, stamp collections, coin collections, and model car collections, to name a few. In occasional instances, these activities will persist into adulthood and will remain prime objects of interest for a lifetime. Sometimes these collections involve elaborate construction and assembly efforts and sometimes, as in the case of model railroads, such interests have brought children and parents together in complex mutual endeavors.

To be sure, not all collections have such salutary effects. Pine cones, dried mushrooms, or other such spoilables may result in scruffy messes that exasperated mothers eventually threaten to or actually do throw out, much to the dismay of the suddenly bereft hoarder. Essentially, as in all such drive derivatives, it is a matter of the level of sublimation involved. The most primitive kind of collecting is really the mere amassing of something such as stones or marbles, whose character is close to its fecal origins, with the collection scattered about in untidy heaps that are the targets of endless promises to pick it all up or get it together, but which somehow continue to spread and to mess. The other end of the spectrum involves the same set of impulses but is managed in better defended, more sublimated fashion. The result is likely to be a carefully and logically arranged display of ancient coins, precancelled stamps, or locally discovered fossils, each with its correct label giving time and place of acquisition, catalogue numbers, and any other important data. Most childhood collections will fall somewhere between these extremes, with some easily available item such as postage stamps or bottle caps kept in a special set of albums or containers that the youngster pores through from time to time with considerable pleasure.

Crafts. In addition to collecting there is a renewed interest in making things, especially if some repetitive obsessive-compulsive quality is involved. All latency children seem to delight in crafts of this character. There is the excitement of watching the way some limited repetitive act (such as threading beads or braiding thongs) can build and organize into an interesting, useful, or beautiful form. Weaving, braiding, macramé, all sorts of assemblings and arrangings become background presences in the homes and lives of such boys and girls. They enjoy models, for example, or cutouts of various kinds, where they must follow very detailed instructions, bring tiny parts together, and indulge in much gluing and pasting. Such a pattern fits beautifully into the anal disposition and a good time is had by id, ego, superego, and all the friends and family.

Grade-school children are great craftspeople. Whittling, soap sculpture, linoleum block carving, lettering and printing, crayon drawing, watercolors—all claim the energy and involvement of many children. The list is potentially endless, and the recent expansion of computer devices has enlarged it. Quite young children have become interested in this aspect or that of electronics, some assembling parts and others operating computers both for learning and for diversion. The impact of this newest dimension of technological experience on ego development remains to be discerned; it is unlikely to be trivial.

Games. Of course, not all activities are so quiet. Without moving into the realm of true sports, children engage in a great many games that provide more room for blending the satisfactions of obsessive detail and muscular interests. Youngsters play jacks and mumbledypeg, they toss cards and jump rope, and they often have doggerel rhymes to go along with some of these activities. Some of the collections of these rhymes make fascinating reading (Opie & Opie 1959). Almost any activity that expresses the unity of repetitiousness (preferably of rhythmic character), detail, rule, and the creation or the preservation of form, will appeal to this age group.

Nor is the inner-city child less involved. An active after-school program may be present and vie with the local community center, the Big Brothers program, and a volunteer grandparent project to provide diversions and activities for a variety of age groups. Such phenomena have saved and helped many children from delinquency and addiction. Even the street itself has its diversions, although these are less likely to make for sublimation. Nonetheless there are sidewalk games that children can draw with chalk, stickball and other group games that youngsters organize, and a variety of types of fantasy play. It is a truism that in many deprived areas the hazards of the street far outweigh its potentials for positive growth. Such potentials are present, however, and some youngsters are able to use them.

Sports. The anal period is a moment in growth much given to muscular activities, to the joy of mastering and expressing the novel integration of mind and body that developmental advance offers the child. Such a celebration of new acquisitions occurs once again in latency, when the growth of the previous years culminates in a larger, stronger, better coordinated body that has both far more endurance and the beginning capacity for true skill. These emergents, plus the joy in rules, details, and performance, lead to the beginnings of organized sports. Earlier in the century such interests found expression in sandlot baseball, city street stickball, driveway or playground basketball, and against-the-house slugball and handball. Currently, most of this spontaneous expression of childhood play has been preempted by more organized patterns in playgrounds, community centers, and school-based programs. The former diversions have not disappeared, but adult-sponsored efforts of a more structured character have largely replaced their spontaneous expression. There is a certain difference between the earlier, child-initiated sandlot baseball and the current adult-organized preparation for Little League competition. However, the basic interest of the time is expressed as readily in the one form as the other—there is a primary joy in body mastery, body movement, body efficiency, and body expression. This, combined with the many other diversions of latency interest, leads to a lively and often intense involvement in the typical sport activities of the period.

This is when youngsters learn to throw and to catch a ball, they begin to sort out into children who are fast runners, are physically strong, or are good fighters—and those who are not. The great accent of the time falls on acquiring skills, and many youngsters can keep occupied at this task all day long. The Little Leaguer who eventually emerges is formed through such patient skill acquisition.

Little girls might share this pattern and get into sports as readily as do boys, although there is probably some selectivity here with respect to preferred sports. Girls with a somewhat different orientation may find their optimum form of self-expression in ballet or other forms of dance. Many ballerinas have their first exposure to this discipline as early as 6 or 7 years. The background of a professional dancer, typically shows lifetime patterns that jelled well before the youngster's 10th birthday. A related although distinctly different universe that claims the passionate involvement of other girls is gymnastics. Some of these tiny children exhibit an extraordinary level of muscular and bodily control. Their capacity for regular, sustained, grueling, arduous, exhausting physical work is equally astonishing. Latency is capable of producing exceptional phenomena of this kind and does so regularly.

The energies of these young people take directions that are as varied as human temperament, environmental opportunity, parental affluence, and the possibilities of a complex culture can make them. This is when so many mothers become dispatchers whose schedules rival those at Pennsylvania Station. This child goes to ballet lessons, that one must be gotten to the track and field gym, the other one is taking karate lessons, and yet another is in child chorus or is studying the flute or any of a long list of other teachable skills.

Learning and School

The natural bent of this age group is toward learning and mastery in the real world. The children are interested in learning how to do things and in the doing itself. This forms the basis of the great civilizer of this epoch of life, learning in school. The entire system of schooling derives from some of these developmental realities and acts as one of the major formers and shapers of the latency ego.

Every child must face a radical transition between play school and kindergarten, on the one hand, and the quite different demands of first grade (and the succeeding school years), on the other. Shade it as you will, it is all the difference between fun and work. Within the ambience of first grade, the child must master cognitive competencies that had formerly been "readiness" issues. Once the transition is made, the child passes beyond preparatory forms; now he faces the challenges of real-life accomplishment and, with that, the possibility of failure. Suddenly, marks and tests and grades are in the picture, objective evaluation of performance is present, and the child must meet this new set of standards—or bear the consequences. This atmosphere is fundamentally different from the one that pervaded prior learning and group environments. In the former settings the pressure was mild; now it is all too likely to become intense. As teacher and school systems become more attuned to developmental realities, children are being held back in kindergarten if they are not "ready," and compensatory and ameliorative techniques are being introduced early if developmental lag is evident.

The importance of such early case finding and intervention can scarcely be overstated; it is here that professionals can address major difficulties with relative ease and initiate preventive or therapeutic techniques. Here the integrity of the perceptual and organizing apparatuses of the central nervous system assumes paramount importance. It is in these early school years that a great array of school-related diagnoses begin to be made: mental retardation, dyslexia, specific learning deficit, attention deficit disorder, and the like. The everyday school routine involves the capacity of the child to perform the various kinds of taking in of information—organizing these data, storing them in memory, making the proper associations to other stored information, formulating a pattern of response and integrating that into his musculo-skeletal apparatus so that performance follows. All the necessary neurological building blocks must be well in place, and adequate educational methods must address the totality of the child in a way that will stimulate and exercise his mind and guide it toward optimal function as it continues to develop. In other words, learning implies a healthy child of good endowment surrounded by a supportive family and attending a good school. Such a set of circumstances does not always happen. A complex array of neurological, social, and environmental elements are necessary and more than that, they need to come into play in proper sequence. Given these stringent requirements, it is almost predictable that in a sizable number of situations these conditions will not be met; when they are not, the child will not learn as he should. This is the basis for the ubiquity of learning-related problems within school systems the country over. Hence, within any catalog of the emergents of latency, the appearance of school-related learning disorders is central.

Thought

As noted earlier, latency involves the instinctual regression to a more anal position and the pervasive influence of this shift. The story of development, however, is characteristically a history of progression and regression occurring simultaneously, and this happens in latency as well. In the cognitive realm quite a different emergent appears, a major advance in the quality and style of thinking. Freud (1911/1958) described this transformation in a remarkable article about the two principles of mental functioning. The more familiar picture of these changes has been depicted for us by Piaget, who called the cluster of new capacities in latency the *stage of concrete operations*. During the preschool, oedipal years, thinking was confined largely to the fantasy-dominated preoperational coping mode. With the advent of latency, however, this gives way to a kind of limited capacity for true logical thought. Piaget (1936/1952) described many innovations in cognitive capacity that appear at this time; for purposes of this discussion the three most important are *classification, seriation,* and *conservation*. These capacities provide much of the infrastructure for latency behavior.

Classification refers to the youngsters' capacity to arrange the phenomena of their world, be it seashells or personality types, into more or less orderly categories. The children can begin to see how larger, more general groups of objects can contain specific subgroups; these in turn can be subdivided into yet smaller and more discrete categories, and quite complex arrays of classes of objects can emerge. Within a tribal society, for example, the youngster can begin to appreciate the shadings and distinctions of the intricate kinship relations within his family, the several connections of that family to its clan, and the way that the clan in turn fits into the larger order of the tribe. Or a Western child may begin to save stamps and to learn all about the different countries and their different types of postage, perhaps even to specialize in the stamps of a particular type within a particular region, or to collect only animal stamps from many countries, and so on. The capacity for classifying leads to much of the collecting behavior that is so important in latency and that offers so much gratification at this developmental moment; once the children begin to think this way, they will exercise this new-found capacity simply because they have it, and, in many instances, enjoy it to an enormous degree.

Seriation is the capacity to arrange things in series. This too comes with latency; some youngsters learn all the statistics associated with certain ball teams or players or get involved in crafts that require repeated operations with minor variations. These children, too, are building on a newfound capacity: the ability to sequence things. They act on this because it is there, they can do it, and, once again, they may derive great pleasure from the practice.

Finally, there is the matter of conservation. This capacity requires that the child be able to abstract the essence of quantity (such as mass or volume) despite changes in its appearance. Although the child will achieve the capacity to think in this fashion by the end of latency, initially he has not mastered it. The child is not yet capable of fully abstract thinking and can therefore be readily deceived by appearances. A lower wide container seems to contain more than a taller narrower one with the same content; the basic essences of mass, volume, extension, and quantity cannot yet be conceptually separated out of each concrete perceptual experience. But the child has taken the first steps, he can acquire elementary arithmethic and grammar, can extract the meaning of a simply written paragraph, and can learn lists and dates. Formal education is underway.

Object Relations in Latency—Dynamics

Having relinquished the parents as objects of erotic love and rivalrous hate, the child develops a new type of relationship. He withdraws the erotic feeling from the parent of the opposite sex and transforms both its sensuous character and its target so that it becomes a muted, idealized admiration of the same-sex parent. The little boy feels drawn toward his father as an admirable model. It seems to him that his father is the strongest person in the world or the smartest, or the best father there is. If another youngster challenges this, the child quickly asserts, "My Pop can lick your Pop." The little girl similarly is apt to seek out her mother as a guide, instructor, and helper. Mother always knows. Many little girls tell their mother everything. (This pattern may persist until puberty and then transform abruptly into defensive avoidance, much to the mother's uncomprehending dismay.)

The tendency toward idealization will often touch both parents. Thus the boy's admiration for his father may well be paralleled by the simple awareness that his mother is the most beautiful woman in the world. Or, should he withhold perfectibility from the mother, he may instead direct it toward a teacher.

With parents and parent substitutes (such as teachers, police officers, clergy, mail carriers, and the like), the child is essentially compliant. This does not mean he is totally submissive; there may be many sites of conflict or at least of protest in the interactions. Under certain conditions the youngster will bridle and point out how unfair it is (it was not his turn to do that chore, why does the other one get away with everything, so and so has a bigger share, etc.). But even though obeying under protest, the average child listens to orders and performs as directed.

At this age, challenges to parents, and to the adult world in general, will not usually take direct form. But the child has a variety of indirect means of asserting himself and opposing his own will to that of the significant other. A socially acceptable way is to play riddles, puzzles, and games. Latency children are great riddlers and will often express a state of covert negativism by posing conundrums. A great many latency jokes are built on riddles. "Knock, knock. Who's there?" or "How many Californians does it take to. . . ?" "How many elephants can get into a VW?" "What's black and white and red [read] all over?" In each case, the child bests the adult, is one up, and comes off triumphant from the engagement. Best of all, the adult enjoys the joke too.

The same sort of scenario takes place in games. The child challenges the grown-up in a socially approved fashion and, if possible, wins the match. The obverse is the pain the child experiences when he is bested, and the adult triumphs within a context that then feels "unfair." Many children in therapy will cheat in games and change the rules because the need to win is so great.

Prologue to Love.   One of the more interesting shifts of erotic interest that sometimes occurs now is a peculiar kind of love relationship that may develop between little boys and girls of 6 or 7. This can be an attachment of great intensity; sometimes the baffled children are overcome by a kind of sweet shyness and cannot speak to one another; sometimes, in the excess of his incomprehensible feelings, the boy will be rude and provocative toward the girl. Occasionally the children feel reciprocally drawn to each other and form a brief intense bond whose poignancy is such that they never forget it, and whose quality remains as a lingering memory of ineffable sweetness all through life. These are usually short-lived relationships that most truly typify the term *innocent*. It is as if the mechanism that will later finally bring the oedipal complex to an end (by turning the attachment out of the family to a real-life lover in the external social world) now takes a trial step.

Peer Relations.   This is, however, a transient episode at best; the direction of latency love is generally away from heterosexuality and toward an affectionate attachment to same-sex others. In particular, it is a time of beginning major interest in peers. Friends become ever more important and the definition of fun often comes to mean being with same-sex friends.

By the same token there is often an increasing distaste for children of the other sex. This is generally more powerful in boys than girls, but the tension between the genders is likely to be felt and expressed by both. Boys speak of girls with disdain, and girls talk about boys with derision. Depending on many variables, this can take the form of good-natured chaffing or really intense rejection and avoidance. In the old-fashioned classroom, for example, where boys sat on one side of the room and girls on the other, a favorite punishment of boys used to be to require them to sit on the girls' side. The culprits were sure to be teased and miserable.

From the psychoanalytic perspective, all of this is in the service of keeping oedipal elements at bay. As the supportive structures of latency fall into place, numerous evidences of these tendencies come into view. Thus, the boy might proclaim a distaste for mushy stuff in the movies. He likes action, lots of it, and a good war movie or a Western might fulfill his needs exactly. The classic Westerns were famous for minimum intimacy, maximum gallantry (limned the more brightly by notable villainy), and at the end of it all, the cowboy in the white hat did not kiss a girl but patted his horse (loud applause from the latency section).

Nor do these feelings stop with fantasy. When Aunt Nellie comes to visit the family after a long absence and plants a kiss on the youngsters cheek after exclaiming how much he has grown, a look of distaste may cross the young boy's face and he will probably make a more or less surreptitious effort to wipe off his cheek. Little girls, with their somewhat less complete oedipal transition from the mother to the father, seem to undergo a less complete defensive transformation at latency. Or, more precisely, they retain a much wider array of options in their affectional style. Some of them remain determinedly heterosexual throughout, whereas others undergo transformations not unlike those of the boys, that is, they are intensely involved with girlfriends, often in the form of complex love–hate relationships, and regard boys as nasty and peripheral.

Overall, throughout early latency, boys and girls are inclined to cleave to same-sex groups; on the other hand, as this epoch continues, the urge toward social engagement with one another grows progressively stronger. This semiovert, semicovert condition makes them very prone to teasing. Let but the chant arise, "John and Mary sitting in a tree, *k-i-s-s-i-n-g*. First comes love, then comes marriage, then comes Mary with a baby carriage," and John is ready to draw blood while Mary talks of leaving town. Because they are both evidently interested in each other, why all the fuss? The answer is simple: The yearnings and fantasies are not fully conscious, not yet fully developed. They are obscure inner images, and the teasing doggerel suddenly exposes them in a vulnerable, unready, and unformed state. The victims are wounded and humiliated—and they react accordingly.

The role of peers through the latency years becomes increasingly central; by the time the youngsters arrive at prepuberty, their peer relationships are often among the prime interests in their lives. Social scientists have directed a great deal of thoughtful attention toward the study of peer interaction. The question of the role of parental management and its impact on peer success—or failure—is of considerable interest. The usual question is that of social competence: To what extent does the style of rearing affect the skills and performance of children as social beings? In terms of the kind and quality of social competence that younger latency children achieve, a number of powerful shaping forces clearly are at work. Thus, during a recent study, Putallaz (1987) evaluated interactions between mothers and their first graders in play sessions and then compared these findings to the way the same children interacted with other children as well as the way the mothers dealt with other mothers. It turned out that all the observed patterns of exchange were significantly related. The salient finding was that "positive, agreeable mothers had positive, agreeable children; mothers who focused on feelings had children who focused on feelings; and disagreeable mothers had disagreeable children" (p. 336).

That the family influence is powerful at this early stage of latency is not surprising. However, a predictable reality of development is that the latency years will find the youngsters turning toward their peers with increasing frequency and mounting intensity, so that as the grade-school years advance, the stresses and rewards of this peer dimension of their existence achieve ever greater valence and emotional force.

A curious echo of this state of affairs is to be found in animal research. Suomi (1983) noted that the social rearing environment of a young Rhesus monkey was an important determinant of that baby's eventual level of social competence. The well-known isolation syndrome is an extreme example of what the formative environment can do to an individual's social competence; the monkey raised for the first 6 months of life without contact with other monkeys is a social cripple thereafter. Once restored to their normal social context, such isolation-reared individuals do not play with peers, they are indiscriminately and inappropriately aggressive, they are sexually deficient, and if they should reproduce, the females are neglectful and abusive toward their infants. In short, the achievement of social skills is at least in part a function of early social experience.

Because a Rhesus monkey matures 4 or 5 times faster than a human infant, by the time such a monkey is finishing its first year, it is socially close to the beginning of latency.

Under more normal conditions, by the 2nd month of life the baby monkey begins to leave its mother occasionally to explore its environment, and thereafter, increasing amounts of time are spent with peers. With the passage of time, the level of peer involvement continues to increase up to puberty, after which the preeminence of peer interaction begins to decline. It is evident that this kind of peer engagement is not simply a repetition of the interactions with the mother; many new qualities are added that never appear in the parent–child exchange. In particular, the kinds of play that peers engage in are not echoes of or echoed in any of the interactions with the mother. Functionally, the between-peers play serves as a sort of practice version of almost all the varieties of adult behavior, be they aggressive, sexual, or affiliative. In effect, this play enhances social skills and prepares the young monkey for later competence in social interaction.

For the human young, early isolation experience is certainly traumatic, and the need to develop social skills during latency has been remarked on by many investigators. Indeed, investigators have made numerous observations in the schoolyard, in the classroom, and in summer camps that bear on this issue. Gerald Patterson (1982), for example, emphasizes that the failure to acquire social skills is part of the profile of many children with conduct disorders.

SEPARATION OF THE SEXES. There seems to be a developmental sequence in the way that social patterns unfold during these latency years. The findings suggest that from kindergarten through the 6th grade, there is a steady pattern of change in both the quality and the content of the various kinds of play among boys and girls. The kindergarten children touch each other easily and the sexes mingle readily at table with no great sexualization of their interactions. As the years progress, however, the initial freedom and lack of self-consciousness give way to charged communicative behaviors that convert many details of ordinary exchange into bearers of numerous additional messages. By the sixth grade, the height of prepuberty, boys and girls tend to sit at different tables for lunch, and every touch is erotized.

Curiously enough, the persistent and increasing erotization is accompanied by a parallel and often more intense competition. Teachers are very aware of these phenomena. By the fourth grade or so an announcement from the teacher that "the girls have finished their work, but the boys have not" can serve as a powerful motivator. Teachers have good reason to recognize as well that cross-gender interaction begins readily to breed excitement; accordingly, the teachers will act to try to keep this at a minimum. For example, in the schoolyard the teacher on duty may keep boys away from the girls' designated play area.

Thorne (1985) spent some time observing the behavior of boys and girls both in classrooms and schoolyards. In describing the group interactions that he studied, Thorne delineates a series of boundary phenomena that he calls *borderwork*, that is, acts that tend to emphasize the gender boundary between boys and girls. These include contests, rituals of chasing and pollution, and group invasions. In spontaneous seating from the fourth grade (approximately 9 years of age) on up, the boys and girls tend to be quite exclusive; the boys who sit closest to the girls are usually low-status members of their group. In spelling bees and math contests, the boys are likely to be pitted against the girls to make the competition keener. In some athletic events (not all), similar divisions occur. This was noted chiefly in team play (the boys' team plays baseball against the girls' team) where the nature of the game limits the membership. In more informal kinds of play, where one group does not oppose against the other, and where everyone has a turn, tension between the genders is usually not prominent.

During a play sequence, when boys have arguments, the outcome is often very different than is the case with girls. If an all-male play group has a falling out over some point in scoring, the boys will often yell and argue with passionate intensity, but they usually settle the matter quickly by one means or another and the play goes on. Where an all-girl population is involved, it is not unusual for such an argument to break up the play for that day; those who feel mistreated or offended by the outcome will simply stop playing.

As the grade-school years advance, various kinds of tag and chasing games assume increasing importance, both as a substitute for and an expression of the erotized tensions in the playground. The names of these forms of play speak for themselves: Girls Chase the Boys; Boys Chase the Girls; Chase and Kiss; Kissers and Chasers; Kiss or Kill. Chasing games often occur in the first three grades as well, but there the activity usually takes the form of fantasy play with one child assuming the role of monster, making monster noises, and chasing victims who flee in mock terror. By the fourth grade, however, the more gender-explicit elements begin to become important, and kissing (the girls usually threatening to kiss the boys) takes the place of the monster.

Allied with this are the pollution games where a given individual or a gender group is declared to be contaminated—to have "cooties"—and a host of touching rituals are specified to avoid or to transfer the cooties from one person to another. Girls are usually regarded as endangering the boys.

Finally, playground invasions are a major element in the excitement and interaction of the genders. Usually boys disrupt girls' games, although it may go either way. Sometimes boys ask to join in a girls' game, cooperate appropriately for a time, and then abruptly "mess it up." The girls respond with almost ritual chasing and tattling to playground attendants.

Within the group context, from a relatively early time girls appear to be more sexual than boys. Thus the kissing activity or the contaminating power of the touch tend to adhere far more to girls than to boys.

Although the more typical friendship patterns at this age are primarily with same-sex peers, sexual interest heightens, often in rather primitive form, as the epoch progresses. Where the general cultural style is uninhibited, there is likely to be much use of obscene language, especially in jokes, and frequent references to perverse sexual practices. The shrinking back and the concealment spoken of earlier seem to be replaced by a kind of counterphobic excess. Occasionally notes are passed from boys to girls— and sometimes girls to boys—suggesting wildly bizarre sexual engagements. When these are caught by teachers, the results can be quite dramatic.

All sorts of odd compromise behaviors tell at once of the curiosity, the uncertainty, and immaturity of the sexual development at this time. One couple, for example, described their problem with an 11-year-old daughter, who was seeking entry into a club at school. The requirement for a girl's initiation into this particular organization was that she had to watch her parents engaging in sexual intercourse and then describe what she had seen before the rapt membership. Presently the parents were sealing the edges of their window blinds and stuffing keyholes to fend off the determined efforts of their insistent offspring. As is so often true in development, latency can be an engaging and intriguing, but not altogether an easy time for all of the participants.

Such difficulties, however, really belong to late latency or prepuberty. During the latency years proper, by and large, both genders reach a low ebb of erotic feelings; there is not much tenderness in the lives of these youngsters. They are, in many ways, little savages and are far more interested in aggressive teasing than in affectional loving. But there are some notable exceptions.

TENDERNESS.   Some latency children show exquisite tenderness toward a pet. A kind of passionate involvement can be present that is almost consuming in its intensity. The pet can be as large as a horse or as small as a kitten, but it moves into the child's life as a commanding presence on whom he lavishes much of that great store of oedipal yearning that he can no longer experience in its original form, but that, for whatever reason, escapes containment.

Sometimes a latency child reacts in a similar way toward a younger sibling, exhibiting a fierce protectiveness and providing bottomless loving care. Little brother or sister is adored, carried around, ministered to, made much of, and, where the occasion demands it, bravely defended. This provides an interesting contrast to the oedipal child's reaction to a new baby, where the commonest sentiment is considerable rivalry. For many a latency girl a new baby in the home becomes, in some curious fashion, *her* baby. She immediately takes over as many functions as she is permitted; she feeds, plays with, changes, dresses, and undresses the baby, she puts the baby down for his nap or tucks him in at night, she consoles the baby when he is unhappy and becomes wise in reading his cues and signals; all in all, she sets up shop as prime competitor to the mother for the role of caretaker and infant rearer. Again, it is a question of the particular home, and the specific moment in the girl's development when the new baby appears. If the latency child has really completed her oedipal work and made a solid identification with the mother, then the pregnancy and the new baby act to confirm this developmental step, and she embarks on this chance to work at and to realize her new identity with enthusiasm and effectiveness. Some derivatives of the earlier oedipal rivalry might also be present to fuel her behavior (in her fantasy she is a better mother than Mom), but her pattern is now a sublimated one, with many positive ingredients that confirm her feminine role as well as her familiar position as a good and helpful child.

Fantasy and Daydreams

Latency is a time of containment of fantasy, and so obsession and ritual become important. The youngsters learn the forms of address, and each morning the class chants, "Good Morning, Miss Jones." Religious rites are of great interest to many of these children, and they often enjoy participating in ceremonies. Many parents find that the children flourish best with predictable, regular routines. Some of the youngsters are fascinated by train, plane, or bus schedules and study them avidly. Their games and play forms often involve much compulsive patterning and repetition (e.g., the doggerel of jump-rope rhymes). In a sense, they seek to bind fantasy through repetitious action.

For a great many children, however, fantasy will not be so readily bound. There are powerful, unanswered yearnings within them that have not been totally managed by the available means that the superego and the ego can bring to bear; these need a safe form of expression. What better outlet to give them than daydreams? And so latency children can become great daydreamers and live out much affectively charged experience of considerable intensity in this realm.

Daydreams are not confined to a single gender; both boys and girls share in this activity although the dream content, which is shaped by the great gender issues of this time, may well be different. Boys will often think of adventure, of traveling in bands (all male), and of carrying out missions. Tolkien's *The Fellowship of the Ring* (1954), the story of such a band of adventurers, is a classic example of the genre; there is no end to the variety of these tales. For many generations King Arthur and the Knights of the Round Table dazzled the imaginations of latency children in the Western world, and the knight in shining armor is very much a latency idea.

Many fantasies of both genders tend toward themes of rescue. The boy dreams of saving maidens fair and earning their undying admiration; the girl dreams both of facing threat or danger and of being saved by some Prince Charming or, like Nancy Drew, of offering rescue to others. Usually the situation is heady stuff: The latency boy dashes into the burning building and guides, or even carries, the terrified occupant(s) out. Like Perseus, he boldly bests fierce monsters and saves the terrified girl from imminent devouring. The girl in her turn faces the perils of Pauline, with an eye to the whereabouts of her ideal rescuer–partner, or becomes Wonder Woman and does the rescuing herself. In both instances the outcome of encounter with either rescued or rescuer tends to trail off somewhere; they live happily ever after. The oedipal theme is still tucked away, only now it is in new garb.

Other fantasies are essentially dreams of glory. The child will be the football hero, the winner of the Indianapolis 500, the gold medalist at the Olympics. The less mature forms of such yearning take even more grandiose character: the youngster is Superman, Wonder Woman, or some figure out of science fiction. Books often yield such heroic models as Tarzan of the Apes or Thuvia, Maid of Mars. More "realistic" youngsters will read the novels designed for them: *Nancy Drew* or *The Hardy Boys*. These are sources of endless pleasure and excitement for the youngsters, who can temporarily resolve all their tensions and uncertainties through transiently merging with heroic roles.

Erotic Fantasies. Fantasies with a more overtly erotic flavor occur as well. A mature woman recalled that as an 8- or 9-year-old she used to have a pleasurable repetitious fantasy whenever she took her bath. She would cover her middle with a washcloth and imagine that a group of men stood all about her and commanded her to remove the cloth. This she would then proceed to do very slowly, very voluptuously, and with great erotic pleasure. A grown man recalled that at 7 and 8 he used to have a repetitious fantasy that involved an imaginary cave in which he imprisoned many young women. All of them pined for his attention and occasionally he would show himself to them, but he would not let them free. The great pleasure in the daydream was in thinking about how much they yearned for his presence.

Most of the fantasies of this time are concerned with looking or showing. Actual physical contact is less evident and not so much the goal of the "story" (although this will vary with the level of stimulation to which a given child may have been exposed). Another kind of fantasy, less obviously erotic, also characterizes this time of life. It is a direct expression of the regression to anality and explicitly involves the theme of torture, often in the form of whipping or beating, but sometimes in the sense of humiliation. The victim might be forced to eat excreta, or be confined in some exposed way so that he or she becomes subject to public regard and teasing. Sometimes the child may perceive himself as victim; more often he is himself the tormentor, or he directs those who are so engaged.

On the other hand, where the need and/or the readiness for fantasy indulgence are less, thoughts tend to shift to the concrete and the immediate. The youngster thinks ahead to playing basketball that afternoon or to meeting friends and telling them about something. The boy or girl may direct much thought toward school-learned topics; for many children education really opens doors into lands of wonder, and they ponder what people are like in another country or how the computer really works. The how-to kind of thinking has considerable developmental importance; this is the age of mastery of many real-world functions.

The Family Romance. There is also considerable rumination about interpersonal themes. Childhood depression and neuroses are usually first diagnosed at this age, and the milder forms of these tendencies are no stranger to latency children. They begin to grasp something of human motivation. They discover the imperfections displayed by grown-ups, and accordingly a gradual deidealization of adults moves these children, more or less quickly, beyond the admiring stance of the earlier epoch. Teachers, relatives, and presently parents begin to emerge in more realistic dimensions, and new qualities enter the relationships. Toward the end of latency the parental image in particular may have lost much of its earlier sheen, some of the intellectual and emotional shortcomings of the father or mother are now seen in more realistic perspective, and a characteristic form of compensatory fantasy ensues. It is called the *family romance* and may appear, in one form or another, at any time in the developmental column during the latter part of latency, prepuberty, or puberty proper (Freud, 1909/1959).

Generally speaking, the child's ruminations take somewhat the following form in this fantasy:

> My parents are not the great folk I thought they were. In some ways they are rather drab, imperfect, not very interesting. I could not have had such ordinary origins, I am made of finer stuff, nobler, purer. Surely I must truly belong elsewhere, perhaps to people of great fame or wealth, to great politicians or multimillionaires. Probably I was just placed with these bumpkins temporarily; they are only caring for me until the time comes to claim my birthright. Someday a great chauffeured limousine or a coach-and-four will drive up, they will ask for me by name, and I will go off to my true family and proper estate without looking back.

So the child muses as he tries to sort himself out in the ever more realistic world his enhanced perception depicts. It is a powerful fantasy and serves to buffer the youngster against the stresses and the disappointments of too much reality, the loss of the ideals. (In the case of the adopted child, the family romance will often center on fantasies concerning the child's biological parents. In some cases this can come to assume extraordinary proportions.)

Identity

At each developmental level the child addresses the matter of identity anew. Identity is a pattern of organization superimposed on the ego to combine its various elements and identifications into an integrated and functional whole. To form an identity, the self musters these elements according to some inner template and gives them coherent form. Once established, identity confirms for the child a sense of being a distinctive person, of possessing a *who-ness* and a *wholeness* that are characteristically his own (Erikson, 1950). A composite structure emerges from the blending of many substructures, all fitted together and superimposed on one another. Thus, the child has a certain identity as a member of a particular family, as a member of a specific religious or ethnic group, as a representative of a given gender, as an aspirant perhaps toward certain career choices, as a bearer of particular ideals or values, and so on. All of these subsets form elements within the larger set of who the child is and how he relates himself both to the inner and outer worlds. Identity is perhaps best understood as a sort of interface phenomenon standing between the subjective complexity of inner experience and the impersonal world of outer experience, giving order to the one and direction to the other. It is a construct that looks both inward to the child's own sense of self and outward to the world of others (and to their perceptions of the child). Thus, on the one hand, identity refers to the child's sense of himself as an ongoing entity with a consolidating continuity of experience and feelings. On the other hand, identity also refers to how the child fits into his social world and the roles he might play in different social contexts. It represents the congruence between how others see the child and how the child sees himself.

Body Image. Not until about the beginning of the latency epoch can the average child produce a drawing that abandons the characteristics of the "potato man" and looks anything like a person. The sense of the outlines of the human body do not appear to achieve even an initial level of precision until this time; not until latency does the child begin to have a first tentative organization of what his body is really like. Heretofore the fantasy additions and preoccupations of the oedipal period may have made this difficult, or perhaps the immaturity of the central nervous system was the stumbling block. In any case, now is when this image first appears in an even remotely valid way.

By the same token, however, this is when the body image is most fragile. The child's sense of his body outlines as permanent, of his gender as immutable, and of his appearance as truly his own are recent developments and are not yet well founded and secure. The youngster is all too alert to any hint on the part of his peers and schoolmates of any deviance or difference that challenges the integrity of this image. If the child encounters a difference, he becomes anxious; perhaps the body outline is mutable, perhaps it too could change. To protect himself, the child must challenge any hint of body difference: He notes such a difference and decries it; he rejects this evidence of deviant vulnerability and derides it; he becomes sadistic and provocative; he teases and excludes; he withdraws from and ostracizes. At best he makes up disparaging nicknames: Shorty, Fatso, Lefty, Rete (retarded), Spaz (spastic), Gimpy.

For the psychoanalyst, the underlying reservoir of castration anxiety that has been repressed but has by no means disappeared is in the background of this behavior. Any hint of body difference seems to evoke the powerful fears of the earlier period—"This is what happens to you if you're bad [incestuous, murderous, oedipal]"—and the youngster is moved to distance himself from the deviant (punished, castrated) one. Such a theoretical stance would also explain the character of peer choice; the boys withdraw from the girls because the sex difference at this early time still spells castration.

Gender Identity. A multiplicity of factors contribute to the state of knowing, feeling, and experiencing the self to be a boy or a girl. Although these factors are present throughout childhood, they change in depth and quality as development progresses. As noted earlier, social designation plays a critical role in the forming of self-concept; such social characterizing is present from birth on. By the 2nd year of life children are already aware of sex differences and on some level are probably alive to the sense of self as male or female; the phallic-stage experience expands and enriches this sense of gender. With the repression at the end of the phallic-oedipal period new adaptations appear. A variety of intrafamilial traditions, models, and expectations come into play: The peer group assumes ever-increasing importance (it proscribes some behaviors, demands others, and sets a powerful stamp on the expression of gender identity); school performance makes its requirements; and cultural styles for clothes, games, pets, and diversion open certain channels for expression and eliminate other possibilities.

In Western society, latency girls can choose among a rather wide spectrum of gender behaviors. They can be at any point on that range of possibilities and still be entirely acceptable, both to themselves and to their world. They can be tomboys, climb trees, play ball, hang around with boys, or ride horseback all day; they can be somewhere in between, enjoying athletics and outdoor activities, playing with boys a good deal of the time, yet giving equal time to dress-up, doll play, and romantic games with other girls; or they can cleave to the other extreme with baby care, baby dolls, girls' groups, and frilly clothes at the center of their interests. Boys, however, have no such latitude. They can be as tough, competitive, and as assertive as they like, or they can be rather quiet. But they cannot appear in any sense effeminate or show any serious interest in playing with girls or enjoying "girlish things." Their peers will reject them, their teachers will raise questions, and their parents will worry about them. They will also worry about themselves: "Why am I different?" they will muse, "What's wrong with me?" Any degree of gender uncertainty will give rise to confusion and depression in this age group. In particular, boys who are called *sissies* by their classmates will go through immensely painful experiences when growing up. This sobriquet is a statement of negative identity status, and brands its wearer with a scarlet letter that no amount of parental comforting and reassurance can readily efface.

Strong currents in American upper-middle-class culture currently seek to curb the assertiveness of boys and augment that of girls. In a variety of ways children are receiving the message that it is good for girls to be competitive and aggressive, and it is good for boys to be tender and emotional. The less direct but associated message is that girls should not be too froufrou and baby doll oriented, and boys should not be excessively macho. This more egalitarian view of gender and gender role is clearly affecting youngsters' development. Time will have to tell whether this effect is fundamental or cosmetic.

Social Role. Identity structuring now must flourish in two realms: in the home, with parents and siblings; and in the school and neighborhood, with peers. Both undergo considerable degrees of evolution during the grade-school years.

IDENTITY AS CHILD. At home, the cardinal shift is toward accepting the identity of self-as-child. This seems so obvious it scarcely needs stating: What else is an 8-year-old to be but a child? This is obvious to a person only until meeting a streetwise ghetto boy who at 8 is a numbers runner, a well-paid lookout for drug traffickers, and a point man for two prostitutes who work his street. At 7 he was initiated into coitus by a 9-year-old girl in the neighborhood; he has been sexually abused by one of his caretaker's boy-friends; he has achieved a certain competence at petty thefts from store counters; and he has had several fights at school (he was beaten up pretty badly once, but otherwise acquitted himself well). He does some of the shopping for the family and baby-sits an infant sib. If asked, he says without smiling that he knows his way around and does not think of himself as a child. Needless to say, the 9-year-old girl who originally seduced him, given her particular set of experiences, might also not feel very much like a child. Hence, the achievement of that particular social identity, the status of *child*, is by no means an automatic given. It is the product of a particular kind of ecological set and emotional support system.

PEER IDENTITY. This breaks down into several subsets, the most important of which are classroom role on the one hand, and place and status in the out-of-school group on the other. Within the classroom, emotional, social, and cognitive pressures maintain a complex state of tensions. The youngster has to cope with the teacher's authority and the school hierarchy; he has to meet the cognitive requirements and stresses of a highly organized and demanding educational system; and he must respond to both of these within a context of peer awareness and reactivity. There are a variety of levels of possible adaptation to these multiple pressures, and one of them is to adopt a classroom identity. A given child may become the teacher's pet, the clown, the disrupter, the dunce, the pariah, the teacher's helper, the gossip, the quidnunc, and so on. Not all children have extreme role positions, but most have a certain sense of how they are regarded, where they fit in, and what role they play within the classroom context.

Within the neighborhood peer group, quite a different set of parameters operate. Here the internal group dynamics find expression without the external authority of school, coach, scoutmaster, or family. Such factors as assertiveness, capacity for leadership, masochistic invitation for exploitation, gender status (sissy, macho, coquette, tomboy), capacity to obtain resources (e.g., money, video games, cookies, or sports equipment), special skills (e.g., competence at ball play, speediness as a runner, ability to dance or sing, skill at an instrument), particular sensitivities and fragilities, vulnerability to teasing, proneness to crying or blushing, position on the aggression spectrum (e.g., truculence, cowardice, provocativeness, bullying, flight readiness)—these and a host of additional qualities determine group status. There are numerous group roles to be filled (scapegoat, leader, assistant, fixer), and everyone must fit into a pecking order. There are, in addition, a complex and shifting hierarchy of in-group and out-group clusterings (those from the rich neighborhood, those from the poor, those with the fancy clothes, those from a particular ethnic group, and many others). These will become far more complex and finely differentiated during adolescence, but they already play a significant role in the life of most children from midlatency onward.

Where children feel disaffected or rejected at home (e.g., where parents are depressed, schizoid, or alcoholic, or are chronically engaged with crises of poverty or ill health), the peer group can come to have far greater significance for a given latency child than it would otherwise attain. This is the relative norm in deprived transitional environments where street gangs flourish. From the view of the police, the gangs are breeding grounds for crime; for the involved youngsters the gang may be the best—or the only—available source of care and belongingness.

THE SUPEREGO IN LATENCY

The superego, once formed, like any other dimension of personality continues to grow and to change. Under optimal circumstances, it will show evidence of positive development that will take it to new heights of richness and maturity. By the same token, however, it will also exhibit the vulnerabilities of all growth: When conditions for healthy maturation are lacking, its advance may be arrested; it may regress to more primitive levels of function; or it may develop in a skewed and unhealthy fashion.

The first major growth phase of the superego comes during latency. With the "conquest" of the oedipal impulses, the superego can enter a state of partial quietude. In effect, the demands for its services are less, and its task becomes one of maintaining the status quo rather than of actively struggling with impulse. This change is only partial, however; new emergents, in fact, engage it, and the superego proceeds to develop in important ways, although in a somewhat different direction.

At the outset, the superego is fairly primitive and not altogether well integrated into personality. As a result, the early latency child may display a curious vulnerability in authority contexts. The child may be unusually sensitive to the teacher's criticism or desperately reactive to some menacing act or threat of exclusion by an older child (Furman, 1980). Because the internalization of superego precepts is so basic to its structure, the resort to defensive externalization is particularly likely at this time. Many children have the strong tendency to attribute awesome power and authority to others, and they often become quite upset by some critical comment or act of exclusion that seems too trivial to merit such a reaction. Under favorable circumstances as latency progresses, the superego becomes more contained, the child perceives the world more realistically, and this kind of reactivity tends to disappear.

Impulse Control

Latency is a time of civilizing. Anal-stage training prepared the individual for social living; during that epoch the mastery of the impulses to mess, soil, and hurt, and the development of a firm set of necessary control apparatuses meshed together to make the child fit for social encounter.

Latency in its turn polishes and refines these apparatuses and begins to synthesize the patterns that ultimately yield a civil, decent, and reasonably well-bred individual. This is the age when manners are first seriously taught and begin to be acquired; when a child reads about chivalry and courtliness and aspires to gallantry and graciousness; and when courtesy becomes (or fails to become) a part of a person's behavioral life. For the first time the child begins to grasp not only what politeness *is* but what it *means*. He learns the forms of address that include "Excuse Me" and "I'm sorry"; "Please" and "Thank you"; "If you don't mind" and "You're welcome"; and he masters the forms of behavior that go along with waiting his turn, sharing, and not grabbing or pushing. Manners are major items in the exchanges between latency children and adults; much of schoolroom training has to do with the forms of decorum. The child's not speaking until he is called on, his requesting permission to leave the room, and his coping with a host of civilities and impulse management issues are the everyday grist for the educational mill. During these years this aspect of socialization goes on continuously, both in and out of school.

The home is, of course, the primary site for such civilizing. The models of the parents (are they courteous to each other; are either of them, or both, respectful in addressing the child?) become salient, pivotal presences in determining the character of the child's forms of address, both to his parents and to others. Some parents, albeit themselves ignoring interpersonal courtesies, nonetheless insist that their young observe these rules. Such teaching may well have its effect, and the child may learn superficial politeness, but he will not readily acquire the underlying message of courtesy—the respect for another person's sensibilities. Manners come down to an awareness of and a sensitivity to other people's interpersonal boundaries; if a person bumps into someone and apologizes, it is not necessarily because of the physical damage done; there may have been no physical damage at all. The apology is rather to smooth out and heal the narcissistic wound thus engendered. The concern is with the thrust into the selfhood of the other; the person senses that what happened is invasive and unpleasant, and tries, with the apology, to soften the blow, to undo that thrust, and to make it right.

This is what the child learns, or fails to learn, when he encounters social proprieties. Such instruction in courtesy is basic; once learned, it forms an interpersonal foundation. In time the child can erect upon it many additional practices involving garb, form of address, and various tokens of respect in manner, voice, and facial expression; in short, the array of interpersonal practices that characterizes the exchange between equals and unequals in any complex variegated society. The primary lessons of this kind are learned in latency. Ideally, they become part of the basic value set and superego organization of the individual so that, thereafter, the child who fails to act with good manners will feel guilty.

The notion of propriety becomes a central issue in training. Bad language, coarse gestures, off-color remarks, highly personal references, the fully panoply of the infamous and the scatological in human exchange are addressed during this era, and the child arrives at some sort of equilibrium. The effects of modeling and identification are painfully evident in such connections. For example, the ready use of obscenities in the home makes it awkward, to say the least, to try to curb the child's recourse to such language. More than that, the language reflects and reinforces a mind-set of its own; the child either keeps the instincts at a distance and reinforces that by keeping instinctually evocative words at a distance, or allows the instincts ready access to consciousness and expression.

Paradoxically, the greatest danger of action on impulse probably occurs where an attempt is made to forbid all thought of what is, in fact, a pressing inner presence. It is one thing to limit the use of dirty words; it is quite another to forbid dirty thoughts of any kind, whether in the form of jokes or indeed of any reference to bathroom themes or sex. The result of *that* kind of rigid rearing is to make for fragile and brittle controls that may all too easily give way. The ideal is the sensible middle ground where anal or sexual issues can be discussed in a matter-of-fact way, without excessive shame or anxiety, and without treating the ping of sexual excitement that such a discussion might evoke as though it were either sinful, funny, or dangerous. But the parents' systematic recourse to obscenity does not help the children learn either propriety or impulse control and, indeed, might introduce a distinct element of hypocrisy into the child's rearing process.

As latency development proceeds, a rather common phenomenon is the appearance of modesty, sometimes of prudery. Frequently this change takes place rapidly; on occasion it seems to come overnight. Thus, a little boy who had never previously made much of a fuss about having someone in the bathroom when he was bathing or urinating might abruptly insist on keeping the door locked. "Keep out of here when I'm using the bathroom," he yells at would-be intruders and henceforth does not want his mother or sisters to see him dressing; sometimes he will not even allow their presence when he is only partially unclothed. In some instances this will extend to the father as well. Like other behaviors this has many roots and may indeed be the end product of a series of complex processes. Whatever else it is, however, it represents part of the latency child's struggle for mastery over phallic phase and oedipal impulses; it is another way of distancing the self from the instincts. The voyeuristic and exhibitionistic impulse are central to this particular set of concerns, but they are part and parcel of the more general press against such inclinations. Sometimes the struggle between modesty and exhibitionistic impulses is most apparent in the earliest formative stages, as in the case of the oedipal-age little boy, who ran naked down the hall after his bath calling to this sister: "No girls allowed to look at my penis!" Somewhere in latency, modesty usually wins out, and the more overt forms of exhibitionism are displaced onto gymnastics, athletic field performance, or stage activities, whereas the bathroom door becomes a sacred portal (Rosenfeld et al., 1984).

Latency Ethic

To a greater or lesser degree, the latency epoch relieves the child of the need to struggle with the consuming oedipal passions of yore. During this era, under optimal conditions, much of the tension in the parent–child relationship diminishes. Roles and territories become clear, child is child and parent is parent. With this, the youngsters are far more available for attachments outside the home, and the new realm of peer engagement becomes the central arena for interpersonal development. But the child presently experiences this ebb and flow of peer interaction as a complex environment with its own hierarchies, threats, principles, punishments, and rewards. At the outset it is a trackless sea of unbounded possibility. The youngster needs a chart to find his path. And it is precisely this work, the inner organization of a map for safely threading a way through the uncertainties of peer interaction, that presently takes form within the superego. This new set of constructs for navigating the shoals of the social environment, is added to the body of principle, taboo, and precept already in place. For the child's built-in inhibition against incestuous yearnings does little for his address to questions of whose turn it is to play or who is really the winner in a particular exchange. A new array of social orderings is necessary, and during latency, this comes to be so organized.

Much of the latency superego is formed within the context of social group pressures. Initially what emerges is an ethic of latency with its own tenets. They involve such assertions as:

Finders keepers, losers weepers.
First come first served.
Everyone was doing it so I did it too.
He did it to me first so I was just getting even.

These "principles" prevail chiefly in early latency; they do not appear earlier, and they are not likely to dominate later. That is to say, they are not likely to do so where development proceeds normally and the person matures well; in many cases, however, such maturing fails to occur. Hence, in many lives such a value set persists as that person's basic ethical stance (Kohlberg, 1964).

These latency positions are largely narcissistic, territorial principles, built on assertions of who a child is, retention of what he has, and revenge for what he has lost. They also reflect the power of the group and its central role in determining what is right and what a person may or may not do. For the psychoanalyst it is not surprising that these principles should prevail. Anal regression is regarded as very much a part of latency, and it is precisely in the anal phase that social pressure, shaming, and the eyes of the significant other are among the determinative forces at work shaping the child's behavior. Moreover, it is also when the critical emergence of territoriality seems to be first in evidence. The ethic of early latency can be construed, first and foremost, as an anal-stage ethic of boundaries and entitlements, possession and retention, pride and retaliation. Dominating it is the basic sense of revenge as a regulating principle; it is this, rather than some abstract conception of justice, that preoccupies the youngster. "Getting even" with someone, getting back at someone, paying back for some injustice—these become matters of consuming interest to the latency child. When an insult is extended, the retort that restores equilibrium is "You're another." There is a fundamental need to assert and maintain an equality of balance in human affairs.

Fairness.   As latency proceeds, however, a more general and abstract position emerges. This new stance becomes the guiding principle for all latency address to ethical issues; it sets a basic style for the resolution of conflict that persists well into every person's later life. In essence it says that the main goal to seek in exchanges with peers is *fairness.* That is to say, the sense of balance, of equal weighting of goods, of respect for everyone's boundaries, of equality of entitlements, of even-handedness in the award of both punishments and plaudits, such general statements as these become the measure of the child's sense of justice and injustice. This concern pervades group interactions, but, even more intensely, it applies to the expectations of treatment by authority figures, such as parents, teachers, scout leaders, coaches, police officers, and the like. "If I got smacked for doing it and now he did it, or she did it, then that person should get the same."

Such issues generate intense emotion. Children experience the maintenance of this balance as a vital dimension of their well-being. If a parent or teacher shows preferential treatment to another child, there is a distinct sense of outrage, a feeling of mistreatment, and on some level at least, a yearning to protest. In many situations protest is unwise, even unthinkable, yet even under such circumstances, the mistreated child at least mutters to himself about the unfairness of it all.

Developmentally, the fairness doctrine probably emerges from the acute sensitivity of narcissistic boundaries and the vulnerability the child experiences at these sites. The nature of the narcissistic reaction is to feel each grievance, each onslaught, as a sort of penetration of the self's perimeter, and to seek relief by undoing that thrust or "getting even." If the child is hurt, he must retaliate with suitable revenge to ease the wound to the sense of self and hence becomes very much caught up in this talion principle. "An eye for an eye and a tooth for a tooth" sound very good to him; in his eyes this is just the fair way to do things. Fairness becomes a guiding principle in his life. Many a child spends long hours puzzling over or bemoaning some episode where he feels he was treated unfairly; there can be a considerable degree of preoccupation with such issues. More than that, he will not only mourn the dents in his periphery, he will seek redress. He will fight where he can; will refuse to speak to the offending other; will be sullen with, pout at, or avoid the authority figure whom he regards as the author of the unfair dealings; and will tend in a host of ways to communicate a sense of outrage. Such motives underlie the spiteful behavior that is so common in latency children. A child mistreats another child just to make that one feel bad (e.g., a toy is broken, a doll disfigured, homework defaced or torn up, "just for spite"). Occasionally it turns out that the author of the vandalism is simply sadistic and his actions are part of a primary pursuit of pleasure. More often, however, the child has experienced a slight or has sensed a personal injury on some level and has reacted in a retaliatory way. In his own view he may be redressing an inner claim to justice that demands such a step. Once the child does equivalent damage, it allays the sense of disequilibrium, at least to some extent. The child is no longer troubled by the nagging, gnawing feeling of things being out of kilter. His sense of proportion is restored, the dent in his sense of integrity is smoothed, the perimeter is no longer sending back shock waves of pain.

Rules. As latency goes on, however, the superego adds another dimension as the outcome of any one of several different processes. For example, it may be a product of advancing cognitive growth (Piaget, 1952), a stage in the unfolding wavefront of moral development (Kohlberg, 1964), or yet another set of anal-stage derivatives—or perhaps all influences come to bear at once. In any case, the result is the child's adherence to rules. The 2-year-old is forever learning the rules to everything; a good many of the no-no's typical of that time of life are, in effect, rules in themselves, or a response to the violation of rules that the child has not yet learned. The acquisition of rules proceeds slowly all through childhood; it is, however, during latency that this faculty comes truly into its own. Prior to this, rules were a means to an end; at this point they become an end in themselves. Rules as such become objects of intense emotional involvement; children negotiate and agree on items; maintain, defend, and fight over them, if necessary; and sometimes invest them with immense affective import. What seems to happen is that rules become part of the individual child's superego and his personal defense perimeter. The rule violation within a social context, for example, a card game or a ball game, now assumes the stature of a personal slight. The child observes the breach with intense concern and may come rushing to the defense and redress of this violation with vociferous energy. Or, the more shy and frightened individual may react by withdrawal, tears, and every evidence of being stricken. A common reaction is "If that's the way you're gonna play, I won't play with you anymore." The particular variety of response manifested has to do with the temperament of that child and with his capacity to assert himself in the face of opposition; obviously, children will vary widely in this respect. But the inner sense of outrage and violation because a rule has been dishonored is probably close to universal.

The ability to abide by rules, however, in itself requires a certain amount of emotional maturity. After all, if a child plays a game, inevitably he will lose on some occasions. And what is the child to do then, particularly the narcissistic child, who cannot tolerate frustration, who has a high level of expectation and a powerful sense of entitlement? Characteristically, such a child changes the rules. The superego imperative is powerful and not lightly gainsaid; except in extreme instances of narcissistic disorder the rules cannot merely be ignored. The child feels the prick of conscience; rules are important, and he must obey them. But the compromise that the child works out is simple: "Alter the rules so that you always win; do so each time if necessary, and deform them beyond recognition if you must, but avoid the agony of defeat; see to it that you win!"

The key variable here is that at least the form of rule structure is maintained. The child does not challenge that rules are real, present, and important; he works within this framework. And this measure of regard for rules is the key; it tells how vital it is to preserve the developmental emergent even in the face of an unusual level of dysfunction.

As latency proceeds, this matter of rules and the issue of fairness tend to converge and to coalesce. A game is fair if it is played by the rules. An exception to the rule is not fair unless both parties agree that the other fellow, or the other team, can also make the same exception. Then, in effect, social agreement dictates altering the rule, and the interaction can proceed. This is important because rules are quintessentially social constructs; they assert consensually arrived at modes of social engagement. A critical aspect of development is to learn about the social character of rules. The children come to understand that by group agreement they can change rules; they can do so in simple game play (e.g., in the next poker hand, deuces will be wild), and they can do so in more complex and subtle situations (e.g., boys vote to allow the tomboy to join in their game).

Where they understand the rules, healthy children feel comfort, and where they violate them they feel guilt. Even if they get away with a violation and win, the win is tarnished; they did not "really" win. When this happens, the reaction is typical of a superego response: Despite the "victory," often they will feel guilty or let down; sometimes they will confess and seek to undo.

Implications for Later Development

This aspect of superego formation is a far cry from the issues of fantasied incest and murder that originally brought that agency of mind into being. By the same token, learning about some violation of rules does not evoke the same reaction as the idea of someone engaging in forbidden sex or parricide. The emotional impact of the one on the sensibilities of most people is not to be compared with the thrust of the other. On the other hand, the matter of rules is far more ubiquitous in everyday life than is the concern with oedipal issues.

In effect, the latency superego builds in the "traffic rules of life." This is the developmental moment when the child lays out these vital social channels and formulates the proprieties and the regulations that govern the everyday intercourse of people. The issues are by no means trivial; when traffic rules are violated, bad things can happen. Withal, however, the large majority of such rules, and their violations, do not have life-and-death implications. They make people impatient, carry a low-grade level of stress, and are annoying without throwing off the individual's equilibrium altogether (e.g., having to wait on line when there seems to be no obvious reason for the delay; keeping the same place in the line even though someone cuts in ahead). Perhaps the ultimate expression of this superego level is evident in such human achievements as *Robert's Rules of Order*, where each item and nuance of group interaction falls under a rule of some kind so that all expression and communication follow a predetermined sequence of orderings and priorities. The law during latency is to follow rules; this emergent sets the standard for the subsequent elaboration of the rule of law.

Ego Ideal

Quite a new way of coping with narcissistic yearnings is discernible in the grade-school child. Ideally, these yearnings have largely been tamed, with only a wholesome residue contained within the ego ideal. For most people, however, this is at best a partial solution. Even after the initial superego formation is relatively complete, a goodly quantum of unsuppressed narcissistic wish still remains loose somewhere in the child's personality. This grandiosity can take many forms, but one of the commonest is to become attached to some semifantasy figure whom the child encounters in the world of entertainment. These can be fictional characters such as Tarzan, comic book figures such as Superman, television heroes such as the Hulk, and a host of others. A little later on in latency idealizations will involve great athletes, actors, racing car drivers, ballerinas, skating champions, and other real individuals. These culture heroes acquire a mythic, semilegendary character that tends to absorb the child's grandiose aspirations and to provide a form of external ideal.

Chapter 15

Late Latency or Prepuberty

INTRODUCTION

Latency has been variously divided into two stages (Bornstein, 1951) or three (Sarnoff, 1976) depending on the proclivities of the various observers. However, all agree that toward the end of this epoch a number of noteworthy changes herald the oncoming advent of puberty proper (Frank & Cohen, 1979). These changes arrive earlier for girls than for boys and include subtle biological changes that can be measured only by endocrine assays; anatomical changes defined by the Tanner stages; and behavioral changes, such as interests, interpersonal patterns, fantasies, and cognitive growth.

DEFINITION

The end of latency flows over into the early precursors of puberty without sharp or set markers. This epoch is variously designated as late latency or prepuberty; it subtends the culmination of the one phase and the immediate foreshadowings of the next. Chronologically this transitional time corresponds to the ages 9 through 11 years for girls and ages 10 through 12 years for boys.

By the time they have reached this epoch, youngsters have achieved a certain competence as latency children. They have good command of their bodies; they are in the fourth, fifth, or sixth grades at school and are veteran scholars; they can express themselves well in an age-appropriate way; they are realistic and alert in their estimation of other people's feeling states and intentions; and they are often becoming rather bumptious, inquisitive, and assertive in their relations with adults. At times they may give the impression of being junior adults in their own right, knowledgeable individuals who know their way around. Usually, they have thoroughly combed their neighborhood and are familiar with its byways; they may have a good store of "wise guy" retorts and can keep up their end of a social exchange; and they can carry out many everyday tasks with competence and self-confidence. More than that, a definite latency identity has emerged. They are well aware of their ethnic, cultural, and family traditions; and they know who they are. Under reasonably favorable conditions, they will have established a clear territory of self with well-demarcated boundaries; and they are more or less ready to defend it against invasion by an intrusive sibling, peer, or, if necessary, adult.

Behaviorally, the general motoric restlessness of the individual child may increase, with perhaps some accompanying display of heightened emotionality, enough to be evident to sensitive parents. A more playful, fun-loving quality may be present, but more touchiness and tears and dramatics may at times also be evident. Some authors tend to emphasize the difficult aspects of the youngster's adjustment. For example, Kay (1972, p. 103, cited in Francis & Marcus, 1975, p. 29) states that the preadolescent boy is

... greedy, voracious, unkempt, unruly, impolite, hostile toward parents, sisters, withdrawn and performs destructive acts. Masturbation and other autoerotic habits are frequent as are sexual activities with other children, which include polymorphous and homosexual pursuits in which he seduces others and lets himself be seduced.

Kestenberg (1961) speaks of premenstrual girls as tending to

talk a blue streak, [and as exhibiting] vague, disjointed profuse communication [and] overall disorganized behavior in pre-puberty, but the same is true of movements, actions and approach to problem solving, and other aspects of functioning in pre-puberty... (p. 32)

To be sure, this is a transitional time. The child is filled with a sense of uncertainty about the future, an awareness of imminent change. He is prey to mixed desires, on the one hand, to hold everything stable and, on the other, to grow up and do what the older kids do. But most youngsters do not betray so surly or so disorganized a picture as has been painted. They certainly have such moments, but in the healthier children, the basic state tends to be one of competence and, for the most part, conformity.

ACTIVITIES

The mastery these youngsters have achieved begins to express itself in many ways. They are often involved in projects of one sort or another; they may join the Boy Scouts or Girl Scouts and actively seek merit badges. They are more responsible, can manage money, and can thus do some of the family shopping or take on regular housekeeping chores. They can make use of public transportation and can even make fairly complicated trips involving numerous bus changes. Many are experts on a bicycle and can travel fast and far in this way.

It is a time of curious social transitions. The youngsters may still pay a reduced rate on the bus or at the movies, yet overnight a given child may convert from having a baby-sitter to being one.

Psychologically, pressure begins to build on the latency identity, with the greatest stress attached to the sense of being a child. The basic respect for the adult usually remains paramount, but there is enough dawning awareness of parental faults and foibles to raise many questions in the youngster's mind and to inspire such fantasies as the family romance. Patterns of compliance to parental authority, albeit not abandoned, are less predictable than they were earlier.

SEXUAL INTERESTS

Sexual interests tend to come to the fore, and the youngsters glory in their newfound, albeit sometimes wildly inaccurate knowledge. It is a time for many sexual myths, for ready misunderstanding of sexual facts, and for much confusion of pregenital and genital ideas. Masturbation is talked about more often and perhaps is more widely practiced than earlier in latency. Accordingly, the emphasis on privacy generally increases, and this often pours over into an interest in codes, secret inks, hidden messages, and the like. Sometimes the youngsters develop special languages, such as pig-Latin, during this epoch. What with the new stirrings of infantile fantasies, the child indeed has something to hide—and to reveal in cryptic covert ways.

ADAPTIVE STYLES

At the same time, the new competencies are unevenly manifested to the social surround. Thus, the boy's room may be a mess, but if the parents have guests in for cocktails and ask the youngster to help serve canapés, to everyone's amazement he may do so in exemplary fashion, utilizing a correct, polite, and solicitous manner and winning praise from all.

Boys

Boys at this stage are often boisterous, knowledgeable, and competent. They may possess an extraordinary level of mastery in any one of several areas, such as sports, model building, animal care, music, or other skills. Many of these youngsters find ways to earn money, usually by providing a neighborhood service (shoveling snow, cutting grass, walking dogs, etc.). Occasionally a young entrepreneur actually develops a little business (e.g., repairing electrical appliances or tutoring younger children).

Many boys of this age are actively interested in sports. Some hang around older players when they can, watch sporting events regularly, and follow the fortunes of their favorite teams with zealous devotion. Others prefer to engage in play themselves, and the high moments of the day occur when like-minded peers get together to start up a game. In general, these boys prefer outdoor play to indoor activities and group interaction to solitary play. Indoor activities will also often include some kind of competitive interaction such as a video or a tabletop game.

Regardless of the site of the play, there is much preoccupation with rules and fairness, and heated arguments are common as issues arise about whose turn it is, whether or not someone touched base, or whether a ball was safe or out. Although passions may rise to fever pitch during such exchanges, soonor or later the matter is settled and the game goes on. From the developmental view, this is a peculiarly important crucible for the formation of those character traits relating to socialization.

Girls

The girls for their part are more curious than before, more assertive, and often more invasive. They, too, have arrived at a high level of competence in a great many realms, and they can take care of themselves and often enough of a younger sibling in an able fashion. Such younger siblings frequently perceive them as "bossy," and indeed the girls tend to take on a parental tone, perhaps more so than do boys.

This is an age of beginning secrecy for girls. They discover the pleasures of gossip and are forever gathering in groups to whisper delicious bits of private information after extracting oaths that the recipient(s) of the communication will never tell. They are also great passers of notes to one another wherein they confide their secrets to relatively public channels of exchange. More reserved youngsters may begin to keep diaries (somehow these, too, often find their way into the public domain).

At this age girls are typically taught about menses, parents initiate training bras, and the sense of bodily transformation becomes a very live issue. Much of the girls' whispering is about who has confided that she likes whom, but the boy must never, ever be told; who has worn this or that undergarment to school; who has had her first period and what she said about it; who is acting like a "slut"; who has had a tiff with her former best friend and is now best friends with whom. The importance of these matters to the youngsters should not be underestimated; who is whose best friend can be an aching, nagging issue that fully preoccupies a particular girl for a considerable time. It can be a serious mistake to ask such a youngster who her best friend is in the presence of her peers; quite possibly she has secretly told each of three different girls that *she* is the one in that preferred status, and she does not dare let any one of them know where matters really stand.

Sometimes more serious issues arise as well, such as whose parents are breaking up or are getting remarried. When adults become preoccupied with their own problems, the youngsters will turn to one another for catharsis, ventilation, or solace.

Giggling is an associated phenomenon that is often part of this excited whispering (Kestenberg, 1961). This behavior serves as a coping device to deal with the anxiety generated by developmental issues. Frequently the giggling is part of a shared social pattern. It may take on a contagious uncontrollable quality, carrying a group of girls to the point of exhaustion; they may have tears in their eyes and sometimes may even have wet themselves. More often than not the girls cannot say why there are in such a state; something was funny, they don't know why.

The dynamic organization of late latency can be thought of as an essentially solid core floating on a sea of change and uncertainty; the paramount fear arising from the developmental stage is loss of control of the self. Girls fear this lack of control in many areas: their height will get out of hand; their breasts will be too large or too small; their menstrual flow will come, or won't come, will be too much, or will fail to be adequate. They worry about having an attractive personality and whether to remain mother's little girl, attached and secure, or to cut free and become a teenager. There are many uncertainties, much anxiety, and hence a great deal of giggling.

An intriguing aspect of this time of life is that so many of these girls are fascinated by horses to an extraordinarily intense degree. It is by no means universal and is probably influenced by many sociocultural factors (e.g., professionals hear little of such things from deprived children). Yet within white American middle-class culture it is a common and sometimes rather an extreme state of affairs. The occasional girl becomes drawn to horses with an ardent intensity that at times seems limitless; she lives, eats, drinks, and thinks horses all the day through. She has pinups of horses, she insists on taking riding lessons, and she presses hard to have her parents buy her a horse. In one such instance, a young girl persuaded her parents to replace her chair at table with a single post barstool on which she then mounted a saddle. She could thus eat all her meals as it were on horseback.

The therapist can speculate readily enough on the psychodynamics of this behavior. Clearly, there could be phallic-phase elements here (having a large living presence between the girl's legs and under her control with perhaps an additional factor of direct masturbatory experience). On a more primitive level, a girl on horseback could achieve a sense of fusion with a symbiotic other, with an associated state of heightened grandiose narcissistic power. Perhaps all are present to some degree, with different emphases for each individual child, or perhaps some other heretofore undescribed motivational set is at work. In any case the phenomenon, when encountered, is striking.

IDEALS

Both the boys and the girls turn to more realistic ideal models than was true in earlier latency. The girls have ballerinas, TV, rock, or video stars, gymnasts and tennis players, astronauts and scientists, all the variety of models that a rich and many-faceted culture can provide. All may become objects of glorification and sometimes of crushes. On the whole, the girls' idealized attachment objects include more heterosexual possibilities than is true for boys at the same developmental level. The girls are drawn both to female and male objects for ideal formation and modeling, and they will declare a mad passion (usually in almost grotesquely excessive terms, as though the hyperbole itself could be a meaningful defense) for this rock star, that folk singer or some other daring young man. It all has a sort of play quality, the girl's trying out of her capacity for loving and attachment in a safe, protected way with an unattainable and securely distant object. It is also a subject with powerful social appeal, which can supply endless material for shared excitement and exchange with girl friends.

The boys tend to admire and to idealize only males. Again a wide variety of choices will be found among any given population, but the chances are that action figures of some kind will predominate. Athletes, racing car drivers, astronauts, or macho TV or screen performers maintain a sizable hold on the imaginations and inner ruminations of a great many boys. Given the performance, competence, and muscle mastery issues of the time, this is not surprising.

However, it is also true that many career choices of a serious kind develop from special interests, such as music, science, medicine, writing, or acting, that sometimes flourish during this epoch. These youngsters are generally less introspective than they are likely to become after puberty, but their commitment to the acquisition of skills may be considerable, and they are drawn toward heroic figures who are recognized masters of such competencies.

DRIVE DEVELOPMENT

Certain characteristic adjustment tasks confront both genders. This is a time when in anticipation of puberty, the earlier pregenital interests begin to surge toward the surface. Although the behavior is variable, there may be occasional—usually transient—breakthroughs of dirtiness or greed. The boys may go in for loud, exhibitionistic belching, and every summer camp counselor knows of the prodigies that they can perform with their stomach gas. The girls, as noted, have many areas of uncertainty about their bodies, and, on some level, may continue to harbor fantasies of growing into full-fledged males as well as full-fledged females; they yearn for a sort of bisexuality that amounts to having everything. Thus some girls have to struggle with the dilemma of whether menarche requires that they relinquish being the star quarterback on their block. For both genders, there is a keen sense of abandoning the protective nurturance of childhood. The girls in particular have to make their peace with the dimly remembered but deeply sensed image of the former overshadowning maternal presence. They are drawn to it as comforting, and they fear it (in part because it is so comforting) as leading to loss of boundaries and autonomous identity. Both genders are aware at some level that growing up means separation as well as independence, and both are apprehensively aware of the uncertainty that comes with impending change.

Body image issues are very prominent at this time. Along with growth, both boys and girls now encounter the beginning stirrings of obscure, unfamiliar, and guilt-evoking ideas that together make for a condition of heightened vulnerability. More than that, the very cognitive achievements—the school learning and the improved capacity to think, recall, and comprehend—combine to make the youngsters more aware of heretofore undreamed-of dangers. As a consequence, for some, the notion arises of damage, in the form of brain cancer, AIDS, or some other physical condition that they have heard about (usually on TV, or perhaps because a family member or neighbor has fallen seriously ill); and they are gripped by the fear that they may have acquired some dreadful disease. They inquire anxiously about its symptoms and worry secretly about their own bodies. Could they have something like that or, on a less conscious level, are they being punished for bad thoughts, for masturbation, for sex play with another child? For most youngsters these are passing, uneasy speculations thrust readily aside in favor of the next diverting activity to claim their attention. For a few, however, these thoughts are brooding, menacing presences that hang like dark clouds over every waking moment and that find their way as well into troubled dreams.

PART V

Adolescence

Chapter 16

Puberty

INTRODUCTION

Other than birth and death, puberty is perhaps the most celebrated phase of human development. It is a loud and clamorous time marked by dramatic transformations of immense personal and social significance. These events take place relatively rapidly in an eye-catching, emotion-laden fashion.

Paradoxically, for the individual boy and girl, some of the changes come silently; the child knows about it after it has happened. A boy looks down and there is a gap between his trousers and his shoe. He is awakened at night by an erotic dream and a nocturnal emission. Suddenly he no longer looks upward to meet his father's gaze; their eyes are on a level. Girls contend with body changes, the phenomena associated with menarche, and the accompanying flood of information and misinformation, but again, these things come when they come, early or late, for the most part without accompanying sensation—they are merely there.

These changes are, for the most part, the secondary sexual characteristics. The primary characteristics determine maleness or femaleness; the secondary group is associated with fertility and reproduction. Although many of the changes are obvious and dramatic, others are silent and not readily available to awareness. Thus, two boys in sixth grade watch Susan walk past. They have known her for years through earlier grades, but now one of them pokes the other and says: "Hey look, she's walking with a wiggle." And indeed she is. Her pelvis has broadened, her trochanters have changed their angle, and her gait has altered accordingly. The metamorphosis was completely silent; she had no awareness of any of this until her classmates called the wiggle to her attention. Once alerted, however, the child must make some decisions. She can decide to stay on a higher plane and ignore the whole thing, she can try anxiously to suppress the wiggle, or she might find it interesting to exaggerate this novel development. But somehow or other she has this to take into her future calculations; she is different now and must adapt to the new reality.

While the youngsters are dealing with all these inner transformations, these same changes are impinging on society. The community begins to view the young people as potential members and to measure them against a host of criteria. An enormous institutionalized educational system awaits them; a wide array of working slots in society are traditionally teenage employment; the youngsters are often objects of prurient interest or, in certain cultures, objects of potential matrimony; the military apparatus will receive some of them; they have extraordinary potential as consumers and whole industries are geared to their preferences; they also pose dangers that major sectors of the police force are designed to address; all in all, the community heralds the adolescent population with mixed emotions.

THE ONSET OF PUBERTY

It is not easy to assert just when puberty begins. Usually this is thought of in biological terms; by such criteria, the girls go into puberty 1½ to 2 years earlier than do the boys. That is to say, the girls will start showing some widening of the areola of the breast and the beginnings of silky pubic hair at about 10 years. Breast development proceeds, and body hair grows, changing its silky character to the coarse curly growth typical of maturity. There is a beginning deposition and redistribution of subcutaneous fat so that the girls' bodies look feminine in contour, and presently, perhaps 12 to 18 months after the first intimations of puberty, menarche occurs. The average girl will start to menstruate at about 12 years. The boys are not really well into puberty until they are 13 or 14.

A common marker for the beginning of female puberty is the first menses. It is, generally speaking, a good landmark although, biologically, it is not an accurate one. But most women remember this event and can often recount the day, the hour, and the circumstance of the first such experience; hence it allows for accurate reporting. There is no comparable initiating moment for boys. Indeed, most men would have a hard time recalling just when it all happened to them. It has been suggested that the first nocturnal emission might serve as an equivalent biological marker for boys, and that may well be the case. Men in our culture, however, are seldom able to say just when that occurred. It is ignored and repressed; boys are usually not prepared for it as girls are for menarche, it is not discussed within the family, and the whole experience is treated as a nonevent. Even its name carries a negative connotation; it is often referred to as a *nocturnal pollution*. Small wonder then that it is treated as something shameful and put out of mind as quickly and as thoroughly as possible. (For a detailed account of the biology of puberty, see Appendix 17–1.)

PSYCHOLOGICAL CHANGES AT PUBERTY

From a psychological view, the pubertal changes give rise to powerful instinctual thrusts. These intense erotic and aggressive impulses seem to arise from the nexus of the biological transformations of the time; they are blends of imagery and feelings that carry with them an immense current of yearning. These impulses now move toward consciousness and, sometimes intermittently, sometimes continuously, they fill the youngster's inner world.

Under normal conditions these emergents are often commanding presences in the youngster's life for months on end. They represent a wide variety of contents from the past: oral wishes—to devour, to consume, to suck in, to vomit out, to bite, to suckle, to kiss, to blend, to fuse, to fellate;

anal motives—to smear, to shatter, to torture, to suffer, to bugger, to be sodomized, to blow up, to rend, to tear, to destroy, to filthify, to wallow; and phallic-oedipal yearnings—to seduce, to yield, to conquer, to compete, to castrate, to be deflowered, to be spayed, to impregnate, to be pregnant, to rape, to be raped, to couple sexually with mother, father, sibling. All these and more course through the youngster's head and channel their way toward full consciousness and even toward enactment.

Perhaps the best model for the events of the time is the image of a beleaguered ego. For what takes place is a steady drumfire of impulse and desire pressing against the inner surface of the ego, hammering at the gates of consciousness, making itself felt throughout the organism. All the coping devices of the ego are called into play to meet the onslaught; these take form as defenses, flights, sublimations, partial yieldings, resorts to fantasy, firm denials, turnings against the self, and in some cases, failures to ward off the enactment of a particular desire. The stress of the time may be considerable, and the evidence of an ego under pressure is pervasive.

Rate of Pubertal Change

Sometimes the onset of puberty is gradual, the adjustments take place smoothly and quietly, the pressure never gets too high or out of hand, and the youngster moves gently through puberty with few problems and enjoys the whole epoch. Sometimes the transition is abrupt—the changeover from child to youth takes only a few months, the youngster is filled with intense passions for which he may be totally unprepared, the undeveloped defenses crumble, and the impulses surge forward, triumphant. A flood of disturbed behavior can follow, such as emotional explosions, seduction, sexual enactments, firesetting, violence, theft, and flight.

The possible paths through adolescence will vary with the power of the instincts, their rate of buildup, the ego's coping capacity, the time span during which the process unfolds, the amount of inner stress the ego must deal with, and the amount and kind of support or pressure that come to or at the ego from without. Puberty can take place under circumstances that complicate its unfolding, for example, a home where a disturbed father seduces each daughter as she develops, combined with a school where a surface morality overlays an undercover youth culture riddled with violence and sensuality. Or puberty can occur under conditions that support and channel its expression, for example, a home where mature parents understand the youngster's experience and buffer, protect, assist with, and redirect the eruptions of the time, perhaps with the help of a school where sensible sex education courses are joined with an atmosphere of high achievement and a rich activity pattern. These external supports and provocations become key factors in the youngster's development.

Paths through Puberty

Studied in aggregate, most youngsters cope reasonably well with the demands of puberty, not without some inner perturbation, perhaps, but with no notable disruption of the social surface of their lives. Offer and Offer (1975) have described and validated statistically three patterns of movement through adolescence: they call them *continuous, surgent,* and *tumultuous.* The point of these findings is that there are several routes through this period, and although they carry with them differing styles of adjustment along with differing levels of upset and problem, young people, for the most part, handle puberty without grave disturbance, severe behavioral difficulties, or deviant social behavior.

AXES OF OBSERVATION

On the other hand, very few youngsters get through this phase without at least some inner struggle. To comprehend this, it is necessary to observe the phenomena of the time in somewhat greater detail. The individual experience of the pubertal child is easiest to understand by studying it along a number of axes of observation, such as perception, cognition, affect, and fantasy. Each of these functions will be affected to some degree by the transformations of the time, each will be impinged upon by instinctual pressures, and each will undergo growth and elaboration in and of itself.

Perception

The pubertal process significantly affects perception. There is a new orientation to so many of the percepts of the world that a radical restructuring of the perceptual frame of reference takes place. For example, a 9-year-old boy throwing a ball against a wall and catching it enjoys his play until a girl in his class walks by, and he has to interrupt the rhythm of his game to allow her to pass. He thereupon gestures to her testily to hurry up so he can resume his sport. If, about five years later, he is throwing the ball against the same wall when a 14-year-old girl happens by, his eyes will fix on her body, and he will follow her progress, unmoving but for his eyes, his ball forgotten, until she is some distance away. When she is in full view, her presence completely takes over his perceptual world; figure and ground are altogether reversed and he does not even think of his game while the intriguing and captivating image of her undulating passage dominates his perceptual field. The same sort of thing will be true at home where, for instance, the mother's or the father's underwear will suddenly intrude into the youngster's awareness framework in a new way, or where TV ads of a suggestive character assume a new valence.

Cognition

Cognition, too, is undergoing a major, perhaps even more radical transformation. This occurs in several ways. On one level, all sorts of hitherto unthought-of ideas intrude into consciousness. Thus, as a youngster tries to concentrate on schoolwork, some configuration in the academic material may trigger an eruption of erotic fantasy that suddenly suffuses him with excitement and fills his mind with disturbing images. Studying is hard under those conditions: Concentration is disturbed, attention is deflected from the academic content, and the focus of interest is turned elsewhere. This sort of breakdown in the smooth functioning of cognition may be sporadic and unusual, or, for a time, it may recur constantly and make for major difficulties in scholarship. It is part of what makes some youngsters do poorly in the sixth and seventh grades, compared with their former academic performance. Teachers' awareness of this vulnerability makes them think twice and three times about what readings to assign to students of this age.

Sometimes the problem is a combination of the perceptual and the cognitive; a boy or girl looks up and meets the eyes of a girl or boy, or sees the other's body from some suggestive vantage point, and a flood of fantasy is released with equivalent results. Or a memory may be evoked that carries with it a cascade of emotional recall that washes everything else away. In any case, thinking is especially vulnerable at this time.

Paradoxically, new cognitive strengths are also emerging. Piaget (1936/1952) suggests that from about 11 years onward, the youngster begins to utilize *formal operations,* that is, abstract thinking. The ability to conceptualize and to generalize is now differentiating, and presently the capacity to think in fully abstract, rational, logical terms will come into full bloom. This is very much a part of adolescent experience, so that the disrupting of the orderly processes of thinking described above parallels the enrichment of the ability to think conceptually. As a result, complex patterns of maturity and immaturity are likely, giving adolescence some of its characteristic color.

Along with these processes comes a rather typical increase in curiosity, especially in the sexual realm. The mounting pressure to know is accompanied by an enhanced capacity to understand, and at this time some youngsters begin to devour knowledge voraciously. Albeit particularly likely to occur in the areas of the erotic and the developmental, this desire to learn may encompass almost any kind of information. For many, knowledge itself becomes important. A sort of epistomological hunger appears, and the youngsters take much pleasure both in learning and in demonstrating how much they know. This interest in knowledge for its own sake can shade over into the defensive as well; some children seek to appear superior, sophisticated, and beyond surprise.

Emotions

With the onset of adolescence the emotional world expands enormously, and in a number of ways these affective developments are among the great changers and shapers of the time. There is a huge increase in the sheer quantity of available emotion. The capacity to experience excitement, thrills, grief, anger, rage, love—all the feelings—is augmented manyfold. These youngsters are more reactive, and often they are upset more easily, or, at any rate, given to far more ready shifts in their emotional state than was true during latency. Adolescence is nothing if not an emotional time, and the richness of feeling that becomes developmentally available is sometimes in itself puzzling and overwhelming to the involved youth.

At the same time many novel emotional experiences, moments of genuinely new affective sensation, create their own brand of turmoil. A person has but to consider the availability of full orgasm to recognize something of what is added at this time, but there is, in addition, the immense impact of first love. All sorts of new fears come up, such as the fear of fragmentation—this is the moment in life when a youngster may first suffer an anxiety attack. The child's outbursts of rage may have an intensity that was unknown earlier in his life, and he may have to contend with strange experiences such as depersonalization. Mood swings occur, with the emotional compass needle gyrating wildly about its axis and the feelings themselves shifting abruptly from one state to another. These phenomena are by no means universal, but neither are they rare. All in all, affect increases enormously.

Fantasy

With all the instinctual messages to supply content and the instinct-derived push to supply affect, it is small wonder that fantasy now expands and flourishes. For many young teenagers, the sudden efflorescence of embarrassing and provocative ideation comes as a shock; it is confusing, confronting, and disturbing. They do not know where these thoughts are coming from, what to make of them, or what to do with them—should they confess them, try to forget them, allow themselves to enjoy them? The child cannot even ask because that would mean telling, and for many youngsters nothing is so distressing as the possibility that other people suspect what is going on in their heads. In the nature of things, the freedom to put some of this into words is at least partly a function of the existing patterns of family and interpersonal relationships. Some family settings encourage the child's free and direct expression of his thoughts regardless of what they are; other families insist on decorum and propriety as the primary guidelines, not only for language and behavior, but for thoughts as well. Ultimately, the youngster never recounts some pubertal fantasies unless he is in the unusual situation of working in analysis and has a well-developed open channel to the analyst.

The effect of these thoughts on the youngster's state of mind should be taken very seriously. One pubertal boy described his problem something like this. It had all started when he read a "dirty" book. Someone had given him a copy of the *Decameron* by Boccaccio, and when he started reading it, he encountered tale after tale of suggestive exploits and earthy behavior. They fascinated him, but at the same time they were shocking and a little repelling. Presently he noticed a change in his world. Somehow, everything he looked at seemed dirty; people all seemed to be soiled, tainted. It was clear to him that this altered quality of his perceptions came directly from reading the book; it suggested voluptuous feelings in all kinds of people including priests, nuns, fathers, mothers, young, old; in short, the world was not a nice clean place, it was a sexual place, a dirty place. And this new perception left him sorely troubled.

Masturbatory Fantasies.   In particular, the fantasies associated with masturbation occupy an especially prominent position in the emotional life of these youngsters. Most children do a certain amount of body exploration and self-play during latency, but the full pattern of masturbation to orgasm characteristically appears at puberty. It is one of the landmark events typical of this time of life. There is probably at least some difference between boys and girls in respect to the frequency with which masturbation occurs. It is said that 95% of boys masturbate and 5% lie. With girls it is somewhat more difficult to assess prevalence precisely. Girls are capable of crural masturbation without using their hands, and they then consider themselves not to have done it and answer accordingly on questionnaires. So the figures are less accurate. A sizable percentage of girls, more than half by all accounts, do masturbate.

In the preceding century, physicians as well as the lay public believed that masturbation caused many illnesses, including blindness, insanity, lecherousness, sensuality, and impotence. Popular folk concepts of health and disease associated it with acne, warts on the hands, and a host of similar problems, major and minor. The question of what begets such ideas of harmfulness has, in fact, obvious answers. Indeed, the theory actually predicts what clinical experience demonstrates. For masturbation is not disturbing to the young person because it involves the sexual apparatus, because there is an ejaculation, or because the boy or girl experiences an orgasm. These are important experiences but they do not themselves cause concern. What seem to do the damage are the fantasies that accompany the act. Masturbation is almost always accompanied by erotic imagery of some kind, and these imagic experiences make the youngster feel guilty, frightened, and troubled.

Oedipal Development in Puberty. The Oedipus complex was laid to rest some years earlier, when the ego and superego succeeded in repressing it and locking it away, out of sight if not out of mind. With the beginning instinctual movement of puberty, however, the full array of repressed strivings becomes activated and starts to surge once again toward consciousness. More than that, the pressures are even greater than before; the growth during the intervening years and the very process of puberty itself give more energy and push to these drives. With this the unthinkable and the forbidden begin to press for conscious recognition and direct expression. But the ego has also been developing; it possesses a richer, more complex organization than it did when the child was 5 or 6. Hence, the defenses of the ego and the efforts of the superego, by and large, keep these impulses at bay. The youngster is troubled, the ego is under pressure, but there is seldom an eruption of conscious incestuous thoughts. The closest the child comes to it is during masturbation, for the oedipal impulse finds its most ready channel to awareness in the masturbatory fantasy.

If a therapist were to obtain the content of such a fantasy from a pubertal youth (no small feat), the emerging image would probably resemble the following scene. The boy says that his typical fantasy is to see a woman undressing. As the masturbatory act proceeds, she takes off more and more of her clothes, revealing more and more of her body. When orgasm approaches, she doffs some particular garment, and with this, he ejaculates. Sometimes the image may involve two people and is a dramatization of coitus or oral sex, sometimes it can take a sadistic form such as whipping or torture. Whatever its character, often a single sequence tends to be repeated with each masturbatory experience.

On inquiry, such a youngster will usually describe the person he sees as "just a woman," nobody he knows. In effect, the defensive organization of the ego is at work. If the youngster is in analysis and can work on the image, the figure will typically turn out to be a representation of some forbidden incestuous object, the mother or perhaps an older sister, whose identity is masked to allow the image access to consciousness. Unfortunately, it is not masked well enough to avoid guilt; somewhere inside there is a subliminal awareness of the forbidden character of the wish—and hence of the act. The superego strikes back, as it must, and a sense of some sort of wrongdoing clouds the experience, giving it an uncomfortable taint.

The degree and the quality of guilt will vary enormously with the youngster's education in sexuality, the level of seductiveness in the home, the basic pattern of ego–superego relationships (well defended, masochistic–submissive, psychopathically evasive, etc.), and, in particular, the youngster's capacity to sublimate. But it is evident why the culture has ascribed so many ills to the masturbatory act: Implicit in the behavior is a tendency to violate one of the group's essential taboos and, hence, the inclination to read into it all manner of dangers and damage.

An occasional boy from a sophisticated home will be well prepared for pubertal development. The parents well have freely and comfortably discussed masturbation, accepted its normality, and stated its universality. When seen later in therapy, the boy is likely to remark that although he knows how normal it is, still, whenever he masturbates, he feels bad for a while afterward, as though he had done something wrong. He does not know why, he just feels that way.

Occasionally, too, the defensive mechanism slips, and the boy has a frankly incestuous fantasy. For example, a youngster might picture his sister in various states of undress while he masturbates. When he comes out of the bathroom, he immediately does something that provokes her; he messes up her school project, calls her a name, or otherwise attacks her "for no reason at all." They thereupon have a fight, and he gets the worst of it. Thus, he pays off for his guilty wish and undoes his trespass.

Menstruation Fantasies.   The girl experiences similar masturbatory sequences but she is also encountering menstruation. The cultural history of this event is interesting. Not too many years ago menstruation was considered to be akin to illness. The woman was "not well" or "indisposed." The nicknames attached to the process tell their own story; women referred to their menstrual periods by saying, "I have a visitor," or "auntie's come," or "grandma's here" or "my friend's arrived." Another term was "I'm falling off," or "falling off the roof." These phrases have largely disappeared from the language, although a parallel term "I've got the curse" has persisted. The implication behind these designations would seem to be that some woman appeared and pushed another women off the roof so that she fell, was injured, and bled. The usage that has never been employed is "mother's come," and hence the likelihood is that the underlying thought is precisely the old oedipal story of mother castrating daughter and causing her to bleed.

Preoccupation with the menses throve on secrecy and mystery. Traditionally, menstruation was regarded as a covert subject, to be spoken of in whispers; men could not possibly understand it, and they should not hear about it. Many women were reared by mothers who were so inhibited that they never warned their daughters or prepared them for menarche, and the tales are legion of girls being shocked and frightened by their first experience of vaginal bleeding. The characteristic remark is "I thought I was bleeding to death." Almost always, someone other than the mother gave the girl whatever explanation she received. Occasionally there would be a girl whose periods came early and who, after she recovered from the initial shock, went on for months and years without telling her mother she was menstruating. A more common story was that of the mother who never said anything, but who gave her daughter a book. At best, it was a murky, conflicted area, filled with tension and mythology and hinting of forbidden mysteries.

The current style of child rearing has changed radically in this respect. For the most part menstruation is now treated as a normal process, children of both sexes learn about it well in advance, books are available in profusion, it is taught in school either in sex education courses or as part of hygiene, and it has, in large measure, been effectively demystified. Many of the nicknames have disappeared, and the equating of menstruation and illness is no longer the norm. This is a major cultural accomplishment and has done a great deal to facilitate feminine development.

Current attitudes about menstruation reflect less the morbid attitudes of the past, but rather the feelings about femininity that emerge from other dimensions of personality growth. Thus, athletic girls given to sports and outdoor activity often regard the menses as a disruptive and awkward intrusion. Such girls find the experience a messy one, the apparatus needed to cope with it unpleasant and ungainly, and the overall necessity of adapting to this part of their bodily functioning a chore and a burden. In contrast to this, youngsters who have little inclination for outdoor sports and instead prefer sewing, cooking, and other traditionally feminine activities will often regard their periods as an experience that enhances their womanliness, and a good thing in its every aspect. They like what happens and what they have to do about this desirable event. Needless to say, most girls fall somewhere in between. They may find the mechanics of menstruation objectionable, but they like being girls, like being grown up, and accept the whole process as a matter of course.

Body Awareness. In a larger sense, the advances of puberty precipitate a marked increase in body awareness. Considering what is happening, it could scarcely be otherwise. The physical alterations are dramatic; height, hairiness, musculature, bosom, sexuality, facial contours, everything is growing and shifting. It becomes a matter of endless fascination for the average boy and girl to document their own growth. Inevitably attention turns in on the self, and the youngster begins to spend a good deal of time in front of the mirror. A state of normal narcissistic involvement appears; the child experiences the self, in particular the bodily self, as fascinating.

The encounter with the mirror is important. The boy studies the progress of muscular growth, he flexes his biceps, expands his chest, strains one arm against the other to watch the ripple and play of muscle patterns, and strikes herculean stances to exaggerate the contours of his torso. The girl studies her face carefully and arranges her hair to frame it in a variety of ways, swept up, hanging over one eye, in a bun at back, piled up on top, hanging free, and on and on. She observes herself in whatever poses she can create: in profile, full face, three-quarter view, head tilted forward, head tilted back, eyes wide, eyes half lidded, and so on. She studies her body and watches the growth of her bosom from its earliest tiny buddings to full-fledged womanhood. She is very conscious of her pubic hair; some girls count and can tell their girlfriends how many hairs they have at a given time. Many girls study the form of their genitals; not infrequently they use a mirror to see how they are made.

Most youngsters have some concerns about their growth. Often the child feels a mild and transient regret at not being taller, shorter, leaner, or fuller than native endowment actually supplies. Handsomeness and prettiness are of inevitable importance although, as a rule, not to catastrophic proportions.

Body Image Problems. On the other hand, handicaps of any kind are likely to become far more portentous issues than heretofore. This is especially true if it is a visible difficulty, such as obesity or a large birthmark, rather than a covert one, such as diabetes. The awareness of difference is always a problem for children; at puberty its impact increases manyfold. The child's intense self-scrutiny and overinvolvement in his own changes and developing contours, the fascinated mirror study so typical of the age, cannot help but make deviance a major source of alarm. Many youngsters go through a great deal of pain with what may be, at best, a trivial disfigurement; sometimes the outside observer cannot even tell what is bothering the boy or girl. Many plastic surgeons have had to ponder the ethics of performing a "nose job" on a youngster with minimal visible deviance in nasal contours.

Perfectly normal variants may have disturbing social overtones. Thus, during pubertal growth, some boys go through a transient episode of enlarged breast development (gynecomastia), which can cause considerable self-consciousness and worry. The physiological state usually clears up spontaneously in a few months; unless properly managed, the psychological impact can last for a long time.

The turning inward and the attention to the self are by no means confined to the body. With the host of new thoughts and fantasies that are now appearing, there is a general redirection of interest inward. The youngster will often appear to the surrounding family to have become self-centered, even selfish. Parents may voice vigorous reproofs in an attempt to correct this unfortunate turn. But the inward drift is not lightly altered; it is a normal, indeed an inevitable consequence of growth, and to some degree everyone goes through such a state. The extent of this tendency can vary markedly however.

Changes in Attachment to Parents—Distancing

The many shifts and changes lead to major transformations in the young-sters' patterns of relationship, and the ties to the parents undergo the first of a series of revolutionary alterations. Both parents and child are moving into an unfamiliar realm where they will need to reestablish their relationship on a vastly different basis involving a new mode of mutual regard. A somewhat mechanical model of the preexisting latency pattern can help describe this transition. The ties between parent and child all during the grade-school years may be regarded as consisting of an array of conduits. One such channel conducts loving care, one carries concerns about health and hygiene, one transmits messages about impulse control and conduct regulation, another handles playfulness and game-type interaction, yet another conveys thoughtful attention to plans and the future, and similarly, a great variety of messages flow back and forth. They become familiar channels that the child regularly depends on and frequently resorts to during any given day. They are a natural and everyday part of life.

Then puberty appears, and the tide of erotic and aggressive yearnings that wells up in the child suddenly floods the conduits with emotions and reactions. All too quickly the channels overload; they become a threat rather than carriers of support. Thus, the need for health care may have routinely involved rectal thermometers, body inspection, questions about bowel function, or at least a hand to the brow to check for fever. Suddenly the youngster is proclaiming, "I don't want you to do that, I can do that myself, I don't want you to look at me, I don't like it when you feel my forehead. . . ."

To be sure, this is not the final word. In early puberty this situation is changeable and unpredictable. For example, if the child falls really ill, he may demand just those interventions and attentions that, at the outset, he so hotly contested. The same holds true for all of these conduits; they are blocked off when the youngster feels able to cope and are immediately reopened and reutilized when he is in a state of need. This sort of oscillating behavior is not easy on the parents, as in the following vignette:

One morning Susan, who is 14 years old, asks her mother, "Mother, what dress do you think I should wear to school today?" Mother has often helped with the selection of clothes, and so she says without hesitation, "Why don't you wear the red one with the puffed sleeves, you haven't worn it for a while." To which Susan responds, "That dowdy old thing?! Why, Mother, how could you even think such a thing, no one but *no one* is wearing puffed sleeves now, why I'd be laughed out of class if I came in with anything like *that;* really, Mother I don't know where you get your taste from." Susan thereupon dons something else and goes grandly off to school where she tells all her friends about the antediluvian tastes she has to contend with at home and what a burden it is.

That evening, however, Susan faces a dilemma. The crowd she goes with has had a lot of parties but always as a group. Tonight, for the first time, they are having a couples party, a boy will call for her, and she is especially concerned with how she will look. She has narrowed her selection down to two dresses and cannot decide between them. So she turns to her mother and asks anxiously, "I don't know which one is nicer—which dress should I wear tonight?" Mother, who has learned something from the morning's experience, says, "Why don't you wear the one you like best, dear?" At which point Susan dissolves in tears and wails, "Oh Mother, I've been trying so hard to figure this out, this is the most important night in my life, and you'd think if a girl asks her own mother for a little help with something the mother would do something for her, but no, you won't help me, you let me down . . . "

Mother, it seems, cannot win. Nor is she supposed to, as a matter of fact, during such a time of change and transformation with its many rapidly alternating emotional states. The youngster is going to swing back and forth from dependency to independence, from neediness to disdainfulness, from close attachment to emphasized distance—and there is often no way for the parent to read all the signals and know where that particular child is at a given moment. There is simply too much flux, too much on-again, off-again behavior for the parent to keep up with it and to chart a course. Usually the adult's best stance under such circumstances is to provide a kind of steadiness, a center of stability around which the teenager's sorties and flights, advances and retreats, can swirl. As a rule the worst thing the parent can do is to take each such gambit seriously, as a breach of ethic, an invitation to heightened intimacy, or as a cause for equivalent emotional reaction. Then the youngster becomes even more reactive and more guilty, and the tension at home can mount by geometric increments. At best, it can be a difficult time for a household.

In many homes the course of events is less dramatic; most youngsters get through their teens without explosive or disturbing interactions. But many young people will evidence their work on the process of detachment in other ways. Thus, it is common to hear young teenagers saying, "I can't talk to my parents, I don't know why, they just don't seem to understand me. I can talk to other grownups, and it's not the same, but my parents—somehow it just doesn't work." The tides of emotion are simply too great to buck, the currents of development are carrying the youth ever farther away, and in one way or another the means for finding distance have to be invoked.

The relatively small proportion of more troubled youngsters may have to resort to tantrums and outbursts as distancing tactics; sometimes periods of moroseness or daydreams of leaving home and getting away from it all are in the forefront. An occasional youngster asks to go live with some other family member or to be sent off to boarding school, and here and there, not so rarely of late, the teenager who feels unloved, unwanted, or simply angry at his family will run away. It has been estimated that currently there are about 1 million such runaways every year.

One of the most helpful devices for dealing with the need for distance has been the telephone, and its use by the American adolescent population has been a major phenomenon of our times. The Group for the Advancement of Psychiatry (GAP) (1968) study of normal adolescence made the point that the phone serves as a perfect counter to heated oedipal tensions in the home; the youngster needs merely to "dial-a-peer" to be out of the situation and in initmate contact with the great antidote for such family embroilment, the safer and more comfortable interaction with the friend. The phone itself makes for a kind of protected intimacy; the caller is guarded from excessive physical closeness but is still in a peculiarly personal relationship with the significant other.

The sensual power of the spoken word has received fewer more dramatic accolades than the spate of reactions to the "dial-a-porn" messages that have become available. For a fixed sum of money, a dialer is put in contact with a husky-voiced other, who will communicate various descriptions of erotic arousal and activity. Occasional parents are said to have had to face a monthly phone bill of thousands of dollars because their adolescent off-spring took advantage of this opportunity.

Abstraction and Depersonalization

In adolescence the youngster feels the sweep of transformation and senses that nothing he has known will ever be quite the same again. All things familiar are now viewed in a new light and measured by new standards, the child's very physique is shifting and altering, and his mind is no longer the same mind as before. He is seized by moments of intense fantasy or drifts off into periods of blankness. A father might snap his fingers in front of such a youngster's eyes and say, "Hey, where were you?"—and the answer might well be a puzzled, "I don't know." And that could very well be true—the teenager does not know. Whatever he was thinking about was repressed immediately and automatically, as though the youth had been falling into thought patterns he could not allow himself to know about.

A more dramatic form of such behavior is the phenomenon of depersonalization. This is a characteristic element that is found primarily, and normally, at this time of life. It affects the perceptual world in particular and involves an odd sense of being divided within the self, as if the youngsters were for a time spectators observing their own behavior, onlookers as well as actors. There is a hard-to-describe sense of detachment from the self, or a split within the self. The adolescent seems to be functioning, going about his business as usual, while at the same time standing outside himself and watching all this take place.

There are a number of associated phenomena as well. The child has a sense of distance from the world; visual images appear to be coming from afar, as though seen through the wrong end of a telescope. Sounds, too, may seem oddly muted and distant, perhaps with an "electronic" quality. Sometimes there is a peculiar feeling of unreality about everything in the outer world, or the self, or both. Occasionally the youngster feels the quality of distance within the self; for the moment he has lost all feeling, or the feelings are wooden, or dead. Or the child has no control of his thoughts, they come marching by of their own volition while he looks on helplessly.

By and large, these are transient phenomena lasting at most a few seconds or a few minutes. Rather rarely an adolescent will get "stuck" in some such state and not be able to snap out of it for hours, or even for days at a time. This is a most uncomfortable frame of mind; properly speaking it is a kind of neurosis and has been called the *depersonalization syndrome.* Some more malignant forms of this condition are associated with temporal lobe syndromes, with dissociative disorders, with borderline states, and with psychosis. But that is quite exceptional; usually it is a far briefer and more transitory situation. In a sense the inner organization of the self is shifting and reorienting, and has not yet all come together.

IDENTITY LOST AND REGAINED

Under the hammering of these drive derivatives the ego experiences a great deal of pressure, and the part of it that constituted the latency identity gives way. Within the ego, the identity is a higher echelon of organization, marshaling together an array of identifications, defenses, coping devices, and character traits so that they form a coherent pattern. As noted in the discussion of latency identity, when this pattern is well established, it gives rise to a subjective sense of who-ness, a feeling of being a particular someone. The someone who the child was during the grade-school years, however, is no longer appropriate to the new intellectual, emotional, biological, and wish life of the pubertal child. He is, in fact, no longer a child, certainly not in the sense that held true during those earlier years. That previous identity structure simply fragments and is resorbed, and, for a time, the youngster does not know for sure who he is or how that person should be; he is a sort of soft-shelled crab who has lost the carapace of identity.

The construction of such an identity is the chief work of early adolescence. The way it is done is not entirely dissimilar to the way a person might go about buying a new dress or suit. In the clothing store the purchaser selects, from among many possibilities, the most eye-appealing items. He or she looks at a number of garments and quickly eliminates them. Others receive more serious consideration, and one after another, the person tries them on for size. The individual keeps the clothes that fit the best and are the most attractive; the rest he or she doffs and discards. In a similar fashion a teenager has a host of people all about, each of whom offers a possible model for emulation. There are family members, neighbors, clergy, and teachers in the immediate surround, and then there is the extended world of heroic figures in sports, national, and world affairs, science, literature, entertainment, and the like. Particular ethinic groups or subcultures may have their own charismatic figures. There are TV idols, movie stars, and rock concert figures. There are characters in history, in fiction, in legend, in myth, in holy writings, and in epic poems. In short, there is no dearth of models or of possible objects of interest and admiration to serve as exemplars, or at least as indicators of the direction a young person might wish to follow. The actual process of identity formation then involves a series of experiments in the configuration of self. The new possibility to be considered is simply accepted as a sort of presence to carry within the self for a while. The following vignette illustrates the way the process works:

One evening a 14-year-old boy is reading about the lives of the saints. He is much taken by the story of St. Francis of Assisi, whose life seems to him particularly noble and worthwhile. He goes to sleep that night thinking about what he read, dreams about it, and wakes up in the morning in a state of inspired resolve. Henceforth he will lead a life of saintliness and beauty; he will devote himself entirely to good works; he will live in a house by the side of the road and be a friend to all. In this frame of mind he gets dressed, comes down to breakfast, and astonishes everyone by his abstemiousness and his willingness to be pleasant to his siblings. Off he goes to school in this elevated mood, and for the first two periods maintains his resolution. But in the late morning, during a break, he notices several classmates clustered together, looking at something and laughing. Drawn by curiosity, he approaches them, looks over somebody's shoulder—and recoils in dismay. What they are studying is scarcely saintly! He tries to recoup, turn his thoughts elsewhere, but alas, it is too late. In a little while he is in the bathroom where he masturbates. When he emerges, he looks different and feels different. He sees himself now as an outcast, a vagabond, a raffish fellow, perhaps a highwayman, an outsider snapping at the heels of humanity, someone set apart from the great united chorus of the good people. And in that state he goes home at the end of the day.

Most likely the boy will become neither outcast nor saint, but the identity garb he will eventually piece together will have within its pattern perhaps a few patches taken from each. The work of designing and building this part of the organization of the self will take time and a good deal more of this kind of experimenting in a variety of contexts.

The girl in front of her mirror, experimenting with various posturings and hairdos is also making efforts at identity formation, a sort of play with the potentials of the self. With her hair so, she is a woman executive, all iron and efficiency. When it sweeps the other way, however, she becomes a femme fatale, enslaving men, using them for her own purposes, and casting them aside when she no longer needs them. Yet another sort of arrangement, and she is a country housewife in a cottage with primroses and children everywhere; still another, and she is a sporting member of the horsey set, riding to hounds. And so she works on her identity, there and elsewhere, and begins to assemble the elements that will ultimately be blended together to give her persona its eventual form.

For certain youngsters, this is a difficult process. Thus, tomboys may greet the pubertal changes with discomfort and may, for a while, deny the womanhood that is thrusting itself upon them. Some girls become anorexic and, in effect, fight the changes in their bodies by starving themselves into flatness and amenorrhea. Because puberty is not necessarily a desired process for any particular boy or girl, the child may enter into the identity work of the time most unwillingly. But sooner or later all who grow this far must do this work, and the construction of identity will proceed henceforth.

As growth proceeds, it carries with it an implicit message of cutting the self loose from the ties to the parents. Part of the identity of being a child had been to accept the self as an attached person living in a state of at least partial dependency. Now the pressures of the time (not the least of which is the pressure to form a new identity) carry the youngster away, sever more and more of these supportive ties, and widen the distance. In a fundamental sense, the youth is losing his parents, losing his original connectedness, drawing away. This is a complex experience with many overtones and multiple sonorities. It carries with it something of the early sense of fear of separation; there is also a quality of depression and a feeling of inner emptiness that, at times, can hurt grievously. There is also a certain elation, a sensation of freedom achieved, even a kind of grandiosity at the perception of attained maturity and acquired autonomy. These feelings blend together in odd ways so that the youngster may feel confused—no matter what he says or does, it is not quite what he meant or intended; or he may feel as if he is losing control—he feels one way momentarily and then the feeling shifts and changes. But the most common experience is a background sense of mild but continuous depression that usually does not come out clearly or have any fixed content. It seems to arise from the general circumstance of losing the stable core relationship that has stood the youth in such good stead for so many years. Little wonder that a certain pervasive sadness colors the child's experience, or that he falls into a brown study from time to time and cannot explain why. It is part of the pain of growing up.

THE PEER GROUP

Caught up in flux and change, loss and acquisition, confusion and achievement, the youngster needs help from somewhere. He can no longer turn to his parents for all the aforementioned reasons—where can he go? The answer is simple—he seeks out others in like straits and turns to them. In brief, the young teenager immerses himself in his peer group because therein he finds the best communication. The group offers an assemblage of others, with similar needs and accomplishments, problems and struggles, and the same hungry quest for substitute objects of attachment. And so the peer group emerges as a central presence of signal importance. In a real sense it becomes at least a partial substitute for the now distanced parents, assuming many of the functions the parents had previously served, and some they would have continued to serve.

Among other things, the peer group becomes the arbiter of morals for its members, and many issues that burden these youngsters come before it—Should you kiss a boy on a first date? How far should a girl go if she really likes a boy? Whose fault is it if a girl gets pregnant?—and so on. The problems that confront these youngsters thus have a forum for address without the potential challenge of parental opprobrium or the danger of embarrassing revelations. This is immensely important to the affected boys and girls; they turn hungrily to the group, and it becomes, for a time, their primary affiliation. Much of how they dress, the jargon they use, the rock star or TV idols they favor, and the behavior they display in social contexts emerges from their identification with the group ideals, the group style, or a particular group leader. The peer group is a great molder of adolescent values, and many a parent has the disturbing experience of having his or her position swept away by the child's flat declaration that "Nobody I know dresses that way [or likes that kind of entertainment or has to go to bed at that hour], so I don't see why I should have to," said with the certainty and assurance of a person who offers an unassailable argument. For a while at least, the peers are likely to constitute a formidable presence in the home of the pubertal youth.

FIRST LOVE

The psychological movement of the time is not only an account of detachment, it is also one of reattachment to new objects. One of these is the peer group itself, and its many important missions, but within its context yet newer formations appear. Not only is there a search for substitute parental presences, there is also an opening up of the affectional world in a novel way. This is a critically important step, for with it, the future breaks with the past, and a whole new universe of possibility opens up. This shift brings the youngster face to face with the issues of adolescent loving, adolescent crushes, and adolescent sexuality, which are of vital import for all subsequent object attachment. This is one of the important crucibles in fashioning the basis for future relationships. Nor is there any preordained sequence for this process. Some youngsters gradually become more and more interested in socializing, first in group interactions, at church groups, and picnics, and parties; then in some essays with the less intense forms of pairing off at ball games, dances, and movies (chiefly on double dates and often with different companions); and presently by a focused interest in a particular partner, with a reaching out toward ever-increasing intimacy. Others begin by falling in love. From the outset there is a plunge into intense attachment accompanied by highly varying degrees of physical involvement. In some instances, puberty starts out with a plunge into promiscuity, with rapid couplings and uncouplings with serial partners.

There is, however, a rather typical sequence for these early pubertal years which displays a more stepwise character. Not infrequently a girl's first love may be with some distant personage who is considerably older and far enough away to have semimythic proportions. Often enough this is part of a group experience; everyone is in love with Elvis Presley, or the Beatles, or some other societal hero; everyone swoons and screams and has them as pinups; and everyone talks about the passions they evoke. In an earlier day, movie figures who were celebrated in fan clubs (Errol Flynn, Clark Gable, etc.) held such status; later the great band leaders or popular singers, such as Frank Sinatra, were lionized by the young. The point is, there is always someone.

Youngsters of different background and temperament will, of course, find highly diverse objects of attachment, but impressionistically these figures seem to be of two general varieties: rebellion objects and idealized objects. The *rebellion objects* embody the strivings for sensuousness and independence, and they might be exhibitionistic, surly, raucous, or freakish; for this kind of choice, the group attachment is helpful but not essential. (There is an extra modicum of security if everyone is rebelling together.) The *idealized objects* convey a sense of wisdom, talent, virtue, and profundity. Sometimes these idealized figures are curiously remote and extreme. One young girl, for example, became fixated on a signer of the Declaration of Independence, a Mr. Pinkney, and studied his life and accomplishments in great depth. For a given youngster, a great scientist or author can become the myth-object. In general, the person selected for such demigod status will often be an idealized parent figure of some sort who is far enough away to be safely out of tangible reach. Whoever the particular choice may be, there is that about him or her to make that individual an acceptable partner for the youngster's daydreams. In a sense this is a first level of displacement of erotic feelings away from the actual parent.

The next step in the process may involve a crush. The youngster finds him or herself drawn powerfully to some neutral adult in the more immediate environment. This may be a teacher, a relative (often an uncle or an aunt), a neighbor, a lifeguard; in any case, it will be some figure whom the teenager sees regularly but with whom there is little likelihood of closeness. The youngster "hangs around" this person, hoping to catch a glimpse of him or her and thus experience the accompanying thrill—and hoping even more to be noticed by the adored one, which brings with it a sensation of overwhelming excitement.

This may continue for a few days, or even a few weeks, after which the attachment is likely to switch to someone else.

On the psychological level, the work involved carries forward the theme of displacement. Now the feelings are turning from the quasifantasy figures toward real people, but the inhibitions continue to be powerful, and there is usually no physical contact between the pubertal youngster and the object of the crush.

The final step in this sequence occurs when the love interest turns toward the boy or girl who lives next door or who is a classmate. With this, the Great Displacement has done its work. The affects, kindled long ago by the heat of oedipal fire, suppressed for so long under the weight of superego admonishment, and bursting forth anew with the resurgent press of pubertal instincts, have finally found their home. They are displaced outward, away from the bodies of the parents and attached at last to an extrafamilial, age-appropriate heterosexual object. It is a moment of developmental triumph; the ego has converted a conflicted incestuous possibility into an accepted and approved pattern of interest and attachment.

None of these steps is necessarily easy. The child writes to a fantasy object who fails to answer, and the youngster is crushed. Or he has poured out his heart to the admired "star," and the answer is a form letter with no personal recognition at all. The youngster develops a crush and is called a pest or told to quit hanging around all the time. Or, finally, what does the boy or girl next door do with the heart that is now so gratuitously bestowed? What happens can be wonderful, a true meeting of hearts and minds, but it can also be painful, humiliating, or exploitative; even at this early age the reaching out for relationship is potentially hazardous. But meeting and overcoming these hazards is very much part of growing up.

Earlier developmental vicissitudes might now also find expression in an unusually configured pattern of attachment. A particular youth may find that his love interests are homosexual; the arousal and excitement, the attachment hunger, and the daydreams turn ever toward a same-sex object. Or there may be a powerful thrust toward donning the clothes of the other sex. This is very much the time of life when such encounters and recognitions, however much adumbrated by previous experiences, now make a firm claim on the vital center of attachment interest. Many youngsters feel a certain relief in knowing that this is their pattern; they are not especially conflicted about their sexual orientation, and it becomes a matter of finding their way with the identity they are now establishing. With others, however, the confirmation of their sexual identity as deviant fills them with the most acute anxiety. The ensuing emotional stresses can be of monumental, even of life-threatening, proportions.

Chapter 17

Mid and Late Adolescence

INTRODUCTION

This period covers the ages of approximately 14 to 17 years for girls and 15 through 19 years for boys. For both, the first encounter with pubertal changes is past, and the patterns of biological growth are firmly established. The girls are well advanced in their development, the menstrual cycle is reasonably regular, the body contours are close to their adult fullness, and maximum height has been attained. The boy too has gone through his growth spurt, erections and occasional nocturnal emissions are an accepted part of life, some sort of masturbatory routine has usually been established, and the first disturbing tangle of puberty is gradually smoothing out. The more advanced pubertal changes are occurring; the boy's voice deepens, and his facial hair begins to grow. He now may shave for the first time, or he may consider growing a mustache or a beard (see Appendix 17–1 for a discussion of the biology of puberty).

NEW DEVELOPMENTS

Both genders have become fully fertile and must consider (or choose to deny) all the awesome implications of that transformation.

Under optimal circumstances the instinctual set has moved in a progressively heterosexual direction. The youngster is interested in the opposite sex, although perhaps not yet in any particular individual or in dating (even before feeling ready, however, the youngster may actually be doing it), and is usually not yet seeking a confirmed partnership with long-range implications.

Body Growth

The body contours are beginning to firm up and certain verities must be faced. The child has passed beyond the growth spurt and is clearly going to be tall or short; the contours of his face have achieved definition, and he is plain or comely; and the general body type is clear—during this epoch it becomes evident that the person is slated to be heavyset, buxom, or slender. Youngsters may have a variety of typical problems: acne, squeaky voice, awkward gait, and braces on the teeth. Biology is a massive presence and sets the conditions for further development.

Cognitive Growth

The intellectual expansion at this time of life is striking. The beginning of Piagetian formal operations tends to take place at about 11 years. As the years advance, this process also proceeds, and by the mid teens, the youth is capable of a wholly new order of thinking, which is visible in a variety of ways. For one thing, the capacity to generalize from specific bits of information is enormously enhanced. The youngster can look at a number of dissimilar items, abstract from them a common underlying principle, and form an overarching generalization that will embrace all the variances. This is a powerful competence. It makes for far more effective problem solving than was possible in latency; the concrete approach typical of that epoch required addressing each individual instance as a separate entity. Now the youngster can discuss a more general principle that governs whole classes of events no matter how dissimilar they seem.

Another such advance is the power to draw fine distinctions. There may be a number of instances of an event that appear superficially to be essentially the same. With the newly emerging capacities, however, the youngster can begin to discern subtle grounds for differentiation; they may look alike, but actually they are quite different because of *A*, *B*, and *C*. This ability will increase the youth's debating capacity manyfold. The parents become aware of these new developments when they try to enforce discipline; suddenly they face all sorts of legalistic objections, fine distinctions, and highly conceptual arguments about principle. The effort to regulate such an individual is quite a different challenge from what it was just a short time earlier.

Yet another competence that emerges is the ability to address concepts as entities capable of study, comparison, and manipulation, of being loved and being hated. Adolescents catch up a wide variety of abstractions in their enthusiasms, including social concepts (such as freedom, equality, rights, justice, truth); religious concepts (God, purity, the absolute, soul, holiness, evil, diabolism, transcendence); or ethical/aesthetic concepts (art for art's sake, the purity of science, the essence of beauty). The youth is becoming ever more capable of such address to the conceptual. In the hands of some young people the results can be extraordinary.

Emotional Growth

The emotional growth of the middle phase of adolescence is no less extensive. The pubertal emotions, as mentioned earlier, offer both qualitative novelty and quantitative richness. These outpourings, however crude and massive, represent an altogether new, albeit callow, level of personality organization. There is a starkness and impetuousness about them that is often very confronting to adults; in their naïveté teenagers tend to be absolute: "If I'm not invited to that party my life is ruined." "This is the most important decision of my whole life." "I can't ever face them in school again." "Don't tell me it's not love! I'm crazy about him[her]." Hearing these declamations most adults tend to smile a little, but no one can be long in the company of a young adolescent in this kind of turmoil without gaining a keen sense of the intensity and pervasiveness of the affect. The judgment giving rise to the feeling may be childish, but the character of the response is too powerful, too emphatic, and sometimes too threatening not to be taken seriously.

Probably because of this change in the quality and structuring of affect, the predisposed youngster now begins to show the signs of classical affective disorder. There is evidence to suggest that children carrying the manic-depressive genetic burden are different from the time of birth on, and it may presently be possible to diagnose the condition in latency or even earlier. However, the full-blown cyclical form of the illness does not usually manifest itself as such until late in adolescence. The basic wiring change in the central nervous system that is necessary for mature affective responses may well act to release the classical expression of the illness.

In any case, much of what is typically adolescent traces back to this development. The frenetic quality of the music these youngsters prefer, the dramatics to which they so often lend themselves, and the intensity with which they experience the inevitable crises of beginning exploration into relationships make it evident that the various symbolic as well as real expressions of a deeply felt emotional life are sharply present. On the other hand, the encounter with first love often has a sweetness and poignancy that many a person can recall vividly ever after. And it may have been a relationship where neither partner ever addressed the other, or where they never touched. Only their eyes met, but this kindled such fires within them, suffused their bodies with such a pervasively thrilling emotion, that the impression remains ineradicable.

For better or for worse, this kind of experience gradually gives way to a different order of response. Again, this usually occurs slowly, although there is much variation. The youngster behaves as though he has acquired a new instrument and is now learning both to tune it and to play it. The boy and girl begin to learn how to manage their emotions, how to modulate the feelings, how to tune them. They ask themselves many questions: "When do you cry, and how many tears? Is it ladylike to really laugh hard? What do you do with your temper—when do you show your anger, and when do you suppress it"?

The culture teaches a great deal about such matters, and the youngsters hear loudly and clearly that such and such is "childish," presumptuous, or whatever. Sometimes these precepts are carried to extraordinary lengths. A woman reported a teenage memory. She had attended a finishing school, and on one occasion she and a group of her girlfriends were playing and cavorting in one of the rooms, with much noise and laughter. Suddenly the dignified headmistress appeared. She clapped her hands to silence the uproar and stated forcefully: "Girls! Please! When a young lady laughs she does so in four syllables, accenting the third: Ha ha *ha* ha."

For the most part parents and teachers do not get quite that picayune in their instruction, but they do model and reward, and punish, various forms of affective communication.

At best, however, these newfound emotions are often hard to handle. This is especially true if they threaten to express some of the forbidden, unconscious wishes of earlier years to devour, to smear, to engage in illicit sex, to kill or destroy—the host of repressed but pressing pregenital and phallic yearnings. Now, carried by the powerful currents of pubertal feeling, these configurations continue to demand expression. The youngster must persist in efforts to prevent a dangerous breakthrough, and he finds a variety of defenses.

One of the best techniques is to push the whole business back out of sight. If the person can keep it all contained and out of awareness, he has solved part of the problem, only to find that in doing so, he creates a new condition. For the impulse has two components, a cognitive content and an emotional charge; the repression may take out the cognitive part, but the affect is often not repressed all the way. It is repressed enough so that the youngster is not aware of its content, but not so far that he is free of its demand. He feels a powerful yearning for something but does not know for what. What he does know is that whatever he wants, nothing he has is that something.

Boredom. Assume that a given youngster is socially popular, has many friends, and is invited to many events. He has a horde of computer games, a VCR, a large-screen TV, a sailboat, a motor bike, an automatic camera, a closet full of fine clothes, and an elaborate stereo system. And he is bored. Nothing interests him, nothing appeals to him, and nothing attracts him. He regards the people about him as blah, he feels that the objects he has acquired are so much junk, and the invitations he receives fail to excite him. He yearns for something but knows not what. All he knows is that he feels stressed and dissatisfied, and he complains irritably that everything is so dull, so *boring*.

Emotional Breakthroughs. An alternative configuration appears when the defenses slip, and some of the feelings do break through. When that happens, it may inspire some of the strange stories so typical of adolescence, such as the sudden runaway or the unexpected emotional flare-up that seems to come out of nowhere. Less frequently the explosion may involve violence, with blows being exchanged or property damaged. These gusts of emotion often are in response to apparently trivial stimuli, a cross word, a trifling bit of teasing, a minor critical admonition. "For no reason," the girl bursts into tears, runs sobbing up to her room, and bars the door for hours. Or the boy shouts a series of obscene words and runs roaring out of the house, slamming the door so hard the glass breaks. For most youngsters, certainly for the healthier ones surrounded by well-functioning families, these are transient episodes, usually followed by waves of guilt that lead to heartfelt apologies and, ultimately, to a firmer grip on the self and a deepening of family warmth. For the more troubled boys and girls—and the more troubled families—such episodes can end with serious consequences. Major runaways, impulsive sexual engagements and pregnancy, suicidal gestures, and acts of vandalism are among the hazards of such emotional flooding and loss of control.

The Sense of Newness. Adolescence, however, is not primarily a mass of antisocial acts or moments of personal torment. It is, among other things, a period of extraordinary encounters with the new. The teenager has so much to discover about himself, his body, his mind, his capacity to function in novel and remarkable ways. The cognitive additions that he has recently acquired open so many doors and yield so many insights. Among the major facets of the emerging revelations is the sense of the self as freshly met and different.

The Sense of Fragmentation. Some of the identity work of the time increases the awareness of personal vulnerability at the same time that it offers unexpected treasures of possibility. Thus the fragile new formations have a feeling of potential fragmentation; there are moments when the youngster feels he or she is flying apart. It is as though the child loses his moorings, internally and externally; too much is happening, he cannot keep it together; everything in life, in the self, is becoming undone. In particular, this impinges on the sense of who-ness. The youngster speaks of not knowing who he is; he does not recognize himself. He looks in the mirror and sees a stranger. He mulls over his own behavior and does not understand it. He tries to sort out his own motivations and behavior, and they make no sense. Occasionally the young person has periods of blankness; he wanders off in his thoughts and does not know where he has been, almost as though, for a moment, the teenager really does fragment and break into some unrecognized, sequestered area.

At the same time the opening up of the child's personal sense of self and of boundaries leads to a (transient) lack of any confining structure that links him to a particular defined identity. All this gives rise to marvelous new feelings. They come and go and take many forms. Sometimes there is a quality of being joined with the universe, fusing with nature, being part of all that is alive, sharing in the whole of creation. For the more religious youth, a readiness for communion with deity may emerge, an ability to feel the great pulse at the core of reality or to sense God's presence everywhere. Although these may be occasional experiences, often they have immense power in the youngster's life and make him feel very special indeed. Such sequences have great shaping force on the sense of the self and may in turn influence career choice.

Talents

Among the other emergents at this moment of development is the discovery of talents and exceptional abilities. It is by no means unusual for special potentialities to realize themselves much earlier, and the range of such abilities may vary all the way from musical gifts to gymnastic competencies. But it is also true that with the unfolding of adolescence, many novel ego strengths appear, and many that have appeared earlier now take on new dimensions. The term *whiz kid* has become part of the language and part of folk culture. But nowhere do these new emergents receive more respect than within the teenage community itself. Here, even lesser degrees of accomplishment are often greeted by a kind of awe. Indeed, it is safe to say that among peers, the general tendency is to overestimate the level of attainment of the talented other. At home many a youngster tells about so and so in his class, who is a genius at music or writing or math. This overestimation of another's endowment is rather typical of the era, and most high schools seem to be filled with geniuses, or so our youngsters would insist. On the other hand, once these students enter college, their extraordinary capacities tend to disappear. Somehow they do not usually display the stellar attributes ascribed to them by their high school peers.

Perhaps it is not so surprising that this happens. This is an extraordinary time of life in so many ways. These young people receive so much cognitive strength, so much emotional richness in such a short time. Suddenly they see into the interstices of life; every day brings some grand illumination; they are immense discoverers. No one has understood all this with such clarity before, no one has felt so deeply about life, love, and suffering—no one could have. They are dazzled by the very extent of their compass, and their sense of self expands accordingly.

A Revised View of Parents

Teenagers look at their parents with new eyes. Here are people living with this knowledge and richness all around them and apparently unaware, unresponsive. For some youngsters, this feeds into the defensive disdain that is already forming: How could the parents be such clods? How could they fail to realize what is going on? This may extend to adults in general; it seems that only the youth appreciate the vitality of reality, only they are aware of what is wrong with the culture, what is really happening. The parents have either failed to get to this point in their own growth, or, worse still, they did get there and for some unaccountable reason fled the field and failed to maintain an appropriate reaction to it all. Sometimes the teenagers manifest a certain hauteur at this point; they patronize their elders. At moments they may behave condescendingly, or they may become downright arrogant.

The Romantic Period: The Time of Poesy

At the same time the inner lives of these teenagers are given over to the many emotions that surge within them. These feelings fill the youngster's awareness with all manner of erotic, grandiose, and exciting impulses. This is very much the romantic period in most people's lives, when they dream of living in keeping with their lusts and vaulting ideas, and reality seems at moments to be hopelessly banal and humdrum. There is often a yearning to transcend the immediate, to break out of the confines of the everyday. In striving to communicate his state of mind, the youngster may be driven to resort to poetry. Conventional language, mere prose, cannot convey the depth and richness of these new affects; he must go beyond these into the realm of art and verse. This may be the only time in a given life cycle when the individual does attempt to write poetry, but it may well be that it is also the only time when the balance of urgent emotions, emerging cognitive strengths, and undeveloped controls stand in quite that relationship.

Sensation Hunger. The new capacities do not confine themselves exclusively to expresion, however. This state of mind carries with it an intense sensation hunger. Many midadolescents long for change, novelty, and newness. Some of these young persons become prey to an urgent desire to leave home, go out into the world, court experience, try new things, see new places. They dream of traveling, going far away, and having all manner of adventures.

Or the departure may be more internal. The youngster seeks to lose the self in rock music or Bach, in dancing or ball games, in athletic competiton or academic scholarship. Here the attempt is to control this sensation hunger (and the many associated inner yearnings) by a flood of external stimuli. The teen does not merely listen to rock music, he has to love it overwhelmingly. And the music itself may not be enough; the listener must add patterns of moving colored lights and perhaps a heavy dose of some mind-altering chemical. The goal is a kind of flooding, a sensory experience of catastrophic proportions. Instead of being its victim, however, the young person has engineered it, created it to order.

Patterns of Containment. The management of such intense charges of emotion is no minor matter. For certain youngsters the optimum safe haven is not so much the controlled expression of and indulgence in these feelings; it is rather a studied turning away from them. Such a youngster cultivates a carefully formulated stance of distance, hauteur, and sophistication. He presents himself to the world as a "cool cat," superior to it all, beyond surprise. The youngster abruptly becomes a worldly woman or a man of the world, who has been around, knows all there is to know about sex or drugs or miscreance, and is a bit above it all. Such a teenager finds maintaining a state of uninvolvement a far safer position than "letting himself go."

The world of childhood has been divided by some authorities into internalizers and externalizers. The one tends to respond to the stresses of life by turning inward in a myriad of ways (some wholesome, some in the form of symptoms and illness); the other would correct any imbalances by seeking to change things in the outside world. Inborn tendencies may be the deciding factor in determining which form of expression a given youth will select for adolescent emotionality. Alternatively, the determinative factor may be learned patterns gleaned from models offered by the social milieu. Many young people do try out certain characteristic forms of turning inward such as the pursuit of mystical experience or a radical engagement with religion. Cults that offer rewarding inner experiences become very attractive to some of the more vulnerable young. Drugs that promise heightening, deepeing, or broadening of, or the attaining of new levels of consciousness may be tried for that reason, and, once essayed, continued in a persistent quest for such an outcome.

Sensuality. Given a capacity for orgasm and a generally heightened sensuality, the adolescent externalizers are often at once fascinated by and frightened of the intensity and seductive power of sensual experience. They may find themselves drawn simultaneously to autoeroticism, heterosexuality, and, often enough, some measure of homosexuality as well. They dream great carnal dreams, try a variety of experiments, and usually make at least some interactive attempts at sexual engagement. Sometimes these are rewarding, sometimes merely humiliating and disillusioning. All too frequently, the initial sexual experiences are incestuous or in some way coercive, and all subsequent intimacy is marred by this initiation. In any case, the yearnings, the fantasies, and the accompanying vulnerabilities in this realm are of extraordinary degree.

This is one of the sites where the sensation-hunger referred to earlier finds direct and pungent expression. The youngsters tell dirty jokes, their language is often studded with crudities, and they tease each other about sexual activity. They read about sex, look at pornography in all its versions, engage in obscene phone calls (either through a "dial-a-porn" service or through calling up someone and expressing lurid erotic ideas), listen to suggestive songs and tout the performers as great artists, and, when circumstances permit, grope for each other's bodies. A sizable percentage of the young first engage in heterosexual (or homosexual) intercourse at this time of life, with all the accompanying guilt, grandiosity, masochism, power play, anxiety, pregnancy scares, actual pregnancy, veneral diseases, and all the other predictable complications of entry into so complex, so primal, and so vital an aspect of human adjustment.

Alcohol

Among the many experiments that adolescents undertake may be an initial engagement with alcohol. This is an important dimension of growing up and needs a great deal of careful attention. Alcoholic beverages play a considerable role in American culture. Alcohol is used as a form of ceremonial practice, for example, to signify completion of a negotiation or a protracted bargaining session; it serves as a social facilitator, perhaps *the* social facilitator at gatherings of various kinds, for example, family get-togethers, business meetings, dinners, parties; it is used as a self-medicating, tension-relieving antianxiety agent in many (most?) homes and as a source of courage in the face of impending stress; it is part of certain religious ceremonies; and it is an ingredient in many quite conventional cooking recipes. Alcohol is far and away the commonest and probably the most serious substance of abuse in the culture. It is ubiquitous to the point of being pervasive, and the way the youngster encounters it, the modeling offered to the youth, what he is led to expect, what is permitted and what is forbidden, all become items of critical importance in development. Most youngsters respond strongly to the twin pulls of alcohol: as one of the provinces of adulthood into which they are seeking entry, and as a powerful mind-altering agent that is at once sensuously pleasurable, disinhibiting, and socially acceptable. The first attraction almost certainly locks them into a pattern of having to try it out; the second will keep the more vulnerable and more needy young people actively involved with it. In any case, most youngsters will have to find out what the much talked of "getting drunk" is all about, and many will slip into a pattern of a certain amount of beer consumption, overt or covert, as part of what it means to have a good time or to be sociable.

IDENTITY

A major step in identity development is the group of markers that serves to assert the unique character of adolescent identity structure, namely, those things that define the youth as at once a nonchild and a nonadult. There are, in fact, a great many such markers.

The Self as Nonchild

The nonchildishness of the self is a proud and touchy business. The parents encounter the first intimations when the youngster turns on them with asperity at some point and states pontifically. "Don't treat me like a child!" The beginnings of the second individuation phase of adolescence (Blos, 1967) involve many such acts of distancing the self from the state of being "childish"; among them perhaps the most common sequence is the pattern of imitating those behaviors regarded as being typically adult. Curiously, the items selected are almost invariably not the adult aspect of adulthood but its regressive dimension. That is to say, when the stresses of adulthood are particularly burdensome, then adults are prone to drink, smoke, or have an affair. The youth inevitably notes precisely these behaviors and reacts to them as the paradigm of what it means to be grown up. He likewise fails to notice that most adults work hard, earn an income, take care of themselves, act responsibly toward others, and do the things that have to be done even if they do not enjoy them. It is the permitted regressions of adulthood that first lay claim to adolescent presumption.

At the same time, there is a deeply felt need to keep the self from being swallowed up by the senior and experienced presence of the close significant adults. For so many years the parents have been omniscient, omnipotent, providing the answers, making the decisions; it is not easy simply to step away and find an individual path. The parental influence is too pervasive and compelling.

Under optimal circumstances the youngster moves away gradually, demarcating appropriate areas of decision and personal freedom, and confirming them by mutual consent and through negotiation with his parents. There is little noise in such a system, and the assumption of independence is not a troubled thing but a comfortable, natural process. In many other homes, however, the psychological and psychosocial hurdles are too great. The youngster is struggling against the invisible parent within as well as with the real parent in the actual environment. No matter what the real one says or does, the inner presence clings and criticizes, and the boy or girl lashes back, thrashes about, and struggles to be free. It can make for some serious difficulties.

Individuation

A curious reality in many of these contexts is the frequent presence of an ideal teenager who exists in the parents' thoughts and who possesses attributes that the parents value. These may be conventional values, such as dressing attractively and doing well in school, but they are not always of that kind. There may also be all sorts of compensatory roles, such as having all the libidinal fun that the parent feels he or she missed out on; fighting back against authority that the parent once submitted to; or failing at school because the parent does not want to be surpassed. The usual image, however, is a collection of virtues that may be mentioned lightly or referred to casually, but that are nonetheless vitally important to the parent. Sometimes the parents hold them up firmly as specific models for emulation. To the extent that such models become internalized presences within the adolescent's mind, he must deal with them during individuation. Simply to follow them may mean dependence; in effect, the youngster is still being a good child. On the other hand, to break away from them might be a formidable task. The teenager might have to fight hard and strive in every possible way to free himself from this clinging or pursuing presence.

The initial step of this work, then, is to achieve an element of psychological separation from the parental attachment. Young people work at the task of psychological separation with some of the devices referred to earlier, such as rebelliousness, a critical or devaluing attitude toward the parents, attachment to the peer group, and inability to speak to the parents about many personal matters. Other more extreme tactics might involve running away, getting married, using patterns of intense opposition (acting to challenge parental principles as totally as possible), engaging in vandalism (e.g., cutting up parents' clothes), or physically assaulting the parents. Most of these radical behaviors are more expressive of the overwhelming attachment and the anguish arising from the inability to free the self than they are true efforts at freedom.

The attainment of psychological freedom is one side of the effort. The other and equally important aspect is the youngster's search for the nature of his own dimensions. What can a given youth do best and what does he want to do? What is the optimal expression of his talents? What is the true object of his preferences? It is in the quest for these answers that a young person begins to assert actual individuality. Sometimes a youngster's personal preference is exactly what the parents would have wished, but what the parents prefer is no longer the issue; the point is: What does the youngster want? This is the proper target for adolescent experimentation and for questing behavior; finding the self is the supreme achievement of this time of life.

Cars and Radios. As part of the search for individuation, modes of transportation and communication become extremely important. Many young people use bicycles, all-terrain vehicles (ATVs), scooters, and motorcycles. When they do obtain cars, they frequently customize them (give them an individual character) in some way. More than that, some teenagers tend to get CB radio equipment into their vehicles, whereupon a curious kind of group process follows. This is particularly evident in rural and suburban areas where young people may spend much of the evening "hacking around," cruising in a crowded car from a home to a drug store with a soda fountain, to a bar with a dance floor, to another home, and so on, round and about town. During all this driving around, mutual contact by radio might pull a whole group of cars to a particular place for a while; or there may be word of a fight going on (always a sure attraction); or someone might show up with a message from other acquaintances about "action" somewhere else, and the whole group might take off on a sort of pseudoquest that goes on for hours.

This kind of boundary work is a pervasive aspect of adolescent adaptation. As the youth works at the issues of differentiation and identity construction, these basic concerns permeate all endeavors. Occasionally they take far more troublesome forms.

Running Away. Running away is a common thought in the minds of youngsters seeking distance, and, unfortunately, a not uncommon act. A large number of young people who would never dream of actually running away compromise by sneaking out at night when no one (especially the parents) knows and joining their friends for some nocturnal frolic. They thus establish their freedom and their difference, assert their identity, have their fun, and no one is the wiser. The more serious runaway pattern is another matter entirely. Instead of preserving the outer surface of family structure, such a defiant flight shatters it and creates a crisis. Sometimes the teenager has been abused or molested and has good reason to hate the home; often enough the runaway youth feels unwanted to begin with. In any case, the youngster responds to the stress of personal differentiation by flying from home attachments to a state of relative, albeit pseudo, independence.

The Use of Drugs. Drug use is a complex behavior that has many roots and a variety of forms of expression. Drugs accomplish two of the most important goals that drive behavior in general: They give pleasure and relieve psychic (and biological) pain. The psychological returns for drug ingestion are not to be underestimated; for many individuals there is a sizable increment of direct hedonic reward associated with use of these agents, a phenomenon that has much to do with the adhesiveness of drug taking to the life course of certain chronic users. On the other hand, it is likely that the pain relief (experientially, the euphoriant, mood-elevating, disinhibiting, antidepressant, and antianxiety qualities) of certain of these chemicals makes them even more seductively inviting as quick fixes for distress. However temporary the effects and however bad the subsequent letdown, by smoking, swallowing, sniffing, or injecting, at least for a little while the person can escape the stress of the moment. For many adolescents that is a pearl of great price, and this is one of the factors that makes attempts at treatment so formidable—and so dubious.

Besides these direct reward aspects, crucial social factors encourage drug use. To begin with, many adults engage in such behavior and offer this model to their young. Within the family, there is talk about it, laughter, evident pleasure, excitement, and cautionary statements of all kinds. For the adolescent this is a command bid in and of itself; the very nature of the developmental issues of the time, draws him immediately to want to indulge in the forbidden pleasures of adulthood.

Then there is the peer group factor. The sophisticates, the toughs, the "cool guys," the in-group, all the status roles so important to the young are often associated with the use of pleasurable but forbidden substances. In general, if the teenager wishes to "belong," then he does whatever the group is doing; in certain contexts this means using drugs. Each group creates its own norms and ethics; for the more vulnerable youngster who needs desperately to belong, the sway of the group style may at that time and place far outweigh the principles of home or the official laws of the community. Thus some teenagers take drugs only when with peers.

On an individual level, there are at least two major sources of pressure on the adolescent to engage in a certain amount of drug use: It is part of the experimenting with the novel and the forbidden that appeals so strongly to many teenagers; and, once essayed, for some of the young, it satisfies the criteria for serving as a masturbatory equivalent. A majority of teenagers probably try out drugs the way they try out all sorts of sensual and frightening experiences, in effect, to see what it is like—to find out what all the talk is about and whether it is true; to see if they will be scared; to see if they can master it. Sometimes they do it simply because they have been told so often not to. For the majority, however, although they may indeed find it pleasurable, it is, in fact, not *that* rewarding, particularly in the face of the many warnings and admonitions directed toward them by adult society. Their judgment, capacity for guilt, reality testing, and preserved degrees of respect for parental values all participate in allowing them to stop the practice after a few tries. For the more vulnerable, however, both for the reasons given above (in particular, the use of the drug as anodyne) and because the drug experience becomes erotized, the hunger, the itch to do it again and yet again, becomes continuing and unrelenting. It takes on very much the character of compulsive masturbation; the youngster literally cannot leave it alone.

Suicidal Behavior. Occasionally the more internalizing sort of young- ster, floundering in a welter of incompatible yearnings (seeking at once a state of sticky adhesiveness and urgent detachment), can see no way out, and, in despair, makes a suicide attempt. Suicidal ideation is frequent, and gestures of highly varying degrees of seriousness are all too common in mid and late adolescence. Really lethal attempts are fortunately considerably rarer but are still common enough to be a major cause of death at this time.

The Work of Differentiation. Instead of turning inward on the self, the more externalizing kind of youngster is likely to express such struggles by lashing out against the parents. Provocative behavior, defiance of rules, deliberate disobedience or violation of family taboos (all the way from refusing to go to church to stealing money from mother's purse) may be resorted to as a way of declaring independence. Negativism is again the easiest and commonest way of attempting to assert identity. A person knows who he is by not being whatever he is told to be; there is clarity in that if nothing else. In fact, the youngster who takes this course is as intensely attached as ever; his very commitment to a systematic violation of the rules makes him completely dependent on them as guides for conduct.

A common mode of asserting difference might be for the youth to confront some political or ethical stance the parents espouse and to assert that he has adopted the opposite view. The son of the political liberal begins to mouth conservative doctrine; the religiously orthodox parents find their offspring hotly defending some heterodox position, or even atheism. The straitlaced mother has to cope with a daughter who stays out all night (sometimes the night has been spent at a girlfriend's house, but the mother does not know that and the effect is the same); in one way or another the youngster has to underscore that he is not following the family line, is no longer bound or attached. He is free to be his own person.

Sometimes those children who have heretofore been most dependent and compliant, as teenagers, begin to thrash about most violently at the ends of their emotional tethers. They have been the most enmeshed and thus have the hardest task of all, to pull away and to develop a separate identity.

The Elements of Identity

As noted in the previous discussions, identity is actually an overarching term for a wide variety of separate formations within personality, each of which constitutes a unique site for new organizations of the self. Thus the adolescent has a particular identity as a member of a siblingship, and of a family; he may have quite a different identity within his peer group. He may have to deal with pervasive issues of gender identity and problems with sexual identity that do not emerge until he has started to seek out and realize sexual interactions. Presumably, hierarchies in psychic structure, with ever wider spans of patterned organization, bring together more and more complex structures into ever more elaborate systems. Chief among these must certainly be the cluster of identity functions that pull the other roles and concepts and subidentities into a certain consistent whole and thus give personality a distinctive stamp. Subjectively, as noted earlier, this allows for the achievement of a sense of who-ness, an integrated sense of self, which is of profound importance in maintaining an individual against the vicissitudes and the buffetings of life's many stresses. Identity work never stops; it continues all through life.

Gender Identity. Identity issues come most vividly to life at mid adolescence; in particular, the matter of gender identity is a very real presence in the thinking of boys and girls, and the work on sexual identity will usually get underway as well.

The questions the youngsters ask themselves are many: "Am I fully a man?" "Am I a real woman?" "Is there something homosexual about me, or am I some kind of mixture?" The boy might ruminate: "I know that girls excite me, but when I'm in the locker room and I find my eyes drawn to the other boys' genitals—does that mean I'm homosexual?" The boy has endless worries about his own genitals and about sexual behavior: "Will I be potent? Am I really frigid? Will I be able to carry through? Am I oversexed?" The occasional boy, who feels woefully inadequate, may seek to compensate by all sorts of identity distortions. In an effort to deny his own yearnings, he may repudiate sensuality and adopt an ascetic position. Or he may take the opposite tack and become excessive in his sexuality, crude, invasive, and exhibitionistic. He may move in the direction of a kind of Don Juanism, trying to prove his virility. Or he may become cruel and abuse the girls he goes with as a substitute for a felt lack of manliness.

Similarly a girl may feel sexually cheated. The boys have everything; they don't get pregnant; they can get away with anything. She may feel unlovable and needy, or she may become revengeful and seductive, teasing boys, or loving and leaving them.

The work on sorting out a gender identity and establishing and confirming a sexual identity goes on for a long time.

Aside from the larger questions about the youngster's erotic self, many issues are products merely of his inexperience and immaturity. Thus, the concerns about love and sex give rise to such questions as "How do you know that you're in love? Is what I feel really love—or is it only passion?"

The shifting, changing codes of our day do not help much in determining the rights and wrongs of sexual conduct. In a given suburb there may be two homes, side by side, where one mother encourages her daughter to preserve her virginity until marriage (with the assurance that sex will mean so much more to her then), and the other puts her 15-year-old on the pill, "just in case." Given so much uncertainty and variability, the youngsters turn to one another for guidance and counsel and seriously debate such matters as "How far should you go on a first date?" and "Is it OK to do it if you're in love?" In a very real sense a culture in transition offers poor support to the emerging personality. There are no solid and socially reinforced markers to indicate the right way to go; the teenager has to figure it out as he goes along. A generation ago words such as purity and chastity had profound cultural meaning; a girl could be devastated by confrontation in these areas. Today a person is not likely to hear any reference to these values even in church. The clergy do not offer such opinions because they would never be taken seriously.

Dating. In the American culture dating is a primary and necessary part of the adolescent pattern, in marked contrast to those cultures where marriages are arranged by parents or by custom. In Western society, forming a liaison requires taking a chance, experimenting, trying out fantasies of self and others by checking them against the realities of actual experience. It is a laboratory in which to study so many things. The young person wonders

> How do I feel with a boy [or girl] next to me? Am I in heaven, scared, attracted, cold, frigid, unable to control myself, dumb... ? How does the other sex react toward me? Am I likable, attractive, pretty sexy, do I have a good "personality," am I a dud, a wallflower? More than that, how do I react to the way I feel they feel? How do I do? Can I handle the situation, am I a failure?

All kinds of feelings can emerge from these experiments, everything from the heights of elation to the blackest depression. One youngster comes away with a sense of despair: Perhaps the boy is convinced that girls "just" do not like him, or the girl believes that boys are not a bit interested in her as a person and only want to take advantage of her. Another boy emerges with a feeling of heightened self-confidence: That girl really seemed to think he was something special; and another girl has a sense that the boy was evidently interested, he was eager to become intimate, but she managed the whole thing just the way she wanted to. A third comes away with an even more inflated, or badly punctured, sense of omnipotence. All kinds of mixtures of positive and negative reaction ensue, but there is also a garnering of experiences, a sharpening of perceptions, a beginning effort toward regarding the self as a potential mate for someone. These interactions are among the powerful shapers of identity of self as male and female; they do much to settle old questions, although they open up as many new ones.

Some boys and girls find that heterosexual dating does not mean much to them. Either they are not heterosexual, or they are just too young for this sort of thing. A rather surprising percentage of such young people really are not much interested in social-erotic experience until they enter their 20s. They may date pro forma because everybody does it, and they may enjoy it a little or not enjoy it a little, but, all in all, they find it more of a chore than a pleasure. Later on, however, there is an increased sense of caring and excitement, and they begin to date in earnest. Such youngsters are decidedly not ready for sex at this time, and premature sexual experience may serve only to heighten their defensiveness and add a quality of anxiety and distaste to their subsequent attempts at intimacy. This is particularly true if the initial experience was incestuous in character.

As noted earlier, a minority of youngsters are much drawn to homosexual objects and find heterosexuality really does not gratify them; they may even find it unpleasant. Their dating experiences are rather shallow and empty, and they are all too aware of the erotic tensions they experience around same-sex contacts. It is not unusual for early sexual experience, with either gender and sometimes with both, to play a substantial role in shaping the sense of sexual identity they eventually adopt.

Social Identity.   Beyond the sexual realm the youth necessarily explores other major dimensions of identity search. For example, the mid and late adolescent begins to face a rich layering of social identity issues. Thus, many young adults carry forward with them into their 20s, and even their 30s, an odd sense of being at play. What they do is not really the act of the fully adult person; it does not really "count." It is as though they feel they are still children playing; their marriage is just "playing house," their work is like a paper route, real enough and earning good money, but still a sort of kid-stuff activity, not yet grown-up or serious. The feeling that accompanies so much of what they do is, "I'm still just a youngster trying things out; I can't really be held responsible. If I make a mistake, if something goes wrong, it doesn't really matter; the real adults [parents] will take care of it."

This sense of juvenility is curious, and in some instances it can persist well into middle adulthood. It colors both work patterns and personal relationships and can serve as a major barrier to marriage. Marriage, after all, is what a person does when he is grown up; the person who feels this way thinks of the self as too young, not yet ready for marriage. The same sort of thinking can also delay initial sexual experience (unless that too is regarded as a form of play).

In the usual situation, somewhere in the late adolescent or early adult years the individual gives up being a child. That is to say, the person accepts the irrevocability of his acts; what he does is serious and final; it cannot be undone. It is the deed of an adult; it matters. Such a person recognizes legal, ethical, and social responsibility for what he says and does—he recognizes the community framework and takes his place in it.

For many young people, however, this is a tremendously difficult step. The lost world of childhood has such appeal, whereas the demands of adulthood are so burdensome. They prefer to strive as best they can to retain their status as a child, to cling to it tightly, to fight hard against the prospect of leaving it. This comes into view in a variety of ways. Some high school students have a major problem with getting college applications out. They just cannot seem to get at them. As deadlines near, the parents get frantic, but nothing gets done. Then there are the many youngsters who drop out during their first year of college. A certain percentage of this group is probably responding to similar promptings. The transition from the status of high school kid to that of college man or woman may be key for them; they are not ready to leave home, to give up their comfortable position of juvenility, or indeed, to make any commitment to the future.

Psychosocial Moratorium.   Erikson (1963) called this state of inconclusive avoidance of decision-making the *psychosocial moratorium*. It is an apt phrase that well describes a great many cases. The point is to avoid commitment: "Don't fence me in," cries the adolescent, "don't ask me to jump either way. Not yet. I'm not ready. I'm not sure what I want."

In some cases, the youngster who goes through this experience suffers chiefly from a fear of the loss of possibility. What is most upsetting to the youth is the notion that by making any particular choice, he gives up the chance to realize all the others, and this would be a terrible loss. He wants to keep his options open, to avoid any given label, to be able to think of himself as going in any direction he chooses, or in all directions at once. So it becomes important to avoid taking the jump and landing on a particular spot; only by avoiding such an action can the person see himself as still being able to land on them all. This hesitancy about making commitments can endure for years.

This stance impinges on many areas. For example, two late adolescents may have "gone together" for a while, and now one of them raises the question of marriage. The other experiences an immediate sense of panic and says, in effect, "Don't push me, I'm not thinking of anything like that." Perhaps this ends the relationship—the need to avoid commitment can override even some rather strong feelings of attachment. The youngster tells the partner, "I really think I'm not ready to settle down, I've got to play the field for a while longer," and off he or she goes. This is a frequent element in many relationships of late adolescence; one partner of a dating couple feels more adult and seeks marriage, whereas the other still experiences the self as a child and views the relationship as a form of play. Much heartache has ensued when these two orientations have clashed.

Curiously enough, some young people do the opposite. They get married as a sort of move in a game; perhaps to get away from home, to score against a rival, to defy the family, or to gain points within the social group. Not until later do they begin to experience the strictures and responsibilities of marriage, and then they get upset. They do not like this game; they do not want to play anymore. The woeful results of such play marriages with no real commitment scarcely need describing.

Career Choice. An important dimension of social identity is career choice. This is another great decision of the time; it involves setting a long-range course for the future that may require a considerable degree of commitment. In some instances the matter of career was set much earlier. In a family where for generations all the men have been military officers, the question of a son's going into military training may never even be raised; the only issue is,—which branch?—and there may be considerable agonizing about that. Or the family has a rich tradition of jurists, and the youth is told, "Well, of course, you will go to law school, no matter what, a law degree is useful; if you decide to change to something else later, you can always do so." In actuality the career choice is preset.

This is often true of working-class families as well. Some families have a long tradition of a certain occupation; all family members share in the work and each up-and-coming member of the clan is expected to participate, learn the skills, and make a contribution. The apprenticeship is automatic. The youngster might rebel by entering some other form of apprenticeship, or he might want to go to college, perhaps to enter a profession. Although the implied upward mobility might gain the approval of one parent, it might strike the other to the heart.

Where choices are less determined, the range for decision making is much wider. A major choice is often which college to attend. This can be an issue fraught with the most dire implications, and youngsters may mobilize enormous energy and emotion concerning it. Once in college, the student must choose a major and decide among courses of study, which causes more turmoil. An occasional young man or woman solves the problem by avoiding all commitment. The trick is for the person to keep changing his major so he is never through with school; he is a perpetual student. This can persist far into adulthood.

Career choice allows for an almost infinite variety of permutations and combinations. There are individuals who maintain some grandiose fantasy of the future. They devalue whatever they have, whatever is offered them. They await the Big Opportunity that will make them independent and wealthy, and they thereby justify a life of waiting and idle noncommitment.

The issue of choice faces youth at every level of the socioeconomic ladder. For the youth growing up in the ghetto, the choice might come down to deciding whether to be a worker or a hustler, whether to look for a regular job or seek to rise in the rackets. Whole theories of delinquency have been built on the principle of subcultures of crime that offer seductive role models to local youth and that powerfully influence their career choices. Profound cultural and subcultural factors come into play, pressing the angry youth or the member of an angry subgroup toward an antisocial stance, and giving major impetus to a particular career possibility. A black child growing up in a ghetto, where one model of "making it" is the local pimp and where numbers running retains general community acceptance and approbation, has a very different set of vectors influencing career selection than does the white child in the perhaps not-so-distant wealthy suburb.

Social Group Choice. The available social groupings are always important for the teenager. In a large high school the cafeteria will provide a ready laboratory for the study of this factor. The usual arrangement is for tables to be freely occupied by whoever happens to sit there. A person who simply observes the seating process for a few days presently will realize that there is one table for the "brains," one for the "hoods," one for the "jocks," one for the leftists, and so on for all sorts of groupings, subgroupings, and splintered groupings. A given youngster might start off his semester with the "grease," but as he perhaps advances in his therapy or does better in his work, he may change tables a time or two and eventually end up sitting regularly with the "brains."

In the later grades the groups will discuss jobs, college choices, apprenticeships, recommendations, applications, and forms—all the paraphernalia associated with career choice, training, and future planning. Whom the individual youth sits with and what they talk about will have a considerable impact on his attitudes, and these factors will join with the role and model of the parents and the inner promptings of his disposition as the forces collectively determining this aspect of identity formation.

Idealism

As adolescence proceeds, a new, critical factor for social identity choice appears and intensifies: the behavioral pattern associated with the term *idealism*. It may be noted fairly early in the adolescent process but is usually most evident from the mid teens forward. Not all teenagers evidence a great deal of idealism, yet all young people probably experience such stirrings within, and for some, it becomes the dominant motif in their lives.

Patterns of Idealism. Idealism, in its simplest form, involves an intense attachment to some concept, usually of religious or humanitarian character, that comes to play an increasingly dominant role in the young person's life. For the most part, this gives rise to a tendency to expound a particular view, to debate its merits, and to advance its ideology. A sizable percentage of youngsters who are caught up with some ideal join others of like mind in organizations that may require going to meetings, marching in demonstrations, joining a vigil, or attending rallies. In the occasional case, where a youth becomes passionately devoted to a given cause or leader, the young person may sacrifice everything for the cause, giving up his own money and property, changing his residence, and demanding familial support and compliance to the rules connected with the new system.

The most intense idealists, once they begin to live out their cause, also display a whole new order of behavior. Upon joining the movement, they tend to leave home, to move into the group's quarters physically, and to immerse themselves totally in both the novel ideas and the new group of fellow believers. Each generation has posed its own problems for parents and society. In the 1930s, the idealistic American young would run off to Spain to join the Lincoln Brigade and fight fascism in Europe. Many died— this is not unusual. One of the occupational hazards of the idealist is that he might be asked to lay down his life for the cause (whatever that may be), and it is not especially rare for the youth to do so. The neophyte is also often asked to give up his wealth and frequently does that too.

During the 1960s, idealistic causes were rife in the United States, and the model figures were the hippies and the Beat generation writers. At the same time there was a huge expansion of the variety and the number of religious and semireligious cults in the population including the Unification Church, Scientology, and the Hare Krishna movement. Many of these groups had a semipolitical character and were involved in assaults on organizations respresenting the status quo, such as the Weathermen and the Students for a Democratic Society.

As this tide abated, the commune movement swept up many of the more idealistic young, antipollution groups claimed quite a few, and government-sponsored agencies, such as VISTA and the Peace Corps, took up a goodly share.

The Sources of Idealism.   Several sources contribute to the development of idealism in the individual. The grandiosity that originated in the symbiotic fusion with the deific mother image is never forgotten by the child; even after the work of separation–individuation, some capacity for (plus the longing for) such a state of oneness lurks in the youngster's personality organization. At the time of superego formation, much of this grandiosity is caught up in the organization of the ego ideal. However, a great deal of residual grandiosity continues to play a role in ordinary personality function. During latency, it takes the form of an interest in superheroes. The surge of adolescent development rekindles much of this earlier yearning for union with an ideal other, only at this point the conditions are notably different.

To begin with, the massive instinctual push of erotic and aggressive impulses during the pubertal epoch greatly expands the youngster's capacity to love and to hate. At the same time, the strength and competence of the ego grow in striking fashion. These factors enable the youngster to cope with the far more intense erotic and aggressive yearnings that churn away within.

The youth is now developing cognitively as well, and one of the great steps forward is his capacity to focus on individual concepts and abstractions with concentrated attention. These things become real to the teenager, capable of being worked with, cared for, or despised. To the extent that he is an idealist, he comes to love certain ideas and to attach his intense erotic yearnings to these purely conceptual entities. Such a youngster becomes inflamed with a passionate love for these abstract conceptions, and as is the way with instinctual loving, he overestimates the objects of his attachment. If he had fixed his affections on another person, then that person would have become the noblest, the sweetest, the purest, the kindest, the most wonderful individual in the world. Because the object of his affections is an idea, a parallel aggrandizement takes place, and it becomes the source of all virtue and wisdom. Everything about it is loved and glorified beyond all reason; it merits the total devotion of the true believer; indeed, everyone should believe.

On the other hand, the aggressive yearnings are either contained by the power of the new ideal or are redirected toward its enemies. Thus the youth loves, determinedly loves, everybody, because he loves some version of deity who commands him to do so. Or he loves the downtrodden and froths with rage at their oppressors.

In this way, the instinctual and cognitive developments of adolescence now reinforce the earlier capacity for idealization through symbiotic fusion, and a formidable state of mind ensues. Adolescent idealism has been a force throughout history and is a major source of energy for confronting, invigorating, and renewing a culture.

It is easy to perceive why such a tendency persists and what evolutionary function it may sustain: The idealism of the adolescent epoch may well be necessary to cancel out the impact of the cognitive discoveries during that era. The last part of adolescence is a dangerous and vulnerable period because the youngsters have a maximum of capacity to understand and a maximum of intensity in the expression of their reactions, whereas their experience and the maturity of their judgment are, relatively, at a minimum. That combination makes for crime, suicide, and accidents, and adolescents manifest these aplenty. It may be that those tendencies would be far worse without the presence of idealism to keep the young people in a state of relative control and compliance. Indeed, contemporary society may have done a great deal to weaken the tendencies toward ideal formation. There has been a shift away from a strong theological orientation with no provision of alternative ideals. In fact, American young are educated in a way that destroys their budding tendencies to idealize. All historic figures are debunked, all causes and *isms* are challenged, and all values are demonstrated to be culturally determined, transient expressions of expediency, and thus merely adaptive. Moreover, what the formal educational system has not effected, the TV barrage has accomplished. The end result is a large sector of teenagers who are cynical, dispirited, and apathetic, and who lend themselves all too readily to cults and drugs.

A final note about idealistic loving. Many of the youngsters who take this turn toward ideas have had problems with their interpersonal relations. They fear to love people or are inhibited in their attempts; ideas and ideals seem safer. As they enter into the group formations that cluster around the charismatic leader or the center of a cult, they find others who share their outlook and presently they find companionship. "We love each other because we love the Cause." And so they are bound ever more tightly to the ideal; it has at once provided a channel for fusion, for erotic love, and for heterosexual attachment. Obviously, this does not apply where the cult is ascetic; under such circumstances the youth worships from afar, which in many such cases is the safest course he can follow.

Idealism usually dies down to a large extent when the individual moves out of adolescence. The presence of idealistic interests seems to vary with the level of instinctual pressure; as the driving fires of adolescence are banked, the involvement with ideals appears to lessen as well. Curiously, an examination of adolescent movements in history establishes that the nature of the ideal does not so much determine the youngsters' feelings as does the total social-cultural context within which it occurs. Thus the notion of an Aryan empire that would last a thousand years had as firm a claim on the masses of German youth in the Hitler era as any ideal of peace on earth and Christian brotherhood has had on its supporters. Unfortunately, negative ideals hold a considerable fascination for many teenagers.

THE SUPEREGO IN ADOLESCENCE

A great deal of superego work normally goes on during this period. At the outset, the upward surging of the instincts acts as an arousing mechanism that triggers the superego into active reaction. Because this agency of mind was brought into being to keep these drives at bay, it must indeed, respond to their arousal.

This response contributes to making the youngster feel constantly under attack; it seems as though someone is always telling him what to do, someone is always "on his back," everything he does receives criticism. To escape the grimness of the inner voices, the youth tends to attach the superego feelings to the parents and reacts accordingly. Relationships at home may become rather tense as the youngster fights back against these "critics." When the new cognitive strengths begin to manifest themselves, the youngster proceeds to assail the superego by questioning these inner values—and the parental exemplification of them. Before too long the questions become a tight, logical scrutiny. The young person challenges the superego: "Why need I believe in God, why should I respect my elders, why shouldn't I know all the family secrets, why should I love my country—look at all the things it does wrong . . . ?"

This reworking of the superego is of vital importance for society because it forces a constant reexamination of cultural positions. Adolescents challenge, test, probe, and think all kinds of values. Under certain cultural conditions none of this may be done in public, and a sort of underground dissidence develops. Under more open conditions teenagers will express a great many doubts, and society tends to tolerate a certain amount of adolescent fire and rebellion as being normal. Obviously, this varies enormously with time, place, and circumstance.

THE END OF ADOLESCENCE

There is no easy way to determine an end point for this time of life. Certainly there is no biological marker; hormonal stability and full expression of growth potential usually occur well before completion of the shifting, changing relationship patterns and identity constructions. The hallmarks of its ending, therefore, have to be psychological in character.

Psychological criteria are multiple in form and rather diverse in character. A few of the more important transformations are as follows:

1. *The Final Renunciation of the Bodies of the Parents as Objects of Erotic or Aggressive Interest.* The youth should have progressed psychologically to the point that he no longer needs to free himself from a disturbing attachment to either parent. Ideally, the way is open now for reestablishing a bond with the parents on the basis of friendship, mutual respect, good memories, reconciliation, and a sense of caring and companionship. There may be elements of ruefulness for prior excesses, along with a factor of significant forgiving on both sides. Sometimes humor and a sort of wry mutual understanding emerge as saving graces. Theoretically, oedipal issues have finally been laid to rest, and any former painful interactions between parent and child are now a thing of memory. Under optimal circumstances, no feelings of rivalry, suffocatingly close attachment, or covert erotic interests tinge the new relationship. This criterion is, however, seldom met. It is an ideal that, in most instances, is not even closely approached. For example, in many families areas remain that parent and child never speak about because they still hurt too much—and always will. There are families where the adolescent leaves, or is thrown out of, the home and never returns. But it is also true that much of the intensity of adolescent *Sturm und Drang* does die out, and, in most instances, a far more comfortable equilibrium is likely to be present at 24 years than was evident at 16.

2. *The Ability of the Adolescent to Transfer Erotic Feelings Outward to an Age-Propinquent Heterosexual Peer.* This standard is far more likely to be met. Nonetheless, here, too, many young people cannot relate well to an appropriate object and remain isolated or perhaps have serial relationships promiscuously in an attempt to fill this emotional void. Many have been able to accomplish only a partial escape from oedipal attachment and seek out partners old enough to be a parent. Others fly to extremes to escape oedipal connection and can love only someone as dissimilar from the parent as possible, for example, members of another race, nationality, or ethnic group. Whatever the innate tendencies that may underlie their expression, homosexual and bisexual

patterns are certainly fostered by particular configurations of early child rearing. These gender styles appear to be increasing in incidence for two possible reasons: Changed cultural attitudes make the expression of such tendencies far more acceptable than heretofore, and the current fashions of rearing children are making for an absolute increase. However, as boys and girls leave adolescence, most of them have established a reasonable relationship with a girlfriend or boyfriend.

3. *The Appearance of Adequate Sublimatory Strengths within the Context of Interpersonal Relations.* In effect, the crude early eroticism and the self-centered narcissism of puberty are not merely better masked, but are now literally transmuted into a new level of tenderness and protective caring that will embrace both spouse and children, and, in time, all of society.

4. *The Acquisition of a Sense of Identity.* The changes and transformations in identity and relationship patterns that were so prevalent during the teenage years should now come to rest, and the person should achieve a steady state. This implies acquiring a sense of identity; there is a certain who-ness, a clarity of role, and a specificity of presence that are acceptable to the person and to the important figures around him. Sometimes however, this part of the process fails, and the adolescent quality persists into adulthood. Such people are spoken of as permanent adolescents, and the term describes them well. The fact is, however, that in their very variability they have come to a steady state of sorts. It is an immature organization, to be sure, but it nonetheless characterizes their adult status. Once their identity of permanent adolescent has stabilized and is recognized for what it is, then the professional can say (albeit paradoxically) that even here, by achieving permanence, adolescence has come to an end at last.

APPENDIX 17–1
THE BIOLOGY OF PUBERTY

Frank and Cohen (1979) define puberty as "the period of bodily development during which the gonads secrete sex hormones in amounts sufficient to cause accelerated growth and the appearance of secondary sex characteristics." Although the statement defines the biological events of puberty, it says little about the many psychological and social aspects of this time of life. Neither in psychological nor biological terms can puberty be considered a single event; it is rather a succession of interrelated processes that combine to give the outcome designated by that word (Petersen, 1979).

It is assumed that somewhere in the brain there is a center that researchers call a *gonadostat*. Its exact nature is uncertain; perhaps it consists of a cluster of cells or a network of clusters; in any case, it acts as a regulating agency. When the proper conditions are reached, it turns on and initiates a sequence of events, each following the other in a series of cause-and-effect cycles that express themselves somatically by the transformations of puberty. What turns the gonadostat on is uncertain. At least two theories have been advanced: the first one is, that the slow accretion of growth during the latency years finally builds the total mass of the body to a level sufficient to serve as a biological trigger; the other theory is that a genetic clock runs a predetermined course, and after so many minutes, hours, or days have passed, it turns on. There are also two hypotheses for the actual mechanisms that initiate puberty. One views the trigger as lying in the hypothalamus, specifically in the neurosecretory cells of the medial basal hypothalamus and the arcuate nucleus. These send neural messages to the median eminence, which actually releases the gonadotropins. The other regards it as originating in the adrenal glands, where the release of androgens and estrogens initiates the so-called adrenarche. There are three important adrenal secretions of this kind: *dehydroepiandrosterone* and *androstenedione*, which are both weak androgens, and *estrone*, a weak estrogen.

Once the process has been triggered, the hypothalamus signals the pituitary to begin secreting gonadotropins. The hypothalamus is the forward portion of the base of the brain; it rests just on top of the pituitary gland, which hangs down from it by a pedicle. The hypothalamus functions in two quite different ways. On the one hand, it can perform the same role as any other brain center by sending out neural messages; on the other, it is also able to secrete endocrines (chemical message bearers that pour directly into the circulating blood) that serve as initiators and regulators of various body processes. In this instance the form of the message is chemical; the hypothalamus secretes a substance called *gonadotropin-releasing hormone* (usually abbreviated to GRH). This pours into a network of vessels (the portal plexus of the pituitary gland) that carries blood from the median eminence of the hypothalamus into the body of the pituitary. The GRH affects the pituitary directly and causes it, in turn, to release substances called gonadotropins. (Thus the hypothalamic secretion, gonadotropin-releasing hormone, is well and simply named; it is the hormone that causes the release of gonadotropin.)

The gonadotropins also take their name from their function; the targets of their activity are the gonads. Specifically, these gonadotropins have the task of initiating, stimulating, and facilitating the growth of the ovary and testis. In this manner they start the more overt pubertal changes.

The gonadotropins are two in number: follicle-stimulating hormone and lutenizing hormone (again, they are best known by their acronyms: FSH and LH). Once in the bloodstream (they are pumped in directly from the pituitary gland), the gonadotropins are carried all over the body, and, among other tissues, they reach the gonads, the ovaries, and the testes. These organs are preprogrammed to respond immediately to the gonadotropins by secreting sex steroids (such as testosterone and estradiol). The sex hormones proper are powerful agents that circulate in the blood and actually bring about the processes of pubertal change. A sensitive feedback loop carefully regulates the level of these sex hormones as they circulate in the blood; presently these hormones reach the hypothalamus, which is attuned to their presence. As soon as the hormone levels rise to a critical point, this triggers a response that turns off the secretion of GRH. This in turn damps down the secretory activity of the pituitary and thus of the gonads, and the endocrine levels fall. Now, however, the trigger works in reverse; as soon as the levels drop *below* a critical point, the whole cycle is initiated once again—a classic self-regulating feedback loop.

In very early puberty, before the secondary sexual characteristics make their appearance, the gonadotropins are released only during sleep; there is a surge approximately every 90 minutes that is terminated by a REM episode. In boys, during the year before physical puberty becomes evident, the concentration of FSH rises significantly; in girls, the levels of both FSH and LH rise before breast development begins. The adrenal secretions are also elevated during this interval.

Thus, during the late grade-school (prepuberty) period, there is an increase in the release of gonadotropins and sex steroids during sleep; the level of adrenal sex steroids rises (a state of affairs called the *adrenarche*), but no change is noted in the secondary sex characteristics.

As the child moves into early puberty, the nighttime secretion of gonadotropin continues, but the concentration of sex hormones (e.g., testosterone and estradiol) increases to higher levels. Other hormones (e.g., thyroid and growth hormones) may also be increasing. The result is that the secondary sex characteristics begin to appear.

In particular, the gonadotropic hormones cause the size and activity of the gonads (ovary and testis) to increase. As these sex organs enlarge and become more active, their secretions play an ever increasing role in bodily development. Boys show an increase in the level of circulating androgens (male hormones such as testosterone or androstenedione), whereas girls experience an increase in their levels of both androgens and estrogen (male and female hormones). In the girls, the androgen secretions arise both from the ovaries and from the adrenal glands (some directly, and some as prehormones that convert to these powerful androgens). It is, however, the change in the level of estrogen that eventually initiates menstruation.

Despite the periodic daily fluctuations in the titer of boys' endocrine secretions, their basic testosterone levels steadily increase as they proceed toward puberty. This increase correlates roughly with their pubertal stage. The rapid rise in testosterone level accompanies the onset of nocturnal emissions, masturbation, and beginning interest in girls (infatuation, dating, talk of falling in love). The final level of androgens that girls achieve is about one-tenth that of the boys. As is true of other hormones, androgen levels vary during the menstrual cycle; however, these levels are at their peak at the time of ovulation. In primates this is usually a time of greatest sexual interest, and it seems that, in general, sexual desire in both sexes tends to correlate with androgen level. Thus, women treated with androgens (for cancer or some other medical condition) generally describe increased sexual arousal.

It is well known that girls experience the adolescent growth spurt some 2 years earlier than do boys. What is less well recognized is that the earliest pubertal changes take place at almost the same time in both sexes; that is, the earliest changes in the male genitals begin, on the average, only a few months later than the earliest changes in the areola of the girls' breasts; ultimately, both achieve complete sexual maturity at almost the same time. In the girls, however, the growth spurt does occur at a much earlier time, and the visible breast development has immediate social meaning, whereas the boy's concealed genital maturation does not. The evident voice changes, facial hair growth and alterations of physique, which are more socially notable evidences of male development, are all later events. Despite many efforts, few adequate studies to date have succeeded in correlating affective, cognitive, behavioral, hormonal, and physical changes in a thorough and well-documented fashion (however, see Nottleman et al., 1987; Steinberg, 1989).

As the boys move through the first stages of the process, the testes increase in size (largely because the seminiferous tubules are growing apace), the smooth scrotal sac of the little boy begins to wrinkle and become vascular, and hair follicles appear in the genital region.

The classic first signs of female development are breast budding, wrinkling and vascularity of the labia majora, and the beginnings of hair growth on and around the vulva. The internal organs, the uterus and ovaries, enlarge as well, and the body fat begins to redistribute so that the girl's body shows the first signs of becoming more "feminine."

As puberty progresses, the boy's penis broadens and lengthens, pubic hair takes on its characteristic pattern, early facial hair appears (usually as a fine mustache at the corners of the upper lip), the testes continue to enlarge, and sperm appear. Voice changes follow, and finally the growth spurt begins. Some breast enlargement may occur at this time, an occasional source of alarm to both the young boy and his family. (This is considered a normal phenomenon; the tissue usually shrinks back within several months.)

As the girls grow, the bony pelvis enlarges, the ovaries, tubes, and uterus move lower into the pelvic cavity and continue to increase in size, the breasts progress beyond budding, and the mammary glands and ducts elaborate. Vaginal epithelium thickens and secretions appear; Bartholin's glands become active. The vagina deepens and its pH becomes acid. Pubic hair spreads from the labia over the mons, and axillary hair appears. Most girls reach close to their maximal height in mid puberty. This is when acne may appear in both sexes as the sebaceous glands become more active.

Now, too, the sleep gonadotropins and sex steroid levels are higher than before, and the peak levels of their secretion begin to appear during the waking hours as well.

Finally, the youngster passes from mid to late puberty. For the boy, penis length reaches its full 15 centimeters, mature sperm are being formed, and the volume of seminal fluid increases. Pubic hair begins to grow more luxuriantly, muscularity becomes more massive, and he has almost reached his full height.

The girl has close to full breast development now, the vagina elongates until it, too, is approximately 15 centimeters, and the girl's body is becoming fully feminine with a marked redistribution of body fat. Menarche occurs during this interval, and within a year or two, the girl will reach maximal height.

Menarche brings a new regulatory mechanism into play. As the ovarian follicle ripens, the concentration of the female sex hormone, estradiol, rises sharply. This affects both the hypothalamus and the pituitary, causing them to secrete GRH and gonadotropin respectively. The consequence is ovulation. At first this is an uncertain arrangement; 55% to 90% of the early cycles are anovulatory (produce no ovum). After menarche has occurred, it takes another 5 years to reach a point where 80% of menstrual cycles produce fertile ova. During this interval, growth hormone is at its height.

In both sexes, the result is that fertility is now at least periodically present.

Coda

In a way, all stories are examples of personality development, for all stories are ultimately accounts of a moment in someone's life when something happened that mattered. Something changed, and thereafter the person(s) involved grew differently. They lost or achieved, they were gladdened, instructed, or damaged, they succeeded or failed, or they became wiser or sadder—some event impinged on their lives that altered the direction of their growth. And so the story of development is the tale of everything that matters.

Development is a complex phenomenon that involves melding the genetic foundation with the environment to produce mature growth. To sort out this chaotic and complex process is the work of the specialists in child development, and it is a major undertaking.

The number of factors that will affect the path of such growth is potentially infinite. Humans are born and develop under widely varying circumstances of climate, geography, economics, social custom, cultural practice, and tribal or local styles that have survived major transformations of both physical and cultural ecology. We are enormously plastic, endlessly adaptive creatures and have molded ourselves to fit and survive under the most unlikely conditions. How we do this, with what strengths, and with what limitations, we are only now beginning to understand.

The story of human development will not be completely realized until the genetic map is complete, and the entire history of childhood has been explored in depth. At present researchers are only at the edge of such an exploration, but the terrain is endlessly fascinating, and the discoveries that surely lie ahead are likely to make future generations of children happier and healthier than they are today. For as the knowledge of how to rear a child starts to crystallize out of the solution of scientific discourse and the research reports, the necessary information will emerge—in what form we can only speculate. It will be applied through means we cannot yet envisage, and children will be reared in some different fashion, about which today we can only dream. This bids fair to promote a revolution in human affairs that holds magnificent promise for the future.

Bibliography

Abraham, K. (1921/1966). *Contributions to the theory of anal character*. New York: Basic Books.

Achenbach, T. M. (1982). Developmental psychopathology (2nd ed.). New York: Wiley.

Adams, P. L., Milner, J. R., & Schrepf, N. A. (1984). *Fatherless children*. New York: Wiley.

Ainsworth, M. D. S., & Wittig, B. A. (1969). Attachment and exploratory behavior of one-year-olds in a strange situation. In B. M. Foss (Ed.), *Determinants of infant behavior* (Vol. 4). London: Methuen.

American Psychiatric Association. (1980). *Diagnostic and statistical manual of mental disorders* (3rd ed.). Washington, DC: Author.

American Psychiatric Association. (1987). *Diagnostic and statistical manual of mental disorders* (DSM-III-R; 3rd ed.–revised). Washington, DC: Author.

Anscombe, G. F. M. (1961). Intentions. In A. I. Melden (Ed.), *Free Action*. London: Routledge & Kegan Paul.

Anthony, E. J. (1957). An experimental approach to the psychopathology of childhood encopresis. *British Journal of Medical Psychology, 30*, 146–175.

Aronson, E., & Rosenbloom, S. (1971). Space perception in early infancy: Perception within a common auditory-visual space. *Science, 172*, 1161–1163.

Azrin, N. H., & Foxx, R. M. (1974). *Toilet training in less than a day*. New York: Simon & Schuster.

Balint, M. (1966). *Primary love and psychoanalytic technique*. Stuttgart, Germany: Ernst Klett.

Baron, M., Risch, N., Hamburger, R., Madel, B., Kushner, S., Newman, M. Drumer, D., & Belmaker, R. H. (1987). Genetic linkage between X-chromosome markers and bipolar affective illness. *Nature, 326*, 289–292.

Barnes, D. M. (1986). Brain architecture: Beyond genes. *Science, 233*, 155–156.

Barnes, D. M. (1987). Alzheimer's protein is also in infant brains. *Science, 238*, 1652.

Bennett, S. L. (1971). Infant–caretaker interactions. *Journal of the American Academy of Child Psychiatry, 10*, 321–335.

Benson, R. M., & Harrison, S. I. (1980). The eye of the hurricane: From 7 to 10. In S. I. Greenspan & G. H. Pollock (Eds.), *The course of life* (Vol. 2, pp. 137–144). Washington, DC: U.S. Department of Health and Human Services.

Berch, D. B., & Bender, B. G. (1987). Margins of sexuality. *Psychology Today, 21*(12), 54–57.

Berlyne, D. E. (1969). Laughter, humor and play. In G. Lindzey & A. Aronson (Eds.), *Handbook of social psychology* (Vol. 3). Boston: Addison-Wesley.

Bernstine, R., Borkowski, W., & Price, A. (1955). Prenatal fetal encephalography. *American Journal of Obstetrics and Gynecology, 70*, 623–630.

Blos, P. (1967). The second individuation process of adolescence. In R. S. Eissler, Freud, A., Hartmann, H., & Kris, M. (Eds.), *Psychoanalytic study of the child* (Vol. 22, pp. 162–186). New Haven: Yale University Press.

Bock, R. D., & Moore, E. G. J. (1986). *Advantage and disadvantage: A profile of American youth*. Hillside, NJ: Erlbaum.

Bornstein, B. (1951). On latency. In R. S. Eissler, Freud, A., Hartmann, H., & Kris, M. (Eds.), *Psychoanalytic study of the child* (Vol. 6, pp. 227–285). New York: International Universities Press.

Bowlby, J. (1958). The nature of the child's tie to his mother. *International Journal of Psychoanalysis, 39,* 350–373.

Bowlby, J. (1969). *Attachment and loss: Vol. 1. Attachment.* New York: Basic Books.

Bowlby, J. (1973). *Attachment and loss: Vol. 2. Separation.* New York: Basic Books.

Bowlby, J. (1980). *Attachment and loss: Vol. 3. Loss.* New York: Basic Books.

Bradley, R. M., & Mistretto, C. M. (1975). Sensory receptors. *Physiological Reviews, 55,* 352–382. (Reprinted from De Snoo, K. (1937). Das trinkende kind im uterus. *Monatsschr. Geburtsh. Gynaekol., 105,* 88–97)

Brandt, I. K., Hsia, Y. E., Clement, D. H., & Provence, S. A. (1974). Propionic-acidemia (ketotic hyperglycinemia): Dietary treatment resulting in normal growth and development. *Pediatrics, 53,* 391–395.

Brazelton, T. B. (1962). A child-oriented approach to toilet training. *Pediatrics, 29,* 121–128.

Brazelton, T. B. (1973). Neonatal behavioral assessment scale. Philadelphia: William Heinemann Medical Books.

Brazelton, T. B. (1982). Mother–infant reciprocity. In M. H. Klaus, T. Leger, & M. A. Trause (Eds.), *Maternal attachment and mothering disorders* (2nd ed., pp. 49–54). Skillman, NJ: Johnson & Johnson Baby Products.

Brazelton, T. B., Koslowski, B., & Main, M. (1973). The origins of reciprocity: The early mother–infant interaction. In M. Lewis & L. Rosenblum (Eds.), *Origins of behavior* (Vol. 1). New York: Wiley.

Bregman, J. D., Dykens, E., Watson, M., Ort, S., & Leckman, J. F. (1987). Fragile-X syndrome: Variability of phenotypic expression. *Journal of the American Academy of Child and Adolescent Psychiatry, 26,* 463–471.

Brenman, M. (1954). On teasing and being teased: And the problem of moral masochism. In R. P. Knight & C. R. Friedman (Eds.), *Psychoanalytic psychiatry and psychology: Clinical and theoretical papers* (pp. 29–51). New York: International Universities Press.

Brooks-Gunn, J., & Lewis, M. (1984). The development of early visual self-recognition. *Developmental Review, 4,* 215–239.

Brossard, L. M., & Decarle, T. G. (1968). Comparative reinforcing effect of eight stimulations on the smiling response of infants. *Journal of Child Psychology and Psychiatry and Allied Disciplines, 9,* 51–59.

Bruner, J. S. (1975). The ontogenesis of speech acts. *Journal of Child Language, 2,* 1–19.

Cadoret, R. J., Cunningham, L., Loftus, R. & Edwards, J. (1975). Studies of adoptees from psychiatrically disturbed biologic parents: Part II. Temperament, hyperactive, antisocial, and developmental variables. *Journal of Pediatrics, 87,* 301–306.

Cann, R. L. (1987, September/October). In search of Eve. *The Sciences,* pp. 30–37.

Cantor, S. (1982). *The schizophrenic child: A primer for parents and professionals.* Toronto, Canada: Eden Press.

Carey, W. B. (1982). Validity of parental assessment of development and behavior. *American Journal of Diseases of Children, 136*(2), 97–99.

Caron, A. J., & Caron, R. F. (1985). Cognitive development in early infancy. In T. M. Field & N. A. Fox, (Eds.), *Social perception in infants* (pp. 107–147). Norwood, NJ: Ablex.

Catterall, J. (1986). Review of *Advantage & disadvantage: A profile of American youth* (Bock, R. D. & Moore, E. G. J., 1986). *Science, 236*(4798), 204–205.

Chess, S., Korn, S., & Fernandez, P. B. (1971). *Psychiatric disorders of children with congenital rubella.* New York: Brunner/Mazel.

Chess, S., & Thomas, A. (1984). *Origins and evolution of behavior disorders: From infancy to early adult life.* New York: Brunner/Mazel.

Chomsky, N. (1957). *Syntactic structures.* The Hague: Mouton.

Chusid, J. (1986). Consequences of paternal nurturing. In A. J. Solnit & P. B. Neubauer (Eds.), *Psychoanalytic study of the child* (Vol. 41, pp. 419–438). New Haven: Yale University Press.

Clemens, L. G., & Coniglio, L. (1971). Influence of prenatal litter composition on mounting behavior of female rats. *American Zoologist, 11,* 617.

Cloninger, C. R. (1987). Neurogenetic adaptive mechanisms in alcoholism. *Science, 236,* 410–416.

Coghill, G. E. (1929). *Anatomy and the problem of behavior.* Cambridge, England: Cambridge University Press.

Collias, N. E. (1956). The analysis of socialization in sheep and goats. *Ecology, 37,* 228–239.

Condon, W. S., & Sander, L. W. (1974). Neonate movement is synchronized with human speech: Interactional participation and language acquisition. *Science, 183,* 99–101.

Conners, C. K. (1980). *Food additives and hyperactive children.* New York: Plenum.

Crowe, R. R., Noyes, R., Pauls, D. L., & Slymen, D. (1983). A family study of panic disorder. *Archives of General Psychiatry, 40,* 1065–1069.

Cytryn, L., McKnew, D. H., Zahn-Waxler, C. & Gershon, E. S. (1985). Developmental issues in risk research: The offspring of affectively ill parents. In M. Rutter, C. E. Izard, & P. B. Read (Eds.), *Depression in young people* (pp. 163–188). New York: Guilford.

DeCasper, A. J., & Fifer, W. P. (1980). Of human bonding: Newborns prefer their mothers' voices. *Science, 208,* 1174–1176.

DeLoache, J. S. (1987). Rapid change in the symbolic functioning of very young children. *Science, 238,* 1556–1557.

Deutsch, C. K., Matthysse, S., Swanson, J. M., & Farkas, L. G. (1990). Genetic latent structure analysis of dysmorphology in attention deficit disorder. *Journal of the American Academy of Child and Adolescent Psychiatry, 29*(2), 189–194.

de Villiers, P. A., & de Villiers, J. G. (1979). *Early language* (p. 21). Cambridge, MA: Harvard University Press.

De Vries, M. W. (1984). Temperament and infant mortality among the Masai in East Africa. *American Journal of Psychiatry, 141,* 1189–1194.

Diamond, M. C. (1987). Environmental influences on the young brain. In J. D. Noshpitz, J. D. Call, R. L. Cohen, S. I. Harrison, I. N. Berlin, & L. A. Stone (Eds.), *Basic handbook of child psychiatry* (Vol. 5, pp. 6–13). New York: Basic Books.

Dinnerstein, D. (1977). *The mermaid and the minataur: Sexual arrangements and human malaise.* New York: Harper & Rowe.

Down, J. L. H. (1983). Observations on an ethnic classification of idiots (*London Hospital Clin. Lect. Rep., 3,* 259). In M. D. Levine, W. B. Carey, A. C. Crocker, &

R. T. Gross (Eds.), *Developmental–Behavioral Pediatrics* (p. 361). Philadelphia: Saunders. (Original work published 1866)

Dubowitz, V. (1980). The floppy infant (2nd ed.). *Clinics in developmental medicine* (No. 76, pp. 1–158). Philadelphia: Lippincott.

Egeland, J. A., Gerhard, D. S., Pauls, D. L., Sussex, J. N., Kidd, K. K., Allen, C. R., Hostetter, A. M., & Housman, D. E. (1987). Bipolar affective disorders linked to DNA markers on chromosome 11. *Nature, 325,* 783–787.

Eisenberg, N. (1987). Interactive behaviors. *Science, 236*(4802), 728.

Emde, N. E., & Harmon, R. J. (Eds.) (1982). *The development of attachment and affiliative systems.* New York: Plenum.

Emde, N. E., & Robinson, J. (1979). The first two months: Recent research in developmental psychobiology and the changing view of the newborn. In J. D. Noshpitz, J. D. Call, R. L. Cohen, S. I. Harrison, I. N. Berlin, & L. A. Stone (Eds.), *Basic handbook of child psychiatry* (Vol. 1, pp. 72–105). New York: Basic Books.

Erikson, E. H. (1950). *Childhood and society.* New York: Norton.

Erikson, E. H. (1963). *Childhood and society* (2nd ed.). New York: Norton.

Fantz, R. L. (1963). Pattern vision in newborn infants. *Science, 140,* 296–297.

Feinberg, I. (1982/1983). Schizophrenia: Caused by a fault in programmed synaptic elimination during adolescence? *Journal of Psychiatric Research, 17940,* 319–334.

Feinberg, I. (1987). Adolescence and mental illness. *Science, 236,* 507.

Ferguson, C. A. (1964). Baby talk in six languages. In J. Gumperz & D. Hymes (Eds.), *The ethnography of communication, 66,* 103–114.

Field, T. M., Huston, A., Quay, H. C., Troll, L., & Finley, G. E. (Eds.) (1982). *Review of human development.* New York: Wiley.

Finkelstein, J. W. (1980). The endocrinology of adolescence. *Pediatric Clinics of North America, 27*(1), 53–69.

Fischer, K. W. (1987). Relations between brain and cognitive development. *Child Development, 58,* 623–632.

Forehand, R. L., & McMahon, R. J. (1981). *Helping the noncompliant child: A clinician's guide to parent training.* New York: Guilford Press.

Fraiberg, S. (1977). *Insights from the blind.* New York: Basic Books.

Fraiberg, S., Adelson, E., & Shapiro, V. (1975). Ghosts in the nursery: A psychoanalytic approach to the problems of impaired infant–mother relationships. *Journal of the American Academy of Child Psychiatry, 14,* 387–421.

Francis, S. J., & Marcus, I. M. (1975). *Masturbation from infancy to senescence.* New York: International Universities Press.

Frank, R. A., & Cohen, D. J. (1979). Psychosocial concomitants of biological maturation in preadolescence. *American Journal of Psychiatry, 136,* 1518–1524.

Freedman, D. A. (1980). Maturational and developmental issues in the first year. In S. I. Greenspan & G. H. Pollock (Eds.), *The course of life: Vol. 1. Infancy and early childhood* (pp. 129–145). Washington, DC: U.S. Government Printing Office.

Freud, A. (1949). Certain types and stages of social maladjustments. In K. R. Eissler (Ed.), *Searchlights on delinquency.* New York: International Universities Press.

Freud, S. (1953). Three essays on the theory of sexuality. In J. Strachey (Ed. and Trans.), *The standard edition of the complete psychological works of Sigmund Freud* (Vol. 7, pp. 3–122). London: Hogarth Press. (Original work published 1905)

Freud, S. (1958). Formulation on the two principles of mental functioning. In J. Strachey (Ed. and Trans.), *The standard edition of the complete psychological works of Sigmund Freud* (Vol. 12, pp. 213–226). London: Hogarth Press. (Original work published 1911)

Freud, S. (1959). Family romances. In J. Strachey (Ed. and Trans.), *The standard edition of the complete psychological works of Sigmund Freud* (Vol. 9, pp. 235–241). London: Hogarth Press. (Original work published 1909)

Freud, S. (1961a). Civilization and its discontents. In J. Strachey (Ed. and Trans.), *The standard edition of the complete psychological works of Sigmund Freud* (Vol. 21, p. 64). London: Hogarth Press.

Freud, S. (1961b). The dissolution of the Oedipus complex. In J. Strachey (Ed. and Trans.), *The standard edition of the complete psychological works of Sigmund Freud* (Vol. 19, pp. 173–179). London: Hogarth Press. (Original work published 1924)

Freud, S. (1962a). Analysis of a phobia in a five year old boy. In J. Strachey (Ed. and Trans.), *The standard edition of the complete psychological works of Sigmund Freud* (Vol. 10, pp. 3–147). London: Hogarth Press. (Original work published 1909)

Freud, S. (1962b). On the grounds for detaching a particular syndrome from neurasthenia under the description "Anxiety Neurosis." In J. Strachey (Ed. and Trans.), *The standard edition of the complete psychological works of Sigmund Freud* (Vol. 3, pp. 90–115). London: Hogarth Press. (Original work published 1895)

Freud, S. (1964). An outline of psychoanalysis. In J. Strachey (Ed. and Trans.), *The standard edition of the complete psychological works of Sigmund Freud* (Vol. 23, p. 189). London: Hogarth Press. (Original work published 1940)

Friede, R. L. (1975). *Developmental neuropathology* (pp. 300–303). New York: Springer-Verlag.

Friedrich, W. N., & Boriskin, J. A. (1976). The role of the child in abuse: A review of the literature. *American Journal of Orthopsychiatry, 46,* 580.

Frijling-Schreuder, E. L. (1969). Borderline states in children. In R. J. Eissler, A. Freud, H. Hartmann, M. Kris, & S. L. Lustman (Eds.), *Psychoanalytic study of the child* (Vol. 24, pp. 307–327). New Haven: Yale University Press.

Frish, R. E., & MacArthur, J. (1974). Menstrual cycles: Fatness as a determinant of minimum weight for height necessary for their maintenance or onset. *Science, 185,* 949–951.

Fullard, W., & Rieling, A. M. (1976). An investigation of Lorenz's "babyness." *Child Development, 47,* 1191–1193.

Fuller, J. L., & Thompson, W. R. (1978). *Foundations of behavior genetics.* St. Louis: Mosby.

Furman, E. (1980). Early latency—Normal and pathological aspects. In S. I. Greenspan & G. H. Pollock (Eds.), *The course of life* (Vol. 2, pp. 1–32). Washington, DC: U.S. Department of Health and Human Services.

Galaburda, A. M., Sherman, G. F., Rosen, G. D., Aboitiz, F., & Geschwind, N. (1985). Developmental dyslexia: Four consecutive patients with cortical anomalies. *Annals of Neurology,* 18, 222–233.

Galenson, E. (1979). Development from 1 to 2 years: Object relations and psychosexual development. In J. D. Noshpitz, J. D. Call, R. L. Cohen, S. I. Harrison, I. N. Berlin & L. A. Stone (Eds.), *Basic handbook of child psychiatry* (Vol. 1, pp. 144–156). New York: Basic Books.

Galenson, E. (1980). Characteristics of psychological development during the second and third years of life. In S.I. Greenspan & G. H. Pollock (Eds.), *The course of life: Vol. 1. Infancy and early childhood* (pp. 443–458). Washington, DC: U.S. Government Printing Office.

Galenson, E., & Roiphe, H. (1976). Some suggested revisions concerning early development. *Journal of the American Psychoanalytic Association, 24,* 29–57.

Georgopoulos, A. P., Schwartz, A. B., & Kettner, R. E. (1986). Neuronal population coding of movement direction. *Science, 233,* 1416–1419.

Gerald, P. S., & Meryash, D. L. (1983). Chromosomal determinants. In M. D. Levine, W. B. Carey, A. C. Crocker & R. T. Gross (Eds.), *Developmental-behavioral pediatrics* (pp. 346–353). Philadelphia: Saunders.

Gerhard, D. S., Egeland, J. A., Pauls, D. L., Kidd, J. R., Kramer, P. L., Housman, D., & Kidd, K. K. (1984). Is a gene for affective disorder located on the short arm of chromosome 11? *American Journal of Behavioral Genetics, 36,* Abstract 3S.

Gershon, E. S., Baron, M., & Leckman, J. F. (1975). Genetic models of the transmission of affective disorders. *Journal of Psychiatric Research, 12,* 301–317.

Gershon, E. S., Hamovitz, J., Guroff, J. J., Dibble, E., Leckman, J. F., Sceery, W., Targum, S. D., Nurenberger, J. I., Jr., Golden, L. R., & Bunney, W. E., Jr. (1982). A family study of schizoaffective, bipolar I, bipolar II, unipolar, and normal control probands. *Archives of General Psychiatry, 39,* 1157–1167.

Gershon, E. S., & Nurenberger, J. I., Jr. (1983). Genetics of major psychoses. In S. S. Kety, L. P. Rowland, R. L. Sicman, & S. Matthysse (Eds.), *Genetics of neurological and psychiatric disorders* (pp. 121–144). New York, Raven Press.

Goldman-Rakic, P. S. (1987). Development of cortical circuitry and cognitive function. *Child Development, 58,* 601–622.

Goldsmith, H. H., Buss, A. H., Plomin, R., Rothbart, M. K., Thomas, A., Chess, S., Hinde, R. A., & McCall, R. B. (1987). Roundtable: What is temperament? Four approaches. *Child Development, 58,* 505–529.

Goldsmith, H. H., & Campos, J. J. (1982). Toward a theory of infant temperament. In N. E. Emde & R. J. Harmon (Eds.), *The development of attachment and affiliative systems* (pp. 161–193). New York: Plenum.

Goren, C. C., Sarty, M., & Wu, P. K. (1975). Visual following and pattern discrimination of face-like stimuli by newborn infants. *Pediatrics, 56,* 544–549.

Gottlieb, D. I. (1988). GABAergic Neurons. *Scientific American, 258*(2), 82–89.

Gould, S. J. (1981). *The mismeasure of man.* New York: Norton.

Graham, C. A. & McGrew, W. C. (1980). Menstrual synchrony in female undergraduates living on a coeducational campus. *Psychoneuroendocrinology, 5,* 145–252.

Graham, J. M. (1983). Congenital anomalies. In M. D. Levine, W. B. Carey, A. C. Crocker, & R. T. Gross (Eds.), *Developmental-behavioral pediatrics* (pp. 363–389). Philadelphia: Saunders.

Graves, P. L. (1980). The functioning fetus. In S. I. Greenspan & G. H. Pollack (Eds.), *The course of life* (pp. 235–256). Washington, DC: National Institute of Mental Health.

Greenacre, P. (1960). Considerations regarding the parent–infant relationship. *International Journal of Psychoanalysis, 41,* 571–584.

Greenberg, J. R., & Mitchell, S. A. (1983). *Object relations in psychoanalytic theory.* Cambridge, MA: Harvard University Press.

Greenberg, M., & Morris, N. (1974). Engrossment: The newborn's impact on the father. *American Journal of Orthopsychiatry, 44,* 520–531.

Greenough, W. T. (1975). Experiential modification of the developing brain. *American Scientist, 63,* 37–46.

Greenough, W. T., Black, J. E., & Wallace, C. S. (1987). Experience and brain development. *Science, 58,* 539–560.

Greenspan, S. I., & Lieberman, A. F. (1980). Infants, mothers and their interaction: A quantitative approach to developmental assessment. In S. I. Greenspan & G. H. Pollock (Eds.), *The course of life: Vol. 1. Infancy and early childhood* (pp. 271–312). Washington, DC: U.S. Government Printing Office.

Greenspan, S. I., Lourie, R., & Nover, R. (1979). A developmental approach to the classification of psychopathology of infancy and early childhood. In J. D. Noshpitz, J. D. Call, R. L. Cohen, S. I. Harrison, I. N. Berlin, & L. A. Stone (Eds.), *Basic handbook of child psychiatry* (Vol. 2, pp. 157–164). New York: Basic Books.

Greif, G. (1985). *Single father.* Lexington, MA. Lexington Books.

Gross, R. T., & Duke, P. M. (1980). The effect of early versus late physical maturation on adolescent behavior. *Pediatric Clinics of North America, 27,* 71–77.

Group for the Advancement of Psychiatry: Committee on Adolescence. (1968). Normal adolescence: Its dynamics and impact. New York: Charles Scribner's Sons.

Gunderson, J. G. (1984). *Borderline personality disorder.* Washington, DC: American Psychiatric Press.

Hagerman, R. I., McBogg, P., & Hagerman, P. J. (1983). The fragile X syndrome: History, diagnosis and treatment. *Developmental and Behavioral Pediatrics, 4,* 122–130.

Hamilton, E., & Cairns, H. (1961). *The collected dialogues of Plato including the letters.* New York: Pantheon Books.

Harlow, H. F., & Harlow, M. K. (1965). The affectional systems. In A. M. Schrier, H. F. Harlow, & F. Stollnitz (Eds.), *Behavior of nonhuman primates* (Vol. 2). New York: Academic.

Haynes, C. F., Wade, T. D., & Cassell, T. Z. (1982). Infant monkeys' achievement of temporal coherence with their social group. In R. N. Emde & R. J. Harmon (Eds.), *The development of attachment and affiliative systems* (pp. 13–30). New York: Plenum.

Hearnshaw, L. (1979). *Cyril Burt, psychologist.* Ithaca, NY: Cornell University Press.

Herbst, D. J., & Miller, J. R. (1980). Non-specific X-linked mental retardation. *American Journal of Medical Genetics, 7,* 461–469.

Hinde, R. A. (1983). Ethology and child development. In P. H. Mussen (Ed.), *Handbook of child psychology* (Vol. 2 pp. 27–95). New York: Wiley.

Hofer, M. A. (1987). Early social relationships: A psychobiologist's view. *Child Development, 58,* 633–647.

Hoffer, W. (1949). Mouth, hand and ego integration. In A. Freud, H. Hartmann & M. Kris (Eds.), *Psychoanalytic study of the child* (Vol. 3/4, pp. 49–56). New York: International Universities Press.

Holden, C. (1987). The genetics of personality. *Science, 237,* 598–601.

Holzman, P. S. (1987). Recent studies of psychophysiology in schizophrenia. *Schizophrenia Bulletin, 13,* 49–75.

Hooker, D. (1952). *The prenatal origin of behavior.* Porter Lectures, Series 18, Lawrence, KS: University of Kansas Press.

Horn, J. M., Lochlin, J. C., & Willerman, L. (1979). Intellectual resemblance among adoptive and biological relatives: The Texas Adoption Project. *Behavioral Genetics, 9,* 177–201.

Horner, T. M. (1985). The psychic life of the young infant: Review and critique of the psychoanalytic concepts of symbiosis and infantile omnipotence. *American Journal of Orthopsychiatry, 55,* 324–344.

Horner, T. M. (1986, October 16–19) *Rapprochement in the psychic development of the toddler: A transactional perspective.* Paper presented to the Annual Conference of the American Academy of Child and Adolescent Psychiatry, Los Angeles.

Hubel, D. H., & Wiesel, T. N. (1986). Brain mechanisms of vision. In J. Wolfe (Ed.), *The mind's eye: Readings from* Scientific American. New York: Freeman.

Hubel, D. H., & Wiesel, T. N. (1953). Receptive fields of cells in striate cortex of very young visually inexperienced kittens. *Journal of Neurophysiology, 26,* 994–1002.

Hunt, J. M. (1984). The role of early experience in intelligence and personality. In M. Endler & J. M. Hunt (Eds.), *Personality and the behavior disorders* (Vol. 1, pp. 511–558). New York: Wiley.

Huston, A. C. (1983). Sex-typing. In P. Mussen (Ed.); *Handbook of child psychology. Vol. 4. Socialization, Personality, and Social Development* (pp. 386–467). New York: Wiley.

Huttenlocher, P. R. (1979). Synaptic density in human frontal cortex: Developmental changes and effects of aging. *Brain Research, 163,* 195–205.

Jakob, H., & Beckmann, H. (1986). Prenatal developmental disturbances in the limbic allocortex in schizophrenics. *Journal of Neural Transmission, 65,* 303–326.

Jensen, A. R. (1969). How much can we boost IQ and scholastic achievement? *Harvard Educational Review, 39,* 1–123.

Jensen, A. R. (1974). Kinship correlations reported by Sir Cyril Burt. *Behavior Genetics, 4,* 1–28.

Judd, F. K., Burrows, G. D., & Hay, D. A. (1987). Panic disorder: Evidence of genetic vulnerability. *Australian and New Zealand Journal of Psychiatry, 21,* 197–208.

Kagan, J. (1967). Stimulus-schema discrepancy and attention in the infant. *Journal of Experimental Child Psychology, 5,* 381–390.

Kagan, J. (1971). *Change and continuity in infancy.* New York: Wiley.

Kagan, J., Keansly, R. D., & Zelazo, P. R. (1978). *Infancy: Its place in human development* (p. 85). Cambridge, MA: Harvard University Press.

Kagan, J., & Lewis, M. (1965). Studies on attention in the human infant. *Merrill-Palmer Quarterly, 11,* 95–127.

Kagan, J., Reznick, J. S., & Snidman, N. (1988). Biological bases of childhood shyness. *Science, 240,* 167–171.

Kamin, L. J. (1981). In S. Scarr (Ed.), *IQ.: Race, social class and individual differences: New studies of old issues* [Commentary]. Hillsdale, NJ: Erlbaum.

Kanner, L. (1943). Autistic disturbances of affective contact. *The Nervous Child, 2,* 217–250.

Kaufman, I. C. (1982). Animal models in developmental psychobiology. In R. N. Emde & R. J. Harmon (Eds.), *The development of attachment and affiliative systems* (pp. 43–46). New York: Plenum.

Kelsoe, J. R., Ginns, E. I., Egeland, J. A., Gerhard, D. S., Goldstein, A. M., Bale, S. J., Pauls, D. L., Long, R. T., Kidd, K. K., Conte, G. M., Housman, D. E. & Paul, S. M. (1989). Reevaluation of the linkage relationship between chromosome 11p loci and the gene for bipolar affective disorder in the Old Order Amish. *Nature, 342,* 238–243.

Kendler, K. S., Heath, A. C., Martin, N. G., & Eaves, L. J. (1987). Symptoms of anxiety and symptoms of depression: Same genes, different environments. *Archives of General Psychiatry, 44,* 451–457.

Kennell, J. (1975). Evidence for a sensitive period in the human mother. In M. H. Klaus, T. Leger, & M. A. Trause (Eds.), *Maternal attachment and mothering disorders* (2nd ed., pp. 39–43). Skillman, NJ: Johnson & Johnson Baby Products.

Kessler, S. (1980). The genetics of schizophrenia: A review. *Schizophrenia Bulletin, 6,* 404–416.

Kestenberg, J. S. (1961). Menarche. In S. Lorand & H. Schneer (Eds.), *Adolescents: Psychoanalytic approach to problems and therapy* (pp. 19–50). New York: Hoeber.

Kidd, K. K. (1982). Genetic linkage markers in the study of psychiatric disorders. In E. Usdin, & I. Hanin (Eds.), *Biological markers in psychiatry and neurology.* New York: Pergamon Press.

Klaus, M. H., & Kennell, J. H. (1976). *Maternal–infant bonding.* St. Louis: Mosby.

Klaus, M. H., Leger, T., & Trause, M. A. (Eds.) (1975). *Maternal attachment and mothering disorders: A round table* (2nd ed.). Skillman, NJ: Johnson & Johnson Baby Products.

Kleeman, J. A. (1967). The peek-a-boo game, I. It's origins, meaning, and related phenomena in the first year. In R. S. Eissler, A. Freud, H. Hartman, & M. Kris (Eds.), *Psychoanalytic study of the child.* New York International University Press, *22,* 239–273.

Klein, M. (1937). *The psychoanalysis of children.* London: Hogarth.

Kohlberg, L. (1964). Development of moral character and moral ideology. In L. C. Hoffman & L. W. Hoffman (Eds.), *Review of child development research* (Vol. 1, pp. 383–432). New York: Russell Sage Foundation.

Kohlberg, L. (1969). Stage and sequence: The cognitive–developmental approach to socialization. In D. A. Goslin (Ed.), *Handbook of socialization theory and research.* New York: Rand McNally.

Kohut, H. (1972). Narcissistic rage. In R. S. Eissler, A. Freud, M. Kris, & A. J. Solnit (Eds.), *Psychoanalytic study of the child* (Vol. 27). New Haven: Yale University Press.

Kolata, G. (1984). Studying learning in the womb. *Science, 225,* 302–303.

Kolata, G. (1987). Early signs of school age IQ. *Science, 236,* 774–775.

Konner, M. (1982). Biological aspects of the mother–infant bond. In R. N. Emde & R. J. Harmon (Eds.), *The development of attachment and affiliative systems* (pp. 137–159). New York: Plenum.

Korner, A. (1973). Sex differences in newborns with special reference to differences in the organization of oral behavior. *Journal of Child Psychology and Psychiatry, 14,* 19–29.

Laplanche, J., & Pontalis, J. B. (1973). *The language of psychoanalysis.* New York: Norton.

Leeuwenhoek, A. van, & Ham, J. (1677). Observations de natis e semine genitale animaculis. *Philosophical Transcriptions of the Royal Society of London, 12*(142), 1040. (Cited from Needham, J. 1959; quoted in J. M. Hunt, 1984)

Leroy, J. G., (1983). Heredity, development and behavior. In M. D. Levine, W. B. Carey, A. C. Crocker & R. T. Gross (Eds.), *Developmental-behavioral pediatrics.* Philadelphia: Saunders.

Levine, M. D., Carey, W. B., Crocker, A. C., & Gross, R. T. (Eds.) (1983). *Developmental-behavioral pediatrics.* Philadelphia: Saunders.

Lichtenberg, J. D. (1983). Psychoanalysis and infant research. Hillsdale, NJ: Erlbaum.

Loehlin, J. C., & Nichols, R. (1976). *Heredity, environment and personality: A study of 850 sets of twins.* Austin: University of Texas Press.

Lorand, S., & Schneer, H. I. (Eds.) (1961). *Adolescents: Psychoanalytic approach to problems and therapy.* New York: Hoeber.

Lorenz, K. Z. (1957). Der Kumpan in der Umwelt des Vogels (Eng. trans.). In C. H. Schiller, *Instinctive Behavior.* New York: International Universities Press. (Original work published 1935)

Lorenz, K. Z. (1943). Die angeborenen Formen möglicher Erfahrung. *Zeitschrift für Tierpsychologie, 5.*

Lourie, R. S., & Nover, R. A. (1980). Applied psychoanalysis and assessment of psychopathology in the first year of life. In S. I. Greenspan & G. H. Pollock (Eds.), *The course of life: Vol. 1. Infancy and early childhood* (pp. 365–379). Washington, DC: U.S. Government Printing Office.

Lucariello, J. (1987). Spinning fantasy: Themes, structure, and the knowledge base. *Child Development, 58,* 434–442.

MacFarlane, A. (1975). Olfaction in the development of social preferences in the human neonate. In R. Porter & M. O'Conner (Eds.), *Parent–infant interaction. Ciba Foundation Symposium 33* (pp. 103–117). Amsterdam: Elsevier.

MacLean, P. D. (1969). A triune concept of the brain and behavior: The Clarence M. Hincks memorial lectures. In T. J. Boag & D. Campbell (Eds.), *A triune concept of brain and behavior.* Toronto: University of Toronto Press.

Mahler, M. (1967). On human symbiosis and the vicissitudes of individuation. *Journal of the American Psychoanalytic Association, 15,* 740–763.

Mahler, M., Pine, F., & Bergman, A. (1975). The psychological birth of the human infant: Symbiosis and individuation. New York: Basic Books.

Mahler, M. S., & Furer, M. (1963). Certain aspects of the separation–individuation phase. *Psychoanalytic Quarterly, 29,* 1–14.

Marks, I. M. (1987). *Fears, phobias, and rituals.* New York: Oxford University Press.

Martin, N. G., Eaves, L. J., Heath, A. C., Jardine, R., Feingold, L. M., & Eyesenck, H. J. (1986, June). Transmission of social attitudes. *Proceedings of the National Academy of Sciences of the United States of America, 83,* 4364–4368.

Masterson, J. (1972). *Treatment of the borderline adolescent: A developmental approach.* New York: Wiley-Interscience.

McCauley, E., Kay, T., Ito, J., & Treder, R. (1987). The Turner Syndrome: Cognitive deficits, affective discrimination, and behavior problems. *Child Development, 58,* 464–473.

McClintock, M. K. (1971). Menstrual synchrony and suppression. *Nature, 229,* 244–245.

McGuinness, D., & Pribram, K. H. (1979). The origins of sensory bias in the development of gender differences in perception and cognition. In M. Bortner (Ed.), *Cognitive growth and intelligence: Essays in memory of Herbert G. Birch* (pp. 3–56). New York: Brunner/Mazel.

Meltzoff, A., & Moore, K. M. (1977). Imitation of facial and manual gestures by human neonates. *Science, 198,* 75–78.

Melden, A. I. (1961). *Free action.* London: Routledge & Kegan Paul.

Mendlewicz, S. S., Simon, P., Sevy, S., Charon, F., Brocas, H., Legros, S., & Vassart, G. (1987). Polymorphic DNA marker on X chromosome and manic depression. *The Lancet, 1,* 1230–1231.

Metcalf, D. R. (1979). Organizers of the psyche and EEG development: Birth through adolescence. In J. D. Noshpitz, J. D. Call, R. L. Cohen, S. I. Harrison, I. N. Berlin, & L. A. Stone (Eds.), *Basic handbook of child psychiatry* (Vol. 1, pp. 63–72). New York: Basic Books.

Mishkin, M., & Appenzeller, T. (1987). The anatomy of memory. *Scientific American, 256,* 80–89.

Modell, A. (1963). Primitive object relationships and the predisposition to schizophrenia. *International Journal of Psychoanalysis, 44,* 282–291.

Morse, P. A., & Cowan, N. (1982). *Infant auditory and speech perception.* In T. M. Field, A. Huston, H. C. Quay, L. Troll, & G. E. Finley (Eds.), *Review of human development* (pp. 32–61). New York: Wiley.

Murphy, K. P., & Smyth, C. N. (1962). Response of foetus to auditory stimulation. *The Lancet, 1,* 972–973.

Mussen, P. H. (Ed.) (1983). *Handbook of child psychology* (4th ed.) New York: Wiley.

Nachman, P., & Stern, D. N. (1983). *Recall memory for emotional experiences in pre-linguistic infants.* Paper presented at National Clinical Infancy Fellows Conference, Yale University, New Haven.

Needham, J. (1959). *A history of embryology.* New York: Abelard-Schuman.

Neuchterlein, K. (1986). Childhood precursors of adult schizophrenia. *Journal of Child Psychology and Psychiatry, 27,* 133–144.

Nottebohm, F. (1984). Learning, forgetting and brain repair. In M. Geschwind & A. Galaburda (Eds.), *Cerebral dominance: The biologic foundations* (pp. 93–114). Cambridge, MA: Harvard University Press.

Nottelmann, E. D., Susman, E. J., Inoff-Germain, G., Cutler, G. B., Jr., Loriaux, D. L., & Chrousos, G. P. (1987). Developmental process in early adolescence: Relationships between adolescent adjustment problems and chronological age, pubertal stage, and puberty-related serum hormone levels. *Journal of Pediatrics, 110,* 473–480.

Nowakowski, R. S. (1987). Basic concepts of CNS development. *Science, 58,* 568–596.

Offer, D. & Offer, J. B. (1975). *From teenage to young manhood:* A psychological study. New York: Basic Books.

Opie, P., & Opie, I. (1959). *The lore and language of school children.* London: Oxford University Press.

O'Rourke, D. H., Gottesman, I. I., Suarez, B. K., Rice, J., & Reich, T. (1982). Refutation of the general single-locus model for the etiology of schizophrenia. *American Journal of Human Genetics, 34,* 630–649.

Page, D. C. (1987). Sex reversal: Deletion mapping the male-determining function of the human Y chromosome. *Cold Spring Harbor Symposium on Quantitative Biology (1986), 51* (Pt. 1), 229–235.

Page, D. C., Brown, L. G., & de la Chapelle, A. (1987). Exchange of terminal portion of X and Y chromosomal short arms in human XX males. *Nature, 328* 437–440.

Parens, H. (1980). Psychic development during the second and third years of life. In S. I. Greenspan, & G. H. Pollock (Eds.), *The course of life: Vol. 1. Infancy and early childhood* (pp. 459–500). Washington, DC: U.S. Government Printing Office.

Parke, R. D. (1982). Father-infant interaction. In M. H. Klaus, T. Leger & M. A. Trause (Eds.), *Maternal attachment and mothering disorders* (2nd ed., pp. 61–65). Skillman, NJ, Johnson & Johnson Baby Products.

Parmalee, A. H. Jr., Cutsforth, M. G., & Jackson, C. L. (1958). The mental development of children with blindness due to retrolental fibroplasia. *The AMA Journal of Diseases of Children, 96,* 641–654.

Pasamanick, B., & Knobloch, H. (1961). Epidemiological studies on the complications of pregnancy and the birth process. In G. Caplan (Ed.), *Prevention of mental disorders in children.* New York: Basic Books.

Patterson, D. (1987). The causes of Down syndrome. *Scientific American, 257*(2), 52–60.

Patterson, G. B. (1982). *Coercive family process.* Eugenen, OR: Castalia.

Pauls, D. L., & Leckman, J. E. (1986). The inheritance of Gilles de la Tourette's syndrome and associated behaviors: Evidence for autosomal dominant transmission. *New England Journal of Medicine, 315,* 993–997.

Pauls, D. L., Pakstis, A. J., Kurlan, R., Kidd, K. K., Leckman, J. F., Cohen, D. J., Kidd, J. R., Como, P., & Sparkes, R. (1990). Segregation and linkage analysis of Tourette's syndrome and related disorders. *Journal of the American Academy of Child and Adolescent Psychiatry, 29,* 195–203.

Petersen, A. C. (1979). Female pubertal development. In M. Sugar (Ed.), *Female adolescent development* (pp. 23–46). New York: Brunner/Mazel.

Peuschel, S. M. (1983). The child with Down syndrome. In M. D. Levine, W. B. Carey, A. C. Crocker, & R. T. Gross (Eds.), *Developmental-behavioral pediatrics* (pp. 353–362). Philadelphia: Saunders.

Pfeffer, C. (1986). *The suicidal child.* New York: Guilford Press.

Piaget, J. (1952). *The origins of intelligence in children* (2nd ed.). New York: International Universities Press.

Piaget, J. (1954). *The construction of reality in the child.* New York: Basic Books.

Piaget, J. (1962). *Play, dreams and imitation in childhood.* New York: Norton.

Pipp, S., & Harmon, R. J. (1987). Attachment as regulation: A commentary. *Child Development, 58,* 648–652.

Piven, J., Gayle, G., Chase, G. A., Fink, B., Landa, R., Wzorek, M. M., & Folstein, S. E. (1990). A family history of neuropsychiatric disorders in the adult siblings of autistic individuals. *Journal of the American Academy of Child and Adolescent Psychiatry, 29,* 177–183.

Plimpton, E. (1981). *Environmental variables and response to maternal loss.* Unpublished doctoral dissertation, School of Graduate Studies, Downstate Medical Center, Brooklyn, NY.

Plomin, R. (1983). Childhood temperament. In B. B. Lahey & A. E. Kazdin (Eds.), *Advances in clinical child psychology* (Vol. 6, pp. 45–93). New York: Plenum.

Plomin, R., & Daniels, D. (1987). Why are children in the same family so different from one another? *Behavioral and Brain Sciences, 10,* 1–60.

Plomin, R., & DeFries, J. C. (1978). Behavioral genetics. *Annual Review of Psychology, 29,* 473–515.

Plomin, R., DeFries, J. C., & MacLearn, G. E. (1980). *Behavioral genetics: A primer.* San Francisco: Freeman.

Plomin, R., Willerman, L., & Loehlin, J. C. (1976). Resemblance in appearance and the equal environments assumption in twin studies of personality. *Behavior Genetics, 6,* 43–52.

Prader, A., Labhart, A., & Willi, H. (1956). Ein syndrom von adipositas, kleinwuchs, kryptorchismus und oligophrenie nach myotonieartigem zustand in neugeborenalter. *Schweiz. Med. Wochenschr., 86,* 1260.

Pruett, K. D. (1983). Infants of primary nurturing fathers. In A. J. Solnit, R. S. Eissler, & P. B. Neubauer (Eds.), *Psychoanalytic Study of the Child* (Vol. 38, pp. 267–277). New Haven: Yale University Press.

Putallaz, M. (1987). Maternal behavior and children's sociometric status. *Child Development, 58,* 324–340.

Rank, O. (1929). *The trauma of birth.* London: Kegan Paul. (Original work published 1924)

Riccardi, V. M. (1977). *The genetic approach to human disease.* New York: Oxford University Press.

Rice, M. L. (1982). Child language: What children know and how. In T. M. Field, A. Huston, H. C. Quay, L. Troll, & G. E. Finley (Eds.), *Review of human development* (pp. 253–268). New York: Wiley.

Richmond, J. B., & Herzog, J. M. (1979). From conception to delivery. In J. D. Noshpitz, J. D. Call, R. L. Cohen, S. I. Harrison, I. N. Berlin, & L. A. Stone (Eds.), *Basic handbook of child psychiatry* (Vol. 1, pp. 11–22). New York: Basic Books.

Rinsley, D. (1980). *Treatment of the severely disturbed adolescent.* New York: Jason Aronson.

Robson, K. S., & Moss, H. A. (1970). Patterns and determinants of maternal attachment. *Journal of Pediatrics, 77,* 976–985.

Roiphe, H. (1979). A theoretical overview of preoedipal development during the first four years of life. In J. D. Noshpitz, J. D. Call, R. L. Cohen, S. I. Harrison, I. N. Berlin, & L. A. Stone (Eds.), *Basic handbook of child psychiatry* (Vol. 1, pp. 118–127). New York: Basic Books.

Rosenfeld, A., Siegel-Gorelick, B., Haavik, D., Duryea, M., Wenegrat, A., Martin, J., & Bailey, R. (1984). Parental perceptions of children's modesty: A cross-sectional survey of ages two to ten years. *Psychiatry, 47,* 351–365.

Rosenn, D. W., Loeb, L. S., & Jura, M. B. (1980). Differentiation of organic from non-organic failure to thrive syndrome in infancy. *Pediatrics, 66,* 698–704.

Rushton, J. P., Russell, R. J. H., & Wells, P. A. (1984). Personality and genetic similarity theory. *Journal of Social and Biological Structures, 8,* 174–197.

Rutter, M. (1987). Temperament, personality and personality disorder. *British Journal of Psychiatry, 150,* 443–458.

Sackett, G. P. (1982). Can single processes explain effects of postnatal influences on primate development? In R. N. Emde & R. J. Harmon (Eds.), *The development of attachment and affiliative systems* (pp. 3–12). New York: Plenum.

Sameroff, A. J., Krafchuk, E. E., & Bakow, H. J. A. (1978). Issues in grouping items from the neonatal behavior assessment scale. *Monographs for the Society for Research in Child Development, 43,* 102–117.

Sander, L. W., Chappell, P. F., & Snyder, P. A. (1982). An investigation of change in the infant–caregiver system over the first week of life. In R. N. Emde & R. J. Harmon (Eds.), *The development of attachment and affiliative systems* (pp. 119–136). New York: Plenum.

Sarnoff, C. (1976). *Latency.* New York: Jason Aronson.

Scarr, S., & Kidd K. K., (1983). Developmental behavior genetics. In P. H. Mussen (Ed.), *Handbook of child psychology: Vol. 2. Infancy and developmental psychobiology* (pp. 345–435). New York: Wiley.

Scarr, S., & Weinberg, R. A. (1980). The influence of "family background" on intellectual attainment. *American Sociological Review, 15,* 674–692.

Scott, E., Ilsley, R., & Biles, M. (1956). A psychological investigation of primagravidae: Some aspects of maternal behavior. *Journal of Obstetrics and Gynecology of the British Empire, 63,* 494–501.

Searle, L. V. (1949). The organization of hereditary maze-brightness and maze-dullness. *Genetic Psychology Monographs, 39,* 279–325.

Sears, R. R., Maccoby, E. E., & Levin, H. (1957). *Patterns of child rearing.* Evanston, IL: Row, Peterson.

Shapiro, T., & Perry, R. (1976). Latency revisited: The age 7 plus or minus 1. In R. Eissler, A. Freud, M. Kris, & A. J. Solnit (Eds.), *The psychoanalytic study of the child* (Vol. 31, pp. 79–105). New Haven: Yale University Press.

Shintoub, S. A., & Soulirac, A. (1961). L'Enfant auto-mutilateur. *Psychiatrie Infantile, 3,* 119.

Shor, J., & Sanville, J. (1978). *Illusion in loving: A psychoanalytic approach to the evolution of intimacy and autonomy.* Los Angeles: Double Helix Press.

Simmons, R. G., Rosenberg, F., & Rosenberg, M. (1973). Disturbance in the self-image at adolescence. *American Sociologic Review, 38,* 553–568.

Smith, G. F., & Berg, J. M. (1976). *Down's anomaly* (2nd ed.). Edinburgh; New York: Churchill Livingstone.

Smith, S. D., Kimberling, W. J., Pennington, B. F., & Lubs, H. A. (1983). Specific reading disability: Identification of an inherited form through linkage analysis. *Science, 219,* 1345–1347.

Smith, S. D., Pennington, B. F., Kimberling, W. J., & Ing, P. S. (1990). Familial dyslexia: Use of genetic linkage to define subtypes. *Journal of the American Academy of Child and Adolescent Psychiatry, 29,* 204–213.

Smotherman, W. P. (1982). Odor aversion learning by the rat fetus. *Physiology & Behavior,* 769–771.

Sontag, L. W. (1940). The significance of fetal environmental differences. *American Journal of Obstetrics and Gynecology, 42,* 996–1003.

Spitz, R. A., Wolf, K. M. (1946a). Anaclitic depression: An inquiry into the psychogenic conditions of early childhood, II. In A. Freud, H. Hartmann & E. Kris (Eds.), *Psychoanalytic study of the child* (Vol. 2, pp. 313–342). New York: International Universities Press.

Spitz, R. A., & Wolf, K. M. (1946b). The smiling response: A contribution to the ontogenesis of social relations. *Genetic Psychology Monographs, 34,* 57–125.

Spitz, R. (1965). *The first year of life: A psychoanalytic study of normal and deviant development of object relations.* New York: International Universities Press.

Spitz, R. (1983). Metapsychology and direct infant observation. In R. Emde (Ed.), *Rene Spitz: Dialogues from infancy selected papers* (pp. 276–286). New York: International Universities Press.

Spruiell, V. (1975). Three strands of narcissism. *Psychoanalytic Quarterly, 44* (Part 4), 577–595.

Sroufe, L. A. (1985). Attachment classification from the perspective of infant–caregiver relationships and infant temperament. *Child Development, 56,* 1–14.

Sroufe, L. A., Fox, N. E., Pancake, V. R. (1983). Attachment and dependency in developmental perspective. *Child Development,* 1615–1627.

Sroufe, L. A., & Waters, E. (1976). The ontogenesis of smiling and laughter: A perspective on the organization of development in infancy. *Psychological Review,* 83, 173–189.

Stein, Z., & Susser, M. (1979). Some effects of the dutch hunger winter of 1944–1945. In M. Bortner (Ed.), *Cognitive growth and intelligence: Essays in memory of Herbert G. Birch* (pp. 244–258). New York: Brunner/Mazel.

Steinberg, L. (1988). Reciprocal Relation between parent–child distance and pubertal maturation. *Developmental Psychology, 24,* 122–128.

Stern, D. (1974). Mother and infant at play: The dyadic interaction involving facial, vocal and gaze behaviors. In M. Lewis & L. Rosenblum (Eds.), *The effect of the infant on its caregivers.* New York: Wiley.

Stern, D. (1977). *The first relationship: Infant and mother.* Cambridge, MA: Harvard University Press.

Stern, D. (1985). *The interpersonal world of the infant: A view from psychoanalysis and developmental psychology.* New York: Basic Books.

Stern, D., Hofer, L. Haft, W., & Dore, J. (1985). Affect attunements: The sharing of feeling states between mother and infant by means of inter-modal fluency. In T. Field, & N. Fox (Eds.), *Social Perception in Infants*. Norwood, NJ: Ablex.

Stern, D., Jaffe, J., Beebe, B., & Bennet, S. L. (1975). Vocalizing in unison and in alternation: Two modes of communication within the mother–infant dyad. *Annals of the New York Academy of Sciences, 263*, 89–100.

Stoller, R. (1976). Primary femininity. *Journal of the American Psychoanalytic Association, 24* (Suppl.), 59–78.

Stolorow, R. D., & Lachman, F. M. (1980). *Psychoanalysis of developmental arrests: Theory and treatment*. New York: International Universities Press.

Sugar, M. (Ed.) (1979). *Female adolescent development*. New York: Brunner/Mazel.

Suomi, S. J. (1983) Social development in Rhesus monkeys: Consideration of individual differences. In A. Oliverio & M. Zappeka (Eds.), *The behavior of human infants*. New York: Plenum.

Suomi, S. J. (1986). Anxiety-like disorders in young nonhuman primates. In R. Gittelman (Ed.), *Anxiety disorders of childhood* (pp. 1–23). New York: Guilford.

Suomi, S. J., Kraemer, G. U., Baysinger, C. M., & Delizio, R. D. (1981). Inherited and experiential factors associated with individual differences in anxious behavior displayed by Rhesus monkeys. In D. Klein & J. Rabkin (Eds.), *Anxiety: New Research and Changing Concepts*. New York: Raven Press.

Svejda, M. J., Pannabecker, B. J., & Emde, R. N. (1982). Parent-to-infant attachment: A critique of the early "bonding" model. In R. M. Emde & R. J. Harmon (Eds.), *The development of attachment and affiliative systems* (pp. 83–93). New York: Plenum.

Tanner, J. M. (1971). Sequence, tempo and individual variation in the growth and development of boys and girls aged twelve to sixteen. *Daedelus, 100*, 907–930.

Tanner, J. M., & Davies, P. S. W. (1985). Clinical longitudinal standards for height and weight velocity for North American children. *Journal of Pediatrics, 107*, 317–329.

Tennes, K. (1982). The role of hormones in mother–infant transactions. In R. M. Emde & R. J. Harmon (Eds.), *The development of attachment and affiliative systems* (pp. 75–80). New York: Plenum.

Thatcher, R. W., Walker, R. A., & Giudice, S. (1987). Human cerebral hemispheres develop at different rates and ages. *Science, 236*, 1110–1113.

Thomas, A., & Chess, S. (1977). *Temperament and development*. New York: Brunner/Mazel.

Thomas, A., Chess, S., & Birch, H. G. (1968). Temperament and behavior disorders in children. New York: New York University Press.

Thompson, R. A., Lamb, M. E., & Estes, D. (1982). Stability of infant–mother attachment and its relationship to changing life circumstances in an unselected middle class sample. *Child Development, 53*, 144–148.

Thorne, B. (1985). Girls and boys together ... but mostly apart: Gender arrangement in elementary schools. In W. W. Hartup & Z. Rubin (Eds.) (1985). *Relationships and development* (pp. 167–184). Hillsdale, NJ: Erlbaum.

Tjio, J. H. & Levan, A. (1956). The chromosome number in man. *Hereditas, 42*, 1.

Tizard, J. (1979). Race and intelligence. In M. Bortner (Ed.), *Cognitive growth and intelligence: Essays in memory of Herbert G. Birch* (pp. 165–186). New York. Brunner/Mazel.

Tolkien, J. R. R. (1954). *The fellowship of the ring.* London: George Allen & Unwin.

Tronick, E., Als, H., Adamson, L. et al (1978). The infant's response to entrapment between contradictory messages in face-to-face interactions. *Journal of Child Psychiatry, 17*, 1–13.

Troy, M., & Sroufe, L. A. (1987). Victimization among preschoolers: Role of attachment relationship history. *Journal of the American Academy of Child and Adolescent Psychiatry, 26*, 166–172.

Tryon, R. C. (1934). Individual differences. In F. A. Moss (Ed.), *Comparative psychology.* New York: Prentice Hall.

Tully, T., & Gergen, J. P. (1986). Deletion mapping of the Drosophila memory mutant amnesiac. *Journal of Neurogenetics, 3*, 33–47.

United States Department of Health and Human Services. (1986). *Vital Statistics of the United States, 1982: Vol. 1. Natality.* Hyattsville, MD: USDHHS.

Vandenberg, S. G. (1984). Does a special twin situation contribute to similarity for abilities in monozygotic and dizygotic twins? *Acta Genet. Med. Gemellol.* (Roma) 33, 219–222.

Vaugh, B., Waters, E., Egeland, B., & Sroufe, L. A. (1979). Individual differences in infant–mother attachment at 12 and 18 months: Stability and change in families under stress. *Child Development, 50*, 971–975.

von Senden, M. (1960). *Space and sight* (P. Heath, trans.). Glencoe, IL: Free Press. (Original work published 1932)

Vosniadou, S. (1987). Children and metaphors. *Child Development, 58*, 870–885.

Walker, D., Grimwade, J., & Wood, C. (1971). Intrauterine noise: A component of the fetal environment. *American Journal of Obstetrics and Gynecology, 109*, 91–95.

Wallerstein, J. S., & Kelly, J. B. (1980). *Surviving the breakup: How children and parents cope with divorce.* New York: Basic Books.

Waters, E. (1978). The reliability and stability of individual differences in infant–mother attachment. *Child Development, 49*, 483–494.

Watson, J. D., & Crick, F. H. C. (1953). Molecular structure of nucleic acids: A structure for deoxyribose nucleic acid. *Nature, 171*, 737–738.

Weinberger, D. R. (1987). Implications of normal brain development for the pathogenesis of schizophrenia. *Archives of General Psychiatry, 44*, 660–669.

Wendell-Amith, C. P. (1964). Effects of light deprivation on the postnatal development of the optic nerve. *Nature, 204*, 707.

White, B. L. (1975). *The first three years of life.* Englewood Cliffs, NJ: Prentice-Hall.

White, R., & Lalouel, J. -M. (1988). Chromosome mapping with DNA markers. *Scientific American, 258*, 40–48.

Wiesel, T. (1982). Postnatal development of the visual cortex and the influence of environment. *Nature, 299*, 583–592.

Wilson, R. S. (1977). Twins and siblings: Concordance for school-age mental development. *Child Development, 48*, 211–216.

Winick, M. (1975). Effects of malnutrition on the maturing central nervous system. *Advances in Neurology, 13*, 193–246.

Winnicott, D. W. (1958). *Collected papers*. London: Tavistock.

Winnicott, D. W. (1953). Transitional objects and transitional phenomena: A study of the first not-me possession. *International Journal of Psychoanalysis, 34,* 89–97.

Wolff, P. H. (1966). *The causes, controls and organization of behavior in the neonate* (Psychological Issues, Monograph No. 17). New York: International Universities Press.

Wolklind, S. N., & DeSalis, W. (1982). Infant temperament, maternal mental state and child problems. In R. Porter & G. M. Collins (Eds.), *Temperamental differences in infants and young children* (Ciba Foundation Symposium 89). London: Pitman.

Wurtman, R. J. (1983). Behavioral effects of nutrients. *Lancet, 1,* 1145–1147.

Yakovlev, P. J., & LeCours, A. R. (1967). The myelogenetic cycles of regional maturation of the brain. In A. Minkouski (Ed.), *Regional development of the brain in early life* (pp. 3–70). Oxford: Blackwell Scientific.

Yarrow, M. R., Campbell, J. D., & Burton, R. V. (1970). Recollections of childhood: A study of the retrospective method. *Monographs of the Society for Research in Child Development, 35*(5), 6.

Zahn-Wexler, C., Chapman, M., & Cummings, E. M. (1984). Cognitive and social development in infants and toddlers with a bipolar parent. *Child Psychiatry and Human Development, 15*(2), 75–85.

Author Index

443

Subject Index